NO GODS NO MASTERS

Book One

NO GODS NO MASTERS

Book One

edited by
Daniel Guerín

translated by
Paul Sharkey

No Gods, No Masters: Book One

ISBN 1 873176 64 3

Library of Congress Cataloging-in-Publication Data
A catalog record for this title is available from the Library of Congress.

British Library Cataloguing-in-Publication Data
A catalogue record for this title is available from the British Library.

The two books of *No Gods, No Masters* consist of the first complete English translation of the four volume French edition (original French title, English translation: *Neither God Nor Master*) published in 1980 by Francois Maspero. Book One consists of Volumes One and Two of the Maspero edition, Book Two consists of Volumes Three and Four of the Maspero edition.

Published by:

AK Press
P.O. Box 12766
Edinburgh, Scotland
EH8 9YE

AK Press
P.O. Box 40682
San Francisco, CA
94140-0682

Kate Sharpley Library
BM Hurricane
London, England
WC1 3XX

Translated by Paul Sharkey
Cover by Clifford Harper
Design and layout work donated by Freddie Baer.

The production of this book is dedicated to the memory of
Tryon Kennen — Radical Faerie, Anarchist Comrade and friend
— by his friend Joey Cain.

TABLE OF CONTENTS

Volume Two of No Gods, No Masters

NO GODS, NO MASTERS: VOLUME I

FOREWORD

I helped compile a version of this anthology for the late Nataf brothers, Andre and Georges, who were running the *Editions des Delphes* publishing house. The reshuffled text we have here, condensed or expanded, is palpably different from that first edition: being more ideological than historical and anecdotal, with fuller introductions, commentaries and notes — being, in short, more didactic. This time the responsibility for the contents is mine and mine alone.

Before proceeding to the text, there is a question that needs answering: Why this title **Neither God nor Master**?

In his 1957 book *The Political and Social Ideas of Auguste Blanqui*, Maurice Dommanget, renowned for his tireless erudition, stated — agreeing here with Louis Louvet's *Worldwide History of Anarchism* — that the catch-phrase *Neither God nor Master* might be an adaptation of a 15th century German proverb to be found in Act I, Scene II of the 1659 tragicomedy, *Peter's Feast, or the Atheist Confounded,* written by Devilliers, a sort of fore-runner of Moliere's *Don Juan*.

In 1870, while the imperial plebiscite was in progress, one of Auguste Blanqui's youngest disciples, Doctor Susini, had issued a pamphlet entitled *The More God, the More Master.*

In the twilight years of his life (1805–1881), during November 1880, Blanqui himself launched a newspaper which he endowed with the title **Ni Dieu ni Maître** (Neither God nor Master).

After the great revolutionary's death, a number of groups and newspapers laid claim to the title. It was displayed on the walls of the Maison du Peuple in the Rue Ramey in Paris. From then on it was the catch phrase of the anarchist movement, even if the latter's inspiration was so very different from — not to say contrary to — Blanquism's.

As we shall see in Volume II of this anthology, Peter Kropotkin, in his *Paroles d'un Révolté* (1885) took the catch phrase for his very own, in the following terms:

> On his death-bed, the man who, more than anybody else, was the embodiment of this system of conspiracy, the man who paid with a life of imprisonment for his commitment to that system, uttered these words, which amount to an entire program: **Neither God nor Master!**

After the bomb outrage mounted by the anarchist Auguste Vaillant against the Chamber of Deputies on December 9, 1893, the bourgeois authorities retaliated by passing the so-called "criminal" laws in order to stamp out anarchism. Following the debating of the bills, onlooker Alexandre Flandin shouted from the gallery in the Palais Bourbon: "Anarchists strive to implement the motto **Neither God nor Master**."

In July 1896, the libertarians of Bordeaux issued a manifesto in which they eulogized "the beauty of the libertarian ideal of **Neither God nor Master**." A little later, Sebastien Faure, writing in *Le Libertaire* of August 8–14 that year, declared: "Blanqui's catch-phrase, **Neither God nor Master**, cannot be dissected, but must be embraced in its entirety. . . ."

During the 1914-1918 war, Sebastien Faure revived the catch-phrase and, once peace had returned, the Libertarian Youth founded in Paris adopted the name **Ni Dieu ni Maître**, as *Le Libertaire* reported on June 25, 1919.

Although, as has been seen, the motto in question had not originated exclusively with anarchists, with the passage of time it came to be theirs. Hence the title given to this anthology.

The text here offered is, in a sense, the hefty dossier of evidence in a trial in defense of a reputation. Anarchism, in fact, has been victimized by undeserved slurs — slurs that have come in three shapes.

For a start, those who defame it contend that anarchism is dead. It is alleged not to have survived the great revolutionary ordeals of our times: the Russian Revolution and the Spanish Revolution, instead of leaving it out of place in this modern world characterized by centralization, large political and economic units and the totalitarian mind-set. As Victor Serge had it, anarchists had no option left but to "switch, under the lash of events, to revolutionary marxism."

Secondly, its detractors, the better to discredit it, offer a quite contentious slant on its teachings. Anarchism is alleged to be

- essentially individualistic, particularist and refractory to any form of organization: preferring fragmentation, atomization, and inward-looking little local units of administration and production;
- incapable of unity, centralization or planning;
- nostalgic for a "golden age;" tending to hark back to obsolete forms of society;
- sinning through a childish optimism, its "idealism" prone to pay no heed to the hard and fast realities of the material infra-structure;
- incorrigibly petit-bourgeois, existing on the margins of the modern proletariat's class movement.

In a word, "reactionary."

Finally, some commentators are especially diligent in commemorating, and craftily publicizing only its deviations, such as terrorism, the maverick outrage, propaganda by explosives.

In the anthology which we offer the reader, the documents can speak for themselves. In re-opening the case for examination, we are not merely seeking, retrospectively, to undo an injustice, nor to make a great display of erudition. For in fact it seems that anarchy's constructive ideas are alive and well and that they can, provided they are re-examined and held up to critical scrutiny, help contemporary socialist thinking to strike out in a new direction. Consequently, this anthology has a bearing upon the realms of thought and of action alike.

The readings were either unpublished or no longer readily accessible, or had been kept hidden in the shadows by a conspiracy of silence. They have been selected on grounds either of rarity or of interest: being doubly interesting by virtue of the richness of the contents or the exceptional promise of their form. Unlike other volumes similar to this, no attempt has been made to arrive at an exhaustive inventory of all the writers subscribing to the libertarian view: nor have we sought to beatify anyone by exception or omission. Attention has focused upon the great masters, and those we have considered their second-rate epigones have been left out. This opening volume of our anthology begins with three of the pioneers of 19th century anarchism: Stirner, Proudhon and Bakunin.

Daniel Guerín, 1977. Photo by Sopie Bassouls

— *Daniel Guerín*

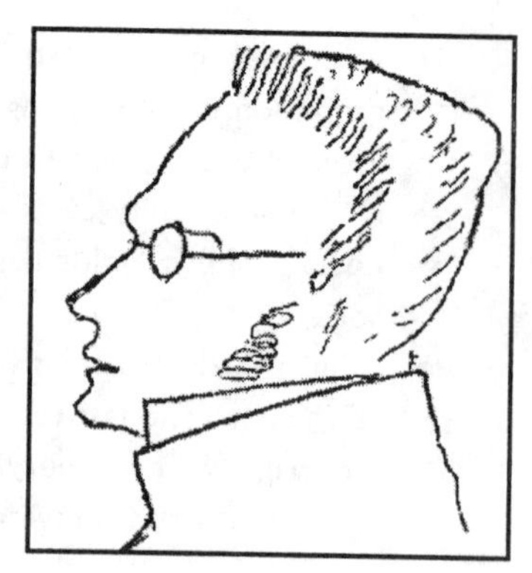

A FOREBEAR: MAX STIRNER (1806–1856)

We reckon we ought to open this anthology with Max Stirner. On two grounds: First, the chronological. In fact, Stirner's earliest libertarian writings date from 1842–1844, which is to say, from a time when Proudhon was publishing his first anarchist scribblings. So, from the point of view of chronology, it really does not matter which of that pair with which we open. If we have opted to open with Stirner, the reason is that he stopped writing well before Proudhon and because it would have been hard to situate Stirner anywhere else in the anthology: Stirner being, in effect, a solitary rebel, a loner.

Even in his contemporary setting, he was a breed apart. He rehabilitated the individual in an age when, in the realms of philosophy, Hegelian anti-individualism was in the ascendancy, and when in the realms of social criticism, the one-eyed approach of bourgeois egoism had led most reformers to place the emphasis on its opposite. After all, is not the term socialism the opposite of individualism? Hence the sound birching meted out to him, somewhat too severely, by Marx and Engels.

Stirner, standing four-square against this societal approach, exalts the intrinsic worth of the "unique" individual — which is to say the individual *nonpareil*, destined by nature to be one of a kind: this notion, be it said in passing, is endorsed by the latest discoveries of biology and also reflects the preoccupations of the contemporary world, eager to rescue the individual from all sorts of oppressive alienations, the alienation implicit in industrial slavery as well as that of totalitarian conformism.

As Stirner told it, the individual, in order to free himself, must sort through the baggage inherited from his forebears and educators, and embark upon a comprehensive effort of "de-sacralization." That effort has to begin with so-called bourgeois morality. To that end, Stirner made Puritanism a special target. The apostles of secularism had quite simply and plainly taken for their own everything that Christianity "has devised against passion." They refuse to heed the calls of the flesh. He deplores secularism's zeal against the flesh, its striking "at the very essence of immortality." How scathing Stirner would have been about the secular morality of the Third Republic in France!

Anticipating contemporary psychoanalysis, our philosopher notes and denounces internalization. From childhood, moral prejudices have been inculcated into us. Morality has turned into "an authority within, from which I have no escape." "Its depotism is ten times worse now than once it was, for it mumbles in my consciousness." "The young are herded to school so as to learn the same old cant, and once they have commended to memory the prattle of their elders, they are pronounced adults." And Stirner becomes the iconoclast: "God, conscience, duty, laws, all of them nonsense which they have packed into our heads and hearts." The real seducers and corrupters of the young are priests, teachers, and fathers who "fill young hearts with figments and young heads with brutishness." Stirner is the fore-runner of May 1968.

Now, from time to time the spirit of his writing led him into certain paradoxes and drew asocial aphorisms from him, leading him to the conclusion that life in society was impossible. But these quite occasional sorties do nothing to traduce the fundaments of his thinking. For all his hermit-like posturing, Stirner aspired to life in a community. Like lost loners, cloistered persons and introverts, he craved companionship. Asked how his exclusivism might allow him to live in society, he replied that only a man who has grasped his "singularity" can enter into relations with his fellows. The individual has need of friends and companionship: if, say, he writes books, he needs an audience. The individual joins forces with his fellows in order to bolster his own power and in order to achieve, through a pooling of resources, what each of them could never achieve on his own. "If behind you there stand millions of others to protect you, together you represent a power to be reckoned with and success will readily be yours."

On one condition, though: such relations with others must be voluntary and freely contracted, and revocable at any time. Stirner draws a distinction between pre-established society, which is constrictive, and association which is a free action. He thereby prefigures the federalism of Proudhon, Bakunin and Kropotkin, as well as Lenin's right to secession.

The author of *The Ego and His Own* is especially identified with contemporary concerns when he broaches the question of the party and specifically invokes the party of his Communist contemporaries. As we shall see, he is scathing in his criticism of the party's conformism. In his view, a monolithic party is no longer an association and has become a corpse instead. So he rejects any such party, though not, of course, the inclination to join a political association: "I can always find plenty of people willing to associate with me without having to pledge loyalty to my colors." He could not join a party, especially if this involved "anything obligatory." The sole condition upon his eventual affiliation would be his not "being swallowed up by the party." "In any event, as he saw it, the party was merely a party, only a part." "The party is freely associated and acts upon its freedom similarly."

There is only one ingredient missing in Stirner's thinking, albeit it is that acknowledgment of it in some shape or form underlies his writings: he cannot quite bring himself to accept that his "egoism" holds equally true for the group. Only out of "selfishness" does he countenance association with others. The Stirnerian synthesis between the individual and society remains wobbly. In the mind of this rebel the asocial and the social are at odds with each other and never quite coalesce. Socially focused anarchists will repudiate him. All the more so as the misinformed Stirner makes the mistake of including Proudhon among the "authoritarian" communists who would condemn the individualist aspiration in the name of some "social duty." Now, while it is true that Proudhon was critical of Stirnerian "worship" of the individual, his entire output is a quest for a synthesis, or rather, a "balance," between defense of the individual and the interests of society, between individual power and collective power. "Individualism is the elementary fact of humanity," "its vital principle," but "association is its complement."

The pages devoted to Stirner which follow open with a review of his life, written by his French disciple, E. Armand (1872-1962).

Max Stirner *by E. Armand*

Who, then, was this Max Stirner whose chief work, *The Ego and His Own*, has been such an unexpected success, having been published in edition after edition, translated, re-translated and distributed, furnishing the matter for doctoral theses in philosophy, for pamphlets and books and commentaries, and countless newspaper and magazine articles in every one of the languages spoken by the civilized peoples of the world?

The Ego and His Own (*Der Einzige und sein Eigentum*) was issued in 1843, only to lapse into oblivion after attracting a few critical articles. Then a German by the name of John-Henry Mackay (John-Henry's Scottish father passed away when his son was two years old: John-Henry was then educated by his mother and a step-father, both of them linguistically and culturally Germans), who would later gain notoriety[1] himself, found his gaze drawn while studying in the British Museum in London in the summer of 1887, to Lange's tome on *The History of Materialism*, in which there were a few lines on Stirner and his book. Eventually he got hold of a copy of *The Ego and His Own* and read it through. So affected was he by the contents that he began to wonder about the man who had written it, about his origins, the course of his life, the circumstances in which he had lived and how he had met his end. He spared no effort in his researches, scouring the public libraries for any and all information about the man who so intrigued him, seeking out the offspring of those who had associated with Stirner some half-century or forty years before, drawing them out, collecting their recollections. He also contacted Stirner's second wife, Maria Danhardt. It was Trojan work, believe me. And what I am about to set out now are the findings of that dogged and protracted pursuit.

Out of his researches came a voluminous tome of biography, *Max Stirner, sein Leben und sein Werk* (*Max Stirner, Life and Work*), the first edition of which appeared in 1897. It is my contention that book, regrettably not translated into French thus far, is of singular assistance in understanding *The Ego and His Own.*

It will surprise no one that, for all his impartiality, Mackay depicted his hero in the kindliest of lights. Not unreasonably, he regarded Stirner as the most daring and significant of thinkers on that side of the Rhine, accounting him one of the successors of a Newton or a Darwin, rather than of a Bismarck, and as towering above Nietzsche who was not, moreover, unfamiliar with Stirner.[2]

(...) Mackay informs us that Max Stirner was merely a pen-name, a *nom de guerre*, and that his hero's real name was Johann Kaspar Schmidt and that he was born in Bayreuth on October 25, 1806. The name Stirner was simply a nick-name given on account of his balding pate (in German *Stirn*). He held on to that nickname in *The Ego* . . . and his other publications. We shall quickly gloss over everything that Mackay has to tell us about his education, his career as a free teacher, his nondescript first marriage which ended with the premature death of his wife and move on to his dealings with the celebrated Berlin coterie of the "The Free" and look at Mackay's revelations.

They were a curious group, a club or coterie which met in the home of one Hippel, an innkeeper famed for the quality of his beverages, whose place was located on one of the busiest streets of the Berlin of his day. Without formality or chairman, all sorts of criticisms were given an airing there and a mockery made of censorship of any sort. The most heated arguments took place there amid the steam emanating from the great porcelain pipes with which anyone who has visited the breweries beyond the Rhine will be familiar: conversations were held over a few glasses. All manner of folk were to be found rubbing shoulders there: there were the group's regulars, sitting in the same position year after year, and there were the casuals, coming and going, popping back and dropping out of sight.

To get the proper measure of the story of this group — which was, to some extent, the incubator of *The Ego* ..., we need to immerse ourselves in the world of the German intellectual between 1830 and 1850. Germany was then turned upside down not just by criticism in matters theological — Strauss's *Life of Jesus* dates from this time — but also by the yearnings for political liberty that were to give rise to the German revolution of 1848.

Among these "Free" the main and primary topics of discussion were politics, socialism (in the communist sense) anti-Semitism (which was beginning to make some headway), theology and the notion of authority. Theologians like Bruno Bauer rubbed shoulders with liberal journalists, poets, writers, students delighted to get away from *ex cathedra* lectures, and even with officers whose conversation extended to more than horseflesh and women and who had the tact to leave their supercilious airs and swagger at the door. There were also a few "ladies" around: Marx and Engels also frequented these circles, albeit briefly.

Bohemians and iconoclasts as they were, the "Free" did not always get a good press or enjoy good repute. It has been argued that there were veritable German-style orgies on Hippel's premises. One occasional visitor, Arnold Ruge, berated them one day: "You want to be free men and you cannot even see the foul mire in which you wallow. One does not free men and peoples with vulgarities (*Schweinerein*). Clean yourselves up before you embark upon any such undertaking." The "Hippel's place gang" was not always flush. One evening the inn-keeper refused to give them any more credit, and so they were forced — Bruno Bauer along with the rest — to pass the hat around in Unter den Linden. On one occasion there was a generous outsider who sized up the situation and, being amused and intrigued, coughed up enough money to restore their credit at Hippel's establishment.

Mackay tells us that Max Stirner was a regular at "Free" get-togethers for ten years. He would show up with his sardonic grin, a dreamy, piercing gaze emanating from the blue eyes behind his wire-rimmed spectacles. Mackay paints him as having been cold, impassive, inscrutable, having no need to confide in anyone and keeping everyone at arm's length: even those with whom he had everything in common were vouchsafed no insight into his joys, his griefs, any of the minutiae of his everyday life. To tell the truth, no one in the circle knew Stirner, not his close friends nor his sworn enemies. His character appears to have spared him passionate love or passionate hatred. Plain, mannerly, sober, virtually without needs or any particular disposition beyond a preference for plainness, this is how Mackay portrays him in the eyes of those closest to him. Strong and self-contained.

At the time when he married again in 1843, this time to Maria Danhardt, an affable, blond, well-to-do sentimental dreamer from Mecklemburg, Max Stirner's star stood at its highest point. Indeed, within months, *The Ego and Its Own* would appear.

The youthful Maria, who had a distinguished education which she had taken in her stride, was also an associate of the "Free" circle. She too was a connoisseur of cigars, smoked the long-stemmed pipe so beloved of students and readily downed old man Hippel's ales. But the marriage was not a happy one. Mackay also had wind of the calumnies to which Stirner had been subjected. He had been accused of living off his wife. Mackay was keen to find what substance there may have been to the charge. He managed to track down Maria Danhardt in London, and found her profoundly religious, elderly and embittered, but with a good enough memory to be able to tell him "that it made her blood boil to think that a man of such erudition and education could have exploited the position of a poor woman like herself, and so abuse her trust as to dispose of her assets as he deemed fit." She went even further and insinuated that this egoist of egoists had derived some curious sadistic thrill from introducing his wife to the "Free" to see her corrupted by the infection there and watch material and moral corruption at work.

How much truth was there in all of this?

Broadly speaking, I go with Mackay's contention. Both of them — especially Stirner, who had always lived in a condition of impoverishment — being poorly versed in financial matters, the likelihood is that the money slipped through the fingers of them both. Of course, the sensitive Maria Danhardt could not understand the deep thinker who had asked her to share his journey through life. And yet Stirner was not without sensibilities, but was first and foremost a romantic. Within a short time of their wedding, they were "co-habitating" rather than living as husband and wife. A point came when separation became inevitable. It was reached in 1845.

(. . .) Far from being slothful, Max Stirner had continued to produce. Neither his conjugal debts not those he had incurred through publication of *The Ego and His Own* had diminished his mind's fertility. And so he set about translating the master works of J.B. Say and Adam Smith which saw publication in Leipzig in 1845–1847, eight volumes complete with his own commentary and notes. 1852 saw the publication in Berlin of his two-volume *History of Reaction*. Also in 1852, we find his annotated translation of J.B. Say's pamphlet *Capital and Interest*, published in Hamburg.

Thereafter, no more mention of him. Mackay shows him to us ground down by poverty, flitting from lodgings to lodgings, all of them tracked down by Stirner's indefatigable biographer. He dropped out of sight, mixing with no one and shunning his old friends. Coping day by day as best he could, he continued to profess to be a journalist, teacher, doctor of philosophy and even rentier, although in point of fact he was a courier, a messenger. In 1853 he was twice thrown into prison for debt. He enjoyed a little respite in his last furnished room rented from his last landlady, a Frau Weiss, who was compassionate towards her tenant. On June 25, 1856 he died from an infection caused by a bite from an anthrax-bearing fly. His Calvary was at an end. He was almost fifty years old. A few people accompanied him on his final pilgrimage: among them, though, were two former "Francophiles," Bruno Bauer and Ludwig Buhl.

Notes to Max Stirner by E. Armand

1. Not just for his poems, several of which have survived, or for his novels, among which we might cite *Die Anarchisten* (*The Anarchists*) and *Der Freiheitsucher* (*Seeker after Freedom*), but also on account of his involvement with the German individualist movement.

2. So much so that the face of the author of *Zarathustra* used to light up at the mention of *The Ego and His Own*, a book that he regarded as the most daring work since Hobbes. "So profoundly at one with Stirner did he feel that in his day he was afraid of being perceived as his plagiarist." (Ch. Andler, *Nietzsche, sa vie et sa pensée*, Volume IV, 1928)

Max Stirner
The False Principles of Our Education[1]

The reader is dealing here with a text that anticipates the contemporary revolutions in education:

(. . .) Freedom of thought once acquired, our time's impulse is to perfect it, in order to exchange it for freedom of the will, the principle of a new epoch. Thus the ultimate object of education can scarcely be knowledge any more: it is, rather, the will born of such knowledge. In short, its tendency will be to create the personal or free man. What is truth but the revelation of what we are? It is a matter of our discovering ourselves, of freeing ourselves from everything extraneous to us, of refraining ourselves or releasing ourselves radically from all authority, of a return to innocence. But schooling does not produce such absolutely true men. And if there be a school that does, it is in spite of schooling. The latter no doubt affords us mastery over things, and, strictly speaking, also affords us mastery of our own nature. But it does not make free natures of us. In fact, no knowledge, no matter how profound and comprehensive it may be, no alert, wise mind and no dialectical finesse can arm us against the snares of thought and will.

(. . .) All sorts of vanity and desire for profit, ambition, slavish enthusiasm and duplicity, etc., are highly compatible with immense learning, as they also are with an elegant classical education. And this whole scholarly farrago, which does not impinge upon our moral behavior, is frequently forgotten by us, especially as it is useless to us: we shake off the dust of the school whenever we leave it. How come? Because education consists exclusively of the formal or the material, or at best of a blend of the two, but not of truth, not of the molding of the true man.

(. . .) Like some other fields, the field of pedagogy too is numbered among those where the point is that freedom should not be allowed access, and opposition not tolerated: what is sought is submissiveness. Effort is invested solely in a purely formal and material training. The stalls of humanism produce only sages; out of the realists' come only "useful citizens"; but in both cases, only submissive creatures are turned out. Our old grounding in "badness" is forcibly suffocated as is the blossoming of knowledge into free will. School life also churns out Philistines. Just as, when we were children, we were taught to accept whatever was foisted upon us, so we later accommodate ourselves to a positive life, we defer to our times and wind up as slaves and supposedly "good citizens."

Where, then, are there signs of a spirit of opposition emerging instead of the submissiveness nurtured thus far? Where is man the creator being molded instead of man the educated? Where is the teacher turning into a collaborator, where the transmutation of knowing into wanting, where, in short, is the aim man the free rather than man the cultivated? We will search in vain: that is how rare it is.

And yet we need to get it into our heads that man's supreme role is neither instruction nor civilization, but self-activity. Does this amount to abandoning culture? No, nor to sacrificing freedom of thought, but rather to transfiguration of it into freedom of the will. On the day when man regards it as a point of honor that he should be alive to or cognizant of self, acting for himself with complete autonomy, with full self-consciousness, and complete freedom, that day he will no longer be for himself a curious, inscrutable object and will begin to banish the ignorance that hobbles and thwarts his full self-knowledge.

Should the notion of freedom but awaken in man, free men dream only of freeing themselves now and for all time: but instead, all we do is churn out learned men who adapt in the most refined manner to every circumstance and fall to the level of slavish, submissive souls. For the most part, what are our fine gentlemen brimful of intellect and culture? Sneering slavers and slaves themselves.

(. . .) The poverty of our current education derives largely from the fact that knowledge has not been translated into ambition, into self-activity, into pure practice. The realists have indeed recognized this shortcoming, but the only remedy they have offered has been to mold "practical" folk as bereft of ideas as they are of freedom. The spirit by which most teachers are driven is dismally poignant proof of what we say. Licked into shape, they themselves lick into shape at best: tailored, they tailor. But all education ought to be personal (. . .) In other words, it is not knowledge that needs to be inculcated, it is the personality that needs to be drawn out of itself. The starting point of pedagogy ought not to be the civilizing vocation, but the calling to shape free personalities and sovereign characters: thus, there must be an end to the sapping of a will hitherto brutally ground down. From the moment that the yearning for learning is no longer sapped, why go on sapping the urge to desire? If the former is cultivated, so too must the latter be cultivated.

The willfulness and "badness" of children are as justifiable as their thirst for knowledge. The latter is enthusiastically stimulated. Let there be work also upon the natural resource of the will: opposition. Unless the child acquires a sense of self, he fails to learn the most important lesson of all. Let there be no repression of his pride, nor of his candor. Against his petulance, I will always have my own freedom. Should his pride turn to obstinacy, the child will do me violence, against which I will react, so I am as free a being as the child. But should my defense be to retreat behind the convenient wall of authority? No. I will oppose him with the inflexibility of my own liberty, so that the child's obstinacy will founder upon that reef. A complete man has no need to play the authoritarian. And should license degenerate into effrontery, that effrontery will weaken in the face of the sweet resistance of a thoughtful woman, her maternal temperament, or a father's firmness: one would need to be very weak to invoke the aid of authority, and anyone who believes he can deal with a cheeky child by cowing him is fooling himself. Commanding fear and respect is something left over from the rococo style of a bygone age.

So, what are we moaning about when we analyze the gaps in our current education? That our schools cling still to the old principle, the principle of learning without will. The new principle is that of the will, of the transfiguration of knowledge. Starting from there, let there be no more "harmony between school and life," but let schooling be life-like, and let the drawing out of the personality be a duty there as well as outside. Let the universal culture of schooling aim at an apprenticeship in freedom, and not in submissiveness: being free, that is really living.

Practical education lags very far behind personal, free education: if the former manages to make headway in life, the latter provides the breath to blow the spark of life into flame: whereas the former prepares the scholar to make his way in a given milieu, the latter ensures that, in his heart of hearts, he is his own man. Not that this work is over once we behave as useful members of society. Only if we are free men, persons creating and acting on their own behalf, can we gain free access to that goal .

The motif, the thrust of the new age is freedom of the will. Consequently, pedagogy ought to espouse the molding of the free personality as its starting point and objective. (. . .) That culture, which is genuinely universal in that the humblest rubs shoulders with the haughtiest, represents the true equality of all: the equality of free persons. For only freedom is equality (. . .) So we stand in need of a personal education (. . .) If we want to hang an "-ism" upon those who live by these principles, I, speaking for myself, would opt for the label of personalists.[2]

(. . .) To conclude and briefly to summarize the end towards which our era should bend its efforts, the elimination of knowledge without will and the rise of the self-conscious knowledge which accompanies the sunburst of free personality, we might say this: knowledge must perish, in order to be resurrected as will and to recreate itself daily as free personality.

Notes to The False Principles of our Education

1. Taken from Max Stirner *Lesser Writings* 1842.

2. Stirner's "personalism" of course has as little to do with the personalism of Emmanuel Mounier as with that of Cruz Martinez Esteruelas. In Stirner's usage, "personalism" means championing the "I" as the Ego.

FROM THE EGO AND HIS OWN

WHAT IS TERMED THE STATE

What goes by the name of State is a warp and weft of dependencies and agglomerations, a common belonging, wherein all who make common cause accommodate themselves to one another and are mutually dependent. It is the ordering of that mutual dependency. Should the king, who, from the top down, confers authority upon everyone, even upon the executioner's assistant, perish, order would nonetheless be maintained in the face of the disorder of bestial instincts, by all who have a sense of order well-anchored in their consciousnesses. Were disorder to triumph, it would spell the end for the State.

But are we really to be convinced by this sentimental notion of mutual accommodation, making common cause and mutual dependency? By that reckoning, the State would be the very realization of love, with each existing for the other fellow and living for the other fellow. But would not a sense of order place individuality in jeopardy? Might one not make do with ensuring order through force, in such a way that nobody "treads on his neighbor's toes" and the flock is judiciously penned or ordered? And so all is for the best in the best of all possible orders, but that ideal order is the State.

Our societies and our States exist without our having fashioned them: they are put together without our consent: they are pre-ordained, having an independent and indissoluble life of their own, being against us individualists. The world today is, as the saying has it, at war with the "existing order of things." However, the meaning of that war is widely misunderstood, as if it were only a matter of swapping what currently exists for some new and better order. Instead, the war should be declared on every existing order, which is to say, on the State, and not on any particular State, much less upon the current form of State. The goal to be achieved is not another State (the "people's State," say), but rather association, the ever-fluid, constantly renewed association of all that exists.

Even without my intervention, a State exists. I am born into it, raised within it and I have my obligations to it, I owe it "loyalty and homage." It takes me under its sheltering wing and I live by its grace. The independent existence of the State is the foundation stone of my lack of independence. Its natural growth, its organic existence require that my own nature should not flourish without let or hindrance, but should be trimmed to size. In order that it may expand naturally, it employs the "pruning" shears on me. The education and training it affords me are tailored to suit it and not me. For instance, it teaches me to abide by the laws, to refrain from trespasses against State property (which is to say, private ownership), to venerate a divine and earthly majesty, etc. In short, it teaches me to be beyond reproach, by sacrificing my individuality on the altar of "sanctity"(anything can be sanctified — other people's property, lives, etc.) That is the sort of cultivation and training that the State is likely to afford me. It prepares me to become a "useful tool," a "useful member of society."

Which is what every State has to do, be it a "people's State," an absolute State or a constitutional State. And it will carry on like that for as long as we are immersed in the erroneous belief that it is an "ego," and, as such, a moral, mystical or public "person."

Freedom of the Individual and Society

Man's primitive condition is not isolation or solitary existence but life in society. Our existence opens with the closest of unions, since, even before we draw our first breath, we share our mother's existence: then, when we open our eyes to the light, we find ourselves at the breast of a human being: her love cradles us, keeps a check upon us and binds us to herself by a thousand ties. Society is our natural state. Which is why, as we come to self-awareness, the union that had at first been so intimate grows increasingly looser and the disintegration of primitive society becomes more and more manifest. If the mother wants to have again, all to herself, the child that but lately was nestling beneath her heart, she has to fetch him from the street and wrest him from the company of his playmates. For the child prefers the company of his peers over the society which he did not enter of his own volition, but into which he merely happened to have been born.

(. . .) Once an association has crystallized in society, it has ceased to be an association, since association is an ongoing act of re-association. It has become an association in an arrested state, it has frozen. It is no more as far as association is concerned, being now merely the corpse of an association: in short, it has become society, community. The [political] party offers us an eloquent instance of this process.

For a society, the State for instance, to gnaw away at my freedom is a matter of small consequence to me. I must resign myself to letting my freedom be whittled away by all sorts of powers, by every being stronger than myself, even by every single one of my peers. Even so, were I the autocrat of all the Russias, I could not enjoy absolute freedom. But, as far as my individuality goes, I do not want anyone tampering with it. Now, it is precisely individuality that society targets and means to subject to its power.

A society to which I affiliate certainly strips me of a few freedoms but it affords me other freedoms in compensation. It matters little, too, whether I deny myself such and such a freedom (through some contract, say). On the other hand, I will stand guard jealously over my individuality. According to the extent of its power, every community more or less tends to set itself up as an authority over its members and to restrict their freedom of movement. It requires of them, and is obliged to require of them, the limited conscience suited to subjects: it wants them subjected and only exists insofar as they are in subjection. Not that that precludes a certain tolerance: on the contrary, society will give a ready welcome to improvement schemes, reprimands and reproaches, just as long as they are of benefit to it: but the criticism that it accepts has to be "friendly." It must not be "insolent and lacking in reverence." In short, there must be no trespass against the substance of the society, which must be regarded as sacrosanct. Society requires that no one should rise above it, that one should stay within the "bounds of the law," that is, that only what is permitted by the society and its laws be allowed.

There is a difference between a society that curtails my freedom and a society that curtails my individuality. In the first case, there is union, agreement, association. But if my individuality is jeopardized, then it is because it is confronted by a society which is a power in itself, a power higher than the Ego, one that is inaccessible to me, one that I may well admire, adore, venerate and respect, but which I may never tame nor use, for the good reason that in its presence I make renunciation and abdication. Society stands or falls by my renunciation, my abnegation, my cowardliness, on what is known as humility. My humility affords its courage. My submissiveness adds up to its dominance.

Where freedom is concerned however, there is no essential difference between the State and the association. No association could be launched, nor could one exist in the absence of certain limitations upon freedom, just as a State is not compatible with boundless freedom. Some limitation upon freedom is inevitable everywhere. For one could not shrug them all off. We cannot, merely because we would like to do so, fly like birds, for we cannot divest ourselves of our heaviness. Nor can we deliberately survive on water alone, like a fish, for we could not do without air, that being a necessity of which we cannot break free, and so on.

(. . .) True, association affords a greater measure of freedom and might be construed as a "new freedom." In effect, it affords an escape from all the constraints inherent in life under the State and in society. However, in spite of those advantages, association nonetheless implies a number of encumbrances upon us.

Where individuality is concerned, the difference between State and association is considerable: the former being its foe, its murderer, and the latter its daughter and auxiliary. One is a spirit that demands our adoration in spirit and in truth: the other is my handiwork, my creation. The State is the master of my spirit: it demands my fealty and forces an article of faith, the creed of legality, down my throat. It wields over me a moral influence, commanding my spirit, dispossessing me of my Ego so as to supplant it as my real self. In short, the State is sacred and, set alongside me, the individual, it is the authentic man, the spirit, the spook.

Association, by contrast, is my own doing, my creature. It is not sacred. It does not impose itself as a spiritual power superior to my spirit. I have no wish to become a slave to my maxims, but would rather subject them to my ongoing criticism. I afford them no citizenship rights within myself. Much less do I wish to commit my entire future to the association, to "sell it my soul," as the Devil would have it, and as is truly the case when the State or any other spiritual authority is involved. I am and will always remain, with regard to myself, more than the State, than the Church, than God, etc., and thus, infinitely more than the association also.

I am told that I must be a man in the company of my peers (Marx, *The Jewish Question*, page 60). I ought to respect them as my peers. As far as I am concerned, no one is deserving of respect, not even my peer. He, like others, is merely an object in which I take or fail to take an interest, a serviceable or unserviceable subject.

If he may be of use to me, then of course I am going to come to an accommodation and enter into association with him, in order to bolster my power and, with the aid of our combined might, to accomplish more than either of us might, in isolation. In such communion I see nothing more than a multiplication of my strength and I afford it my consent only as long as that multiplication brings its benefits. That is what association means.

Association is not sustained by any natural or spiritual tie, and it is not a natural alliance, a meeting of minds. In a natural alliance such as the family, tribe, nation, or even humanity, individuals are of no account except as specimens of the same ilk, the same species. In a meeting of minds, religious community or Church, the individual is only one member governed by a shared mentality. In both cases, what you describe as Ego has to be snuffed out. As a unique individual, you can assert yourself alone in association, because the association does not own you, because you are one who owns it or who turns it to your own advantage.

(. . .) The State makes efforts to stem the covetous: to put that another way, it seeks to turn them exclusively in its own direction and to satisfy them with what it has to offer them. It simply does not occur to it to assuage them out of any affection for the covetous. Instead, it labels as "egoist" the man who cannot control his appetites, and "egoist" man is its enemy. It views him that way because the State lacks the capacity to reach an accommodation with the "egoist" and to understand him. The State being what it is, it could hardly be otherwise, for it is concerned only with itself, could not care less about my needs and only turns its attention to me in order to slay me, that is, to turn me into another Ego, a good citizen. It takes its measures to "improve morals." And what does it do to win over individuals? It sets in motion the means particular to the State. It never wearies of affording everyone a share in its "benefits," in the benefits of instruction and culture. It makes you a present of its education. It throws open to you the doors of its educational establishments, affords you the means of acquiring property through your industry, which is tantamount to enfeoffment. In return for the award of this feof, all it asks of you is the fair return of eternal gratitude. But there are "ingrates" who omit to pay their dues (. . .)

In association, you invest all of your power, all that you own, and you bring it to bear. Society exploits you and exploits your labor power. In the first case, you live as an individualist, whereas in the second, you have to labor in the master's vineyard. You are indebted to society for all that you have and you are obligated to it and laden down with "obligations to society." In the case of association, it is you who are the user, and as soon as you see no further advantage in it, you drop out of it, without further obligation to it and owe it no further loyalty.

Society is more than you and overwhelms you. Association is nothing more than an instrument in your hands, a sword that gives an added cutting edge to your capabilities. Society, on the other hand, claims you for its very own. It can survive equally well without you. In short, society is sacrosanct, association your property. Society makes use of you, but it is you that makes use of association.

From The Ego and His Own (1843)

Concerning the Party

The Party, whose praises have been sung of late, also comes under the heading of Society.

The Party has its place within the State. "Party, Party, who would not belong to it!" But the individual is unique and thus no Party member. He enters freely into association and equally freely reclaims his freedom. The Party is only a State within the State and, in this tiniest of beehive societies, it is as essential that peace should prevail as in the largest. The very people who clamor loudest for there to be an opposition within the State thunder against the slightest quibble inside the Party. Which goes to prove that all that they too want is that the State should be one. It is not with the State but with the unique individual that that all parties are incompatible.

In our day, there is nothing so commonplace as the sound of one being exhorted to keep faith with his Party, nothing being so reprehensible in the eyes of Party members as an individual who deserts his Party. He must follow his Party always and everywhere: he absolutely must approve its principles and support them. To be sure, things are not taken to the lengths of certain closed societies (like the religious orders, the Jesuits, etc.) which hold their members to their beliefs or to their statutes. But the Party ceases to be an association the moment that it seeks to impose certain principles through constraint and defend them against all attack. In that instant the Party is born. As a Party, it is part and parcel of established society, of a deceased association: it has turned into something akin to an *idee fixe*. An absolutist Party, it is not prepared to see doubts cast upon the infallibility of its principles by its members. The latter could only succumb to doubts if they were sufficiently individualists to want to remain something outside of their Party, which is to say, "impartial observers." They cannot be impartial as Party members. Only as individualists.

Should you be a Protestant and belong to that Party, you can only argue on behalf of Protestantism, or at best "purify" it, but not repudiate it. Being a Christian and one of the adepts of the Christian Party, you cannot withdraw from it as a member of that Party, but only if impelled to do so by your individualism, which is to say, by your "impartiality." However much the efforts made by Christians, through to Hegel and the Communists, to strengthen their Party, they have not been able to do any better than this: Christianity encapsulates eternal truth and one should confine oneself to demonstrating and justifying it.

In short, the Party does not countenance "impartiality" and it is precisely there that individualism comes into play. What matters the Party to me? I will always find enough folk who will enter into association with me without having to take a pledge to my flag.

Anyone shifting from one Party to another is promptly labeled a "turncoat." This because Morality requires that one keeps faith with one's Party, and renunciation of it is tantamount to staining oneself with the mire of "infidelity." Only individuality acknowledges no injunction to "fidelity" and "commitment": it permits everything, including apostasy and desertion. Unwittingly, the moralists let themselves be guided by that principle when they have to sit in judgment of a deserter defecting to their own Party: they certainly are not embarrassed by proselytization. They ought simply to take cognizance of the fact that one ought to behave immorally if one wishes to behave as an individual; in other words, one should abjure one's belief and even break one's pledge in order to make one's own decisions, instead of being guided by considerations of a moral nature.

In the view of rigid moralists, an apostate is always under a cloud and does not readily earn their trust: he carries on him the stain of "infidelity," which is tantamount to saying: of immorality. Among the common people, this outlook is virtually universal. As for the enlightened folk, they are, in this regard as in every other, wallowing in uncertainty and turmoil. The contradiction inevitably spawned by the principle of morality is one that they do not wittingly perceive, on account of the confusion of their ideas. They dare not dismiss apostates as immoral, because they themselves flirt with apostasy, with the desertion of one religion for another, nor are they willing to turn away from the moralizing viewpoint. They could truly seize upon an opportunity to shrug free of it!

And do individuals, the Unique ones, form a Party? How could they be Unique ones if they were members of a Party?

Might it be that one should not join any Party? In joining a Party, in entering into its orbit, I enter into association with it, one that lasts for as long as the Party and I subscribe to the same objective. But, while I may well subscribe to the Party's inclinations today, tomorrow that will no longer be the case and I will become "unfaithful" to it. The Party has no powers to bind me, nothing to commit me and I have no regard for it. If it pleases me no longer, I become hostile towards it.

Inside every Party fighting for its survival, the membership is all the less free or all the less "unique," according to the degree to which they are deprived of their individuality and kowtow to the Party's slightest whims. The Party's independence entails dependency for the Party's members.

A Party, whatever its nature may be, can never dispense with a profession of faith. Because its members have to believe in its principles and not cast doubt upon, or question them. As far as they are concerned, these principles have to be certain, beyond doubt. In short, one has to belong body and soul to the Party, failing which one is not a real Party member, but, more or less, an individualist. Do but cast doubt upon Christianity and you are no longer a true Christian, but are committing the presumption of calling Christianity into question and hauling it before your individual tribunal. You have sinned against Christianity, against the cause of a Party (. . .) But that is all the better for you, as long as you do not let yourself be frightened: your effrontery is of help to you in recovering your individuality.

So, someone will ask, can an individualist never take sides? Of course he can. On condition that he does not let himself be gobbled up by the Party. The Party is only ever, as far as he is concerned, a part. He is part and he partakes.

Revolt and Revolution

Revolution and revolt ought never to be mistaken for synonyms. The former consists of the overthrow of the existing order of things, of the existing State or society, and is thus a political or social act. The latter, while inevitably involving a transformation of the existing order, does not take such transformation as its starting point. It starts from the fact that men are not at ease with themselves. It is not a strapping on of battle-armor, but an uprising of individuals, a rebellion that cares nothing for the institutions it is likely to spawn. The Revolution has new institutions as its objective. Revolt induces us to no longer let ourselves be governed, but rather to shift for ourselves. Revolt does not look to the "institutions" to come for any wonders. It is a fight against what already exists. Should it succeed, what already exists will collapse on its own. It merely sets my Ego free from the existing order of things. Which, from the moment that I bid it farewell, perishes and starts to rot.

Now, since it is not my aim to overthrow what already exists, but rather to rise above what exists, my actions are in no way political or social: they have no object other than myself and my individuality: they are "selfish." Institutions are a requirement of the Revolution. Revolt wants to see us rise up or stand up. The choosing of a constitution was the preoccupation of revolutionary leaders: the entire political history of the Revolution seethed with constitutional strife and constitutional issues, just as the talents of social reformers proved extremely fertile in social institutions (like the phalansteries and others). But revolt strives to wrestle free of any constitution.

Counter-Criticism[1]

In the following text, Stirner, writing in the third person, replies to several of his critics. The first part was published in the third 1845 issue of the review Wigand's Vierteljahrschrift as "Authors of Reviews of Stirner." First of all, Stirner replied to Ludwig Feuerbach, author of The Essence of Christianity, regarding which Stirner had been especially scathing in his own book. In the second 1845 issue of the same review, Feuerbach had published, anonymously, an essay entitled "Regarding The Essence of Christianity relation to The Ego and His Own." Stirner next replied to Moses Hess, who had attacked him in a little 28-page pamphlet published in Darmstadt in 1845 as The Last Philosophers. The second portion of this Counter-Criticism was published under the *nom* de plume of G. Edward in the fourth 1847 issue of Otto Wigand's review *The Epig*iones as "The reactionary philosophers. A reply to Kuno Fischer's The Modern Sophists," wherein, again in the third person, Stirner replied to a criticism from Kuno Fischer, which had appeared in 1847 as "The Modern Sophists," in the Leipziger Revue and which was essentially directed against him.

Today's reader will doubtless be interested, not so much in the arguments and quibbles of a Stirner grappling with his adversaries as in the way in which he draws a distinction between his own individualist "egoism" and vulgar egoism, and the manner in which he reconciles his individualism with the spirit of association.

What is Stirnerite Egoism?

A certain notion of egoism, whereby it is taken simply to mean "isolation," has gained currency. But what can egoism have to do with isolation? Do I (Ego) become an egoist if, say, I shun men's companionship? I isolate myself and live alone of course, but that does not make me any more of an egoist than the rest who continue to coexist with men and revel in it. If I isolate myself, it is because I no longer delight in society; if I remain within it, it is because men still have much to offer me. Remaining in their company is every whit as egotistical as isolating myself from them.

When it comes to competition, to be sure, everyone is on his own. But should competition some day disappear, because concerted effort will have been acknowledged as more beneficial than isolation, then will not every single individual inside the associations be equally egoistic and out for his own interests? The counter to that is that it will, though, not be at his neighbor's expense now, but rather for the good reason that the neighbor will no longer be so foolish as to let anybody else be a parasite upon him.

And yet it is said: "The man who thinks only of himself is an egoist." But that would be a man who does not know and cannot appreciate any of the delights emanating from an interest taken in others, from the consideration shown to others. That would be a man bereft of innumerable pleasures, a wretched character. Why then should that runt, that loner be declared to be more egotistical than richer natures? Is the oyster more of an egoist than the dog, the Black more of an egoist than the German, the poor, despised Jewish second-hand clothes dealer more of an egoist than the enthusiastic socialist? And the vandal destroyer of works of art that leave him cold, is he more of an egoist than the painstaking connoisseur who treats them with the utmost care, because he has an interest in and taste for them? And if there should be someone — we shall pass over the question of whether there is any evidence for the existence of anything of the sort — who takes no "human" interest in men, who cannot appreciate them as men, would he not be a wretched egoist, rather than a genuine Egoist? (. . .) The person who loves a human being is, by virtue of that love, a wealthier man than someone else who loves no one: but what we have here is not a contrast between egoism and non-egoism, for both these human types are merely obedient, each after its fashion, to their respective interests.

"Even so, everyone ought to take an interest in people and should love people!" Well now, let us see where that duty, that commandment to love has got us! For the past two thousand years, men's hearts have been stuffed with it, and yet the socialists are complaining today that our proletarians are treated with less consideration than slaves in Ancient times, and yet those same socialists once again are peddling, albeit with much greater stridency, that commandment to love.

You want men to display an interest in you? Well then, make it an obligation upon them to feel some for you, and stop being uninteresting saints who wear their blessed humanity like a sacred garment and clamor like beggars: "Respect our human nature, for it is sacred!"

The Egoism for which Stirner acts as spokesman is not the contrary of love, nor of thoughtfulness, and is not inimical to a sweet life of love, nor to commitment and sacrifice: it is not hostile to the tenderest of cordiality, nor is it the enemy of criticism, nor of socialism: in short, it is not inimical to any interest: it excludes no interest. It simply runs counter to un-interest and to the uninteresting: it is not against love but against sacred love, not against thinking, but against sacred thinking: not against socialists, but against the sacred socialists, etc.

The "exclusivism" of the authentic Egoist, which some would represent as "isolation" or "detachment" is instead a full participation in whatever arouses interest, to the exclusion of whatever does not.

There has been a refusal to give due credit to Stirner for the most significant chapter of Stirner's book[2], the chapter on "My Intercourse," intercourse with the world and the association of Egoists.

Notes to What is Stirnerite Egoism?

1. Taken from his *Lesser Writings.*
2. *The Ego and His Own.*

Moses Hess and the Two Sorts of Egoists' Associations

(...) Hess contends that "our entire history has thus far been nothing but the history of egoist associations, the fruits of which, the slavery of Antiquity, Roman serfdom and modern, axiomatic, universal servitude, are all too familiar to us all." For a start, Hess here uses (...) the expression "egoist association" rather than Stirner's term "Egoists' association." His readers (...) will assuredly not be long in finding it accurate and indubitable that the associations to which he refers were indeed "egoist associations." But is an association, wherein most members allow themselves to be lulled as regards their most natural and most obvious interests, actually an Egoists' association? Can they really be "Egoists" who have banded together when one is a slave or a serf of the other? No doubt there are egoists in such a society, and on that basis it could with some semblance of justification be described as an "egoist association" but, my word! the slaves did not seek out such company out of egoism, and are, rather, in their egoist heart of hearts, against these splendid "associations," as Hess describes them.

Societies wherein the needs of some are satisfied at the expense of the rest, where, say, some may satisfy their need for rest thanks to the fact that the rest must work to the point of exhaustion, and can lead a life of ease because others live in misery and perish of hunger, or indeed who live a life of dissipation because others are foolish enough to live in indigence, etc., such societies are described by Hess as "egoist associations" and he ventures quite candidly and intolerably to take these "egoist associations" of his as synonymous with Stirner's "Egoists' associations." True, Stirner does happen to use the expression "egoist association" too, but that expression is, for one thing, spelled out as an "Egoists' association," and, for another, is appropriate, whereas what Hess calls by that name is more of a religious society, a communion held as sacrosanct by right, by law and by all of the pomp and circumstance of the courts.

Things would be different had Hess agreed to look at egoist associations in real life and not just on paper. Faust was in the midst of such associations when he cried out: "Here I am a man, here I can be one (...)" Goethe spells it out for us in black and white. Had Hess paid close attention to real life, to which he is said to adhere so closely, he might see hundreds of egoist associations of that sort, some ephemeral, some enduring. Even at this very moment there may be some children gathered outside his window and becoming playmates: let him observe them then, and he will spot joyful egoist associations. Maybe Hess has a friend, a beloved: in which case, he may know how the heart has its reasons, how two beings come together egoistically in enjoyment of each other, neither of them thereby "losing out." It may be that he comes across good pals in the street who invite him to accompany them to a cafe: does he take up this invitation so as to do them a kind service, or does he go along with them because it holds out the prospect of pleasure to him? Should they thank him warmly for his "sacrifice," or do they appreciate that, together, they all make up, for an hour or so, an "egoist association?"

Feuerbach's Abstract "Man"

(. . .) Feuerbach forgets that "man" does not exist, that he is an arbitrary abstraction and he sets him up as an ideal. Is it any wonder that in the final analysis he turns him into a generic, mysterious, impersonal being endowed with secret "powers" which, like the Greek gods alongside Zeus, confer a polytheistic function upon him? (. . .) Stirner counters this watchword, this phraseology of "humanism," with that of "Egoism." What? You require of me that I be a "man," you require of me that I be "mannish?" What? Haven't I been "man," "naked little being" and "mannish" since my cradle days? That is, beyond question, what I am, but I am more than that: I am what I have become through my own efforts, through my development, through my appropriation of the outside world, of history, etc.: I am "unique." But, deep down, that is not what you want. You do not want me to be a real man. You would not give a farthing for my uniqueness. You want me to be "Man," such as you have construed him, as an ideal, exemplary type. You want to make the "plebeian egalitarian principle" the guiding light of my life.

I match you principle for principle, requirement for requirement, with the principle of Egoism. I only want to be Me. I abhor nature, I despise men and their laws, as well as human society and its love, with which I sever every general connection, even that of language. Your claims of obligation, to your "thou shalt," to the pronouncements of your categorical verdict, I refute en bloc with the "ataraxia" and serenity of my Ego. It is out of sheer condescension that I make use of language. I am the "Unspeakable" and it is quite right that I should show myself, that I should appear. I ask you, do I not, with my brow-beating Ego and discarding everything human, have as much right on my side as you, with your brow-beating humanity that bluntly stigmatizes me as "non-human" when I offend against your catechism, in declining to permit any tinkering with my self-enjoyment?

Does that amount to saying that Stirner, with his "Egoism," is seeking to deny everything that belongs to us all, to declare it non-existent, that, out of negation pure and simple, he wants to make a *tabula rasa* of all private property in our social organization, which none may escape? Does it mean that he wishes to turn his back on all human community, to turn into a chrysalis, which would be tantamount, so to speak, to committing suicide? That is, my word, a rather crass misunderstanding (. . .) But Stirner's book does contain a weighty "deduction," a very important and mighty conclusion, which cannot, in most cases of course, only be read between the lines, but which has eluded the philosophers completely. For the reason that they do not know the real man, nor even themselves as real men, only ever dealing with "Man," "Spirit" of itself, a priori, with the name only and never with the thing, the person as such. Which is what Stirner is saying, in a negative way, through the irresistible, incisive criticism with which he analyses all of the illusions of idealism and strips the veil from all of the lies of disinterested commitment and sacrifice: which, naturally, his glorious criticisms have yet again striven to construe as an apotheosis of blind, selfish interest, of the narrowest egoism.

(. . .) Stirner himself has described his book as a sometimes "clumsy" articulation of what he intended to say. It is the laborious product of the best years of his life: and yet he agrees that it is, to some extent, "clumsy," insofar as he is grappling with a language corrupted by the philosophers, debauched by the henchmen of the State, of religion and of other beliefs, a language that has been turned into a generator of an unfathomable mishmash of ideas.

PIERRE-JOSEPH PROUDHON (1809–1865)

Pierre-Joseph Proudhon died in Paris on January 16, 1865, at the age of fifty six years, prematurely worn out by his colossal cerebral endeavors. How can we sum up in a few words the personality of this erstwhile workman, the son of peasants, a self-made man and autodidact?

Quite apart from all his other qualities, he was one of the greatest writers in the French language and the critic Saint-Beuve devoted an entire book to him.

Proudhon's was a protean genius, his complete output (to which must be added the 14 volumes of his *Correspondence*, the five volumes of his Carnets currently being published and the unpublished manuscripts revealed to us by Pierre Haubtmann's doctoral thesis) prolific. He was at one and the same time, the father of "scientific socialism," of socialist political economy and of modern sociology, the father of anarchism, of mutualism, of revolutionary syndicalism, of federalism and of that particular form of collectivism that has recaptured a fresh relevance today as "self-management." His views on history, and, especially, on the French Revolution and on Napoleon display an intuitive perspicacity that place him in the company of Michelet. Lastly and above all, he was the first person to anticipate and prophetically denounce the dangers implicit in an authoritarian, Statist, dogmatic socialism.

The 1848 revolution provided him with an opportunity to step, not without courage, into the revolutionary arena, and under the second Bonaparte, the subversive boldness of his writings earned him harassment, imprisonment and exile.

His original and paradoxical turn of mind, highlighted by a mightily plebeian zest, all too often induced him to let his bubbling cauldron of a mind spurt out outrageous ideas — about war, progress, feminism, racism, art, sexuality, etc. He preached a fanatically puritanical morality. He never quite broke free of the Christian education of his early years, and in his mightiest tome, one of the most vitriolic and most devastating indictments ever devised by anti-clericalism, Justice appears, when all is said and done, as a thinly disguised synonym for God.[1] Nor did he successfully discard the strong idealistic stamp which he owed to his reading (at one remove) of the works of Hegel, and his stolidly legalistic mentality remained yoked to the materialist conception of history.

Simultaneously revolutionary and conservative, enamored of liberty and order alike, Proudhon has been claimed by the most contradictory ideologies. In his lifetime, although widely read and the focus of sensational publicity, he plowed an exceptionally lonely furrow.

Marxism, greatly indebted to him and which was not always acting in good faith in its attacks upon him, has long since eclipsed him. Although torn, in terms of action, between Blanquism, parliamentary reformism, anarchism and Statism, and, in terms of theory, between Hegelian philosophy and English political economy, marxism is, apparently at any rate, more coherent than were Proudhon's sometimes chaotic visions. The redoubtable temporal power and intellectual dictatorship exercised in the usurped name of Marx and also to the advantage of the October Revolution and its red epigones' betrayal thereof, have wronged Proudhon's memory. Until quite recently, he was somewhat misunderstood, misrepresented, forgotten about. The belief was that there was nothing more that needed saying about him once he had been hung with the insulting label of "petit-bourgeois." But even in the "marxist" camp, they are starting to re-read him and the insults have become less shrill.

The Young Proudhon: A Self Portrait

Of my private life I have nothing to say: it does not concern others. I have always had little liking for autobiographies and have no interest in anyone's affairs. History proper and novels hold no attractions for me except insofar as I can discern there, as within our immortal Revolution, the adventures of the mind.

(...) I was born in Besançon, on January 15, 1809, son of Claude-François Proudhon, cooper and brewer, native of Chasnans, near Pontarlier in the department of Doubs, and of Catherine Simonin, from Cordiron, in the parish of Burgille-les-Marnay, in the same department.

My paternal and maternal forebears were all free plowmen, exempt from corvées and impositions, from time immemorial.

(. . .) Up to the age of twelve years, my life was virtually entirely spent out in the fields, busy either with minor farm tasks or with tending cattle. I was five years a drover. I know of no way of life that is at once more contemplative and more realistic, more contrary to the absurd spiritualism that furnishes the basis of education and the Christian life, than that of the field hand.

(. . .) How I once relished running through the long grass, which I should have loved to browse upon, like my cattle: running bare-foot along the paths alongside the hedges: my legs working (. . .) trampling (grinding) the green shoots of *turquies*[3] into the deep, fresh dirt! On more than one warm June morning, it happened that I stripped off my clothes and took a bath in the dewy grass.

(. . .) I made scarcely any distinction between what was me and what was not. I was everything that I could touch with my hand, gaze upon and that was somehow serviceable to me; the not-I was anything that might harm or resist me. All day long, I gorged myself with blackberries, rape-seeds, oyster plants, green peas, poppy seeds, toasted cobs of maize, all sorts of berries, sloes, *blessons*, alders, wild cherries, sweetbriers, *lambrusques*, and wild fruits; I stuffed myself with enough salad to choke a petit bourgeois of refined education, and the only effect it had upon my stomach was to give me a ravenous appetite come evening. The soul of nature does no harm to her own.

(. . .) How many downpours I wiped away! How many times, drenched to the bone, I dried my clothes upon my body, in the north wind or in the heat of the sun! How many baths taken at a moment's notice, in the river in summer-time, in springs in the winter-time! I would clamber up trees; delve into caves; ran frogs to ground, rooting around in their holes, risking encounters with a ghastly salamander; then roasting my quarry whole over the coals. In every living thing, man and beast alike, there are secret affinities and animosities of which civilization has made us insensible. I loved my cows, but with a one-sided affection; I had my favorites among the hens, the trees, the rocks. Someone had told me that the lizard is man's friend; I honestly believed it. But I always waged war without quarter against snakes, toads and caterpillars. *What harm had they done me*? None. I do not know; but experience of human beings has always made me despise them the more.

Proudhon the Compositor

(. . .) I left school for the workshop. I was nineteen years old. Having become a producer in my own right and a driver of bargains, my everyday toil, the training I had received and my sharper mind allowed me to probe the matter more deeply than I had hitherto known how to do. All in vain — the mystery deepened.

But, I used to tell myself everyday as I "set up" my lines, what if the producers should somehow agree to market their products and services at pretty much cost price and thus at value? There would doubtless be fewer rich people around, but there would be fewer bankrupts too. And, with everything being cheap, we should have a lot less destitution (. . .) No positive experiment has demonstrated that minds and interests cannot be so balanced out that peace, an unbreachable peace, should sprout from them and wealth become a general rule. (. . .) The whole point is to come up with a harmonizing, evaluative principle of equilibrium.

After some weeks working in Lyon and then in Marseilles, steady work[4] being still in short supply, I set out for Toulon, arriving there with just three francs 50 centimes to my name. I had never been happier or more confident than at that straitened moment. I had not yet learned how to reckon life's debits and assets — I was young. In Toulon, there was no work: I had arrived too late and missed the "boat" by 24 hours. A thought occurred to me and it seemed a real inspiration at the time: while up in Paris the unemployed workers were attacking the government, I resolved for my own part to make my petition to the authorities.

I went to the city hall and asked to speak to the mayor. Ushered into the magistrate's office, I produced my passport to show him:

"Here, monsieur," I told him, "this document cost me two francs and, following information supplied with regard to me by the police superintendent of my district, along with two known witnesses, it promises me and enjoins the civil and military authorities to afford me assistance and protection should the need arise. Now, you will know, Mr. Mayor, that I am a printer's compositor, that, since Paris, I have been searching for work, without success, and that I am down to the last of my savings. Theft is punished and begging prohibited; not everybody can live off their investments. That leaves work, a guarantee of which, it seems to me, looks like the only thing likely to fulfill the purpose of my passport. Consequently, Mr. Mayor, I have come to place myself at your disposal."

I was one of that breed which, a little later, took up the slogan of *Live by working or die fighting!* which, in 1848, gave the Republic *three months to eliminate poverty* and, come June, scribbled *Bread or lead!* upon their banners. I was wrong and today I admit as much — may my example be a lesson to my peers.

The man to whom I had turned was a small, plump, pudgy, smug fellow wearing gold-rimmed glasses and he certainly was not prepared for my formal demand. I made a note of his name, as I like to know those whom I hold dear. He was a Monsieur Guieu, known as Tripette or Tripatte, a former attorney at law, one of the new men unearthed by the July dynasty and a man who, although wealthy, would not turn his nose up at a scholarship for his children. He must have taken me for someone who had escaped the insurrection which had just shaken Paris when the general was buried.[5]

"Monsieur," he said to me, skipping back to his armchair, "yours is an unusual request, and you have misconstrued your passport. It means that, should you be attacked; should you be robbed, the authorities will leap to your defense: and that is all."

"Forgive me, Mr. Mayor, but in France the law protects everyone, even the guilty whom it cracks down upon. The gendarme does not have the right to strike the murderer who stabs him, except in self-defense. If a man is put in prison, the governor cannot seize his effects. The passport, as well as the record book, for I carry both, suggests something more to the working man, or it means nothing at all."

"Monsieur, I am going to award you 15 centimes per league so that you can go home again. Which is all that I can do for you. My powers go no further."

"That, Mr. Mayor, is alms and I want no part of it. Whenever I get back to my own district, upon discovering that there is no work to be had, I am going to seek out the mayor of my commune, just as I have sought you out today: so that my return trip will have cost the State 18 francs, with no benefit to anybody."

"Monsieur, that is outside of my powers . . ."

And he would not budge from that. Defeated and driven back on to the terrain of legality, I tried another tack. Perhaps, I wondered, the man is worth more than the official: quiet manner, Christian face, less mortification: but the best fed ones are still the best:

"Monsieur," I resumed, "since your powers do not allow you to accede to my request, let me have your advice. If need be, I can make myself useful other than in a printing works, and I will not turn my nose up at anything. You are familiar with the area: what work is there? What would you advise me?"

"To take yourself off, Monsieur." I gave him a dirty look.

"Fine, Mr. Mayor," I told him between clenched teeth. "Let me assure you that I will not forget this interview."

Leaving the city hall behind, I left Toulon via the Italian approach road. (...) For two years I roamed the world, studying, questioning the little people to whose social circumstances I found my own were closer — with scarcely the time to read and less for writing.

(...) So much for my life to date and indeed my life is still the same: living in workshops, witnessing the people's vices and virtues, eating my daily bread, earned by the sweat of my brow, obliged to help my family and help with my brothers' education out of my modest earnings: and, in the middle of it all, reflecting, philosophizing, jotting down the tiniest details of unexpected observations.

Wearying of the precarious, impoverished circumstances of the working man, I eventually wanted to attempt, along with one of my colleagues, to set up a little printing establishment. The meager savings of two friends were pooled and all of their families' resources committed to this lottery. The treachery of business life crushed our hopes — our method, toil and parsimony had availed us nothing: of the two partners, one wound up in the corner of a wood to perish of exhaustion and despair and the other now has nothing left for it but to repent of his having squandered his father's last crust of bread.

Public Debut

(...) My public life began in 1837, in the middle of the Philippian[6] corruption. The Besançon Academy had to award a three year scholarship bequeathed by Monsieur Suard, secretary of the Academie Française to young penniless natives of Franche-Comte destined for a career in letters or sciences. I entered the lists. In the memorandum which I forwarded to the Academy and which is in its archives, I told it:

> Born and raised in the bosom of the working class, belonging to it yet in my heart and in my affections, above all by a community of suffering and hopes, my greatest delight, were the Academy to vote for me, would be to work tirelessly, through philosophy and science, with all of the energy of my will and all of my mental powers, for the physical, moral and intellectual betterment of those who I am pleased to account my brothers and companions: so as to be able to plant among them the seed of a doctrine that I regard as the law of the moral universe, and, pending the success of my efforts, to act, gentlemen, even now as their representative in dealings with you.

As may be seen, my protests date from a long time ago. I was still young and full of faith when I articulated my wishes. It is for my fellow-citizens to say whether I have kept faith with them. My socialism received its baptism from a learned company: I had an academy for my sponsor, and, had my vocation — long since fixed — wavered, the encouragement that I then received from my honorable countrymen would have confirmed it beyond relapse.

I immediately set to work. I sought no enlightenment from the schools of socialism then in existence, these beginning even then to fall out of fashion. Likewise I left the party members and journalists, overly preoccupied with their day to day struggles to spare a thought for the implications of their own ideas. Nor did I sample, nor seek out the secret societies — all these people seemed to me to be as far removed from the aim I was pursuing as the eclectics and the Jesuits.

I opened my work of lonely conspiracy with a study of socialist antiquities, which I reckoned was necessary if I was to identify the movement's theoretical and practical law. I found those antiquities first in the Bible. Speaking to Christians, the Bible had to be the primary authority for me. An essay on the sabbatarian institution — examined from the viewpoint of morality, hygiene, family and civic relationships — earned me a bronze medal from my academy. So I hurtled headlong away from the faith in which I had been raised into pure reason, and even then, by some freak which I took to be a good omen, I was applauded for having portrayed Moses as a philosopher and socialist. If I have now gone astray, the fault is not mine alone: was there ever such a seduction?

But I was studying primarily with an eye to practicality. I cared little for academic laurels; I did not have the time to become a scholar, much less a literatus or archaeologist. I tackled political economy right away.

I had taken it as the basis for my opinions that any principle which — taken to its logical conclusion — would result in a contradiction, had to be regarded as mistaken and rejected: and that if that principle had given rise to an institution, that institution itself was to be regarded as contrived: as a utopia.

Armed with that criterion, I selected as my topic for examination the oldest, most respectable, most universal and least controversial thing that I had found in society: property. What befell me, we know. After a protracted painstaking, and above all impartial analysis, I arrived — like an algebrist led by his equations — at this startling conclusion: property, no matter the angle from which it is examined or the principle to which it is related, is a contradictory idea. And as the negation of property implies that of authority, I immediately deduced from my definition this no less paradoxical corollary: that the authentic form of government is anarchy.

(. . .) I thought my work sufficiently unsettling by itself to merit public notice and to arouse the curiosity of scholars. I forwarded my essay to the

Academy of Moral and Political Sciences. The benevolent reception that greeted it, the praises which the rapporteur, Monsieur Blanqui,[7] felt it appropriate to bestow upon its author, gave me reason to think that the Academy, without claiming responsibility for my theory, was satisfied with my work, and I pressed on with my researches.

Dialectics intoxicated me; a certain fanaticism particular to logicians had planted itself in my mind and turned my memorandum into a pamphlet. The Besançon courts having seen fit to initiate proceedings against that pamphlet, I was brought before the Doubs departmental court of assizes on the four-fold indictment of attacking property, incitement to contempt of government, insulting religion and giving offense to morals. I did what I could to explain to the jury how, in the current state of commercial intercourse, use value and exchange value being two unknown quantities perpetually at war with each other, property is quite illogical and unstable, and that this is the reason why workers are increasingly poor and property-owners less and less wealthy. The jury appeared not to understand much of my proof; it stated that this was scientific matter and thus beyond its competence, and it delivered a verdict of acquittal in my favor.

Notes to Pierre-Joseph Proudhon (1809–1865)

1. See *De la Justice dans la Révolution et dans l'Eglise* 1958.
2. The extracts below are lifted from *De la Justice. . .*, from *Lettres à l'Académie de Besançon*, 1837: from *Confessions d'un révolutionnaire pour servir à l'histoire de la révolution de évrier* 1849.
3. *Turquie*, a name the peasants gave to maize (having mixed it up with so-called Turkey wheat, which in fact originated in the New World).
4. Long-term printing work: to this day, printing presses are divided into ones that are "de labeur" (long-term) and those which are "de presse" (occasional).
5. The reference here is to the funeral of General Maximilien Lamarque (1770–1832) which had just provided the occasion for a huge popular demonstration that degenerated into riots.
6. The reference is to the 1830–1848 reign of king Louis-Philippe.
7. Adolphe Blanqui (1798–1854) a bourgeois economist and brother of the great revolutionary Auguste Blanqui.

Property is Theft[1]

Had I to answer the following question: What is slavery? and answer with a single word — Murder — my reasoning would be grasped immediately. I would not need any protracted discourse to demonstrate that the power to strip a man of his mind, his will, his personality, is a power over life and death, and that making a man a slave is tantamount to murder. So why cannot I answer this other query: What is property? in similar vein — Theft — without being assured that I would not be heeded, even though this second proposition is merely a recasting of the first?

I undertake to discuss the very principle of our government and our institutions, property: I am within my rights; I may go astray in the conclusion that will emerge from my inquiries: it amuses me to place my book's concluding thought right at the start of it — again I am within my rights.

One writer teaches that property is a civil right, sprung from occupancy and sanctioned by law; another contends that it is a natural right, its source in labor, and those teachings, contradictory as they may seem, are encouraged and applauded. My contention is that neither labor nor occupancy nor law can create property; that it is a cause-less effect: am I to be held reprehensible?

What a brouhaha erupts!

— Property is theft! That's the tocsin of '93! the mayhem of revolutions!

— Calm yourself, reader; I am not an agent of discord, a seditious firebrand! I am a few days ahead of my times: I spell out a truth whose emergence we strive in vain to stem; I am writing the preamble to our future constitution. If our preoccupations would but let us hear it, this definition, Property is theft, which sounds to you such a blasphemy, would act as a lightning conductor; but how many are the interests and prejudices that oppose it! Philosophy will not, *alas!*, alter the course of events: destinies will be worked out regardless of prophecy; moreover, should justice not be done and our education completed?

— Property is theft! What an inversion of human ideas! Proprietor and thief were forever contradictory terms, just as the entities they describe are antipathetic; every language has articulated this contradiction in terms. So on what authority would you assail this universal convention and throw down the gauntlet to the human race? Who are you to refute the reasoning of peoples and ages?

— What is my puny person to you, reader? I, like you, am of a century when reason bows only before fact and proof; my name, like your own, is seeker after truth[2]; my mission inscribed in the words of the law: *Speak without hatred and without fear — tell what you know.* Our species' task is to build the temple of science, and that science embraces man and nature. Now truth discloses itself to all, to Newton and Pascal today, to the shepherd in the valley and the journeyman in his workshop tomorrow. Everyone has his contribution to make, and, mission accomplished, he vanishes. Eternity goes before us and comes after us: between those two infinities, what is the span of mortal man, that the century should take him under its notice?

So, reader, forget about my title and my character, and concern yourself with my arguments alone. My aim is to remedy the universal error of universal convention: It is to the faith of humankind that I appeal the opinion of humankind. Make so bold as to follow me and, if you have an open mind, if your conscience is free, if your mind can blend two propositions in order to arrive at a third, my ideas will infallibly become your own. In opening with my final conclusion, my intention was to inform and not to taunt you: for I am certain that if you will but read me, I will command your assent. The matters of which I must speak to you are so simple, so palpable, that you will be stunned that you never noticed them, and you will say to yourself, "I never thought about that." Others will offer you a display of genius cracking the secrets of nature, and gushing sublime oracles — here you will encounter only a series of experiments in justice and right, a sort of assaying of the weights and measures of your conscience. The operations will be carried out before your very eyes, and it is for you yourself to gauge the outcome.

In addition, I offer no system: I seek the end of privilege, the abolition of slavery, equality of rights, the rule of law. Justice, nothing but justice; such is my discourse in sum — I leave to others the care of disciplining the world.

I said to myself one day: Why so much pain and misery in society? Must man be forever unhappy? And, without dwelling upon the all-purpose explanations of the peddlers of reform who record the general distress — some the cowardice and incompetence of the authorities, others plotters and disturbances, still others ignorance and widespread corruption. Weary of the interminable battles of rostrum and press, I have sought to plumb things for myself. I have consulted the master scientists, read a hundred volumes of philosophy, law, political economy and history, and it has pleased God to have me live in an age when so much reading was useless to me! I have made every effort to locate precise information, comparing doctrines, measuring answers alongside objections, forever manipulating equations and reductions of arguments, weighing syllogisms by the thousands in the balances of the most scrupulous logic. By this tiresome route, I have gleaned several interesting facts, which I will impart to my friends and to the public just as soon as I rest from my labors. But, it has to be said, I reckoned that first I should acknowledge that we had never understood the meaning of such commonplace and sacred words as justice, equity, liberty; that our thoughts on each of these things were unfathomably obscure; that in the end, that ignorance was the sole cause both of the pauperism that consumes us and of all the calamities by which the human race has been afflicted.

My mind started at this curious discovery — I doubted my very reason. What! I said, could it be that you have discovered that which eye has not seen, nor ear heard, nor intellect penetrated! Tremble, wretch, that you should mistake the visions of your ailing mind for the plain truths of science! (. . .)

So I resolved to devise a corollary to my reckonings, and these were the conditions which I myself imposed upon this new undertaking: is it feasible that mankind should have been so long and so universally mistaken in the application of the principles of morality? How and why might it have gone astray? Given its universality, might that error not be invincible?

These questions, upon the solution of which I made the accuracy of my observations dependent, failed to withstand analysis for long.

(. . .) Yes, all men hold and repeat that equality of circumstance is the same thing as equality of rights: that property and theft are synonymous terms; that all social pre-eminence, awarded or, more properly usurped on the pretext of superior talent and service, is iniquity and banditry; all men, I say, bear witness to these truths in their souls: it is simply a matter of making them cognizant of them.

The Advent of Liberty[3]

Community[4] is oppression and servitude. Man is quite willing to bow before the law of duty, serve his country and oblige his friends, but he wishes to work at what pleases him, when it pleases him, and for as long as it pleases him; he wants to be able to arrange his own schedule, obedient to nothing except necessity, to choose his own friends, his recreations, his discipline; to serve out of conviction, and not upon command; to make sacrifices out of self-interest, and not from slavish obligation. Community is essentially contrary to the unfettered exercise of our faculties, our noblest inclinations, our innermost feelings; anything that one might devise to reconcile it with the requirements of individual reasoning and will would suffice only to change the substance while retaining the name. Now, if we genuinely quest after truth, we must steer clear of quibbles over words.

Thus, community is trespass against autonomy of conscience and equality. The first, by constricting the spontaneity of mind and heart, the spirit of enterprise in action and in thought. The second, by offering equal reward to industry and laziness, talent and stupidity — even to vice and virtue.

(. . .) Which form of government shall we prefer?

- Ah, you may well ask — one of my younger readers will doubtless say — you are a republican.

- Republican? Yes, but the word is meaningless. *Res publica* means public business. Now, anyone seeking public office, regardless of the form of government, can call himself a republican. Kings, too, are republicans.

- Well then: are you a democrat? — No.

- What! A monarchist, then? — No.

- Constitutionalist? — God forbid!

- Are you an aristocrat, then? — By no means.

- Do you want a mixed government? — Far from it.

- What are you, then? — I am an anarchist.

- I understand: you are being sardonic. Your sarcasm is directed at government.

- Not in the least — you have just heard my authentic and duly deliberated profession of faith: although very much enamored of order, I am, in the fullest sense of the term, an anarchist. Listen to me.

In order to satisfy his needs as directly and comprehensively as possible, man looks around for a rule: in its inception, that rule is, as far as he is concerned, a living, visible, tangible thing: it is his father, his master, his king. The greater a man's ignorance, the more implicit his obedience, the more absolute his confidence in his leader. But man, whose habit it is to accommodate himself to a rule — which is to say, to discover it through deliberation and reasoning — deliberates upon the orders of his leaders. Now, such reasoning is a protest against authority, an inkling of disobedience. The moment man looks into the well-springs of the sovereign will, from that moment that man is a rebel. If he obeys now, not so much because the king commands, but because of the king's logic, it can be stated that henceforth he acknowledges no authority, and that he has set himself up as his own king. Woe betide anyone who dares lead him and has only the cachet of a majority to offer him, by way of an endorsement for his laws: for — sooner or later — the minority will become the majority, and the shortsighted despot will be toppled and all his laws annulled.

As a society achieves enlightenment, royal authority retreats: this is a fact to which the whole of history bears witness. At the birth of nations, men had no need to reflect and reason: without method, without principle, not even knowing how their reason might be employed, they did not know if theirs was the right view or if they were deceiving themselves; so overwhelming was the kingly authority that there was no acquired knowledge to challenge it. But little by little, experience conjures usages into existence, and these customs. Then these customs are phrased as maxims, articulated as principles, in short, are translated into laws, to which the king as the embodiment of law is required to pay homage. A time comes when customs and laws are so numerous that the will of the prince is, so to speak, bound by the general will. Upon assuming the crown, he is required to swear that he will govern in accordance with custom and practice, and that he is himself only the executive arm of a society whose laws are made without him.

Thus far, everything happens instinctively, and, so to speak, unbeknownst to the parties concerned; but let us take a look at the inevitable conclusion to this trend.

As he educates himself and is exposed to ideas, man ends up acquiring the notion of science, which is to say, a notion of a system of knowledge reflecting the reality of things and making deductions from observation. Whereupon he searches for the science or system of brute bodies, the system of organized bodies, the system of the human mind, the system of the world; how could he fail to search for the system of society as well? But, having reached that peak, he realizes that truth or political science is something quite independent of the sovereign will, the majority view or popular beliefs: that kings, ministers, magistrates and peoples, being so many wills, are of no consequence to science and deserving of no consideration. In a flash he realizes that, if man is born sociable, his father's authority over him ceases the day when, his mind fully-fledged and his education complete, he becomes his father's partner: that his real master and king is demonstrated truth: that politics is a science, not an art: and that the calling of the lawmaker boils down, in the final analysis, to a methodical questing after truth.

Thus, in a given society, man's authority over his fellow-man is in inverse proportion to the intellectual development attained by that authority, and the likely duration of that authority can be calculated on the basis of the pretty well general longing for true government, which is to say, government in accordance with science. And likewise, the rights of might and the entitlements of cunning diminish in the face of the widening province of justice, and should end by melting away into equality. Similarly, sovereignty of the will retreats before the sovereignty of reason, and will wind up fading into a scientific socialism. Property and royalty have been in decline since the world began: just as man looks for justice in equality, so society looks for order in anarchy.

Anarchy, absence of master, of sovereign — that is the form of government to which we draw closer day by day, and which the inveterate habit of mistaking the man for the rule and his will for the law makes us regard as the last word in disorder and the exemplification of chaos. The story is told that a 17th century Parisian bourgeois, having heard tell that in Venice there was no king, the fellow was dumbfounded beyond recovery, and thought that he would die from laughter upon first hearing anything so ridiculous. Our prejudice is like that: we all more or less want a leader or leaders, and right now I have in my hand a pamphlet whose author, a communist zealot, dreams, like a second Marat, of dictatorship.

(. . .) This synthesis of community and property we shall nominate liberty.

In order to identify liberty, then, let us not amalgamate community and property indiscriminately — that would be absurdly eclectic. Through analytical method, we seek out the kernel of truth in each, in accordance with the wishes of nature and the laws of sociability, and we discard the foreign bodies within. And the end-result provides an apt expression for the natural form of human society — in a word — liberty.

Liberty is equality, because liberty exists only in a state of society, and, outside of equality, there is no society.

Liberty is anarchy, because it countenances no government of the will, only the authority of law, which is to say, of necessity.

Liberty is infinite variety, because it respects every will, within the limits of the law.

Liberty is proportionality, because it affords full scope to merit's ambition and to emulation of glory.

Liberty is essentially organizing: in order to ensure equality between men, equilibrium between nations, agriculture and industry, centers of education, trade and distribution are distributed in accordance with the geographical and climatic conditions of each country, the type of product, the character and natural talents of inhabitants, etc., on a scale so fair, so wise, and so well married that there is nowhere a population surplus or deficit, no excessive or insufficient consumption or production. The science of public entitlement and private entitlement — real political economy — begins right there.

(. . .) Politics is the science of liberty: man's government of his fellow-man, no matter the name under which it lurks, is oppression: society's highest perfection lies in the marriage of order and anarchy.

The end of the old civilization is nigh: under a new sun, the face of the earth is going to be remade. Let us leave a generation to die out; let us leave the old prevaricators to perish in the desert — the blessed earth will not cover their bones. Young man, outraged by the corruption of the times and consumed by a yearning for justice — if you hold your country dear, and have any feeling for the interests of humanity — make bold and embrace the cause of liberty. Strip off your ancient selfishness and immerse yourself in popular tide of nascent equality. There, your rehydrated soul can drink deep of a sap and an unknown vigor: your wit, gone flabby, will recover irrepressible energy; your heart — even now shriveled perhaps — will be rejuvenated. Your purified eyes will see everything in a new light: new sentiments will inspire new thoughts in you; religion, morality, poetry, art, language, will loom taller and more beautiful; and, certain then of your faith, thoughtfully enthusiastic, you will greet the dawning of universal regeneration.

Notes to Property is Theft

1. Taken from *What is Property?* 1840
2. In Greek *skeptikos*, examiner, a philosopher who makes a profession of seeking out the truth (Proudhon's note)
3. This title has been devised by us. (D. Guérin)
4. By "community," Proudhon means, as he himself puts its elsewhere, the "communist system," a "faceless, mystical tyranny," "the human person stripped of its prerogatives." (See below, Proudhon "Against 'Communism'")

THE SYSTEM OF ECONOMIC CONTRADICTIONS[1]

(. . .) I realized that the first step towards an understanding of revolutions within society was to draw an inventory of the whole list of its antinomies, a catalogue of its contradictions.

I would be hard put to give those who have not read it an idea of that work[2]. I will make the attempt, however, employing language accessible to every book-owner today; for, if I could, in a few lines, succeed in giving a clear idea of what I consider the authentic economic method, it is unlikely that it would not soon override every conviction.

In my first memorandum, in a frontal assault upon the established order, I said things like, Property is theft! The intention was to lodge a protest, to highlight, so to speak, the inanity of our institutions. At the time, that was my sole concern. Also, in the memorandum in which I demonstrated that startling proposition using simple arithmetic, I took care to speak out against any communist conclusion.

In *The System of Economic Contradictions*, having recalled and confirmed my initial formula, I added another quite contrary one rooted in considerations of quite another order — a formula that could neither destroy the first proposition nor be demolished by it: Property is freedom. Property is theft; Property is freedom: those two propositions are equally demonstrable and co-exist, one alongside the other, within the *System of Economic Contradictions*.

I adopt the same approach with regard to each of the economic categories, the division of labor, competition, the State, credit, Community, etc.: demonstrating, turn and turn about, how each of these concepts, and, consequently, how the institutions deriving from them have a positive aspect and a negative aspect; how they give rise to a double series of diametrically different outcomes: and in every case I concluded that what was required was agreement, conciliation or synthesis. Thus property features here alongside other economic categories, with its *raison d'être* and it reason not to exist, which is to say, as a two-edged element of the economic and social system.

Put like that, it seemed sophistry, afflicted with error and bad faith. I shall strive to render it more intelligible, taking property as my example.

Property, considered as encompassing the range of social institutions, has, so to speak, a double-entry record: one is the record of the benefits that it brings and which derive directly from its essence: the other is the entry for the drawbacks it entails, the expenses it causes, these also deriving, like the benefits, directly from its nature. The same holds true for competition, monopoly and the State, etc.

In respect of property, as of all economic factors, harm and abuse cannot be dissevered from the good, any more than debit can from asset in double-entry book-keeping. The one necessarily spawns the other. To seek to do away with the abuses of property, is to destroy the thing itself; just as the striking of a debit from an account is tantamount to striking it from the credit record. The best that can be done against the abuses or drawbacks of property, is to amalgamate, synthesize, organize or balance them with a contrary factor, which is to it what the creditor is to the debtor, the investor to the director, etc., (as in, say, community), so that, without the two principles' altering or destroying each other, the advantages of the one can compensate for the disadvantages of the other, just as — in accounting, the entries — once matched one against the other, give a final result, which is either entirely loss or entirely profit.

The solution to the poverty problem thus consists of taking the book-keeper's expertise to fresh heights, setting down the entries for society, recording the credits and debits of each institution, with the general accounts or divisions in the social ledger being, not the terms of ordinary accountancy such as capital, funds, general merchandise, orders and deliveries, etc., but those of the philosophy of legislation and politics, like competition and monopoly, property and community, citizen and State, man and God, etc. Finally, and to round off my analogy, the entries must be kept up to date, that is to say, there must be a precise recording of rights and duties, so that at any given moment one can gauge the scaleof order and disorder and a balance be arrived at.

I have devoted two volumes to explaining the principles behind this system of accounts which I shall call, if you like, transcendent; twice since February,[3] I have rehearsed these elementary ideas, which bookkeeping and metaphysics have in common. Conventional economists have laughed in my face; political ideologues have politely invited me to write for the people. As for those whose interests I have taken so much to heart, they have treated me even more badly.

The communists cannot forgive me for having made a critique of community, as if a nation was one huge polyp and there were no rights of the individual alongside society's rights.

The property-owners wish a fatal illness upon me for having said that property, alone and of itself, is theft; as if property did not derive the whole of its value (rent) from the traffic in products and thus were not dependent upon a phenomenon higher than itself, the collective strength and solidarity of labor.

Finally, the politicians, whatever their colors, are insurmountably repelled by anarchy which they construe as disorder; as if democracy could be achieved other than by distribution of authority and as if the true meaning of the word "democracy" was not dismissal of government.

(. . .) In society, the theory of antinomies is at once the representation and the basis of all movement. Mores and institutions may vary from people to people, just as a trade and mechanics vary from century to century, from town to town; the laws that govern their evolutions are as inflexible as algebra. Wheresoever there are men banded together for work; wheresoever the notion of exchange value has taken root and where, due to the separation of industries, there is traffic in values and products. There, regardless of society's being upset, in deficit or bankrupt with regard to itself, and regardless of poverty and of the proletariat, the antinomial forces of society, inherent in every exercise of collective effort, as well as in every individual motive, have to be kept in a constant equilibrium, and the antagonism perpetually reproduced by the essential tension between society and the individual has to be perpetually redirected into synthesis.

Notes to The System of Economic Contradictions

1. Extract taken from *Confessions d'un révolutionnaire* op. cit.
2. The reference is to the book *Système des contradictions économiques ou Philosophie de la misère,* two vols., 1846, to which Marx was to reply the following year with his *Poverty of Philosophy*.
3. A reference to the Parisian revolution of February 1848.

Proudhon in the 1848 Revolution

The 1848 revolution was a political revolution, its social content being as yet faltering and confused. Proudhon was torn by it. An apolitical anarchist, he was in danger of being a foreign body in it. But the tide of events turned him into a journalist-cum-parliamentarian: like it or not, he had no option but to get involved.

Prior to the popular explosion in February, he had been nothing short of reticent. He could sense that the monarchy was approaching its end, but he did nothing to speed its demise. For Louis-Philippe's adversaries and for the "poor democrats," he had nothing but contempt: "The greatest good fortune that could befall the French people, would be for a hundred Opposition deputies to be thrown into the Seine with a millstone about their necks. They are worth a hundred times less than the conservatives, for they are more hypocritical than the latter." He even looked upon the Guizot government's ban on public gatherings as quite natural. As he was later to admit, the approach of the republic struck terror into him.

The advent of it first "dumbfounded" him and he prematurely wore "mourning for the republic and carried the burden of the calumnies about to strike socialism." However, he very quickly recovered and welcomed the revolution. In his Carnets, he noted: "Today's victory is the victory of Anarchy over Authority," only to let his uneasiness surface once again: ". . . or else it is a mystification." "There is no going back from this fait accompli; it is foolish to look backwards. I would not have made the revolution of February 24 : but the people's instinct has decided otherwise. . . . I stand by them all." "No matter what happens, I will stand by the people." "You wrought the revolution and here you have the revolution."

Proudhon's anxiety, which was to be largely justified by ensuing developments, sprang from his libertarian conception of the social revolution. "The social revolution is seriously compromised if it is delivered by political revolution," he was noting as early as 1845. And, later: "Power in the hands of the proletariat (. . .) will be an embarrassment until such time as the social revolution has been made." With hindsight, he was to agree: "I am the only revolutionary who did not put his shoulder to the February coup de main, because I wanted a social revolution." The disagreement between himself and the democrats was total. They were, above all else, politicians. They aimed to carry on the tradition of the Revolution of 1793 and "establish true socialism at the instigation of the government." They proclaimed "the need for the Revolution to be imposed from the top down, rather than proposed from below," as Proudhon wanted. And the founding father of anarchism forcefully asserted: "Socialism, by virtue of the very fact that it is a protest raised against capital, is a protest raised against power. Now, the Mountain meant to achieve socialism from a position of power and, worse still, to make use of socialism in order to achieve power.

Inevitably, under pressure from the workers, the political revolution was to broach the social question, which democrats were not at all equipped to resolve. "The social revolution cropped up without anybody at the top or at the bottom having any apparent understanding of it. . . . The Revolution, the Republic and socialism, each one reliant upon the others, was approaching with giant steps. . . . That revolution, which was about to erupt in the political order, was the birth date of a social revolution that was in no one's vocabulary.

No one, that is, except Proudhon. Since 1846, he had had a very settled idea of it. It fell to him to launch a "crucial revolution" an "economic revolution." He had his own "solution to the social question." In the form of the mutual association, what we today would describe as self-management. "I am the Revolution," he noted proudly in his Carnets. The panacea he proposed was a curious blend of realism and utopia. Realism when he called for a proliferation of workers' production associations as the only way of side-stepping capitalism and Statist nationalization alike. Utopia, when he deluded himself that his system would spread like an oil stain and wind up progressively taking over the whole of industry, without violent expropriation, thanks to interest-free loans granted to workers' associations by a "People's Bank," a sort of mutual fund operating outside of the orbit of any State control.

But politics snatched Proudhon away from his panaceas. Defeated at first in the April elections, he was returned as a deputy in the follow-up elections on June 4-5, 1848, by some 77,000 votes. A few weeks earlier he had been thundering: "Universal suffrage is counter-revolution." As will be seen anon, he was to concede now that: "When I think of everything that I have put down on paper and published over the past ten years regarding the State's role in society, bringing the authorities under control and the revolutionary incapacity of government, I am tempted to think that my election on June 1848 was the result of incomprehension on the part of the people."

A fortnight later, the workers from the faubourgs rose up to register their protest at the closure of the "national workshops," a sort of work scheme that had been devised for the purpose of reducing unemployment. But Proudhon had taken his parliamentary calling too seriously: "As for me, the memory of the June events will forever be a burden of guilt upon my heart. . . . Out of parliamentary cretinism, I failed in my duty as a representative. I was there to see and saw not: to raise the alarm and did not cry out!"

But whenever the disturbances in the Faubourg Saint-Antoine were crushed savagely by General Cavaignac's[1] troops, Proudhon took to the streets. He went to the Place de la Bastille. To a questioner, he replied: "I am listening for the sublime hour of cannon fire." While a terror-stricken bourgeoisie screamed hysterically, he insisted that the rebels be not slandered. He eulogized the unselfishness and lofty morality of the working classes. "The combatants of June (. . .) they used you ill who, in the name of the authorities, made you a promise that the authorities were powerless to keep."

After the June events, Proudhon was no longer quite the same man. He spoke a class language. Aggressively proclaiming his socialism. From mid-July on, he was up to his neck in the fray. He mounted the parliamentary rostrum to turn it into an instrument of social struggle. "Whether it was hubris or lightheadedness," he was to write, "I reckoned that my time had come. It was up to me, I told myself, to throw myself into the whirlwind. From my seat in the audience, I hurled myself — a new actor — into the drama." He tabled a bill which was designed simultaneously to hit the rich and exonerate the poor: a one third levy upon all income, with a one-third discount on all rents or farm dues. The suggestion provoked widespread scandal. On the finance commission, "Monsieur" Thiers, the spokesman for the bourgeoisie, cut lumps out of Proudhon. On July 31, Proudhon explained himself in a great speech delivered before the assembly. Exasperated by interruptions and insults, he turned provocateur. He "questioned" the "propriety of proceeding with social liquidation," only to add: "In the event of refusal, we would proceed with the liquidation without you." (Violent grumbling). And, by way of reply to his interrupters, he added also: "When I say "we," I identify myself with the proletariat, and when I say "you," I am identifying you with the bourgeois class."

A deputy cried out; "That's social warfare!"

The speech closed with what were adjudged these inflammatory words: "Capital will not be making a come-back. Society is wise to it.- Proudhon was to comment: "Which meant: the social question has been posed and you will resolve it or you will not have an end of it.- "It was no longer I who was speaking from the rostrum, it was all toilers!

The scandal created by this parliamentary outburst was tremendous and Proudhon's bill was rejected virtually unanimously by 691 votes to two, the latter being Proudhon and a certain Greppo. Proudhon was to deliver this forceful comment: "From July 31 forward, I became, to borrow the expression of one journalist, the bogeyman (. . .) I have been preached at, toyed with, eulogized, placarded, had my life story rehearsed, been caricatured, condemned, insulted, cursed (. . .) In anonymous letters, the bigots have threatened me with the wrath of God: pious women have sent me blessed medals (. . .) Petitions have been forwarded to the National Assembly, asking that I be expelled as unfit.

The by-elections of September 17, 1848 provided Proudhon with a further opportunity to espouse a clear-cut revolutionary stance. Swallowing his repugnance vis-á-vis universal suffrage yet again, he gave his endorsement through his newspaper to the candidacy of François-Vincent Raspail. A scientist renowned for his work in the fields of botany and organic chemistry, and a specialist in the medical uses of camphor, Raspail (1794–1878) had earned a reputation as "doctor to the poor" and in 1846 had been prosecuted for practicing medicine unlawfully. On February 24, 1848, he had been one of the first to march on the city hall and proclaim the Republic there. Later, he had declined all public office and gone on to launch a newspaper in which he was scathingly critical of the provisional government. Alongside Auguste Blanqui, he had been one of the leading lights behind the mighty demonstration by the popular clubs which had stormed into the Palais Bourbon on May 15, declaring the assembly dissolved and installing a short-lived insurgent government in the city hall. That same evening, along with Barbès and a handful of others, Raspail had been arrested and committed to the Vincennes fortress.

Consequently, it was as a prisoner that he offered himself to the electors of the Seine department in the partial elections. Raspail romped to victory. "Socialism," Proudhon was to relate, "made the elections of September 17. Even as everything stood ready to crush him, 70,000 men answered his call by way of protesting against the June victors, and appointed Raspail to represent them. The democratic election committee held its meetings in the offices of Le Peuple. In the face of an extreme backlash, the democracy adopted its most vigorous mouthpiece as its flagship (...) The issue was no longer a choice between monarchy and democracy, but rather between labor and capital."

Within a few weeks, at a banquet, Proudhon proposed a resounding "toast to the Revolution." He resolutely added the adjective "socialist" to that of "democratic," arguing that from now on there was no way of "disentangling the Republic from socialism." "Only the people, shifting for itself, without intermediaries, can carry through the economic Revolution launched in February."

But the June revolt and the horrific repression of it had not just radicalized the vanguard: it had also, to a much greater extent, given a fillip to the counter-revolution. Except in the Seine department, the by-elections had favored the conservatives and a newcomer, Prince Louis Bonaparte, nephew of the great Napoleon, had successfully had himself returned by 300,000 votes across five departments. Whereupon he put himself forward as a candidate in the presidential elections of December 10.

Proudhon once again urged Raspail to run in those elections.[2] At first, his newspaper had urged abstention, before urging that votes be spoiled by way of protest. By then, Louis Bonaparte, General Cavaignac (the butcher from June) and the bourgeois democrat Ledru-Rollin had already declared their intentions to run. What good would it do for Raspail to run? Proudhon was to explain: "Raspail's candidature was specifically prompted by Ledru-Rollin's." By voting for Ledru-Rollin, the democracy "was coming out in support of the governmental thesis and was no longer socialist (...) The honor of its future opposition required that it register its protest.

In the tide of reaction that swept the provinces of France, especially in rural areas, Ledru-Rollin's candidature stood no chance. But, as Proudhon explains, even if it "stood no chance of success and it were up to us to contrive its failure, we should have done so." Raspail's candidacy was a gesture of defiance towards the bourgeois democrats who had proven themselves bankrupt in their exercise of power since the February revolution.

In the end, it was the Prince who carried the day, by a huge majority. Proudhon had this to say about this stunning result: "France has appointed Louis Bonaparte president of the Republic, because it is weary of parties, because all of the parties are moribund." And he went on to explain that the righteous horror inspired by General Cavaignac had, in any case, "herded most democrats in the direction of Napoleon." The Revolution had given up the ghost.

The incoming regime wasted no time before throwing Proudhon into prison. As a result of which he had plenty of time to probe and draw the lessons of the revolution's failure. This was his chance in 1848, if not to venture quite so far as anarchy "which, like any other principle, is more indicative of an ideal than of a reality," then at least to attack State centralization. Citizens had to be "enjoined to recover possession of themselves." "Departments and communes [had to recover] control of their affairs, control of policing, the disposition of funding and of their troops."

Unless these minimum requirements were met, "all talk of revolution was hypocrisy." But the men of 1848 "held back as they were by the general prejudice and that fear of the unknown that stalks the greatest minds, lacked daring." "The political question was devolved . . . upon the National Assembly: whereupon it was foreseeable that it would be buried there. There, the understanding was that the people, being a minor, could scarcely be trusted to its own counsel: governmentalism was upheld with increased vigor." "The flaw, the very great flaw of the government (. . .) resides in its failure to demolish. Power has to be disarmed," its "nails and teeth drawn," "half of the army let go, and troops banished from the capital." Instead of which, the government raised twenty-four battalions of the National Mobile Guard, made up of volunteers. "What then did it intend to do with all these soldiers? June was to teach us the answer to that.

Proudhon had arrived at the following libertarian conclusions from his scrutiny of the historical precedent of 1793: "Clubs had to be organized. The organization of popular societies was the fulcrum of democracy, the corner-stone of the republican order." "If there was one institution that democratic authorities should have respected, and not just respected but also fostered and organized, it was the clubs." "Everything was done the wrong way round in February (. . .) Instead of restoring to the people its fertility of initiative by subordinating the authorities to its wishes, an attempt was made to resolve, from positions of authority, matters on which time had not [enlightened] the masses." "The provisional government, having none of the genius of revolutions (. . .) wasted days and weeks on pointless trial and error, agitations and circulars." "Driven by the breath of opinion, it strove to latch on to some initiative. A dismal venture!" Aside from the odd positive measure, "everything else was merely farce, bluster, nonsense and flying in the face of common sense. We could say that power has a stultifying effect on men of intellect.

And Proudhon gave a sound thrashing to those who, like the members of the Popular Front government of 1936, had but one thought in their heads: keeping within the bounds of the law. "The whole of their ambition (...) has been to render a true accounting like good stewards. Haunted by the memory of '93 (. . .) not wishing to be taken for wreckers, nor to usurp the nation's sovereignty, they have confined themselves to the maintenance of order (. . .) They reckoned that by straying from the legal path and pitching (. . .) the people into Revolution, they would have forfeited their mandate. It was noised abroad that the Revolution was going to throw the State into disarray, that democracy was anarchy (. . .) Rather than resort to summary, extra-legal methods against the rich (. . .) they have set integrity in the place of policy. (. . .) They were filled with honor and scruples (. . .) slaves of legality, incorruptible guardians of democratic decency." As Colette Audry has written apropos of Leon Blum, they were determined to be "just."[3] They took "delicacy to the lengths of meticulousness, respect for persons, opinions and interests to the lengths of [self-] sacrifice."

Among the bankrupters of 1848, the one whom Proudhon bore the most animosity was Louis Blanc. In his estimation, Blanc bore the heaviest responsibility, in that he styled himself a "socialist." On 17 March 1848, Louis Blanc had been one of the organizers of a huge popular demonstration that had attracted upwards of 100,000 workers. But he had prevented its being turned into a gauntlet thrown down to the government to compel it to take a more vigorous line with regard to those sabotaging the Revolution. Proudhon could not forgive Blanc this let-down. "What! Here we have a man convinced that the men in power, his colleagues, are hostile towards progress: that the Revolution is in jeopardy unless they are successfully replaced: he knows that opportunity is rare, and, once past, is never repeated: that he has but one chance to strike a decisive blow: and when that chance comes along, he seizes upon it only to hold back those who offer him their commitment and their muscle!" And, to conclude his embittered description, the imprisoned Proudhon lets slip this bittersweet comment: "The revolution evaporated like drawn-off alcohol."

But this swingeing criticism of its unsafe steersmen was not the only lesson that Proudhon drew from the 1848 Revolution: as we shall have occasion to see, it prompted him in his vigorous and innovative condemnation of the State and of power generally.

PROUDHON JOINS IN THE FRAY[4]

The February Revolution erupted. As indeed might be imagined, I had no inclination to throw myself into this politico-social mess where Monsieur Lamartine[5] was translating the commonplaces of diplomacy into poetic prose; where there was talk of bringing the whole of commerce, of industry, and soon of agriculture, one after another, into associations or State control; of buying out all property and working it along administrative lines; of centralizing capital and competences in the hands of the State; then of carrying this governmental regime out to the peoples of Europe at the head of our victorious armies. I felt that there was greater usefulness in pressing ahead with my laborious studies behind the scenes, in the conviction that that was the only way in which I could be of service to the Revolution, and in the certainty that neither the provisional government nor the neo-Jacobins would steal a march on me.

(. . .) While I, alone of my persuasion, was slicing through the carapace of the old political economy. While P. Leroux, Villegardelle, Vidal[6] and a handful of others were pressing ahead in different directions with this scientific task of demolition, what were the organs of democracy up to? What were they about? Alas! Allow me to remind them, least the socialists alone bear the responsibility for the misfortunes of the Republic: they were indulging their parliamentary preoccupations; stubbornly sidestepping social issues lest they frighten their subscribers, and preparing to cloak February in mystery. Through this deliberate oversight, they were organizing the national workshops; they were drafting the provisional government's decrees and unwittingly laying the foundations of the reasonable, moderate republic. *Le National*, no harm to it, heaping curses on socialism, was pushing through the fortifications of Paris; *La Réforme*, smugly well-meaning, was standing by universal suffrage and by the governmentalism of Louis Blanc. They were allowing utopia to flourish when it ought to have been pulled up by the roots:

(. . .) Nevertheless it took the experience of February for our Statesmen to be convinced that a revolution is not prescribed nor improvised.

(. . .) Thus, democracy spent itself in the pursuit of that power which it is precisely designed to annihilate through diffusion. All party factions had fallen, one after another; with the Executive Commission dismissed, we were on to the next generation of republicans, rubbing shoulders with the doctrinarians. Unless we could stem this retreat, or at least accommodate it within the constitutional orbit, the Republic was in peril — but that required a complete change of tack. We had to stand in opposition, and place the authorities on the defensive, widen the battle-field, and simplify the social question by generalizing it: stunning the enemy by the audacity of our proposals, henceforth lobbying the people rather than their representatives, steadfastly countering the blind passions of the reaction with the philosophical and revolutionary idea of February.

One party did not play along with this tactic: it demanded a steadfast, even eccentric individualism, a spirit forged for protest and negation. Whether it was hubris or lightheadedness, I thought that my time had come. It was up to me, I told myself, to throw myself into the turmoil. The democrats, seduced by the memories of our glorious revolution, sought to re-enact the drama of 1789 in 1848: while they staged their comedy, we strove to make history. The Republic's fate was now in the hands of God. While one blind force was pulling the authorities in one direction, might we not manage to push society forwards down another? The directions of minds having changed, it would follow that the government, in persisting with reaction, would then, unwittingly, spark off revolution. And from my seat in the audience, I hurled myself, a new actor, into the drama.

My name had caused enough of a sensation over the preceding 18 months for me to be forgiven for offering a few explanations, a few apologies for my notoriety. For good or ill, I had had my portion of influence upon my country's fate: who could tell if that influence, stronger now precisely because it was concentrated, might yet be brought to bear? Thus it was important that my contemporaries should know what I wanted, what I had done, what I am. I am not bragging, I would simply be flattered if, after reading, my readers were to be left with the conviction that there is neither folly nor fury in my actions. The only vanity my heart has ever entertained was the belief that no man had conducted his entire life with more deliberation or more discernment than I have.

But I discovered to my cost that in the very moments when I thought myself most free, I was still, amid the torrent of political passions to which I was seeking to give some direction, merely an instrument of that immoral providence that I deny and repudiate. Perhaps the history of my deliberations, which cannot be disentangled from that of my actions, may prove of some advantage to those who, whatever their views, like to look to experience for justification of their ideas.

(. . .) The revolution of contempt brought low the government that had established the materialist principle of interests. That revolution which condemns capital, by that very action ushers and carries labor into government. Now, accordingly to the widespread prejudice, labor, having become government, ought to proceed along governmental lines: in other words, it is up to government henceforth to do that which had been done without it and in spite of it, to seize the initiative and prosecute the revolution. Because, that prejudice contends, the revolution has to come from above, since it is up above that one finds intellect and strength.

But experience testifies and philosophy demonstrates, contrary to that prejudice, that any revolution, to be effective, must be spontaneous and emanate, not from the heads of the authorities but from the bowels of the people: that government is reactionary rather than revolutionary; that it could not have any expertise in revolutions, given that society, to which that secret is alone revealed, does not show itself through legislative decree but rather through the spontaneity of its manifestations; that, ultimately, the only connection between government and labor is that labor, in organizing itself, has the abrogation of government as its mission.

(. . .) As for myself, and I make no bones about it, I have given my all to political disorganization, not out of revolutionary impatience, not out of love for some empty notoriety, not out of ambition, envy or hatred, but in anticipation of inevitable backlash and, in every instance, out of the certainty I had that democracy could achieve nothing of any good through the governmental hypothesis to which it persisted in clinging. As for the masses, meager though their intelligence might be and weak though I know their virtue to be, I found them less frightening in the midst of anarchy than at the ballot box. Among the people as among children, crimes and trespasses have more to do with shifting impressions than perversity of the soul, and I found it easier for a republican elite to complete the people's education in a setting of political chaos than to have it exercise its sovereignty, with small prospect of success, through the ballot box.[7]

Proudhon the Unseated Candidate (April 1848)[8]

(. . .) Along came the April elections. I deluded myself into running as a candidate. In the circular that I addressed to the voters in the Doubs, dated April 3, 1848, I stated:

> The social question has been posed; you will not get out of it. If it is to be resolved,. we must have men who marry the extreme of the conservative mentality with the extreme of the radical spirit. Workers, reach out to your employers, and you employers, do not shun the advances of those who were your wage-slaves.
>
> After all, what is it to you whether I have been more or less touched with good fortune? It is not enough, if I am to earn your votes, that I should have only poverty to offer, and your votes are not on the look-out for an adventurer. However, if I should fail to reveal my calamitous existence to you, who will commend me to your notice? Who will speak for me?

When I said that, the influence of democracy was still at its height. I had not awaited a turn of luck before preaching universal reconciliation as the object and meaning of socialism.

April 16 put paid to my prospects as candidate. After that dismal day, people wanted to hear no more about extreme radicalism: they preferred to compromise everything by throwing themselves into the embrace of extreme conservatism.

As a defeated candidate, a publicist without readership, I had to turn away from the press. Day in and day out, I was told: write books; they are more worthwhile than newspapers. I agree: but nobody reads books. And while the author of *La Philosophie positive*, Monsieur Auguste Comte, could scarcely muster a couple of hundred loyal followers for his course, *Le Faubourien*, *Le Pere Duchene* and *La Vraie Republique* lead the country. You spend ten years of your life writing your manuscript: fifty amateurs buy a copy, then along comes the journalist who tosses you on to the rubbish heap and that is that. Books now have no purpose other than the training of journalists; in our day, the highest form of literature is the Paris early edition, the penny dreadful.

Proudhon the Successful Candidate (June 4, 1848)[9]

When I think of everything that I have said, written and published over these past ten years regarding the State's role in society, bringing the authorities to heel and government's disqualification from revolution, I am tempted to believe that my election in June 1848 was the result of some incomprehension on the part of the people. Those ideas have been in my head ever since my earliest deliberations; they are coeval with my conversion to socialism. Study and experience have expanded upon them; they have guided me constantly in my writings and actions; they have inspired all of the actions for which I shall answer; curious that after the reassurance they offer and which is the best that an innovator has to offer, I may have appeared momentarily to the society which I take for my judge and the authorities with whom I want no truck, as a formidable agitator.

After the Workers' Revolt of June 1848

Proudhon's confession of guilt[10]

(. . .) This rising is of itself more terrible than any of those which have taken place over the past 60 years. . . . Thiers[11] was seen recommending the use of artillery to bring it to an end. Atrocious massacres have been carried out by the Garde Mobile, the army and the National Guard. . . . The rebels have displayed indomitable courage. . . . Terror reigns in the capital. . . . In the Conciergerie, at the city hall, forty eight hours after victory[12], there is shooting: they are shooting wounded, unarmed prisoners. . . . The most disgusting slanders are being peddled about the rebels in order to incite vengeance against them.

(. . .) After the June events, I raised no protest against the abuse that a few ignoramuses might have made of a few of my aphorisms and reneged upon my popular inclinations: I did not insult the dying lion. But nor did I wait for the events of June before attacking governmental tendencies, and manifesting my sympathies with intelligent conservatism. I have always had and always will have the authorities against me: are those the tactics of an ambitious man and a coward? In addition, drawing up a balance sheet for the authorities, I proved that a governmental democracy is nothing but a monarchy resuscitated.

(. . .) As for me, the memory of the June events will forever be a burden of regret upon my heart. It pains me to confess it: up until the 25th, I anticipated nothing, knew nothing, guessed nothing. Returned a fortnight before as a representative of the people, I had entered the National Assembly with all the timidity of a child and the ardor of a neophyte. Assiduously attending meetings of the bureau and committees from nine o'clock onwards, I would not leave the Assembly before evening, weary from fatigue and disgust. Ever since I had set foot on the parliamentary Sinai, I had lost all contact with the masses: as I became absorbed by my legislative tasks, I had lost sight completely of current affairs. I knew nothing either about the situation of the national workshops or the government's policy, nor the intrigues underway inside the Assembly. One would have to have spent some time in the isolator called the National Assembly to have any idea how men utterly ignorant of a country's state are nearly always the ones who represent it.

I set to work to read everything that the distribution office issued to representatives: proposals, reports, pamphlets, down to *Le Moniteur* and the *Bulletin des Lois*. Most of my colleagues on the left and the extreme left were in the same perplexed frame of mind, wallowing in the same ignorance of everyday happenings. The national workshops were spoken of only with a sort of fright, because fear of the people afflicts all who are numbered among the authorities; as far as the authorities are concerned, the people is the enemy. Every day, we voted fresh subsidies to the national workshops, shuddering at the incompetence of the authorities and our own powerlessness.

Disastrous apprenticeship! The impact of this representative mess amid which I had to live was that I had a grasp of nothing: and on the 23rd when Flocon stated from the floor that the rising was being directed by political factions and had foreign backers, I fell for that ministerial canard, and I was still asking on the 24th whether the rising really had been prompted by the dissolution of the national workshops! No, Monsieur Senard, I was not a coward in June, the insult you flung into my face in the Assembly: I was, like you and like many another, an imbecile. Out of parliamentary cretinism, I failed in my duty as a representative. I was there to see and saw not; to raise the alarm and did not cry out. I was like the dog that failed to bark at the enemy's approach. I, elected by the plebs, a journalist of the proletariat, ought not to have left those masses without guidance and without counsel. One hundred thousand regimented men deserved my attention. That would have been better than my moping around your offices. Since then, I have done what I could to make up for my irreparable shortcoming.

Notes to Proudhon in the 1848 Revolution

1. General Louis-Eugène Cavaignac (1802–1857), the butcher of the conquest of Algeria and later butcher of the Parisian proletariat in June 1848.
2. For Raspail's candidature, see below.
3. Colette Audry *Léon Blum ou la politique du juste 1955*
4. *Confessions d'un révolutionnaire.*
5. Alphonse de Lamartine (1790–1869), better known as a poet, but a one-time Legitimist turned moderate republican: he played a significant political role in the provisional government that emerged from the revolution of February 1848.
6. Pierre Leroux (1797–1871), socialist of Saint-Simonian stamp, with overtones of religiosity. François Villegardelle (1810–1856), at first a Fourierist and later a communist. François Vidal (1814–1872), simultaneously close to the Saint-Simonians and the Fourierists, played an important role on the Luxembourg Commission during the 1848 Revolution.
7. Extract lifted from *La Revolution sociale démontrée par le coup d'Etat du 2 décembre* (1852)
8. *Confessions d'un révolutionnaire.*
9. *Confessions d'un révolutionnaire.*
10. *Carnets de Proudhon* Vol. III, 1968, p. 68: *Confessions d'un révolutionnaire.*
11. Adolphe Thiers (1797–1877) reactionary statesman and butcher-to-be of the Commune in 1871.
12. Proudhon means of course the victory of the government forces.

Peoples' Election Manifesto

The Manifesto below is one of the most telling of Proudhon's writings. Within it, one finds, side by side, an inspired anticipation of contemporary self-management, a somewhat utopian and, to be sure, petit bourgeois "mutualist" notion of social reorganization, a rather aberrant preoccupation with preserving property on a small scale, and a reluctance to impose taxes upon it or upon larger scale property, and, finally, a revolutionary socialist stance vis-á-vis participation in presidential elections which Proudhon regarded as a "dismal affair," and a straightforward opportunity to set out his program.

The central electoral committee, comprising delegates from the fourteen Seine arrondissements and designed to make preparation for the election of the president of the Republic, has just concluded its operations.

Citizen Raspail, the people's representative, has been selected unanimously as the candidate of the social democratic republican party.

The central committee is to publish its circular to electors without delay.

As for ourselves, who have associated ourselves intellectually and emotionally with that candidature, who, in that context, have seen fit, in defense of the dignity of our views, to stand apart from other, less advanced factions of the democracy, we consider it our duty here to recall what our principles are: that being the best way of justifying our conduct.

Our principles!

Throughout history, men who have sought popular endorsement in order to succeed to power have abused the masses with alleged declarations of principle which, in essence, have never been anything other than declarations of promises!

Throughout history, the ambitious and scheming have, in more or less pompous language, promised the people:

Liberty, equality and

Work, family, property and progress;

Credit, education, association, order and peace;

Participation in government, equitable distribution of taxes, honest and inexpensive administration, fair courts, movement towards equality of income, emancipation of the proletariat and eradication of poverty!

So much have they promised that, coming after them, it has to be confessed, there is nothing left to be promised.

But then again, what have they delivered? It is for the people to answer: Nothing!

The true friends of the people must henceforth adopt a different tack. What the people expects of its candidates, what it asks of them, is not promises now, but practicalities.

It is upon these practicalities that they suggest men should be judged: and it is upon such that we ask that we be judged.

As socialist-democrats, we belong, in truth, to no sect, no school. Or, rather, if we were obliged to come up with a description of ourselves, we should say that we are of the critical school. For us, socialism is not a system: it is, quite simply, a protest. We believe, though, that from socialist works is dedicated a series of principles and ideas at odds with economic convention, and which have been absorbed into popular belief, which is why we call ourselves socialists. Professing socialism while embracing nothing of socialism, as the more artful do, would be tantamount to gulling the people and abusing its credulousness.

Being a republican is not the last word: it is not the last word to acknowledge that the Republic ought to be surrounded by social institutions; it is not enough to inscribe upon one's banner, **Democratic and social Republic** — one must plainly point up the difference between the old society and the new. One has to spell out the positive product of socialism: and wherein and why the February Revolution which is the expression thereof, is a social revolution.

For a start, let us recall socialism's underlying dogma, its pure dogma.

The objective of socialism is emancipation of the proletariat and eradication of poverty, which is to say, effective equality of circumstances between men. In the absence of equality, there will always be poverty, always be a proletariat.

Socialism, which is egalitarian above all else, is thus the democratic formula par excellence. Should less honest politicians be mealy-mouthed about admitting it, we respect their reservations, but they ought to know that — in our view — they are no democrats.

Now, what can be the origin of this inequality?

As we see it, that origin has been brought to light by a whole series of socialist criticisms, particularly since Jean-Jacques [Rousseau] — that origin is the realization within society of this triple abstraction: capital, labor and talent.

It is because society has divided itself into three categories of citizen corresponding to the three terms in that formula — that is, because of the formation of a class of capitalists or proprietors, another class of workers, and a third of talents — that caste distinctions have always been arrived at, and one half of the human race enslaved to the other.

Wheresoever an attempt has been made to separate these three things — capital, labor and talent — effectively and organically, the worker has wound up enslaved: he has been described, turn and turn about as slave, serf, pariah, plebeian and proletarian, and the capitalist has proved the exploiter. He may go variously by the name of patrician or noble, proprietor or bourgeois — the man of talent has been a parasite, an agent of corruption and servitude. At first he was the priest, then he was the cleric, and today the public functionary, all manner of competence and monopoly.

The underlying dogma of socialism thus consists of reducing the aristocratic formula of capital-labor-talent into the simpler formula of labor! . . . in order to make every citizen simultaneously, equally and to the same extent capitalist, laborer and expert or artist.

In reality as in economic science, producer and consumer are always one and the same person, merely considered from two different viewpoints. Why should the same not be true of capitalist and laborer? of laborer and artist? Separate these qualities in the organization of society and inexorably you create castes, inequality and misery; amalgamate them, on the other hand, and in every individual you have equality, you have the Republic. And that is how in the political order, all these distinctions between governors and governed, administrators and administered, public functionaries and tax-payers, etc., must some day be erased. Each citizen must, through the spread of the social idea, become all; for, if he be not all, he is not free: he suffers oppression and exploitation somewhere.

So, by what means is this great amalgamation to be brought to pass?

The means is indicated by the affliction itself. And, first of all, let us try to define that affliction better, if possible.

Since the organic origin of the proletariat and of poverty is located in the division of society into two classes: one that works and owns not, and another that owns but works not and, consequently, consumes without producing. It follows that the affliction by which society is beset consists of this singular fiction according to which capital is, of itself, productive, whereas labor, of itself, is not. In fact, for all things to be equal in this hypothesis of the separation of labor and capital, then, because the capitalist profits by his capital without working, so the worker should profit from his labor, in the absence of capital. Now, that is not the case. So, in the current system, equality, liberty and fraternity are impossible: and thus, poverty and proletariat are the inevitable consequence of property as presently constituted.

Anyone knowing that but not confessing it is lying equally to bourgeoisie and to proletariat. Anyone courting the people's votes but keeping this from it is neither a socialist nor a democrat.

We say again:

The productivity of capital, which Christianity has condemned under the designation of "usury," is the true cause of poverty, the true origin of the proletariat, the never-ending obstacle to establishment of the Republic. No equivocation, no mumbo-jumbo, no sleight of hand! Let those who profess to be socialist democrats join us in signing this profession of faith; let them join our company. Then, and then only, will we acknowledge them as brothers, as true friends of the people, and will we associate ourselves with their every act.

And now, what is the means whereby this affliction can be eradicated, this usury terminated? Is it to be an attack upon net product, seizure of revenue? Is it to be, while professing utmost regard for property, the ravishing of property by means of levy, as it is acquired through work and enshrined by law?

It is on this count above all that the true friends of the people stand apart from those whose only wish is to command the people; it is on this count that true socialists part company with their treacherous imitators.

The means of destroying usury, is not, let us repeat, the confiscation of usury: it is by countering principle with principle, in short, by organizing credit.

As far as socialism is concerned, the organization of credit does not mean lending at interest, since that would still be an acknowledgment of capital's suzerainty: it is, rather, organizing the workers' mutual solidarity, introducing their mutual guarantees, in accordance with that vulgar economic principle that anything that has an exchange value is susceptible to becoming an article of exchange and can, in consequence, furnish the basis for credit.

Just as the banker lends money to the businessman who pays him interest upon the loan. Or the estate-owner lends his land to the peasant who pays him a rent for it.

Or the house-owner lets his tenant have lodgings in return for payment of rent. Or the merchant lets his goods go to the customer who pays on the installment plan.

So the worker lends his labor to the employer who pays him by the week or by the month. Every one of us vouchsafes something on credit: do we not talk about selling on credit, working on credit, drinking on credit?

Thus labor can make an advance of itself, and can be as much the creditor as capital can.

Furthermore, two or more workers can advance one another their respective products, and, if they were to come to an arrangement regarding permanent transactions of this sort, they would have organized credit among themselves.

This is what those labor associations are to be admired for having grasped which have spontaneously, without prompting and without capital been formed in Paris and in Lyon, and which, merely by liaising with one another and making loans to one another, have organized labor as we said. So that, organization of credit and organization of labor amount to one and the same. It is no school and no theoretician that is saying this: the proof of it, rather, lies in current practice, revolutionary practice. Thus application of one principle leads the people towards discovery of another, and one solution arrived at always opens doors to another. If it were to come about that the workers were to come to some arrangement throughout the Republic and organize themselves along similar lines, it is obvious that, as masters of labor, constantly generating fresh capital through work, they would soon have wrested alienated capital back again, through their organization and competition; they would attract to their side, to start with, small property, small traders and small industries; then large-scale property and large industries: then the very biggest ventures, mines, canals and railways: they would become the masters of it all, through the successive affiliation of producers and the liquidation of property without the proprietors' being despoiled or indemnified.

(...) Such is the undertaking upon which the people has spontaneously embarked before our very eyes, an undertaking that it prosecutes with admirable vigor, weathering all difficulties and the most frightful privations. And we ought not to weary of saying that this movement was initiated, not by the leaders of schools, and that the primary instigation came not from the State but from the people. We are merely its spokesmen here. Our creed, the democratic and social creed, is not a utopia any more: it is a fact. This is not our doctrine that we are preaching, these are the people's ideas that we have taken up as themes for our explorations. Those who sneer at them, who prattle to us of association and Republic and yet do not dare to acknowledge the true socialists, the true republicans as their brothers are not of our ilk.

Committed to this idea these ten years past, we have not waited for the people to triumph before lining up on its side.

(. . .) Should the government, the National Assembly, the very bourgeoisie sponsor and assist us in the accomplishment of our undertaking, we will be grateful for that. But let none try to distract us from what we regard as the people's true interests; let none try to deceive us with the empty sham of reforms. We are too clear-sighted to fall for that again, and we know more of the workings of the world than the politicians who regale us with their admonitions.

We should be delighted if the State were to contribute through its budgetary provisions to the emancipation of the workers. We would look only with mistrust upon what is termed State organization of credit, which is, as we see it, merely the latest form of man's exploitation of his fellow-man. We repudiate State credit, because the State, in debt to the tune of eight billions, does not possess a centime that it could advance by way of a loan: because its finances repose solely upon paper of obligatory usage: because obligatory usage necessarily entails depreciation, and depreciation always hits the worker rather than the proprietor: because we associated workers or workers in the process of association, need neither the State nor obligatory usage in the organization of our intercourse: because, in the end, credit from the State is always credit from capital, not credit from labor, and still monarchy rather than democracy.

Under the arrangement suggested to us and which we reject with all of the vigor of our convictions, the State, in the awarding of credit, first has to secure capital. For such capital, it must look to property, by way of taxation. So we still have this reversion to principle when the point is to destroy it; we have displacement of wealth, when we ought to have its creation; we have withdrawal of property, after it has been declared by the constitution to be inviolable.

Let others of less advanced and less suspect ideas, meticulous in their morals, support such ideas, and we will not question their tactics. But we, who wage war, not upon the rich but upon principles: we whom the counter-revolution never wearies of vilifying: we have to be more demanding. We are socialists, not despoilers.

We do not want progressive taxation, because progressive taxation is the validation of net product and we wish to do away with net product, through association: because, if progressive taxation fails to divest the rich man of all his wealth, it is merely a concession made to the proletariat, a sort of ransom for the right of usury, in short, a trick; and if it seizes all income, it amounts to confiscation of property, to expropriation without prior indemnification and is of no public use.

So let those who claim to be primarily politicians invoke progressive taxation by way of a reprisal against property, a punishment for bourgeois selfishness: we respect their intentions and if it should ever happen that they get the chance to implement their principles, we will bow to the will of God. As far as we representatives of those who have lost everything to the rule of capital are concerned, progressive taxation, precisely because it is an enforced restitution, is off-limits to us; we will never propose it to the people. We are socialists, men of reconciliation and progress: we seek neither reaction nor *loi agraire.*

We do not want levies upon State revenues, because such a levy is, like progressive taxation in the case of rentiers, mere confiscation, and in the case of the people, mere sleight of hand, trickery. We believe that the State is entitled to repay its debts, and thus to borrow at the lowest rates of interest: we do not think that it is licit for it, under cover of taxation, to default upon its commitments. We are socialists, not bankrupters.

We do not want taxes upon inheritance because such a tax is likewise merely a retreat from property, and, property being a constitutional right acknowledged universally, the wishes of the majority must be respected with regard to it because that would be a trespass against the family; because, in order to emancipate the proletariat, we need not indulge in such fresh hypocrisy. Under the law of association, transmission of wealth does not apply to the instruments of labor, so cannot become a cause of inequality. So, let the assets of the deceased proprietor pass to his most distant and often his most impoverished relative. We are socialists, not stealers of inheritances.

We do not seek taxes upon luxury items, because that would be to strike a blow against the luxury industries: because luxury items are the very badge of progress: because, with labor in the ascendant and capital subordinated, luxury must extend to each and every citizen. Why, having encouraged property, would we retaliate against proprietors for their pleasures? We are socialists, not begrudgers.

(. . .) We do not want to see the State confiscate the mines, canals and railways; that would be to add to monarchy, and more wage slavery. We want the mines, canals, railways handed over to democratically organized workers' associations operating under State supervision, in conditions laid down by the State, and under their own responsibility. We want these associations to be models for agriculture, industry and trade, the pioneering core of that vast federation of companies and societies woven into the common cloth of the democratic social Republic.

Nor do we want government of man by his fellow-man any more: have those who are so quick to seize upon the socialist formula given it any thought?

We want savings in State expenditure, just as we want the worker to enjoy the full range of the rights of man and the citizen, the attributes of capital and of talent. For which reason we ask for certain things that socialism suggests, and which men who purport to be particularly political fail to understand.

Politics tends to lead to specialization and indefinite proliferation of jobs: socialism tends to amalgamate them all.

Thus we believe that virtually the totality of public works can and should be carried out by the army; that such participation in public works is the primary duty that the republican youth owes to its homeland; that, as a result, the army budget and the public works budget duplicate each other. That represents a saving of more than 100 millions: politics overlooks that.

There is talk of trades education. We believe that agricultural training comes in the form of agriculture: the school for arts, crafts and manufacture is the workshop; the school for commerce is the counting-house; the mining school is the mine; the navigation school the navy; the administration school the civil service, etc.

The apprentice is as necessary to the job as the journeyman; why put him to one side in a school? We want the same education for everybody: what good are schools which the people sees as only schools for aristocrats and which represent a double drain upon our finances? Organize association, and by the same token, every workshop becoming a school, every worker becomes a master, every student an apprentice. Elite figures are turned out as well and better by the workshop as by the study hall.

Likewise in government.

It is not enough to say that one is opposed to presidency unless one also does away with ministries, the eternal focus of political ambition. It is up to the National Assembly, through organization of its committees, to exercise executive power, just the way it exercises legislative power through its joint deliberations and votes. Ministers, under-secretaries of State, departmental heads, etc., duplicate the work of the representatives, whose idle, dissipated life, given over to scheming and ambition, is a continual source of troubles for the administration, of bad laws for society and of needless expense for the State.

Let our young recruits get this straight in their heads: socialism is the contrary of governmentalism. For us, that is a precept as old as the adage: *There can be no familiarity between master and servant.*

Besides universal suffrage and as a consequence of universal suffrage, we want implementation of the binding mandate. Politicians balk at it! Which means that in their eyes, the people, in electing representatives, do not appoint mandatories but rather abjure their sovereignty! That is assuredly not socialism: it is not even democracy.

We seek unbounded freedom for man and the citizen, along as he respects the liberty of his neighbor:

Freedom of association. Freedom of assembly.

Freedom of religion.

Freedom of the press.

Freedom of thought and of speech.

Freedom of labor, trade and industry. Freedom of education.

In short, absolute freedom.

Now, among these freedoms, there is still one that the old politics will not countenance, which makes a nonsense of all the rest! Will they tell us once and for all if they want freedom on condition or unconditional freedom?

We want the family: where is there anyone who respects it more than we do? But we do not mistake the family for the model of society. Defenders of monarchy have taught us that monarchies were made in the image of the family. The family is the patriarchal or dynastic element, the rudiment of royalty: the model of civil society is the fraternal association.

We want property, but property restored to its proper limits, that is to say, free distribution of the products of labor, property minus usury! Of that we need say no more. Those who know us get our meaning.

Such, in substance, is our profession of faith.

(. . .) And now to this small matter of the Presidency.

Assuredly, it is a serious business knowing on the one hand whether the people should vote or abstain: and, on the other, under what colors, under what profession of faith the election would proceed.

(. . .) The central electoral committee has decided unanimously to support citizen Raspail in his candidacy for the presidency.

Raspail, returned by 66,000 Parisian and 35,000 Lyonnnais votes; Raspail, the socialist democrat;

Raspail, the implacable exposer of political mythologies;

Raspail, whose work in the field of healing has elevated him to the ranks of the benefactors of mankind.

In lending our backing to this candidature, we do not, as the honorable Monsieur Ledru-Rollin had written somewhere, intend to endow the Republic with a possible chief: far from it. We accept Raspail as a living protest against the very idea of Presidency! We offer him to the people's suffrage, not because he is or believes himself possible, but because he is impossible: because with him, presidency, the mirror-image of royalty, would be impossible.

Nor do we mean, in calling for votes for Raspail, to issue a challenge to the bourgeoisie which fears this great citizen. Our primary intention is reconciliation and peace. We are socialists, not muddleheads.

We back Raspail's candidacy, so as to focus the eyes of the country all the more strongly upon this idea, that henceforth, under the banner of the Republic, there are but two parties in France, the party of labor and the party of capital.

The Authority Principle[1]

Here, after the revolutionary tempest of 1848 had passed, Proudhon draws the lessons from it: an unanswerable indictment of the State and of authority.

The Governmental Prejudice[2]

The form in which the earliest men thought of order within society was the patriarchal or hierarchical form, which is to say, in essence, authority and, in operation, government. Justice, which was later dissected into the distributive and commutative, at first showed itself to them under its first aspect only: a superior bestowing upon his inferiors the portion that was their due.

Thus the governmental idea arises out of family practice and domestic experience: consequently, there was no objection voiced, government appearing as natural to society as the subordination that obtains between the father and his children. Which is why Monsieur de Bonald[3] was correct in saying that the family is the embryo of the State, whose essential categories it reproduces: the king being the father figure, the minister being the mother, the subject the child. For that reason too, the fraternity socialists who accept the family as a building-block of society, all arrive at dictatorship, the most exaggerated form of government. Monsieur Cabet's administration in the States of Nauvoo[4] is a splendid example of this. How much longer will it be before we grasp this ideal connection? The primitive conception of order through government is the common property of all peoples: and while the efforts made right from the beginning to organize, curtail, and modify the operations of authority and tailor them to general needs and to circumstances, demonstrate that negation was implicit in affirmation, the certainty is that no rival hypothesis has been advanced; the spirit has remained the same throughout. As nations have emerged from the savage and barbarous state, we have seen them promptly embark upon the government path, run the gamut of institutions which are always the same, and which all the historians and publicists categorize under these successive headings: monarchy, aristocracy and democracy.

But here is a matter of greater seriousness.

The governmental prejudice having permeated every recess of the consciousness, striking the reason in its seat, every other outlook has long since been rendered impossible, and the most daring of thinkers have as a result ventured the opinion that while government was undoubtedly a scourge, and a blight upon society, it was nevertheless a necessary evil.

Which is why, right up to our own day, the most liberating revolutions and all of freedom's stirrings have repeatedly culminated in a pledge of loyalty and submission to authority: why all revolutions have served only to reconstitute tyranny: and I no more except from this rule the Constitution of '93 than the one in 1848, even though both were the most advanced expressions of French democracy.

What has sustained this mental pre-disposition and made this fascination for so long invincible is that, following the supposed analogy between society and the family, government has always been presented to men's minds as the natural agent of justice, the protection of the weak and the keeper of the peace. As a result of this providential and sacrosanct attribute, government ensconced itself in men's hearts and minds alike. It became part of the mental furniture of the world: it was citizens' faith, their innermost and invincible superstition. If it should weaken, it was said of it, as it was of religion and of property: it is not the institution which is evil, but the abuse of it. It is not that the king is mischievous, it is his ministers: **"Ah, if only the king were aware!"**

And so, added to the hierarchical and absolutist aspects of a governing authority, there was an ideal that addressed the soul and conspired unceasingly against the yearning for equality and independence: while the people, every time there was a revolution, thinking to effect reforms, obedient to the promptings of its heart and the vices of its government, was betrayed by its very own ideas. In the belief that it was entrusting its interests to the authorities, it had always in reality acted in its own worst interests: instead of a protector, it found itself a tyrant.

Experience shows, indeed, that always and everywhere, government, no matter how popular it may have been in its origins, has sided with the best educated and wealthiest class against the poorest and most numerous one: that after having shown its liberal face for a time, it has gradually become exceptional and exclusive: finally, that instead of securing freedom and equality for all, it has toiled doggedly at destroying these things, on account of its natural predisposition towards privilege.

(. . .) The negation of government, which is, in essence, Morelly's utopia[5], which beams out a hastily extinguished light, through the sinister demonstrations of the Enragés and Hébertistes and which would have emerged from the teachings of Babeuf, had Babeuf been able to think his own principle through and make deductions from it — that great and telling negation traversed the whole of the 19th century, all misunderstood.

But an idea is imperishable: it is forever being reborn out of its opposite (. . .) Eventually, in the fullness of political evolution, the following hypothesis was to emerge: government, merely by its practice, will give birth to Socialism as its historical postulate.

Saint-Simon[6] was the first to trace the connection, albeit in faltering terms and with a still vague grasp of the phenomenon:

"The human species," he wrote in 1818,

> has been fated to live first under governmental and feudal rule:
>
> It has been doomed to pass from governmental or military rule to administrative or industrial rule, after having made sufficient progress in the positive sciences and in industry:
>
> Finally, it has been doomed by [the manner of] its organization to pass through a long and violent crisis in the course of its transition from the military to the peaceful system.
>
> The present time is an age of transition:
>
> The transitional crisis opened with Luther's preaching: since that time, minds have been of an essentially critical and revolutionary bent.

(. . .) The whole of Saint-Simon is encapsulated in those few lines, written in the style of the prophets, but too hard to digest for the times in which they were written, too condensed for the young minds which were the first to latch on to the noble innovator.

(. . .) What was Saint-Simon's meaning?

From the moment that, on the one hand, philosophy supplants faith and replaces the old notion of government with that of contract: when, on the other hand, in the wake of a revolution that has done away with the feudal regime, society seeks to develop its economic potential and achieve harmony within it: from that moment forth, it is inevitable that government, being repudiated at the level of theory, is progressively demolished in practice. And when Saint-Simon, in describing the new order of things, keeps to the old style and employs the word "government" together with the qualification "administrative" or "industrial," it must be obvious that the term, coming from his pen, takes on a metaphorical or rather analogical meaning to which only the uninitiated could be blind. How could there be any misreading of Saint-Simon's thinking after reading this even more explicit passage. I quote:

> If one looks at the course taken by the education of the individual, one finds, in primary schooling, that the act of governance is the primary factor: and in schooling beyond that level, one sees the act of governing the children continually lessening in intensity, while teaching plays an increasingly important role. The same has

been true of the education of society. Military, which is to say feudal (governmental) action, must have been stronger in its infancy; it has always had to assert its importance: and administrative power must, of necessity, wind up triumphant over military power.

To these extracts from Saint-Simon we ought to add his famous *Parabole* which struck the world of officialdom like an ax in 1819, and in consequence of which its author was arraigned before the assizes on February 20, 1820 and acquitted. The length of that all too notorious piece prohibits us from citing it.

As may be seen, Saint-Simon's negation is not a deduction from the notion of contract, which Rousseau and his sectarians had corrupted and dishonored over an 80 year period: rather, it flows from another flash of quite experiential and a posterior intuition, as befits an observer of events. What contract theory, prompted by providential logic, had supposedly anticipated in society's future prospects ever since Jurieu's[7] day — to wit, the end of governments — Saint-Simon, putting in an appearance in the heyday of the parliamentary scrimmage, registers as part and parcel of the law of human evolution. Thus, the theory of right and the philosophy of history, like two surveyor's staffs planted one behind the other, led the mind towards an unknown revolution: one more step and we are grappling with the phenomenon.

(. . .) The 18th century, as I believe I have demonstrated more than amply, had it not been derailed by Rousseau's classical, backward-looking, declamatory republicanism, would, by extrapolation upon the contract idea, which is to say by the juridical route, have arrived at negation of government. Saint-Simon deduced that negation from his scrutiny of history and of the education of mankind. If I may cite myself at this point when I alone represent the datum of revolution, I in turn derive it from analysis of economic functions and from the theory of credit and exchange. In order to establish this conclusive discovery, I need not, I think, review the various books and articles wherein it is encapsulated; they have created enough of a sensation over the past three years.

Thus the Idea, the incorruptible seed, has survived down through the ages, from time to time illuminating the man of good intentions, until the day when an intellect cowed by nothing picks it up, incubates it and then hurls it like a meteor at the galvanized masses.

The idea of contract, thrown up by the Reformation by way of a counter to the idea of government, traversed the 17th and 18th centuries without a single publicist's disclosing it, without a single revolutionary's taking it under his notice. Instead, the most illustrious elements within Church, philosophy and politics conspired to fight against it. Rousseau, Sieyès, Robespierre, Guizot, that whole school of parliamentarians, were the standard-bearers of reaction.[8] One man, very belatedly alerted by the degradation of the guiding principle, brought this young and fruitful idea once more into the light: unfortunately, the realistic aspect to his doctrine blinds his own disciples: they fail to see that the producer is the negation of the governor, that organization cannot be reconciled with authority: and for a further 30 years the formula was lost from sight.

(. . .) The idea of anarchy had scarcely been planted in the popular soil before there instantly sprang up so-called conservatives to water it with their calumnies, fatten it upon their violence, warm it beneath the cloches of their hatred and afford it the support of their inane reactions. Thanks to them, it has today mooted the idea of anti-government, the idea of labor, the idea of contract: it grows, it climbs, its tendrils wrap themselves around the workers' societies: and soon, like the little mustard seed in the Gospels, it will blossom into a huge tree whose branches will cover the whole of the earth.

The sovereignty of reason having replaced that of revelation: The notion of contract taking over from that of government: Historical evolution necessarily steering humanity into fresh practice: Economic criticism even now registering that under this new regime, the political institution must be absorbed into the industrial organism:

We fearlessly conclude that the formula for revolution can no longer be either direct legislation, nor direct government, nor simplified government: but is — no more government.

Neither monarchy nor aristocracy nor even democracy, insofar as this third expression might imply some government, operating in the people's name and purporting to be the people. No authority, no government, not even popular government: therein resides the revolution.

From Absolute Authority to Anarchy

(. . .) Any idea is established or refuted by a series of terms that is, so to speak, its agent, the last term being an irrevocable demonstration of its truth or error. If evolution, instead of taking place merely in the mind, in the form of theories, is simultaneously effected through institutions and acts, it constitutes history. This is the case with the authority principle or government.

The first term in which that principle is displayed is absolute authority. That is the purest, most rational, most emphatic, frankest and, all things considered, least immoral and least irksome formulation of government.

But absolutism, in its unadorned form, is odious to reason and to liberty: throughout the ages, peoples' consciousnesses have bridled at it; in the wake of consciousness, rebellion has made its objections heard. So the principle has been forced into retreat: it has retreated step by step, through a series of concessions, each of them more inadequate than the next, the latest of which, pure democracy or direct government, amounts to impossibility and absurdity. The first term in the series being absolutism, its fateful, final term is anarchy, taken in its broadest sense.

We shall now review, one by one, the main staging-posts in this great becoming.

Humanity asks its masters: "Why do you seek to rule over me and govern me?" To which they reply: "Because society cannot do without order: because a society has need of men who are obedient and who labor, while others command and direct: because, since individual talents differ, interests conflict with one another, and passions compete and the particular advantage of the individual runs counter to the common good, there is a need for an authority to prescribe the limits of rights and duties, some arbiter to settle disputes, some public force to see that the sovereign's verdict is carried out. Now, power, the State, is precisely that discretionary authority, the arbiter that renders unto each person that which is his, the force that guarantees and enforces the peace. Government, in short, is the principle and guarantor of order in society: commonsense and nature both proclaim it."

Throughout the ages, from out the mouths of all authorities, you will hear the same, unvarying message — in the tomes of the Malthusian economists, in the newspapers of the reaction and in the testimonials of republicans. The only thing that differentiates them one from another is the extent of the concessions they intend to make to freedom on this principle: those concessions are illusory concessions which add to so-called temperate, constitutional, democratic etc., forms of government a seasoning of hypocrisy, the taste of which merely leaves them more unpalatable.

Thus government, in its simplicity, offers itself as the absolute, necessary, *sine qua non* condition for order. Which is why it always, regardless of what mask it may wear, aspires to absolutism: indeed, according to the principle, the stronger the government, the nearer perfect order. Those two notions — government, and order — therefore, allegedly, have a cause and effect relationship with one another: government being the cause and order its effect. That indeed was the reasoning of primitive societies.

(. . .) But that reasoning is nonetheless false, and its conclusion wholly untenable, since according to the logical classification of ideas, government's relationship with order is not at all, despite what heads of State may claim, that of cause with effect, but rather the relationship of the particular to the general. Order being the general, government being the specimen. In other words, there are several ways of looking at order: who can prove to us that order in society is that which it pleases society's masters to describe as such?

On the one hand, they invoke the natural inequality of talents, from which they arrive by inductive reasoning at the conclusion that there should be a natural inequality of conditions: on the other, they cite the impossibility of reducing divergent interests to unity and of reconciling sentiments.

But at best that antagonism should be viewed as a problem to be resolved, not as a pretext for tyranny. Inequality of talents? Divergence of interests? Well now, you sovereigns with your crowns, fasces and sashes, that is precisely what we mean by the social question: and do you believe that it can be banished by baton and bayonet? Saint-Simon was quite right to take those two words, governmental and military, as being synonymous. Government bringing order to society is Alexander cutting the Gordian knot with his sword.

Who then, ye shepherds of the peoples, authorizes your belief that the problem of contradictory interests and unequal talents admits of not resolution? That class differences naturally follow from them? And that, in order to preserve that natural and providential differentiation, force is no merely necessary but legitimate? I contend, on the contrary — and all those whom the world describes as utopians because of their repudiation of your tyranny contend with me — that a solution to that problem can be found. Some have thought to discover it in community, others in association, still others in massive industrialization. For my own part, I say that the it lies in the organization of economic forces under the aegis of the supreme law of contract. Who tells you that none of these hypotheses is true?

By way of a counter to your governmental theory, which has no derivation other than your ignorance, no principle other than a sophistry, no method other than force, no purpose other than exploitation of human endeavor, of the progress of labor and of ideas, you place in my mouth this liberal theorem: find some form of compromise which, reducing divergence of interests to unity, identifying the particular good and the general good, substituting inequality of education for innate inequality, resolves all political and economic contradictions; where every individual is equally and synonymously producer and consumer, citizen and prince, administrator and administered: where his freedom is forever expanding, without his being required ever to forswear any of it: where his well-being increases indefinitely, without his being able to suffer trespass by society or his fellow-citizens against either his property, his labor, his income or his interest, "opinion" or sentiment-based dealings with his neighbors.

What! Such specifications strike you as impossible to meet? The social contract, when you think of the terrifying multitude of relationships that it has to regulate, seems to you the most unfathomable thing conceivable, something akin to the squaring of a circle and to perpetual motion. Which is why, war-weary, you lapse again into absolutism, into force.

Consider however that if the social contract can be agreed between two producers — and who could doubt that, reduced to such simple terms, it would be susceptible to resolution? — it can be agreed between a million too, since we are still talking about the same commitment, the number of signatories, while rendering it more and more effective, adding to it not one iota. Whereupon your powerlessness argument falls apart: it is laughable and leaves you without a defense.

In any event, you men of power, this is what the producer, the proletarian, the slave, the man whom you would have work in your place, has to say to you: I ask for no man's property and no man's *brasse*,[9] and am not disposed to countenance the fruits of my labors becoming another man's prey. I too want order, every bit as much as, and more than, those who breach it with their alleged government: but I want it to be a product of my will, a condition of my labor and a testimonial to my reason. I will never tolerate its coming from someone else's will, foisted upon me with servitude and sacrifice as its preconditions.

On Laws

In the face of the impatience of peoples and the imminence of rebellion, government was forced to yield: it promised institutions and laws: it has stated that its most fervent wish was that everyone might enjoy the fruits of his labor in the shade of his vine or of his fig tree. Its position required as much of it. Since, in fact, it posed as judge of the law, sovereign arbiter of men's fates, it could not purport to lead men according to its whim. King, president, directory, committee, popular assembly — whatever — power must have a code of rules to live by; without that, how can it ever establish discipline among its subjects? How can citizens abide by its order, if they are not notified of it: if, right after being notified, it is rescinded: if it should change from day to day, from hour to hour?

The government, then, has to make laws, that is to say, impose limits upon itself: because everything that is a rule for the citizen becomes a limitation upon the prince. He will pass as many laws as he finds interests: and since interests are beyond number and the relationships that are struck up multiply into infinity, and there is no end to antagonism, the law-making will have to operate non-stop. Laws, decrees, edicts, ordinances, writs will shower down upon the poor people like hailstones. After a time, the political ground will be covered with a layer of paper, which the geologists need only register as the "papyraceous" formation in the earth's rotations. In three years, one month and four days, the Convention issued 11,600 laws and decrees: the Constituent Assembly and Legislative Assembly were scarcely any less prolific: the Empire and governments since have done likewise. At present, the *Bulletin des Lois* registers, they say, upwards of 50,000; if our representatives were to do their duty that enormous figure would soon be doubled. Do you think that the people and the Government itself can preserve its reason in this maze?

True, we have come a long way since the primitive institution. In society, the government plays, so they say, a father's role: now, what father ever bothered to enter into a compact with his family? To issue a charter to his children? To strike a balance of power between himself and their mother? In his governance, the paterfamilias is prompted by his heart: he does not prey upon his children but supports them through his own toil: by his love, he considers nothing except his family's interests and circumstances: the law to him is what he wishes, and everyone, mother and child, trust in that. The petty State would be lost, if there was the slightest resistance to the father's actions, if those actions were limited in their prerogatives and predetermined in their effects. What! Might it be that the government is not a father to the people because it is subject to regulations, makes compromises with its subjects and makes itself the prime slave of a rationale — be it divine or popular — which is not its own ?

Were that the case, I do not see why I should conform to the law myself. Who offers me a guarantee of its justice and sincerity? Whence does it come to me? Who made it? Rousseau teaches correctly that in a truly democratic and free government, the citizen, in obeying the law, is obeying only his own will. Now, the law has been made without my participation, and in spite of my absolute dissent, regardless of the trespass it may inflict upon me. The State does not negotiate with me; it offers nothing in return, it holds me to ransom. So where are the ties, of conscience, reason, passion or interest that place me under an obligation?

But what am I saying? Laws — for him who thinks for himself and should be accountable for his own actions only, laws for him who aims to be free and feels called to become so? I stand ready to negotiate, but I want no part of laws: I acknowledge none: I protest against every order with which some authority may feel pleased on the basis of some alleged necessity to over-rule my free will. Laws! We know what they are and what they are worth. Gossamer for the mighty and the rich, fetters that no steel could smash for the little people and the poor, fishing nets in the hands of government.

You say that few laws will be passed and that they will be kept simple and be good ones. There we have another concession. The government really must be guilty if it admits its trespasses like that!

A small number of laws and excellent laws at that? Impossible. Must not government regulate every interest, sit in judgment of every challenge? Now, by the very nature of society, interests are innumerable, relations variable and infinitely fluid: So how can there be only a few laws made? How could they be straightforward? How could the best of laws not soon be despicable?

They talk of simplification. But if there can be simplification on one count, there can be simplification on another: instead of a million laws, one will do. And what might that law be? Do not do unto others that which you do not wish done unto yourself. The law of the prophets. But obviously that is no longer a law: its is the basic formula of justice, the rule governing all intercourse. So legislative simplification brings us back to the idea of contract and consequently to negation of authority. Indeed, if the law is singular, if it resolves all of society's antinomies, if it has everybody's consent and endorsement, it will suffice for the social contract. In promulgating it, you are proclaiming the end of government. So who is stopping you from proceeding at once with this simplification?

The Representative System

(. . .) There are not two sorts of government, any more than there are two sorts of religion. Government is government by divine right or it is not: just as religion is from Heaven or it is not. Democratic government and natural religion are two contradictions, unless one would rather look upon them as two mystifications. The people no more has a consultative voice in the State than in the Church: its part is to obey and to believe.

Also, just as principles cannot fail and men are alone in enjoying the privilege of inconsequentiality, so government, according to Rousseau, as well as under the '91 Constitution and all succeeding ones, is still, regardless of the election procedure, only government by divine right, a mystical and supernatural authority over-riding freedom and conscience, while seeming to woo their support.

Follow this logic:

> Inside the family, where authority is implanted in men's hearts, government proceeds from procreation:
> In savage and barbarous settings, it proceeds from patriarchy, which meets the preceding definition, or of force:
> In priestly settings, it proceeds from belief;
> In aristocratic settings, it proceeds from primogeniture, or caste;
> In Rousseau's system, which has come to be ours, it proceeds from fate, or numbers.

Procreation, force, belief, primogeniture, fate, numbers — all of them equally unintelligible and unfathomable things, which it is pointless to reason about and which we would do better to just accept: these are, I will not say the principles — authority like liberty recognizes only itself as a principle

— but the different modalities by which power is bestowed in human societies. For every primitive, superior, preceding and incontrovertible principle, the popular instinct has, down through the ages, always looked for an expression that was equally primitive, superior, preceding and incontrovertible. As regards the production of power, force, belief, heredity or numbers are the fluid forms assumed by this ordeal; they are the judgments of God.

So, do numbers make a more rational, more authentic, more moral appeal to your mind than belief or force? Does the ballot box seem more reliable to you than tradition or heredity? Rousseau rails against rule of the strongest, as if force, rather than numbers, represented usurpation. But then what are numbers? What is the index of them? What are they worth? What is the relationship between the more or less unanimous and genuine views of voters and that thing which lords it over every opinion, every vote, truth and right?

What! That thing is all that I hold most dear, my liberty, my labor, the survival of my wife and children; and when I try to come to an accommodation with you, will you defer it all to a congress whose formation is entrusted to the whim of fate? When I show up ready to enter into a contract, are you telling me that we have to elect arbiters who, without knowing me, and without hearing from me, will determine my innocence or guilt? I ask you, what has that congress to do with me? What assurances can it offer me? Why should I make the huge and irrecoverable sacrifice to its authority of accepting whatever it will have been pleased to determine is the expression of my wishes, the just measure of my rights? And whenever that congress, at the end of proceedings of which I hear not one word, should venture to force its decision upon me as law, and proffer me that law at the point of a bayonet, let me ask, if it be true that I am a part of the sovereign, what becomes of my dignity? And if I am to regard myself as a supplicant, what becomes of contract?

The deputies, it is argued, will be the most capable, most upright, most independent men in the land: selected on that basis by an elite of citizens who have the most interest in order, liberty, the welfare of the workers and progress. A cleverly devised initiative, which is dependent upon the candidates' kind hearts!

But why might the honorable bourgeois who make up the middle class have a better grasp of my true interests than I do? Look, what is at stake is my labor, the exchange of my labor, the thing which, next to love, is least tolerant of authority. (. . .)

(. . .) And you are going to hand over my labor, my love, by proxy and without my consent! Who can assure me that your proxies will not use their privilege to turn power into an instrument of exploitation? Who can guarantee me that their small number will not deliver me up, bound hand and foot and in conscience, to corruption? And should they refuse to succumb to corruption, should they manage to make the authorities see reason, who can guarantee me that the authorities will be willing to give way?

On Universal Suffrage

(. . .) The solution has been found, cry the undaunted. Let every citizen participate in the ballot; there is no power capable of standing in their path, no seduction capable of corrupting them. So thought the founders of the Republic after February.

A few add: let the mandate be binding and the representative liable to recall at all times: and the law's integrity will be guaranteed and the lawmaker's loyalty assured.

Drawing us into the mess.

I have no belief at all — and with good cause — in the sure-footed intuition of the multitude which is supposed to enable it to discern the candidates' merits and worthiness at a glance. There are examples galore of persons elected by acclamation who, even as they strode the platform to parade before the intoxicated onlookers, were at work on the hatching of their betrayals. The people would be doing well if at its rallies it could pick out one honest man for every ten scoundrels. . . .

But, once again, what are all these elections to me? What need have I of proxies, or indeed of representatives? And since I must set out my wishes, can I not articulate them without help from anyone? Will the cost to me be any greater, and will I not be all the surer of myself than of my advocate?

I am told that the thing must be settled: that it is not feasible for me to look to such a diverse range of interests; that, when all is said and done, a whole panel of arbiters whose membership will have been appointed by the unanimous vote of the people, holds out the promise of an approximation to truth and right that is much superior to the justice of an unaccountable monarch, as represented by insolent ministers and magistrates whose tenure places them, like the prince, far beyond my reach.

For a start I see no need to settle at that price: above all, I do not see it as being settled. Neither election nor vote, even should they be unanimous, resolve nothing. We have had recourse to both, to varying degrees, over the past sixty years, and what have we settled? What have we even defined? What illumination has the people obtained from its assemblies? What guarantees has it won? Say that its mandate comes up for renewal ten times a year, and there is a monthly re-endorsement of its municipal officers and judges — would that increase its income by as much as one farthing? Would it go to bed each evening more confident that there would be food on the table the next day, food for its children? Could it even answer that it will not be facing arrest and being dragged off to prison?

I appreciate that on matters not susceptible to normal resolution, or with regard to mediocre interests and trivial incidents, there should be reference to an arbitrator's verdict. Such compromises have the moral consolation of testifying to the presence in men's souls of something loftier than justice — the sentiment of fraternity. But in matters of principle, apropos of the very essence of rights and the direction with which society is to endowed: apropos of the organization of industrial forces: apropos of my labor, my subsistence, my life: apropos of the very hypothesis of government that we are dealing with — I recognize no conclave: I want to shift directly and individually for myself: universal suffrage strikes me as a real lottery.

Government and People

(. . .) Let me pass right on to the final hypothesis. Whereby the people, restored to absolute authority and acknowledging itself in its entirety as the despot, would deal with itself accordingly: where, as a result, it would amass all powers, as is only fair, and vest all authority — legislative, executive, judicial and otherwise, if such there be — in itself: where it would make all of the laws, issue all the decrees, ordinances, edicts, writs and judgments: issue all the orders: take to its bosom all its agents and functionaries, from the top of the hierarchy to the bottom: conveying its wishes directly to them without intermediary: overseeing and ensuring that those wishes were implemented, by imposing proportionate responsibility upon everybody: would sit in judgment of all endowments, civil lists, pensions and incentives: would, finally, as de facto and de jure king, enjoy all the honors and prerogatives of sovereignty — power, money, pleasure, leisure, etc.

(. . .) Regrettably, that set-up, which is, I dare say, generally and in its details, beyond reproach, runs up against an insurmountable difficulty in practice.

Because a government implies a converse term, and if the people as a body, *qua* sovereign, becomes the government, we will search in vain for the governed. The object of government is, let us remind ourselves, not to reduce the divergence of interests to unity — in which respect it acknowledges its utter incompetence — but rather to maintain order in society, in spite of conflict of interests. In other words, the object of government is to make up for absence of economic order and industrial harmony. So should the people, in the interests of its liberty and sovereignty, take charge of the government, it can no longer concern itself with production, since, by the very nature of things, production and government are two irreconcilable factors, and attempting to marry them together would be tantamount to sowing division everywhere. So, once again, where will the producers be? Where will the governed be? Where the administered? Where the judges? Or the executed?

(. . .) We must move on to the extreme hypothesis, whereby the people joins the government en masse, exercising every authority and spends all of its time in deliberations, voting and implementing, like in an insurrection, of one mind throughout, with nothing above it — not president, not representatives, not commissioners, not the *pays legal* and not the majority: in short, where it alone, as a body, makes the laws and is the sole functionary.

But if the people, thus organized for the exercise of power, effectively no longer has anything above it, let me ask this: what does it have beneath it? In other words, where is government's converse? Where are the farmers, the industrialists, the businessmen, the soldiers? Where are the toilers and the citizens?

Will it be the contention that the people is everything at once, that it produces and legislates simultaneously, that labor and government are conjoined within it? Which is an impossibility. Because since government on the one hand has the divergence of interests as its *raison d'être*, and on the other — no resolution involving authority of majority being admissible — the people alone and without exception is competent to pass laws, then, as the debate attending legislation will be dragged out by the sheer numbers of the lawmakers, and since the affairs of State will be inflated as a direct consequence of the numbers of statesmen, there will be no time left over for citizens to attend to their industrial duties: it will take all of their time — and then some — to deal with the business of government. There is no middle ground: one either works or one rules.

(. . .) This, moreover, is how things were done in Athens, where, over a number of centuries, save for a few intervals of tyranny, the people as a body went to the public square to engage in discussions from morning to evening. But the 20,000 citizens of Athens who were sovereign, had 400,000 slaves to do the work for them, whereas the French people has no one in its service and a thousand times as much business to transact as the Athenians. Let me repeat my question: apropos of what will the people-become-legislator-and-prince make laws? On behalf of which interests? To what end? And while it is governing, who is to feed it? (. . .) The people as a body becoming the State, the State loses all reason to exist, in that there is no people left any more: the governmental equation then adds up to . . . zero.

Away with Authority

Is the principal, crucial idea of this revolution not, in effect — away with authority, whether in the Church, the State, over the land, or over money?

Now, no more authority means that one has never seen and never grasped the compatibility of the interests of the individual with the interests of all, the identity between collective sovereignty and sovereignty of the individual.

No more authority! which is to say no more repayment of debts, the abolition of servitude, the lifting of mortgages, farm rents returned, dues payable to church, courts and State all done away with; interest-free loans, free trade, freedom of association, fixed share prices; guaranteed inexpensive education, work, property and housing; an end to antagonism, to war, to centralization, to government, to priests. Is that not society knocked off its axis, working in reverse, turned upside down?

No more authority! Which means free contract in place of absolutist law; voluntary compromise instead of State arbitration; equitable and reciprocal justice, instead of sovereign distributive justice; rational morality, instead of revealed morality; the balance of forces replacing the balance of powers: economic unity instead of political centralization. Once again, is not that what I will venture to call a complete overhaul, a turn-around, a revolution?

One can get the measure of the gap between these two systems from the difference between their styles.

One of the most solemn moments in the evolution of the authority principle was when the Ten Commandments were handed down. The voice of an angel commands the people prostrate at the foot of Mount Sinai:

Thou shalt adore the Eternal one, and none but Him. Thou shalt swear by Him only.

Thou shalt mark his feast days by idleness and thou shalt pay him His tithe. Thou shalt honor thy father and thy mother.

Thou shalt not kill.

Thou shalt not steal.

Thou shalt not commit fornication. Thou shalt do no wrong.

Thou shalt not be covetous and bear no false witness.

For this is the Eternal's ordinance, and it is the Eternal who has made thee what thou art. The Eternal alone is the only wise and worthy sovereign. The Eternal punishes and rewards. The Eternal can make thee happy or unhappy.

All legislation has borrowed this style and all, when speaking to man, employ the sovereign formula. Hebrew gives its commands in the future tense, Latin in the imperative form, Greek in the infinitive. The moderns do likewise (. . .) whatever the law, from whatever mouth it emanates, it is sacred once it has been uttered by that fateful trump which is, in our day, the majority.

"Thou shalt not gather together:

Thou shalt not publish:

Thou shalt not read:

Thou shalt respect thy representatives and the functionaries whom the result of the count or the whim of the State will have given thee:

Thou shalt obey the laws which their wisdom will have made for thee:
Thou shalt faithfully pay thy taxes:

And thou shalt love the government, thy lord and thy God, with all thy heart, all thy soul and all thy mind: because the government knows better than thee what thou art, what thou deservest, what is appropriate for thee, and it has the power to punish those who offend against its commandments, as well as to reward, even unto the fourth generation, those whom it favors."

O personality of man! Can it be that you have been wallowing in such abjection for the past 60 centuries! You claim to be blessed and sacred, and you are only the tireless, cost-free prostitute of your servants, your monks and your henchmen. You know it and it pains you! To be governed is to be watched over, inspected, spied upon, directed, legislated for, regulated, penned up, indoctrinated, preached at, monitored, assessed, censured and commanded by beings who boast neither the entitlement, the expertise or the virtue.

To be governed is to be, at every wheel and turn and every movement, noted, registered, inventoried, priced, stamped, rated, appraised, levied, patented, licensed, authorized, annotated, admonished, thwarted, reformed, overhauled and corrected. It is to be, on the pretext of public usefulness and in the name of the general interest, taxed, exercised, ransomed, exploited, monopolized, brow-beaten, pressured, bamboozled and robbed: then, at the slightest sign of resistance, at the first murmur of complaint, repressed, fined, vilified, irritated, hounded, reprimanded, knocked senseless, disarmed, garroted, imprisoned, shot, mown down, tried, convicted, deported, sacrificed, sold, betrayed and, to cap it all, toyed with, gulled, offended and dishonored. So much for government, so much for its justice, so much for its morality! And to think that there are among us some democrats who claim that government is a good thing: socialists who, in the name of liberty, equality, and fraternity support this ignominy: proletarians who put themselves forward as candidates for the presidency of the Republic! Such hypocrisy! . . . . Revolution is quite another matter. The quest for first causes and final causes has been stricken from economic science as it has also from the natural sciences.

In philosophy, the idea of progress is supplanting the idea of the absolute.

The Revolution is taking over from revelation.

Reason, abetted by experience, discloses the laws of nature and of society to man, then says:

These laws are the laws of inevitability itself. No man had a hand in their making: no one foists them upon you. They have been discovered little by little, and my only purpose is to bear witness to them. If you abide by them, you will be just and good: if you breach them, you will be unjust and mischievous. I have no other incentive to offer you (. . .) You are at liberty to accept or refuse.

If refuse it is, you belong to the company of savages. Withdrawing from the communion of the human race, you become suspect. You have no protection. At the slightest insult, the first person to come along can strike you, without attracting any accusation other than having needlessly used violence on a brute beast.

If, on the other hand, you enter into the compact, you are part of the society of free men. All of your brethren enter into a commitment with you, promising you loyalty, friendship, assistance, service and trade. . . .

Which is what the social contract adds up to.

Notes to The Authority Principle

1. Extracts lifted from *Idee generale de la révolution au XXe siécle* 1851.
2. The subtitles have been added by Daniel Guérin.
3. Louis de Bonald (1754–1840), reactionary philosopher and poodle of the monarchy and religion.
4. A community which the French communist Etienne Cabet (1788–1856), author of *Voyage en Icarie,* attempted to launch in the United States.
5. Other of the *Code de la Nature* 1755.
6. Henri de Saint-Simon (1760–1825), founder of so-called Saint-Simonian "utopian" socialism.
7. Pierre Jurieu (1637-1713), French Protestant theologian and adversary of absolutism in general and of Louis XIV in particular.
8. Jean-Jacques Rousseau (1712-1778), author of *The Social Contract: Joseph Sieyes* (1748–1836), theoretician of the Third Estate: Maximilien Robespierre (1758-1794), parliamentary revolutionary leader: François Guizot (1787–1874) historian and conservative politician and head of government during the latter years of the reign of Louis-Philippe.
9. *Brasse,* in the old French, meant the length of two arms.

Proudhon and Worker Candidates (1863–1864)

The texts we are about to present below (the Manifesto of the Sixty, and Proudhon's two letters to the workers) revolve around a tactical electoral issue: Should the ballot box be used as a weapon against Napoleon II's dictatorship, or not? But the controversy goes a lot further back, and is heavy with implications for the future. For one thing it signals the opening of a breach between the working class and the stalwarts of bourgeois democracy — its determination, more or less faltering as yet, to assert itself politically as a "separate" class; then again, it pits, one against the other, two contrasting views of workers' political action: anarchist abstentionism, and socialists' emancipation through the ballot box

When the imperial regime held general elections on May 31 and June 1, 1863, there had been no consultation of the electorate since 1857. On which occasion, although the support of the peasantry had been secured in the vast majority of provinces, in Paris the victory had nonetheless been a narrow one: the regime won by 110,536 votes as against the 96,299 for the democratic opposition. Five liberal deputies had thus been returned. They included Proudhon's friend, Alfred Darimon. But Proudhon had stayed in the background, and, while the "democratic-socialist" candidate owed his election to the prestige of his mentor, he had not, however enjoyed his support.

In 1863 Napoleon III had decided to consult the country once more, because what was described as the "authoritarian Empire" was afflicted by aging and venality. The despot also felt a need to revive a sham parliamentary life in the country and to bolster His Majesty's overly fragile opposition. In Paris, the results of the poll were celebrated by democrats who secured a quite considerable majority: taking 153,000 votes in comparison with the Imperial authorities' 82,000. In France as a whole, 35 deputies from the opposition were returned to the legislature.

According to Proudhon, at least half of those 153,000 votes had come from the working class. Yet no working man was elected. Of the nine candidates from the list of victors in Paris — of the democrats, six were journalists or men of letters and three were lawyers. However, a workers' committee had been appointed with worker candidates, including Henri Tolain, an engraver, who would very shortly figure among the founders of the First International. In a memorable pamphlet entitled *A Few Facts about the Paris Elections*, Tolain offered this explanation: "The loud voice of universal suffrage is all we have with which to make ourselves heard. . . . The people wants to govern itself. . . . What can the people expect . . . if it does not take its affairs into its own hands?" But the worker candidates won only a derisory number of votes (one got 332, another only 11:

Tolain had withdrawn his candidacy a fair while before the election). The bourgeois democracy looked upon these candidacies with such contempt that its spokesman, Jules Ferry, in his pamphlet *The Election Contest of 1863*, quite simply passed over them without a mention.

Proudhon adopted tactics that were very much his own, the tactics of active abstention. He was the driving force behind an abstentionist committee whose activity was intense: meetings, handbills, posters, all crowned by a cracking manifesto, and publication, on the eve of the election, of a pamphlet bearing his name and entitled *Sworn Democrats and Refractories*. He was astute enough not to rehearse his anarchistic ideas on the topic and took care not to attack the very principle of universal suffrage "the democratic principle par excellence." But, he reasoned, under the Empire, universal suffrage could not operate with complete independence, on a number of grounds which he went on to enumerate: the absence of freedom of assembly, of press freedom, and of municipal freedom. Electoral legislation tailored to suit the authorities made a nonsense of the vote. Finally, and above all else, candidates were manipulated into pledging oaths of loyalty to the Emperor.

Against that backdrop, abstention was, as far as the voter was concerned "a culpable gesture of indifference or sterile dignity," merely "an act of conservation, an appeal to law and entitlement." It was "an essential faculty of the voter." "Part of electoral law." "Merely a declaration by the country to the government that, in this context . . . the voters' vote means that the head of the Empire renounces this dictatorship and simultaneously calls upon citizens to do their electoral duty and perform a true act of sovereignty.

In passing, Proudhon was to shoot down recourse to plebiscite on tendentious or deliberately misconstrued issues, and his criticisms would be equally applicable under Gaullism: "Abstention or silent voting . . . are to be obligatory, being the pre-condition, the prime and most sacred of duties, when the matter put to the vote is equivocal, insidious, inopportune or unlawful." And Proudhon concluded:

> From the present essay and from the abstention committees . . . it will be apparent that there exists an elite that . . . declines to vote, and which bases its refusal upon the fact that universal suffrage, freedom's instrument and guarantee, would turn against it if the vote's guarantees were less than full and its forms less than sincere.

But this language, which was in danger of seeming a touch aristocratic, went unheeded by the popular electorate. In the Seine department, there were only 4,556 spoiled votes, and, across the country, "passive" abstentions, which had numbered 143,000 in 1857, plummeted to 86,000. However, the 4,556 spoiled votes themselves far outnumbered the few hundreds cast for the worker candidates.

On March 20 and 21, 1864, there were follow-up elections. Once again Tolain placed a workers' candidacy before the electors of Paris — his own — and this time he did not back out. He won only 424 votes, As in the previous year, the worker candidates had been sacrificed to candidates from the bourgeois democracy, who had two deputies returned. By way of backing for Tolain's candidacy, a 60-member workers' committee had drafted a Manifesto. This is the text with which we open and which was to be passed down to posterity as the first public expression of the working class's consciousness.

To begin with, Proudhon was enthusiastic as he read this document But a second glance diminished his ardor and praises In his view, this arrival on stage by the "worker plebs" was "at once a great victory and a great failing" He set out his reasoning in a book expressly written for the occasion; published in its unfinished form a little after his death, it was his political testament, *On The Political Capacity of the Working Classes*.

The authors of the *Manifesto*, Proudhon explained there, had not "promoted and proposed the candidacy of one of their number other than on the basis of his worker status." Being a worker, they reckoned that he "represented the working class better than anybody." The significance of this action did not elude the perspicacious Proudhon: "Let me say that this gesture . . . is indicative in the working classes of a hitherto unprecedented revelation, of its cooperative consciousness: proof that half and more of the French nation has stepped on to the political stage, bearing an idea which, sooner or later, must transform society and government from top to toe. . . . A social phenomenon of incomparable transcendence has been made manifest inside society: the arrival in political life of the most numerous and poorest class, hitherto scorned as possessed of no consciousness."

But after paying that tribute, Proudhon nevertheless took issue with the "Sixty." Not unreasonably, he saw the 1863–1864 elections as a "real low blow," "a sort of comedy laid on in order to buy time and harness the Revolution," "the instrument of a political deal." It was senseless to enter the imperial system. Instead, what was required was a radical breach with the authorities. As for the democratic opposition, he was scathing: their candidates made their stand "on the terrain of imperial legality." "They represent nothing, mean nothing and know nothing." The opposition's policy was "in principle, its professed anti-socialism." The worker candidates had made the mistake of holding out the olive branch to this opposition and offering it their support.

PARIS, ONE ELECTION EVENING (JUNE 1, 1863)

Monday, June 1, 1963, around ten in the evening: Paris is in the grip of a muffled agitation, reminiscent of that of July 26, 1830 and February 22, 1848. However unmoved one might be by impressions on the streets, one would have thought oneself on the eve of a battle. On every side, Paris, returning to political life after a 20 year interval, was wakening from her slumbers, feeling herself alive, stirred by the breath of revolution.

Ah! — cried those who had set themselves up as leaders of the movement — Paris right then was Monsieur Haussman's new, monotonous, tiresome city, with its ramrod-straight boulevards and its gigantic hotels and magnificent but deserted quays with its sluggish river bearing only stones and sand to its railway stations which, in replacing the ancient city's gates, have destroyed its *raison d'être* with her gardens, her new theaters, her new barracks, her tarmac, her legions of street-sweepers and her frightful dustiness. This was the old Paris, whose specter appeared by starlight to booming cries of "Long live liberty!"

Paris then, watchful guardian over the nation's freedoms, had arisen to the summons of her orators and answered the importuning of the government with the driest of rebuttals. Independent candidates had scored a formidable majority. The democratic list had been returned to a man; the results of the count were known. The administration had been defeated: its men had been rejected by some 153,000 votes to 82,000. The people, responsible for this coup, mulled over its success: the bourgeoisie had been split: one segment had indicated uneasiness, the other allowed its delight to erupt.

— Some coup! said one. What a slap in the face!

— A serious business, added another. Very serious. Paris being with the opposition, the Empire has lost its capital. . . .

(. . .) Then, on June 1, 1863, there was an eclipse of the moon. The sky was splendid, the evening magnificent. Tender and light, the breeze seemed to share the refreshing, not to say, harmless earthly emotions. The whole of Paris was able to monitor the phases of the phenomenon which, having begun at 56 minutes past nine — just as the polling booths were completing the count — was all over by 16 minutes past one in the morning.

— Thus, opined the wits, is despotism eclipsed by liberty. Democracy has reached out its great hand and a shadow has fallen over the star of December 2: hierophant-like, M. Pelletier, one of those elected and today the parliament's most irritating orator as far as those who read his words or listen to them are concerned, did not fail, in one of his pamphlets, to interpret the threat in this augury.

— More a case, retorted the losers, of the eclipse of Paris's reason. It's a repeat of your fiascoes of 1830 and 1848, and it may well turn out worse for you than in 1830 and 1848!

Manifesto of Sixty Workers from the Seine Department (February 17, 1864)

On May 31, 1863, the workers of Paris, more preoccupied with the opposition's victory than with their selfish interests, cast their votes for the list published in the newspapers. Without hesitation, without haggling over their support and prompted by their devotion to liberty, they offered startling and irrefutable evidence of it. And so the opposition's victory was complete, just as had ardently been desired, but it was assuredly more overwhelming than many had dared hope.

A worker candidate was fielded, it is true, but championed with a moderation that everyone was forced to acknowledge. Only secondary and partisan arguments were advanced in his defense, in view of an exceptional situation that afforded these general elections an especial character: his defenders refrained from raising the widespread problem of poverty. It was with a huge store of propaganda and arguments that the proletariat attempted to make its presence felt: the proletariat, that bane of modern society, even as slavery and serfdom were the banes of Antiquity and the Middle Ages. Those who acted thus had foreseen their defeat, but they saw fit to blaze a trail. It seemed to them that such a candidature was necessary if the profoundly democratic mentality of the great city was to prosper.

In the forthcoming elections, the situation will no longer be the same. By having nine deputies returned, the liberal opposition has been largely gratified in Paris. No matter who they were, selected on the same basis, the newly elected would add nothing to the import of the vote on May 31. Whatever their eloquence, it could scarcely add to the roar emanating today from the slick and sparkling words of the opposition's orators. There is not a single item of the democratic program that we would not be as eager as they to see realized. And let us state once and for all: we employ that word, democracy, in its most radical and clear cut sense.

But whereas we are in agreement on policy, can the same be said of social economy? The reforms we seek, the institutions we demand and the freedom to found them, are these accepted by all who represent the Liberal Party in the legislative body? That is the rub, the Gordian knot of the situation. One fact offers a peremptory and painful demonstration of the difficulties attending the workers' position. In a country where the Constitution is founded upon universal suffrage, in a land where everyone invokes and advocates the principles of '89, we are compelled to justify worker candidates, to spell out in detail and at some length the hows and the whys, simply in order to ward off, not just unfair charges that we are faint-hearts and out and out conservatives, but indeed the fears and misgivings of our friends.

Universal suffrage has marked our coming of age politically, but we have yet to emancipate ourselves socially. In France, a democratic country, that liberty which the Third Estate was able to win with so much vigor and perseverance, must be extended to every citizen. Equality of political rights necessarily implies equality of social rights. It has been repeated time and time again: there are no classes any more: ever since 1789, all Frenchmen are equal before the law.

But we who have no property beyond our arms, we who suffer, on a daily basis, the lawful or arbitrary conditions of capital, we who live under emergency legislation such as the law on combinations and Article 1781 which infringe our rights as well as our dignity, we find it hard to credit that claim.

We who, in a country where we have the right to choose our deputies, still do not have the wherewithal to learn to read: we who, being unable to assemble or enter freely into association, are powerless to organize apprenticeship training, and who watch as that priceless tool of industrial progress turns into a privilege of capital, cannot afford to delude ourselves so.

We whose children often spend their younger days in the degrading and unhealthy factory environment, or as apprentices, which is at present simply a condition bordering upon slavery: we whose women-folk are obliged to quit the home for overly demanding toil at odds with their natures and destructive of the family: we who have no right to come to some arrangement among ourselves for the peaceable defense of our wages, and to make provision against unemployment, we state that the equality written into the law has yet to pass into our mores and yet to be carried into practice. Those who, bereft of education and capital, cannot have recourse to liberty and solidarity to withstand selfish and oppressive demands, inevitably suffer the over-lordship of capital: their interests remain subordinated to other interests.

That interests are not regulated, we know: they elude the law: they can only be reconciled through specific agreements as fluid and changeable as those interests themselves. Unless freedom is afforded to all, such reconciliation is not feasible. We will pursue the acquisition of our rights peaceably and lawfully, but vigorously and with persistence. Our emancipation would soon demonstrate the progress achieved in the mentality of the laboring classes, that countless vegetating multitude dubbed the proletariat, which, having recourse to an apter description, we shall call the wage slaves.

To those who reckon that they see the organization of resistance and strike action in any demand on our part for freedom, we say: you do not know the workers: they pursue a goal much greater and more fecund than that of expending their efforts in day to day strife in which the adversaries on both sides would ultimately achieve naught but ruination for some and misery for the rest.

The Third Estate used to say: What is the Third Estate? Nothing! What should it be? Everything! We are not about to say: What is the worker? Nothing! What should he be? Everything! But this we will say: the bourgeoisie, our senior in respect of emancipation, was, in '89, able to swallow up the nobility and eradicate unjust privileges; it is not for us to destroy the rights deservedly enjoyed by the middle classes, but rather to secure for ourselves the same freedom to act. In France, the democratic country par excellence, every political right, every social reform, every instrument of progress cannot remain the prerogative of the few. By the very nature of things, the nation that has an innate sense of equality has an irresistible tendency to make that a universal inheritance. Any instrument of progress that cannot be made comprehensive, and vulgarized so that it contributes to the common weal, penetrating even to the lowest strata of society, is not completely democratic, in that it represents a privilege. The law should be capacious enough to permit every individual, individually or collectively, to develop his gifts, utilize his resources, his savings and his intelligence, without any term's being set to that other than the next man's liberty and not the next man's interest.

Let no one accuse us of dreaming up *lois agraires*, fanciful equality which would place us all upon a Procrustean bed, with its division, its maximum and its enforced levies, etc. No! It is high time that we had an end of these calumnies peddled by our enemies and swallowed by the uninformed. Freedom of labor, credit, solidarity — those are our dreams. On the day they become real, to the greater glory and prosperity of a country which we hold dear, there will be no bourgeois and no proletarians, no bosses and no workers any more. Every citizen will be equal in rights.

But, we are told, all these reforms you require can be demanded by elected deputies every bit as well as you and better than you: they are the representatives of all and appointed by all.

Well, our answer comes, No! We are not represented, and that is why we broach this question of worker candidates. We know that there is no talk of industrial, commercial, military, journalist candidates, etc., but the phenomenon exists even if the name does not. Does the vast majority of the legislative body not comprise great proprietors, industrialists, businessmen, generals, journalists, etc., who tacitly vote or speak only in offices and then only on issues in which they have a specialist interest?

A very tiny number speaks out on broad issues. To be sure, we think that workers elected should and would champion the broad interests of democracy, but even if they were to confine themselves to championing the sectional interests of the most numerous class, what a specialization that would be! They would supply a want in the legislative body, where manual labor has no representation. We who have in our service none of these things — no fortune, no connections, no public office — are indeed obliged to give our candidates a plain and telling description and to call things by their proper name insofar as we can.

We are not represented, for, in a recent sitting of the legislative body, there was a unanimous expression of sympathy in favor of the working class, but not one voice was raised to articulate, with moderation but with firmness, our aspirations, desires and rights, as we understand them.

We are unrepresented — we who refuse to credit that poverty is the will of God. Charity, a Christian institution, has radically proven and itself acknowledged its powerlessness as a social institution.

No doubt, in the good old days, in the days of divine right, when, being imposed by God, kings and nobles thought themselves the fathers and elder brothers of the people, when happiness and equality were relegated to Heaven, charity had to be a social institution.

In the age of popular sovereignty and universal suffrage, it is no longer such, and can now be nothing more than a private virtue. Alas! The vices and infirmities of human nature will always leave plenty of scope for the exercise of brotherliness: but undeserved misery, the sort that, in the form of sickness, inadequate pay and unemployment, traps the vast majority of well-intentioned working men in a hellish circle from which they strain in vain to break free: THAT misery, let us state emphatically, can be eliminated and will be. How come no one has made that distinction before? We have no wish to be clients or dependents: we wish to become equals: we reject alms: we seek justice.

No, we are not represented, for no one has said that the spirit of antagonism is daily growing weaker among the popular classes. Enlightened by experience, we bear no man hatred, but we do wish to alter things. No one has said that the law on combinations is only humbug these days and that, instead of eradicating the evil, kept it alive by barring every escape route to the man who believes himself oppressed.

No, we are not represented, for, in the matter of trades councils, a queer confusion has taken root in the minds of those who recommended them: according to them, the trade council would be made up of employers and workers, a sort of professional panel, referees charged with deciding, day to day, upon whatever matters may arise. Now what we ask is a council made up exclusively of workers, elected by universal suffrage, a Trades Council along the lines, say, of the Chamber of Commerce, and in reply they give us a tribunal.

No, we are not represented, for no one has mentioned the considerable movement afoot among the working classes in the organization of credit. Who is aware that this very day there are 35 mutual credit societies quietly operating in Paris? They bear the seeds of what is to come after: but if they are to germinate fully, they will require the sunshine of liberty.

In principle, few intelligent democrats challenge the legitimacy of our demands, and none of us abjures the right to pursue them for ourselves.

Opportunity, the competence of candidates, the probable obscurity of their names, in that they would be chosen from among workers practicing their trade at the time of selection (with the specific purpose of clarifying the meaning of their candidature) — these are matters brought up in order to suggest that our scheme is impracticable and that publicity would in any case fail us. For a start, we hold that after 12 years of patient waiting, the opportune time has arrived: we cannot accept the necessity of waiting for the next general elections, which is to say, a further six years. In which case it would have taken 18 years for the time to be ripe for the election of workers — 21 years on from 1848! What better constituencies could be chosen than the first and the fifth? The prospects for success must be better there than anywhere else.

The vote on May 31 has resolved the great issue of liberty beyond all challenge in Paris. The country is calm: is it not wise and politic to put to the test today the power of the free institutions which are to smooth the transition from the old society rooted in wage slavery to the society of the future which is to be founded upon common title? Is there not a danger in waiting until moments of crisis, when passions become unduly inflamed by widespread distress?

Would not the success of worker candidates have an immeasurable moral impact? It would prove that our ideas are understood, that our feelings of conciliation are appreciated: and that at last the refusal to implement in practice what has been acknowledged as fair in theory has ended.

Could it be true that worker candidates would need to be possessed of those eminent oratorical and publicist gifts that single a man out for the admiration of his fellow-citizens? We think not. It would be enough for them to be able to appeal to justice, by spelling out plainly and clearly the reforms for which we ask. Moreover, would not the votes of their electors afford their words a greater authority than the most illustrious orator could claim? Springing from the ranks of the masses, the import of those elections would be all the more sensational in that those returned would have been the obscurest and most unknown of figures up until then. Finally, the gift of eloquence and universal expertise, have these ever been demanded as necessary qualifications of the deputies appointed hitherto?

In 1848, the election of workers set the seal upon political equality: in 1864 such election would set the seal upon social equality.

Other than by flying in the face of the evidence, one is forced to acknowledge that there is a special class of citizenry in need of direct representation, in that the precincts of the legislative body are the only place where workers could worthily and freely articulate their wishes and stake their claim to the rights enjoyed by other citizens.

Let us examine the current position without bitterness or prejudice. What does the democratic bourgeoisie want that we did not want along with it equally fervently? Universal suffrage without impediment of any sort? We want that. Freedom of the press, freedom of reunion, governed by a common entitlement? We want that. Complete separation of Church and State, a balanced budget, municipal exemptions? We want all that.

Now then! But for our support, the bourgeoisie would have a hard time securing or retaining these rights, these liberties, which are the very essence of a democratic society.

What do we want more especially than it, or at any rate more sorely, in that we have a greater interest in it? Free and compulsory primary education and freedom of labor.

Education nurtures and reinforces the sense of human dignity, which is to say, awareness of rights his duties. The enlightened man appeals to reason and not to force in the realization of his desires.

Unless we have freedom of labor by way of a counter-balance to freedom of trade, we will witness the emergence of a financial autocracy. The petit bourgeois, like the workers, will soon be nothing more than its servants. Is it not apparent today that credit, far from becoming widely accessible, has instead a tendency to be concentrated into a few hands? And does not the Bank of France offer a glaring example of contradiction of every economic principle? It simultaneously enjoys a monopoly upon the issuance of paper money and a free hand in the unrestricted raising of interest rates.

Without us, let us say again, the bourgeoisie cannot establish anything with security: without its backing our emancipation may be postponed for a long time yet.

So let us unite in a common object: the triumph of true democracy.

Sponsored by us and backed by us, worker candidates would be living proof of the serious, enduring unity of democrats without regard to distinctions of class or position. Are we to be left to our own devices? Are we to be compelled to seek, alone, the triumph of our ideas? For everyone's sake, let us hope not.

Let us recapitulate, in order to avoid any misunderstanding: the essentially political import of the worker candidates would be this:

A reinforcement, a complementing of the activity of the liberal opposition. In the most modest terms, it has requested the requisite freedoms. Worker deputies would sue for the requisite economic reforms.

That is an honest summation of the general ideas articulated by the workers in the run-up to the May 31 elections. So, a worker candidate would have a lot of difficulties to overcome before he could run. And might with some justification be accused of being a late-comer. Today the ground is clear and since, as we see it, the necessity for worker candidates has been thrown into even sharper relief by what has happened in the inteval, we have no hesitation in breaking new ground in order to fend off the reproach leveled at us in the last elections.

We are airing this matter publicly so that, when the period of canvassing first begins, agreement may be achieved all the more easily and promptly among those who share our view. We say candidly what we are and what we want.

We seek the lime-light of publicity, and we appeal to the newspapers which labor under the monopoly created by the requirement for prior authorization: but it is our conviction that they will do us the honor of affording us their hospitality, thereby indicating that they favor authentic freedom: by affording us the means to communicate our thoughts, even though they may not be in agreement with them.

With all our hearts we yearn for the moment of debate, the election period, the day when the credos of the worker candidates will be in everyone's hands, when they will stand ready to answer every query. We are relying upon the support of those who will be won over when our cause is the cause of equality, indissolubly bound up with liberty — in short, the cause of justice.

(Signed by 60 signatories)

P.J. Proudhon: No Candidates![1]
Proudhon's letter to workers

Passy, March 8, 1864

To workers,

You ask, citizens, what I think of the Manifesto of the Sixty workers which has appeared in the press? Above all, you are eager to know if, after having come out in May against candidatures of every sort, you should abide by that line or, on grounds of circumstance, support the election of a comrade deserving of your sympathies. I had not been expecting, I confess, to be consulted by anyone on such a matter. I had thought the election campaign spent, and in retirement, my thoughts focused only upon mitigating its dismal effects insofar as I was able. But since, on grounds that strike me as quite personal, your confidence in my opinion has felt obliged to, so to speak, put me on the spot, I will not hesitate to answer your question, the more so as my thinking could scarcely be anything other than an interpretation of your own.

To be sure, I was delighted at the awakening of the socialist idea: in the whole of France just then, who more than myself was entitled to rejoice in it? To be sure, I hold, along with you and with the Sixty, that the working class is not represented and is entitled to representation: how could I believe otherwise? Does not workers' representation, today as in 1848, signal socialism's arrival in legislative, political and governmental terms?

We are told that since '89, there have been no more classes: that the notion of worker candidates tends to resurrect them: that, if a working man is acceptable as a candidate, just the way one would accept a sailor, an engineer, a scholar, a journalist, a lawyer, this is because that working man will, like his colleagues, represent society and not a specific class: that, otherwise, the fielding of this working man would be a step backwards, an illiberal, even a dangerous move, by virtue of the misgivings, the alarm, the hostility that it would inspire in the bourgeois class.

Such is the logic of the adversaries of the Manifesto, who do not even realize that they contradict themselves. But, as I see it, it is precisely on account of its specific character, and as the manifestation of one class or caste — for I do not recoil from the word — that worker candidature has value: stripped of that, it would be meaningless.

What! Is it not a fact that, in spite of the Revolution, French society is profoundly split into two classes: one, which lives exclusively by its labors, and whose wages are generally less than 1,250 francs annually, for a family of four, a sum that I take to be the rough average of the national product: another, which lives off something other than its labors, assuming that it does work, and lives off the income from its properties, capital, endowments, pensions, subsidies, shares, salaries, honors and stipends? Is it not a fact that, in terms of the division of wealth and produce, there are still, as once there were, two categories of citizen among us, commonly described as bourgeoisie and plebs, capitalism and wage slavery? But the whole of our political organization, political economy, industrial organization, history, literature and society repose upon that distinction which only bad faith and a foolish hypocrisy seem to deny.

Society's division into two classes — one class of waged workers, another of proprietors-capitalists-entrepreneurs — therefore enjoying indisputable de facto status, the implications of that ought not to come as a surprise to anyone: it is that there has always been some question as to whether that distinction did not also have a *de jure* existence: whether it fell within the province of nature, compatible with justice: whether it might not be possible to bring it to an end, which means contriving some amalgamation of the classes: in short, whether, by means of improved implementation of the laws of justice and economics, one might not successfully do away with a dismal distinction which every man would wish at heart to see eradicated?

That question, scarcely a new one, is what has been described in our day as the social question: it is the whole and all of socialism.

Well, now! What say the Sixty? They, for their part, are convinced that the social question can be resolved in an affirmative sense: with moderation and firmness, they note that for quite some time, it has been stricken from the agenda, that the time has come to re-table it: to that end, and as a signal or earnest of that resurrection, they propose that one of them stand as a candidate: that, by virtue of his being a working man and precisely because he is a working man, they reckon that he can represent the working class better than anyone else.

And these men are accused of designs upon the re-establishment of castes? Some would have them barred as reactionaries, professing dangerous opinions, from representation of the nation, and their Manifesto has even been denounced as inciting some citizens to hate their fellow-citizens! The press thunders, the supposedly democratic opposition shrieks its displeasure, and there are cries of importunity and recklessness and what not. There are dark hints about the police! With a show of consummate disdain, the question is posed whether the Sixty would claim to know more about their interests and their rights, and about defending them, than Messrs J. Favre, E. Ollivier, Pelletan, J. Simon, etc?[2]

Contemptible.

Thus far at any rate, I am quite in agreement with you, citizens, and with the Sixty, and it is gratifying that not for a single moment did you imagine that I could feel differently than yourselves. Yes, class distinction enjoys a de facto existence in our democratic France, and it has yet to be proved entirely that this phenomenon is rooted in entitlement, albeit that there are no grounds for imputing it to anyone. Yes, except for 1848, national representation has been the prerogative of one of those classes: and, unless the representatives drawn from said class make a prompt commitment to effect the fusion sought, justice, common sense and universal suffrage require that the second of those classes be represented like the other, in proportion with its population figures. In mooting that ambition, the Sixty are not in any sense insulting the bourgeoisie, are not threatening it, but are standing up to it like the youngest son to his older siblings.

(. . .) Such language, as candid as it is modest, ought to reassure the faintest of hearts: and the bourgeoisie, the middle class especially, would be ill-advised to be alarmed by it. Whether it knows it or not, its true ally, its savior, is the people. So let it with good grace concede the workers' entitlement to national representation and not, I say again, merely as citizens and despite their worker status, but rather on the basis that they are workers and members of the proletariat.

That said, let me move on to the second point. Whether, in the present circumstances, exercise of the eligibility right is indeed, as far as the working class is concerned, the best way of bringing about the reforms for which it sues, whether such a conclusion on the part of the Manifesto does not conflict with the aim its authors have set themselves, whether it is not at odds with their principles: in short, can socialism, under the current regime, do what it managed to do in 1848 without injury to its dignity and faith? Men of some import in the democracy, whom no one ever suspected of compromise with the enemy, who themselves refrained from voting, nevertheless reckoned it their duty, out of sympathy with the working class and by way of testimony to their distancing themselves from an opposition which was misunderstood, not to oppose the workers' decision and to wish their candidature well. While acknowledging sentiments in which I share, I regret that I can make no such concession, and on this count I take issue with the Sixty.

Consider this: the imperial government, established by coup d'état, identifies as the prime cause of its success its defeat of red socialist democracy, that to this day that is still its *raison d'être*, which it has never overlooked that in its policy, and that there is at present nothing to indicate that it has any inclination nor indeed capacity to change. Under that government, the financial and industrial fiefdom, long incubated over the thirty three years of the Restoration and the July monarchy, has completed its organization and climbed into the saddle. It has supported the Empire, which has rewarded it for its sponsorship. The big companies have formed their coalition: the middle class, the authentic expression of French genius, has found itself being ground down more and more in the direction of the proletariat.

The Republic, through the introduction of universal suffrage, provided Democracy with a moment of effervescence, but the conservative aristocracy soon recaptured the upper hand, and, come the coup d'état, it might be said that power was a foregone conclusion for the side that had best used the reaction against the socialist tendencies. On which basis we may say that, under the regime that has ruled over us since 1852, our ideas, if not our persons, have been, so to speak, placed outside of politics, outside of government, outside of the law. To none but us has access to the periodical press, the preserve of the old parties, been denied. Whereas sometimes a proposition inspired by our principles was put to the authorities, it quickly foundered — I know of what I speak — when rebuffed by contradictory interests.

Confronted with a state of affairs where our destruction is the salvation of society and property, what can we do but accept our reprobation in silence, and, since the government has ventured to impose this draconian condition, separate ourselves radically from it? Entry into its precincts, where we may be sure to find all our enemies, old and new, defectors to the Empire and non-defectors, ministry folk and opposition folk, embracing the prescribed conditions, seeking representation in the legislative body — that would be an absurdity, an act of cowardice! All that we are permitted to do under the existing law is register a protest in great elections, through the negative content of our bulletins. Bear this in mind — that in the system of compression by which democracy is oppressed, it is not such and such a financial measure, such and such an undertaking, such and such an expenditure, such and such an alliance, such and such a treaty, policy or law that we must debate: they have no need of us for that: our opinion is ruled null and void in advance. Such debates are the preserve of the constitutional opposition, friend or foe. For there is room for every view but ours in the Constitution: can you doubt it, after the brouhaha that erupted everywhere after publication of the Manifesto? Now, in order to exercise our separatism, we need neither representatives nor candidates: in legal terms, all we require is a single word, veto, the most vigorous message that universal suffrage can deliver.

Let us clarify out thought with a few examples:

May we, by word of mouth, in writing, or through the actions of men authentically ours, pledge fidelity to the 1852 Constitution, to which we see all our enemies, Legitimists, Orleanists, ex-Republicans, clericals agog to pledge themselves? No, we cannot, for that oath, injurious to our dignity, incompatible with our principles, would imply apostasy on our part, even should we remain, as so many others have after their oath, the personal enemies of the Emperor. The Constitution of '93, by enshrining the sovereignty of the people, swept away the civic oath required under the '91 Constitution to these three terms: Nation, Law and King. Let Napoleon follow that example and then we shall see. Meanwhile, no representatives and no candidates!

There are some who say that the pledge imposed upon deputies is meaningless: that it is not binding upon the maker, provided that, in the act of making it, he understands that his pledge is being made, albeit under the name of the Emperor, to the nation: that, furthermore, the pledge does not imply any support for imperial policy. Finally, that it is not for electors to overcome this scruple, which is a matter of concern to the candidates only. In bygone times, the Jesuits alone possessed the secret of salving consciences: Has that secret now been passed down to the Ecole Normale? Such moralists, now matter how high their reputation for virtue may stand, ought to be deemed the most infamous human creatures by the socialist democracy. So, no representatives and no candidates!

Just now, I referred to the periodical press monopoly introduced and especially directed against us. From the outcome of the May elections, we know what it cost us to have had a week's dalliance with it. Do you think that abolishing ministerial authorization would be enough to do away with that monopoly? Then you are well wide of the mark. We want neither hide nor hair of a regime that has been depraving our political morals, misrepresenting ideas and misleading opinion for 12 years now. Authorizing such corruption of the public mind — be it for six months, for a day, or through the election of a socialist deputy — would amount to declaring ourselves accomplices of that corruption and unworthy ever to be heard. So, no representatives and no candidates!

We want no conditions upon the exercise of universal suffrage, and why? Not just because natural population clusters have been subverted by arbitrary constituency boundaries: we leave it to the Imperial government's competitors to bleat while they await their chance to imitate it. Nor is it because of administrative interference either. In meetings summoned to decide the government's fate, those who rail loudest against such interference are careful to say that, in the minister's shoes, they would not refrain from it. Chiefly because, with a monopoly over a tame press, with centralistic prejudices in the ascendant, with the rarity and inadequacy of summons, with double, triple, quintuple and decuple candidatures and with that absurd principle — of which electioneers are so enamored — that a true representative of France should not be known to his electors: with the mishmash of categories, opinions and interests, things are so combined as to smother the democratic spirit in its corporative and local manifestations, as well as in its national manifestations, with the masses denied a voice and reduced to bleating flocks, never having learned to make their presence felt and to have their say.

To call for the emancipation of the plebs and then to consent, in the plebs' name, to a method of election which is tantamount to rendering it seditious or dumb. What a paradox! So, no representatives and no candidates!

Note, citizens, that in all of this I am sticking to politics alone and deliberately steering clear of economic and social considerations. How many further arguments I could adduce against this candidatures fantasy, which would assuredly not have possessed the people, had we been able in time to explain this proposition, the truth of which you are doubtless starting to discern: that an opposition vote is one thing, a protest vote another and a duly recorded constitutional vote, bearing the stamp of the returning officer another, and a democratic and social vote quite another. In May 1863, the people thought it was voting for itself and as sovereign: it voted only for its bosses and as client. As for the rest, I know that by now you have no illusions left: the worker candidates, if my sources are accurate, say as much themselves. So, what good are representatives! What use are candidates?

Everything that has been done since November 24, 1860, in government and in opposition, indicates a reversion to the regime of 1830, with the sole modification that the title of emperor is to replace that of king, and the Bonaparte dynasty replace that of the Bourbons. Leaving to one side the dynastic issue, with which we need not concern ourselves, can we democrats lend a hand with this about-turn? It would be a betrayal of our past to worship that which we have put to the torch, or put to the torch that which we have worshipped. Now, that is necessarily what must happen if we let ourselves be represented in a legislative body, among an opposition three fourths of which have come around to the idea of a constitutional, bourgeois monarchy. So, no representatives and no candidates!

Many among the workers fail to appreciate clearly these deep-seated incompatibilities between the present or forthcoming political regime, into which they are invited to step, and their democratic social aspirations. This will help them get to grips with the thing:

It is axiomatic that in a country racked by revolutions such as ours is, succeeding governments, although their slogans may change, still close ranks against a third party, and take turns at the duties imposed upon them by this redoubtable inheritance. Now, that is a condition which, should the opportunity arise, we are prohibited from accepting. We — the outlaws of 1848, 1849 and 1852 — cannot agree to the undertakings, deals and all the acts of power devised with an eye to our extermination. That would amount to a betrayal of ourselves, and the world should know that. At present, the public debt, consolidated and outstanding, with growth rates at three percent, stands at 14 thousand 600 millions.

So much for the financial expression of charges accrued since 1789 and bequeathed to one after another of our various governments. It is the plainest and most clear-cut product of our political systems, the most splendid bequest to posterity of seventy five years of conservative, bourgeois rule. If need be, we would assume responsibility for that debt up until 24 June 1848: but we are within our rights to repudiate it after that. And since it is unacceptable that the nation should be declared bankrupt, it would be up to the bourgeoisie to pay off the residue. We await its decision. So, citizens, no representatives and no candidates!

In the Manifesto of the Sixty there is an unfortunate choice of terms. In politics, they profess to be in agreement with the opposition: this is an unduly large concession, inspired by the generous intention of bridging, in part at least, the gulf separating democracy from its representatives, and it must be put down to a slip of the pen. In all sincerity, we can no more be happy with the opposition's politics than with its economic and social ideas: if the latter be mistaken, how could the former be above reproach? The opposition's politics is not the criticisms which parties fling at each other regarding their actions, such as the Mexican expedition, the state of Algeria, the swelling budget, etc.; nor is it the banal demonstrations in favor of freedom, the philanthropic jeremiads, the sighs heaved over Poland, or the more or less explicit support for the trade agreement. On all such matters of pure detail, we should have our reservations about the opposition's criticisms, not just as socialists and communists, but as politicians and democrats.

The opposition's politics is above all its declared anti-socialism, which necessarily places it in the reactionary camp against us. Messrs. Marie and Jules Favre have said as much, in the opening debate, and in a tone never to be forgotten: "We are no socialists!" At which words the entire Assembly erupted into applause: not a single voice was heard to object. So we are within our rights to say that, on the very principle of their politics, members of the so-called democratic opposition are in agreement with the government: they outdo the government itself in their anti-socialism: how could they fail to become ministers some day?

The opposition's politics is its love for parliamentarism, which will draw it willy-nilly into a bloc with the imperialist majority, under the 1830 arrangement: it is its enthusiasm for centralization and unification that shines through all its speeches, in spite of all its declaiming about municipal freedoms and sycophancy towards Parisians. Remember, a high degree of centralization alone can satisfy high ambitions and you will notice that, should France ever have the misfortune to find opposition personnel summoned to take their turn at overseeing this much-cherished centralization.

The opposition's politics is its constitutional dynastic oath: it is the solidarity with the actions of the government to which it consents, if only by drawing its deputy's stipend; it is the compliments, the praises, the thanksgiving which it mixes with its criticisms, the share it claims of its successes and glories.

The opposition's politics is its conduct in the May 1863 elections. When we saw it, once it had usurped the oversight of the count, trampling suffrage underfoot, fielding everywhere candidates utterly irreconcilable with the spirit of the Revolution, showing itself to be more scheming, more tyrannical, more corruptive than the administration, against which it then strove to focus the public revulsion, so as to whiten its own record. Ah, the elections of May and June 1863, fought by an opposition that posed as puritanical; these elections overturned the result of 1851: have you considered that, citizens?

That is what the opposition's politics is about. And you would send your colleagues to join it? No, no! No representatives and no candidates!

To those who would now take us to task for halting the popular upsurge, and who might still have the courage to flaunt the title of men of action which they awarded themselves nine months ago, let me answer that the inactive, the inert, the slumberers are themselves, whose splendid discipline has served the views of the reaction, and at a single stroke, cost democracy thirty years of civic virtue, sacrifices and propaganda. What, then, has this rigorous action produced?

1. A thunderous declaration from Messrs. Marie and Jules Favre: "We are no socialists!" Yes! Your representatives have disowned, reneged upon you, as they did in 1848: they declare war on you and you congratulate

yourselves upon your actions! Are you waiting until they spit in your face?

2. The lamentable result of the oath. The democracy, led by its new tribunes, fondly imagined that the oath of obedience to Napoleon III, and of fidelity to the 1851 Constitution, could not but be a sublime perjury on the lips of its representatives. It was intoxicated with this notion, and it has sadly deceived itself. Our sworn deputies will no more have the courage to breach their oath than to keep it. Can you see them beating about the bush, sustaining heavy losses, swimming between the waters of treachery and fidelity? Traitors to democracy when in cahoots with the Empire, traitors to the Empire when closeted with democracy. Privy councilors and table companions of His Majesty, are still more honest and less hypocritical. Thanks however to this policy, the Restoration of the Orleanist system, with M. Thiers at the helm, is visibly underway. M. Thiers and his cronies, positing monarchy as in principle essential for the organization of power, and declaring themselves to be, by virtue of the very same principle, indifferent as to the dynasty chosen, that being a simple question of personalities according to them, are perfectly at home here. Nothing prevents them from taking the oath, and the more that Napoleon affords them cause to keep it, the more content they are.

   Also, since the taking of all these oaths, a matter of such high significance and import for the Orleanists, but which the country can watch democrats do only with disgust, the party of constitutional, parliamentary monarchy has bounced back completely: supported by the weightiest and most enlightened faction of the Bonapartists, it believes that its victory is assured: it has secured over the Republican party the only advantage it has retained since 1852, the advantage of logic and political honesty.

3. The conclusion to this deplorable intrigue? Democracy, the preponderance of which should have been established once and for all by the 1864 poll, momentarily hailed as sovereign following the election of the new incumbents, now no longer matters, pending the advent of new order, except as the instrument of a political re-plastering job, against which our every effort must henceforth be deployed in defending ourselves.

As for ourselves, whom some have dared to label idlers, puritans, stick-in-the-muds and eunuchs, sure in the knowledge that we could not reply, this is what we have done and what we have achieved. Our success has been splendid enough for us not to lose heart:

At first we told ourselves:

In our own right and ante-dating the 1852 constitution, we have the right to vote. We have the right to vote or not to vote.

If we vote, we are free to choose between the administration's candidate and the opposition's candidate, just as we are to protest against each by selecting a candidate of a hue opposed to them both (which is what the authors of the Manifesto propose).

Finally, we have the right to protest against election of any sort, either by depositing blank votes or by voting for some citizen who would not meet all of the criteria for eligibility, who, say, might not have taken the oath, if in our judgment electoral law, as practiced, does not offer sufficient guarantees for universal suffrage, or on any other grounds.

The point, therefore, was to find out what would be the most useful way for us to vote. Those who have argued that the vote must necessarily designate a candidate, that universal suffrage by itself was bereft of meaning, and that it derived all of its value from the choosing of a man — those people have overwhelmed the public, and they have lied.

We have opted then for the protest vote, by means of blank vote or equivalent, and this was the outcome:

Out of 64 departments we have been able to monitor, there were 63,000 protest votes — 4,556 of them in Paris: proportionally speaking, that makes around 90,000 for the whole of France.

We would have numbered 100,000 in Paris and a million across the 89 departments, had we been allowed to make our voice heard and explain our thinking.

Those scattered votes were enough to sink several candidates from the so-called democratic opposition. They might have sunk them all, and the government might have been left all alone with its elected deputies, facing a protesting democracy, had the monopoly press not smothered our voice.

Do you believe that those 90,000 voters who, in spite of their enforced silence, in spite of calumny, in spite of regimentation of the people, without having managed to communicate or reach agreement, managed to stand firm and, by their protest, preserve the inviolability of democracy, are a minority without virtue? Do you think that this party, seemingly weak in numerical terms, lacks energy? There were 20 of us and our call has been heard over the opposition's racket by 90,000 men. Suppose that the 153,000 in the capital, who cast their votes for the newcomers, had registered a protest as we did, do you think that that protest would have had less of an impact than the harangues with which the opposition has regaled us? What have you to say about that now, citizens?

Faced by a veto from 160,000 voters, augmented by some of the 86,000 who purely and simply abstained, would the administration's candidates with their 82,000 votes have been bragging about representing the capital? Would we be less informed as to our financial situation, the European situation and electoral strengths and so many other matters about which the government and its friends are so wont to prattle, simply because we might not have heeded the pleas of a half dozen lawyers? Would it not be a thousand times better for democracy's honor and its future prospects, had we left the government to debate with its own representatives and to wash its dirty linen at home, as Napoleon I used to say, than to have besmirched our consciences, hitherto unblemished by oath?

Democrats, your line of conduct has been determined for you. Over the past 15 years, a blind reaction has busied itself casting you out of the law, out of the government, out of politics. The situation in which you have been placed is not of your making: it is the handiwork of a conspiracy by the old parties. They are prompted by a single thought, and that thought is incompatible with achievement of that political, economic and social justice, for which you yearn with all your might. A single oath unites them, the symbol of their confederacy, a snare set for the vanity and zeal of democrats. It is scarcely your fault if, hemmed in by their concert, you are condemned to resort to reprisals against them. Which is why I tell you with all of the vigor and all of the sadness my soul can muster: separate yourselves from him who was the first to stand apart, even as the Roman people in another age stood apart from its aristocrats. It is through separation that you will win: no representatives, and no candidates!

What! Having declared yourselves the equals of the bourgeoisie, the repositories of the new thinking, the hope of generations unborn; having displayed the grandeur of your destiny to the world, can you not devise anything better than to pick up, sub-contracted, those aged bourgeois institutions, the futility and corruption of which have been pointed out to you a hundred times over by the government itself? Your dreams would be of doctrine, the balance of representation and cant! Given the chance to be original, you would act as blatant imitators. That, take it from me, is merely the logical conclusion to the Manifesto of the Sixty: labor democracy declaring by its vote that it is abandoning opposition and that, until better times arrive, is renouncing, not the vote, but having itself represented. Through this manifesto, labor democracy has struck a patrician pose: by electing a representative, you would fall back into the ranks of the liberated. Is there an outstanding man among you? Vote him a civic crown, do not make a prostitute, do not make a candidate of him.

For my own part, I do not think that I need tell you that I abide by my resolutions.

Had I no other grounds for perseverance than remembrance of events in which I have been implicated, things in which I have participated, hopes that I helped arouse, out of respect and in remembrance of so many citizens who have suffered and perished since 1848, so that the people's liberties may succeed, and whom I have encountered inside prison and in exile, I would repudiate all compromise and I would say: no representatives, no candidates!

Fraternal greetings to you, citizens.

P.J. Proudhon

Notes to Proudhon and Worker Candidates (1863–1864)

1. The title is our own. The text has been lifted from Proudhon's *Correspondance*, XIII, pp. 247-266.
2. Jules Favre (1809–1880), one of the leaders of the liberal opposition under the Second Empire. Emile Ollivier (1825-1913), ditto, and was later head of government of the so-called liberal Empire between 1867 and 1870. Pierre Marie (1795–1870) former member of the provisional government of 1848 and organizer of the National Workshops. Jules Simon (1844–1896), philosopher and liberal politician.

Proudhon Against "Communism"[1]

Here, in retrospect, Proudhon attacks the type of State and "communistic" socialism preached by Louis Blanc during the 1848 Revolution from the so-called Luxembourg Commission.[2]

Collective sovereignty

In essence, the Luxembourg system is the same as those of Cabet, R. Owen,[3] the Moravians, Campanella, More, Plato and the earliest Christians: a communist, governmental, dictatorial, authoritarian and doctrinal system. It starts from the premise that the individual is essentially subordinate to the group, that his rights and his very life derive from that alone, that the citizen belongs to the State, the way the child does the family, that he is in the power, the possession, in manu, of the State and owes it full submission and obedience.

By virtue of that underlying principle of collective sovereignty and submission of the individual, the Luxembourg school tends in theory and in practice to relate everything to the State — or the community. Work, industry, property, commerce, public education and wealth, as well as law-making, the courts, police, public works, diplomacy and war — they are all turned over to the State for subsequent assignment and distribution, in the name of the community, to every citizen, member of the wider family, in accordance with his aptitudes and needs.

The first movement and first thought of labor democracy, in seeking out its law and offering itself as the antithesis of the bourgeoisie, must have been to throw its maxims back in its face; this is strikingly evident from a first glance at the communist system.

What is the principle underlying the old, artisanal or feudal, post-revolutionary or divine right society? Authority, whether descended from Heaven or deduced from the nation as a whole as Rousseau does. The communists in their turn have spoken and acted thus. They trace everything to the rights of the collective, the sovereignty of the people: their concept of power or of the State is absolutely identical to that of their former masters. Whether it goes by the name of empire, State, monarchy, republic, democracy or community, the thing is self-evidently the same throughout. For followers of that school, the rights of man and the citizen derive from the people's sovereignty: even liberty itself is an emanation from that. The Luxembourg communists, the Icarians and all the rest can, with an easy conscience, pledge loyalty to Napoleon III; their profession of faith is, in principle, in agreement with the 1852 Constitution: and is even a lot less.

"Communism," Overblown Statism

(. . .) Property was still a concession from the State, the sole natural proprietor of the earth, as the representative of the national community. The communists abide by that — as far as they also are concerned — the individual is indebted for his assets, his faculties, his honors and even his talents, to the State. The difference lay in implementation only. For a reason or out of necessity, the ancient State had loosened its hold: a host of noble or bourgeois families had stepped out of the primitive indivision and they have formed tiny sovereignties within the larger one.

Communism's object was to reincorporate all such fragments of its inheritance into the State. Under the Luxembourg system, society's democratic revolution was to be merely a restoration, which is to say, a step backwards.

Thus, like an army which has captured the enemy's guns, communism merely turned their own artillery against the army of proprietors. The slave has always aped his master (. . .)

On Association

When it comes to methodology, quite aside from the public order authority to which it does not yet have access, the Luxembourg party settled upon and preached association. The idea of association is a new one in the world of economics: the divine right states, ancient and modern alike, are the ones that have launched the mightiest associations and supplied the theories for them. Our bourgeois legislation, (the civil code or commercial code) has adopted many of their categories and concepts. What have the Luxembourg theorists added to that? Absolutely nothing. For them, association has very often been merely common ownership of assets and earnings. Occasionally, it has been construed as simple partnership or cooperation, or indeed a collective or share-holder company.

Labor associations have more often been taken to be mighty, numerous companies of workers subsidized, commanded and directed by the State, which draw in the bulk of the working class, enjoy a monopoly of works and undertakings, meddling in every industry, all farming, all trade, every office and all ownership, leading to a vacuum in private establishments and undertakings, and finally overwhelming and crushing every individual initiative, all private property, all life, all liberty and all wealth, precisely as the great limited companies are doing today.

The Supposed Dictatorship of the Masses

Thus, in the minds of the Luxembourg men, public ownership was to lead to elimination of all property; association to destroy all private associations, or amalgamate them all into a single one; competition, turned in upon itself, was ultimately to bring about elimination of competition; collective liberty was to gobble up all freedoms, corporative, local and individual alike.

With regard to government, its guarantees and forms, the problem is similarly disposed of. In that, as in association and the rights of man, it was the same old story: the same old formula recurs, albeit in its communist hyperbole. The political system, according to the Luxembourg theory, might be defined in the following terms: a compact democracy, seemingly rooted in dictatorship of the masses, but wherein the masses merely have the opportunity to consolidate universal slavery in accordance with formulas and guidelines borrowed from the former absolutism:

Indivisibility of power.

Voracious centralization.

Systematic demolition of all individual, corporative and local thought, these being deemed sources of discord.

Inquisitorial policing.

Abolition, or at any rate, curtailment of family, and especially of inheritance.

Universal suffrage, so organized, then, as to serve as a permanent endorsement of this anonymous tyranny, through the preponderance of mediocrities or nonentities, who always enjoy a majority over competent citizens and independent characters who are considered suspect and of course are few and far between. The Luxembourg school has proclaimed it loud and clear: it is against the aristocracy of competence.

On Spontaneity

The important thing to grasp about popular movements is their utter spontaneity. Does the people act in response to incitement or suggestion from without, or rather on the basis of some inspiration, intuition or innate idea? However great the caution with which this feature is spelled out in the study of revolutions, it will never be enough. Make no mistake, the ideas that have always stirred the masses were hatched earlier in the brain of some thinker. Where ideas, opinions, beliefs and errors are concerned, the masses have never led the way, nor could they even today. In every act of mind the individual is the pioneer: the relation of terms tells us as much.

But whereas every thought that arises in the individual has to go on to captivate peoples, not all of the ideas are good and useful. We specifically argue that the most important thing, especially for the philosophical historian, is to observe how the people clings to certain ideas in preference to others, generalizing them, developing them after its fashion and converting them into institutions and customs that live on as traditions until such time as they fall into the hands of legislators and magistrates who will turn them into articles of law and rules for the courts.

The Revolution is No One's Doing

A social revolution like the '89, which keeps worker democracy before our eyes, is a transformation wrought spontaneously in each and every part of the body politic. It is one system supplanting another, a new agency taking the place of a decrepit body.

But such substitution is not effected in the twinkling of an eye, the way a man changes his clothes or his colors, nor is it commanded by a master with a ready made theory, or at the dictation of a revelationist.

A genuinely organic revolution, a product of universal life, while it does have its messengers and its executors, is truly the doing of no one.

Notes to Proudhon: Against "Communism"

1. See *On the Political Capacity of the Working Classes* 1864.
2. Following a demonstration by trades bodies outside the city hall on 28 February 1848, the provisional government launched a "Government commission for workers," housed in the Luxembourg Palace and chaired by Louis Blanc: it assembled employers' and workers' representatives there. That commission also consulted specialists in social issues. The work of the commission was carried out during the period between March 1 and May 16. In the end it ventured to draw up a labor organization plan and drafted the social legislation which was subsequently promulgated by the provisional government.
3. Robert Owen (1771–1858), English "utopian" socialist and promoter of the earliest producers' and consumers' cooperatives. The Moravians, a religious sect founded in Bohemia in the 15th century, were characterized by a very rigorous asceticism, being intent upon living a life of sanctity and charity, away from the world. Campanella (1568-1639), Italian philosopher and author of *The City of the Sun.* Thomas More (1478-1535), Lord Chancellor of England and author of the political and social novel, *Utopia.* Plato (429-347 BC.), author, among other things, of the dialogues *The Republic and The Laws.*

MIKHAIL BAKUNIN (1814–1876)

The Revolution of February 1848, as Seen by Bakunin[1]

Mikhail Bakunin, a Russian émigré, rushed to Paris at the time of the February revolution.

The February revolution broke out. As soon as I discovered that there was fighting underway in Paris, I borrowed a passport from a person of my acquaintance, by way of preparing for any eventuality, and set off for Paris. But the passport proved useless: "The Republic has been proclaimed in Paris" — those were the first words we heard uttered at the border. The news sent a shiver down my spine: I arrived in Valenciennes on foot, the railway line having been destroyed: there were crowds everywhere, shouts of enthusiasm, red flags on every street, in every square and on every public building. I was obliged to make a detour, the railway being impassable in a number of places, and I arrived in Paris on February 26 , within three days of the proclamation of the Republic. Even on the way there, I relished it all.

That huge city, the focus of European culture, had suddenly been turned into a savage Caucasus: in every street, virtually everywhere, barricades towered like mountains stretching to the level of the roof-tops: atop these barricades, amid the rubble and broken furniture, like Georgians in their gorges, were workmen in picturesque smocks, blackened with dust and armed to the teeth: fat grocers — faces rendered stupid by fright — peered fearfully from their windows: there was not a single vehicle on the streets or in the boulevards: gone was all the old smugness, all the odious, monocled, wise-cracking dandies and in their place my noble working men, triumphant, enthused crowds brandishing red flags, singing patriotic anthems and intoxicated by their success.

And amid this unbounded rejoicing, this intoxication, they were all gentle, humane, compassionate, decent, modest, well-mannered, friendly and high-minded to a degree possible only in France and there, only in Paris. Thereafter and for over a week I lived alongside these workers in the barracks in the Rue de Tournon, right next to the Luxembourg Palace; that barracks, previously reserved for the municipal guard, had now, like many another, been turned into a republican stronghold serving as a billet for Caussidière's army. I had been invited to move in there by a democrat friend of mine who was in command of a detachment of 500 working men.

Thus I had occasion to see the workers and to study them from morning to evening. Never and nowhere, have I discovered in any other class of society so much high-minded unselfishness, nor so much truly touching integrity delicacy of manners and light-hearted friendliness married with heroism as among those simple uneducated folk who have always been and will always be worth a thousand times more than their leaders!

Especially striking about them was their profound sensibility to discipline: in their barracks, established order, laws and constraints were out of the question: but would to God that any regular soldier could obey with as much precision, and divine as well the wishes of his officers and maintain order as strictly as these free men: they asked for orders and asked for leadership, eagerly obedient to the merest detail; in their onerous service, lasting whole days at a time, they endured hunger and still their friendliness was undiminished and they were still light-hearted. Had these folk, had these French working men been able to find a leader worthy of them, capable of understanding them and taking them to his heart, that leader might have accomplished miracles with them.

(. . .) That month spent in Paris . . . was a month of intoxication for the soul. Not only was I intoxicated, but so was everybody else: some from a crazed fear, others from a crazed ecstasy of senseless expectations. I rose at five o'clock or four o'clock in the mornings, went to sleep at two o'clock, was on my feet all day long, attending every assembly, meeting, club, parade, march or demonstration: in short, I drank in the intoxication of the revolutionary atmosphere through every one of my senses and through every pore.

It was a fiesta without beginning and without end: I saw everyone and saw no one, for every individual was subsumed into the same, countless, meandering crowd: I spoke to everybody but could remember neither my own words nor others', for my attention was at every step held by new events and objects, by unforeseen developments.

This widespread feverishness drew a modicum of sustenance and reinforcement from news coming in from other parts of Europe: all one could hear was comments such as the following: "There is fighting in Berlin: the king has fled after having made a speech! There was fighting in Vienna: Metternich has taken to his heels and the republic has been proclaimed there. The whole of Germany is in revolt: the Italians have won in Milan and in Venice: the Austrians have sustained an embarrassing defeat! The republic has been proclaimed there: the whole of Europe is turning republican. Long live the Republic!"

It looked as if the whole universe had been turned on its head: the incredible was becoming the norm, the impossible possible, and the possible and normal losing all meaning. In short, the state of mind was such that, had someone turned up and announced: "God has just been driven out of Heaven and a Republic proclaimed therein," everybody would have believed him and no one would have been surprised in the slightest. And the democrats were not the only ones to succumb to this intoxication. Quite the contrary: they were the first to come to their senses again, obliged as they were to set to work to consolidate power that had fallen into their lap against all expectations and as if by miracle.

The conservative party and dynastic opposition, (the latter having become, overnight, more conservative than the conservatives themselves) — in short, all of the men of the old regime — believed even more than the democrats in every seeming miracle and far-fetched development: they had even stopped believing that two plus two make four and Thiers himself had declared: "There is but one option open to us now, namely, to seek oblivion." That fact alone explains the alacrity and unanimity with which all the provincial towns and every class in France recognized the Republic.

Note for The Revolution of February 1848, as Seen by Bakunin

1. Extracted from Confession (1857 Letter to the Tsar), Paris 1932.

BAKUNIN, AS SEEN BY JAMES GUILLAUME

Following his short passage through Paris during the 1848 Revolution, Bakunin, galvanized by the example before his very eyes, shot off to participate in the popular uprising in Dresden (May 3, 1849). As a result of which he was sentenced to death in Saxony and then in Austria in 1850, being eventually handed over by Austria to the Russian government. In his native land he underwent very lengthy and harsh incarceration. Then in 1861 he successfully escaped from Siberia and made his way to London. It was after the uprising in Poland against the tsarist empire (1863–1864) and, doubtless, more especially after the conversations that he had with Proudhon — a Proudhon whose death was not far off — in Paris towards the end of 1864, that Bakunin became an anarchist. Consequently we join James Guillaurne's biography of Bakunin at that point only:

(. . .) When the Polish uprising erupted in 1863, he [Bakunin] attempted to reach the activists leading it: but the organization of a Russian Legion failed, and Lapinski's expedition came to nothing: and Bakunin, who had gone to Stockholm (where his wife joined him) in hope of getting the Swedes to intervene, had to return to London (in October) without having succeeded in any of his ventures. He then traveled to Italy, from where, in mid–1864, he made a second trip to Sweden; he returned via London, where he called again on Marx, and Paris, where he paid another call on Proudhon.

In the wake of the war of 1859 and Garibaldi's heroic expedition in 1860, Italy had just begun a new life: Bakunin stayed in the country until the autumn of 1867, staying first in Florence and then in Naples and its environs. He had devised a plan for a secret international organization of revolutionaries, with an eye to propaganda, and, when the time came, to action, and from 1864 onwards, he managed to recruit a certain number of Italians, French, Scandinavians and Slavs into that secret society, which he dubbed the "International Brotherhood" or the "Alliance of Socialist Revolutionaries."

In Italy, Bakunin and his friends applied themselves in a particular way to combating the Mazzinians[1], who were authoritarian, religious republicans whose watchword was *Dio e popolo* (God and people). A newspaper, *Liberta e Giustizia,* was launched in Naples; in its columns, Bakunin spelled out his program. In July 1886, he informed Herzen and Ogareff[2] of the existence of the secret society, briefing them on its program, by which his two old friends were, as he himself admitted, "greatly shocked." At that point, according to Bakunin, it had supporters in Sweden, Norway, Denmark, England, Belgium, France, Spain and Italy, and also numbered Poles and Russians among its membership.

In 1867, bourgeois democrats from a number of countries, mainly French and Germans, launched the League of Peace and Freedom, and summoned a congress in Geneva that caused a sensation. Bakunin still clung to a few illusions regarding democrats; he attended the congress, where he made a speech, became a member of the League's central committee, established his home in Switzerland (near Vevey) and, over the ensuing year, strove to steer his fellow committee members towards revolutionary socialism. At the League's second congress in Berne (September 1868), along with some cronies who belonged to the secret organization founded in London in 1864 . . . he attempted to have the League pass blatantly socialist resolutions, but after a few days' proceedings, the revolutionary socialists, being in a minority, announced that they were quitting the League (on September 25, 1868), and on the very same day, they launched a new grouping under the name of the International Alliance of Socialist Democracy, with a program drawn up by Bakunin.

That program, encapsulating the conclusions at which its author had arrived at the end of a protracted evolution that had begun in the Germany of 1842, stated, among other things:

> The Alliance proclaims itself atheist: it seeks the definitive and complete elimination of classes, and political, economic and social equality for persons of both sexes: it wants the land, the instruments of labor, as well as all other capital, having become the collective property of the whole of society, to be available only for the use of toilers, which is to say, of agricultural and industrial associations. It acknowledges that all the existing political and authoritarian States, being reduced progressively to simple functions in the administration of public services in their respective countries, will have to melt into a worldwide union of free associations, agricultural and industrial alike.

With its establishment, the International Alliance of Socialist Democracy had testified to its desire to be a branch of the International Workingmen's' Association, whose general statutes it accepted.

September 1868 had seen the appearance in Geneva of the first issue of *Narodnoye Dyelo*, a Russian newspaper written by Mikhail Bakunin and Nikolai Zhukovsky; it published a program entitled "Program of the Russian Socialist Democracy," which was essentially identical to the program that the International Alliance of Socialist Democracy was to adopt a few days later. But the paper had a change of editorial staff from the second issue onwards and came under the control of Nikolai Outine,[3] who gave it a quite different slant.

The International Workingmen's Association had been launched in London on September 28, 1864, but its organization was not finalized and its statutes not adopted until its first congress was held in Geneva between September 3 and 8, 1866.

While passing through London in October 1864, Bakunin, who had not seen Karl Marx since 1848, had had a visit from him; Marx had called on him for the purpose of offering an explanation of the calumny[4] once published by the *Neue Rheinische Zeitung* and put back into circulation by some German journalists in 1853. At the time, Mazzini and Herzen had come to the defense of the libeled Bakunin who was incarcerated in a Russian fortress: on that occasion, Marx had stated once again in the English *Morning Advertiser* that he had had no hand in that libel, adding that Bakunin was a friend of his, and he repeated as much to Bakunin.

In the wake of their conversation, Marx had encouraged Bakunin to join the International: but once back in Italy, Bakunin had thought it better to devote himself to the secret organization mentioned earlier; apart from the General Council in London, the International, in its beginnings, represented little more than one group of mutualist workers in Paris, and there was nothing to hint at the importance that it was about to assume. It was only after its second congress in Lausanne (September 1867), after its two court cases in Paris and the great strike in Geneva (1868) that the association attracted serious attention and became a power whose role as a lever of revolutionary action could no longer be ignored. At its third congress in Brussels (September 1868) collectivist ideas were mooted, in competition with cooperativism. In July 1868, Bakunin was inducted as a member of its Geneva branch and, once he had quit the League of Peace and Freedom at its Berne congress, he settled in Geneva in order to be in a position to take an active hand in that city's labor movement.

Immediately propaganda and organizing activity were given a great fillip. A trip to Spain by the Italian socialist Fanelli[5] led to the foundation of branches of the International in Madrid and Barcelona. The francophone branches in Switzerland came together into a federation that took the name of the *Fedération romande* and had a mouthpiece of its own in the newspaper *L'Egalité*, launched in January 1869. Battle was then joined with phony socialists who were hobbling the movement in the Swiss Jura and this ended with a majority of Jura workers coming over to revolutionary socialism. On several occasions, Bakunin traveled to the Jura to speak on behalf of those fighting against what he termed "reaction wearing the mask of cooperation": this was the origin of the friendship that he struck up with the militants of that region. In Geneva itself, a dispute between the instinctively revolutionary socialist construction workers and the so-called "manufacturing" watch-makers and jewelers eager to participate in election campaigns, was resolved thanks to

Bakunin, who campaigned vigorously from the pages of *L'Egalité* and there, in a series of remarkable articles, he spelled out the program of the "policy of the International," on the basis of the regrettably ephemeral success of the revolutionary element. The International's sections in France, Belgium and Spain acted in concert with the francophone Swiss section and it was anticipated that at the next general congress of the Association, collectivism would be carried by a majority of votes.

The London-based General Council had refused to admit the International Alliance of Socialist Democracy as a branch of the International, on the grounds that the new society represented a second international body and that its presence within the International would have a disorganizing effect. One of the grounds for this decision was Marx's animosity towards Bakunin, in whom the illustrious German communist believed he saw a "schemer" keen to "turn the International upside down and turn it into a tool in his hands": but, independently of Marx's personal feelings, the fact is that the idea of launching a second organization alongside the International was an unhappy one, as Bakunin's Belgian and Jura friends indicated to him, whereupon he yielded to their persuasion and recognized that the General Council's decision had been right. As a result, the Alliance's central bureau, after consultation with the organization's membership, announced, with their agreement, that it was being disbanded; the local group that had been set up in Geneva became an ordinary branch of the International and was recognized as such by the General Council (July 1869).

At the fourth general congress in Basle (September 6-12, 1869) virtually every one of the International's delegates came out in favor of collective ownership: but it was apparent that there were two distinct schools of thought among them: some, the Germans, the German-speaking Swiss and the English were State communists; others, the Belgians, the francophone Swiss, the Spaniards and virtually all of the French were anti-authoritarian communists, or federalists, or anarchists, who called themselves collectivists. Bakunin of course belonged to the latter grouping, as did the Belgian De Paepe and the Parisian, Varlin, among others.[6]

(. . .) The secret organization launched in 1864 had been wound up in January 1869, following an internal crisis, but several of the members of it had kept in touch with one another, and their band of friends had been joined by a few new Swiss, Spanish and French recruits, of whom Varlin was one; this free association of men who combined into a revolutionary brotherhood for collective action must, one might think, have afforded greater strength and cohesion to the great movement of which the International was the expression.

In the summer of 1869, a friend of Marx's had reprinted in the Berlin *Zukunft* the old chestnut that "Bakunin was an agent of the Russian government," and Liebknecht[7] had repeated the allegation on a number of occasions. When Liebknecht visited Basle for the congress, Bakunin invited him to explain himself before a panel of honor. There, the Saxon socialist stated that he had never made any allegations about Bakunin but had merely repeated something he had read in the press. The panel agreed unanimously that Liebknecht had acted with culpable frivolousness and forwarded to Bakunin a written statement carrying the signatures of the panel-members; Liebknecht, acknowledging that he had been in error, offered his hand to Bakunin and in everyone's presence the latter burned the panel's statement, lighting his cigarette with it.

After the congress of Basle, Bakunin left Geneva and withdrew to Locarno (Tessin); he had been prompted to do so by considerations of a strictly personal character, one being the need to settle somewhere where the cost of living was cheap and where he would have the peace and quiet to devote himself to the translation work he intended to do on behalf of a St. Petersburg publisher (initially, this consisted of translating the first volume of Marx's *Das Kapital*, which had appeared in 1867). But Bakunin's departure from Geneva unfortunately left the gate open for political schemers who, by associating themselves with the chicanery of a Russian émigré, Nikolai Outine, only too well known for the part he played in the International for us to hang a label on him here, they succeeded within a few months in throwing the Geneva branch of the International into disarray and in gaining the upper hand and taking over the editing of *L'Egalité*.

Marx, blinded completely by his resentment and petty jealousy with regard to Bakunin, had no hesitation in allying himself with Outine and the pseudo-socialist clique of Geneva politicos, men of the "Temple Unique."[8] while, at the same time, in a *Confidential Bulletin* circulated to his friends in Germany (March 28, 1870), he did his best to ruin Bakunin in the eyes of German socialist democrats, by representing him as the agent of a Pan-Slavist party, from which, Marx alleged, he received an annual stipend of 25,000 francs.

The scheming of Outine and his Geneva confederates contrived to provoke a split in the Federation romande: the latter split (April 1871) into two factions, one of which, by common agreement with the Internationalists in France, Belgium and Spain, had come out in favor of the revolutionary policy, stating that "any working class participation in governmental bourgeois politics cannot but result in the consolidation of the existing order of things," whereas the other faction spoke up for "political intervention and worker candidates." The General Council in London, as well as the Germans and the German Swiss, sided with the latter faction (the Outine and Temple Unique faction), while the French, the Belgians and the Spaniards sided with the other (the Jura faction).

At that point, Bakunin was quite engrossed in Russian matters. As early as the spring of 1869, he had come into contact with Netchayev[9]: at that time he still believed that it might be possible to organize a sweeping peasant uprising in Russia.... It was then that he penned, in Russian, the appeal known as *A Few Words to Young Friends in Russia* and the pamphlet *Science and the Revolutionary Cause Today*. Netchayev had returned to Russia, but had had to flee once more following the arrests of almost all his friends and the destruction of his organization, and by January 1870, he was back in Switzerland. He insisted that Bakunin drop his translation of *Das Kapital* in order to devote himself wholly to Russian revolutionary propaganda.... In Russian, Bakunin wrote the pamphlet *To the Officers of the Russian Army* and, in French, the pamphlet *The Bears of Berne and the Bear of St. Petersburg*; he also brought out a few editions of a fresh run of *Kolokol*[10] and was tremendously busy for some months, but in the end he realized that Netchayev was intending to use him as a mere pawn and was resorting to Jesuitical measures in order to secure himself a personal dictatorship. Following a definitive show-down in Geneva in July 1870, he severed all connections with the young revolutionary. His unduly trusting nature had been abused, as had the admiration he had at first felt for Netchayev's maverick vigor. "Needless to say," Bakunin wrote to Ogareff (August 2, 1870) in the wake of this falling-out, "we made complete fools of ourselves. How Herzen would poke fun at us both, were he here, and how right he would be! Ah, well! There is nothing for it but to swallow this bitter pill which will make us the wiser hereinafter."

Meanwhile war had just broken out between Germany and France and Bakunin monitored its progress with passionate interest and intense absorption. "You are only a Russian," he wrote to Ogareff on August 11th, "whereas I am an internationalist." As he saw it, the crushing of France by a feudalistic, militaristic Germany signaled the victory of counter-revolution: and the only way to fend off that defeat was to appeal to the French people to rise up en masse, in order, simultaneously, to beat off the foreign invader and rid itself of home-grown tyrants who kept it in economic and political servitude. To his socialist friends in Lyon he wrote:

> The patriotic movement of 1792 is nothing by comparison with the one you must now mount, if you would save France. So arise, friends, to the sound of the Marseillaise, which, today, is once again France's legitimate anthem, aglow with relevance, the anthem of liberty, the people's anthem, the anthem of mankind, because France's cause is again, at last, mankind's cause. By playing the patriotic card, we will salvage the world's freedom. Ah, if only I were a young man. I would not be writing letters. I would be in your midst!

A contributor to *Volksstaat* (Liebknecht's newspaper) had written that the workers of Paris were "indifferent to the present war." Bakunin was outraged to find them credited with such criminal apathy: he put pen to paper to show them that they could not remain impervious to the German invasion and simply had to defend their freedom against the armed hordes of Prussian despotism:

> Ah, were France invaded by an army of proletarians — Germans, English, Belgians, Spaniards, Italians — displaying the colors of revolutionary socialism and proclaiming the final emancipation of labor to the world, I would have been the very first to cry out to France's workers: 'Welcome them with open arms, for they are your brothers, and join forces with them to sweep away the putrefying remnants of the bourgeois world!' But the invasion by which France is dishonored today is an aristocratic, monarchical and military invasion. By staying passive in the face of this invasion, French workers would not only be betraying their own freedom, but would also be betraying the cause of the proletariat the world over, the sacred cause of revolutionary socialism.

Bakunin's thoughts on the situation and the means by which France and the cause of freedom might be saved were set out by him in a short pamphlet which appeared, uncredited to any author, in September, under the title *Letters to a Frenchman on the Current Crisis.*

On September 9, 1870, Bakunin left Locarno to make his way to Lyon, arriving there on September 15th. A "Committee for the Salvation of France" had been set up and he was its most active and most daring member, immediately making preparations for an attempt at a revolutionary uprising: that movement's program was made public on September 26 through a red poster bearing the signatures of delegates from Lyon, Saint-Etienne, Tarare and Marseilles: although a foreigner, Bakunin had no hesitation in adding his signature to those of his friends, claiming his share of their danger and responsibility. After having announced that "having become impotent, the administrative and governmental machinery of the State has been abolished" and that "the people of France were reverting to complete self-possession," that poster moved that committees for the salvation of France be formed in every federated commune and immediately despatch two delegates from the committee of every departmental capital "to join the revolutionary Convention for the salvation of France." A popular revolt on September 28 left the revolutionaries in possession of the city hall in Lyon, but treachery on the part of General Cluseret and the cowardice of some of those in whom the people had placed its trust aborted this attempt; Bakunin, against whom the procurator of the Republic, Andrieux, had issued an arrest warrant, successfully reached Marseilles, where he went into hiding for a time, while trying to put another revolt together; meanwhile, the French authorities were peddling the rumor that he was a paid agent of Prussia, and that the government of National Defense had proof of this: for its part, Liebknecht's *Volksstaat* carried these lines with regard to the revolt of September 28 and the program set out in the red poster: "The press bureau in Berlin could not have done a better job of furthering Bismarck's purposes!"

On October 24, despairing of France, Bakunin left Marseilles aboard a ship whose skipper was friendly with friends of his, returning to Locarno via Genoa and Milan. On the eve of his departure, he wrote to the Spanish socialist, Sentiñon, who had come to France in hope of participating in the revolutionary upheaval:

> The people of France is no longer revolutionary at all. The militarism and bureaucracy, aristocratic arrogance and Protestant Jesuitry of the Prussians, in tender alliance with the knout of my dear sovereign and master, Emperor of all the Russias, are going to prevail on the continent of Europe, for God knows how many decades. Farewell to all our dreams of imminent emancipation!

The revolt that erupted in Marseilles on October 31, seven days after Bakunin left, merely confirmed him in his gloomy assessment: the revolutionary Commune that had set itself up in the city hall when the news came of Bazaine's surrender, was only able to survive for five days and abdicated on November 14 in favor of commissioner Alphonse Gent, Gambetta's envoy.

Back in Locarno where he spent the whole winter in isolation, grappling with material discomfort and black misery, Bakunin wrote, by way of a sequel to his *Letters to a Frenchman*, a review of the new situation in Europe: it appeared in the spring of 1871 under the telling title *The Knouto-Germanic Empire and the Social Revolution*. News of the Parisian uprising on March 18 came as a partial rebuttal of his gloomy prognostications, demonstrating that the Parisian proletariat at least had retained its vigor and spirit of rebellion. But the heroics of the people of Paris were to prove powerless to galvanize an exhausted and defeated France: attempts made in several provincial locations to propagate the communalist movement failed, and the brave Parisian insurgents were overwhelmed by superior numbers. And Bakunin, who had arrived among his friends in the Jura (April 27) so as to be closer to the border with France, had to make his way home to Locarno (June 1) without having had the opportunity to act.

This time, though, he was not disheartened. The Paris Commune, the target of hatred from all of the concerted reactionaries, had lighted a glimmer of hope in the hearts of all victims of exploitation[11]; in the heroic people which had shed its blood in torrents for the emancipation of mankind, the world's proletariat saluted, as Bakunin phrased it, "the modern Satan, the great rebel, beaten but not broken." The Italian patriot Mazzini had added his voice to those cursing Paris and the International; Bakunin wrote an *Internationalist's Answer to Mazzini* that appeared in both Italian and French (August 1871): that essay had a tremendous impact in Italy and among the youth and workers of that country it brought about a shift in opinion that, before 1871 was out, had led to the creation of numerous branches of the International. A second pamphlet, Mazzini's *Political Theology and the International* rounded off the task begun: and Bakunin, who, by despatching Fanelli to Spain in 1868, had been godfather to the International in Spain, found himself, as a result of his polemic with Mazzini in 1871, godfather to the Italian International that was to throw itself with so much fervor into the fight, not just against the bourgeoisie's rule over the proletariat, but also against the efforts of men who, at that point, were bent upon enshrining the authority principle in the International Workingmen's Association.

The split inside the Federation romande, which might have been resolved amicably, had the General Council in London so desired, and had its agent, Outine, been less treacherous, had worsened and gone beyond remedy now. In August 1870, Bakunin and three of his friends had been expelled from the Geneva branch for having indicated their support for the Jurassians. In the immediate wake of the war of 1870–1871, agents of Marx arrived in Geneva to reopen old sores: the membership of the Alliance branch thought that they were offering proof of their peaceable intent by announcing that their branch was being wound up, but the Marx-Outine camp did not disarm: a new branch, the so-called revolutionary socialist propaganda and action chapter, launched in Geneva by refugees from the Commune and which the erstwhile members of the Alliance branch had joined, was refused admission by the General Council. Instead of a general congress of the International, the General Council, led by Marx and his friend Engels, summoned a secret conference in London in September 1871: it comprised almost exclusively of Marx loyalists with whom the latter had arrived at decisions that did away with the autonomy of the International's branches and federations, awarding the General Council an authority that flew in the face of the Association's fundamental statutes: at the same time, the conference sought to organize, under General Council auspices, what it termed "the working class's political action."

As a matter of urgency, the International, a wide-ranging federation of groupings organized for battle on economic terms against capitalist exploitation, had to be spared the overlordship of a tiny coterie of Marxist and Blanquist sectarians. The Jura sections, in concert with the Geneva-based propaganda branch, came together in Sonvilier on November 12, 1871 into a Jura Federation, and issued a circular to all other federations of the International, inviting them to join with it in resisting the trespasses of the General Council and in vigorously reasserting their autonomy.

"The society to come," the circular read, "should be nothing other than the universalization of the organization with which the International will have endowed itself. So we should take care to assimilate that organization as closely as possibly to our ideal. How could one expect an egalitarian and free society to emerge from an authoritarian organization? That would be an impossibility. It is incumbent upon the International, being the future human society in embryo, to stand here and now as a faithful reflection of our principles of liberty and federation and to eschew from its ranks any principle tending towards authority and dictatorship."

Bakunin gave an enthusiastic welcome to the Sonvilier circular and threw himself wholeheartedly into spreading its principles around the Italian sections. Spain, Belgium and most of the branches reorganized in France in defiance of the Versailles backlash, as secret chapters, and most of the branches in the United States took the same line as the Jura Federation: and the thwarting of the attempt by Marx and his allies to establish their domination over the International was soon assured. The first half of 1872 was marked by a "Confidential Circular" from the General Council; it was written by Marx and published in a pamphlet entitled *The Alleged Splits in the International.* In it, the main militants of the autonomist or federalist camp were personally attacked and libeled, and the protests that had erupted on all sides against certain actions of the General Council were represented as the products of intrigues mounted by members of the late International Alliance of Socialist Democracy. These, under the direction of the supposed "mysterious pope of Locarno" were alleged to be working to destroy the International. Bakunin summed up this circular as it deserved when he wrote to friends: "The sword of Damocles with which we have for so long been threatened has just fallen on our heads. It turns out to be not so much a sword as Mr. Marx's usual weapon, a pile of rubbish."

Bakunin spent the summer and autumn of 1872 in Zurich, where (in August), at his instigation, a Slav branch was launched that was made up almost exclusively of Russian and Serbian male and female students: it affiliated to the International's Jura Federation. From April onwards, he was in touch from Locarno with a number of young Russians living in Switzerland and had organized them into a secret action and propaganda group. . . . Friction with Petr Lavrov[12] and differences of opinion among a few members were to lead to the winding up of the Slav section in Zurich in 1873.

Meanwhile, the General Council had decided to summon a general congress for September 2, 1872: but as the venue for the congress, it selected The Hague, the better to be able to field, from London, large numbers of delegates equipped with courtesy or fictitious mandates, all of them committed to the Council's policy, and to make access to the congress all the more difficult for delegates from more remote federations and impossible for Bakunin. The newly constituted Italian federation refrained from sending delegates: the Spanish federation sent four, the Jura Federation two, the Belgian Federation seven, the Dutch Federation four, the English Federation five: those twenty one delegates, the only ones truly representative of the International, formed the core of the minority. The majority, numbering forty men, who in fact represented no one but themselves, had made up its mind in advance to do all that might be asked of it by the coterie of which Marx and Engels were the leaders. The only move by the congress of The Hague with which we need concern ourselves here was the expulsion of Bakunin, a decision made on the last day (September 7th), by which time two thirds of the delegates had left, by twenty seven votes in favor with seven against and eight abstentions. The case made by Marx and his supporters in requesting, after a derisory sham inquest held in camera, that Bakunin be expelled, rested upon the following two arguments:

> That proof exists, in the form of draft statutes and letters signed Bakunin, that that citizen tried and perhaps was successful in founding in Europe an organization by the name of the Alliance, with statutes wholly different in social and political viewpoint from those of the International Workingmen's Association: that citizen Bakunin has had recourse to fraudulent procedures designed to appropriate to himself all or part of someone else's fortune, which amounts to embezzlement: that, furthermore, he or his agents have had recourse to intimidation in order to evade honoring their commitments.

It was that latter part of the marxist indictment, with its allusion to the advance of 300 rubles Bakunin had received for the translation of *Das Kapital*, and to the letter written by Netchayev to the publisher Poliakov, that I described earlier as an attempted moral assassination.

A protest at such infamy was immediately made public by a group of Russian émigrés: here are the essential passages from it:

> Geneva and Zurich, October 4, 1872 — At our friend Mikhail Bakunin, they have dared to hurl the charge of embezzlement and blackmail. We do not feel it necessary or timely here to enter

> into discussion of the alleged facts upon which they felt that the curious allegation made against our countryman and friend might be made to rest. Those facts are well known to us, known even in the tiniest details, and we will make it our duty to present them in their true light just as soon as we are allowed to do so. At the moment we are precluded from doing so by the unfortunate circumstances of another countryman who is no friend of ours, but whose harassment at the hands of the Russian government even now ties our hands.[13] Mr. Marx, whose adroitness we have no wish in any event to dispute, has miscalculated badly on this occasion at least. Decent men in every land will doubtless feel nothing but outrage and disgust in the face of such crude intrigues and such a flagrant breach of the most elementary principles of justice. As for Russia, we can assure Mr. Marx that all his maneuvers will be forever wasted: Bakunin is held in too high a regard there and is too well-known for this calumny to touch him.... (This was followed by eight signatures).

In the wake of the congress in The Hague, another international congress met in Saint-Imier (Swiss Jura) on September 15: present were delegates from the Italian, Spanish and Jura federations, plus representatives from the French and American sections. This congress unanimously declared that it "utterly rejects all of the resolutions of the congress of The Hague, and does not in any way recognize the powers of the incoming General Council appointed by that." That General Council had been relocated to New York. The Italian Federation had endorsed the Saint-Imier resolutions in advance, by way of the votes it passed at the Rimini conference on August 4: the Jura Federation endorsed them at a special congress held on the very same date, September 15. Most of the French branches wasted no time in sending their whole-hearted endorsements: the Spanish Federation and the Belgian Federation in turn confirmed these resolutions in their congresses held in Cordoba and Brussels during Christmas week of 1872; the American Federation did likewise at a session of its Federal Council (New York, Spring Street) on 19 January 1873, as did the English Federation, which included two old friends of Marx, Eccarius[14] and Jung, whom his conduct had prompted to part company with him,[15] in its congress on January 26, 1873. The New York-based General Council, seeking to exercise the powers vested in it by the congress in The Hague, announced on January 5, 1873 that the Jura Federation was being "suspended," having been found to be intractable: the only result of which action was that the Dutch Federation which had initially intended to remain neutral, shrugged off its reservations and joined seven other federations of the International in declaring on February 14, 1873 that it would not recognize the suspension of the Jura Federation.

Publication in the latter part of 1873 by Marx and his tiny band of loyalists of a pamphlet by the name of *The Alliance of Socialist Democracy and the International Workingmen's Association*, riddled with the crudest misrepresentations of the facts merely inspired disgust in those who deplored the dismal outpouring of blind hatred.

September 1, 1873 saw the inauguration in Geneva of the sixth general congress of the International; the federations of Belgium, Holland, Italy, Spain, France, England and the Swiss Jura were represented at it. The Lassallean socialists from Berlin had sent a sympathy telegram signed by Hasenclever and Hasselmann. The congress set to work to overhaul the statutes of the International: it declared that the General Council was being done away with, and it turned the International into a free federation which no longer had any directing authority at its head:

"The Federations and Sections making up the Association," stated (Article 3 of) the revised statutes, "retain their complete autonomy, which is to say, the right to organize themselves as they deem fit, to run their own affairs without outside interference and to determine for themselves the path they mean to follow in order to arrive at the emancipation of labor."

Bakunin was worn out by a long life of struggles: imprisonment had aged him prematurely and his health was seriously undermined; his yearning now was for rest and retirement. When he saw the International reorganized on the basis of the victory of the principle of free federation, he reckoned that the time had come when he might take his leave of his colleagues, and to the members of the Jura Federation he addressed a letter (published on October 2, 1873) requesting that they accept his resignation as a member of the Jura Federation and of the International. He added:

> I no longer feel that I have the strength required for the struggle: consequently, I could only be a burden upon the proletariat's camp and not a help. I therefore withdraw, dear comrades, full of gratitude to you and sympathy for your great and blessed cause, the cause of humanity. I shall continue to follow your every move with a brotherly concern, and I will greet every one of your new triumphs with joy. I will be yours until death.

He had only three years left to live.

His friend, the Italian revolutionary Carlo Cafiero[16] offered him the hospitality of a villa that he had just bought near Locarno. Bakunin lived there until mid-1874, wholly absorbed, it appears, by this new lifestyle, in which he at last discovered peace, security and relative comfort. Yet he had not stopped thinking of himself as a soldier of the Revolution: when his Italian friends had laid the groundwork for an insurrection, he traveled to Bologna (July 1874) to participate in it, but the revolt, being poorly coordinated, came to nothing and Bakunin was obliged to return to Switzerland in disguise.

(. . .) By 1875, Bakunin was only a shadow of his former self. In June 1876, in hope of finding some relief from his afflictions, he left Lugano for Berne: on arrival there on June 14, he told his friend, Dr. Adolf Vogt: "I have come here for you to get me back on my feet again or to die. . . ." He died at noon on July 1.

Notes to Bakunin, as Seen by James Guillaume

1. Mazzinians, followers of Giuseppe Mazzini (1805–1872), an Italian republican plotter and one of the architects of Italian unification.
2. Nikolai Ogareff (1813–1877), Russian poet, co-publisher with Alexander Herzen of the journal *Kolokol* (The Bell) in London, and a correspondent with Bakunin.
3. Nikolai Outine (1815–1883) a Russian émigré living in Switzerland. A marxist, he took part in the congress of the League of Peace and Freedom in Berne in 1868 and in the London conference of the International in 1871: editor of the journal *L'Egalité* in Geneva in 1870–1871.
4. According to this calumny the revolutionary Bakunin had been an agent of the Russian government. See below.
5. Giuseppe Fanelli (1827–1877), initially an Italian republican along with Mazzini and Garibaldi: he broke with Mazzini over his statist centralism: he became a friend and collaborator of Bakunin from 1864. In October 1868, Bakunin sent him to Spain to establish there a branch of the International as well as of his International Alliance for Socialist Democracy, even though Fanelli spoke no Spanish.
6. On Cesar de Paepe, see below: Eugene Varlin (1839–1871), French Internationalist and Communard, was shot in the Rue des Rosiers on 28 May 1871 by the Versailles counterrevolution.
7. Wilhelm Liebknecht (1826-1900) introduced marxism to Germany and founded the Social Democracy at the Eisenach congress (1869).
8. This was the name of the premises on which the Geneva Internationalists used to meet, an erstwhile Masonic lodge. (James Guillaume's note).
9. Sergei Netchayev (1847–1882), a young Russian revolutionary. He met, captivated and influenced Bakunin while in Switzerland, winning him over, for a time, to his terrorist and nihilistic ideas: extradited, he died in prison in Russia after lengthy suffering.
10. The journal *Kolokol* was published in the West by the Russian revolutionary Alexander Herzen (1812–1870).

11. See below for Bakunin's essay on the Paris Commune.
12. Petr Lavrov (1823-1900), mathematics teacher turned anti-State revolutionary: escaping from Siberia, he went to Paris and was a sympathizer with the Commune: he then spent some time in Switzerland and afterwards London, before finally returning to Paris to die there.
13. Netchayev had just been arrested in Zurich on 11 August 1872: Switzerland handed him over to Russia on 27 October 1872. (James Guillaume's note.)
14. Hans Georg Eccarius (1818–1889), German tailor and member of the Communist League and then, from 1864, in London, of the International: secretary of the General Council from 1867 to 1871: fell out with Marx at the time of the split in The Hague in 1872, and although no anarchist, joined the "anti-authoritarian" International. Hermann Jung (1805–1870), a Swiss watch-maker settled in London, and a friend of Marx, was treasurer of the International's General Council.
15. The Blanquists had already broken with Marx on September 6 at the congress in The Hague, accusing him of having betrayed them. (James Guillaume's note).
16. See below. Carlo Cafiero (1846–1892), Italian anarchist, initially friendly with Marx, then became a disciple of Bakunin and finally a libertarian communist alongside Kropotkin, Elisee Reclus, etc.

Whom Am I?[1]

I am neither a scientist, nor a philosopher nor even a professional writer. I have written very little in my life-time, and have only ever done so in self-defense, so to speak, and then only when heartfelt conviction obliged me to overcome my instinctive repugnance towards any public display of the inner me.

Who am I then, and what is it that now impels me to publish this work? I am a zealous quester after truth and a no less passionate foe of the malignant fictions which the party of order, that official, privileged representative of interest in every past and present religious, metaphysical, political, juridical, economic and social turpitude, seeks to utilize to this day in the brutalization and enslavement of the world.

I am a fanatical lover of liberty, regarding it as the only setting amid which men's intellect, dignity and happiness can increase and grow: not the quite formal liberty doled out, measured and regulated by the State, that ageless lie that in reality never stands for anything other than the privilege of the few, based upon the enslavement of the whole world: not the individualistic, selfish, petty and fictitious liberty peddled by the school of J.J. Rousseau, as well as by all those other schools of bourgeois liberalism, which look upon so-called universal rights, as represented by the State, as a limit upon the rights of the individual, which necessarily and always results in the rights of the individual being whittled away to nothing.

No, I mean the only liberty truly deserving of the name, the liberty that comprises of the unrestricted expansion of all of the material, intellectual and moral potentialities existing in every person in latent form: the liberty that acknowledges no other restrictions than those laid out for us by the laws of our own natures: so that, strictly speaking, there are no restrictions, because those laws are not foisted upon us by any external law-maker living either alongside or above us: they are, rather, immanent, and inherent within us, representing the very foundations of our being, material, intellectual and moral alike: instead of finding them curtailments, we should look upon them as the actual conditions and effective grounding of our liberty.

I mean that liberty of every individual which, far from stopping in front of the liberty of one's neighbor as in front of a boundary-marker, instead discovers in it an endorsement of itself and its extension into infinity: the freedom of the individual uncircumscribed by the freedom of all, freedom in solidarity, freedom in equality: freedom triumphant over brute force and the authority principle which was never anything other than the idealized expression of that force: liberty which, having once toppled all heavenly and earthly idols, will lay the groundwork for and organize a new world, the world of solidary humanity, upon the ruins of all Churches and all States.

I am a staunch advocate of economic and social equality, because I know that, outside of such equality, liberty, justice, human dignity, morality and the welfare of individuals as well as the prosperity of nations will never be anything other than so many lies. But, while I am a supporter of liberty, that primary condition of humanity, my reckoning is that equality should be established in the world by means of the spontaneous organization of labor and of collective ownership of producers' associations freely organized and federated into communes, and, through the equally spontaneous federation of those communes — but not by means of State supervision from above.

This is the point which is the main bone of contention between the revolutionary socialists or collectivists and the authoritarian communists who argue in favor of absolute initiative on the part of the State. Their goals are the same: both parties wish to see the creation of a new social order rooted exclusively in the organization of collective endeavor, inescapably incumbent upon each and every body in consequence of the force of things, in equal economic circumstances for all and in collective appropriation of the instruments of labor.

Except that communists imagine that they can bring this about through development and organization of the political power of the working classes and principally of the urban proletariat, abetted by bourgeois radicalism, whereas revolutionary socialists, enemies to any and all equivocal connivance and alliance, take the contrary view that they can only achieve that goal through the building-up and organization, not of the political, but rather of the social and thus anti-political power of the laboring masses of town and country alike, including all men of goodwill from the upper classes who, breaking with their entire past, might frankly be willing to join hands with them and embrace their program in its entirety.

From this derive two different methods. The communists believe they have a duty to organize the work force in order to take over the political power of States. The revolutionary socialists organize with an eye to the destruction, or, if one would prefer a more polite expression, the liquidation of States. The communists are supporters of the principle and practice of authority, whereas revolutionary socialists place their trust exclusively in liberty. One and all are equally supporters of science which is bound to kill off superstition and supplant faith, but the former would like to impose it: the others will strive to disseminate it, so that human groups, once won over, may organize themselves and federate spontaneously and freely from the bottom up, on their own initiative and in accordance with their real interests, but never according to some pre-ordained plan foisted upon the ignorant masses by a handful of superior intellects.

The revolutionary socialists reckon that there is a lot more practicality and wit in the instinctive aspirations and actual needs of the popular masses than in the profound intelligence of all these doctors and teachers of humanity who still seek to put their shoulders to the wheel of so many failed attempts to bring them happiness. Revolutionary socialists, on the other hand, think humanity has let itself be governed for a long time, indeed, for too long a time, and that the source of its afflictions resides, not in this or that form of government, but in the principle and in the very practice of any government whatever.

There at last is the contradiction, now become historic, that exists between the communism scientifically developed by the German school and in part embraced by the American and English socialists, on the one hand, and Proudhonism, extensively expanded upon and taken to its logical consequences, on the other, as embraced by the proletariat of the Latin countries.[2]

Notes to Who Am I

1. The title is of Daniel Guérin's devising. The extract is lifted from *La Commune de Paris et la notion de l'Etat 1870* as it appears in *Oeuvres* IV, p. 249ff.

2. (Bakunin's note) It has also been embraced and will be embraced more and more by the essentially anti-political instincts of the Slav peoples.

God and the State

The Individual, Society and Liberty

(. . .) Starting from the condition of gorilla, it is only with very great difficulty that man attains consciousness of his humanity and appreciation of his liberty. At first, neither that consciousness nor that liberty are accessible to him: he is born a brute beast and slave and becomes human and progressively emancipated only in the context of a society which necessarily predates the inception of his reason, speech and will: and this he can only do through the collective endeavors of all past and present members of that society which is, in consequence, the basis and natural point of departure of his human existence. It follows from that that man does not attain his individual freedom or personality unless these are complemented by those of all of the individuals around him, and then thanks only to the toil and collective might of society, outside of which he would remain, of all the savage beasts existing upon earth, unquestionably the most stupid and most miserable. In the materialists' interpretation, which is the only natural and logical one, society, far from diminishing and curtailing it, is instead the creator of the liberty of individual human beings. It is the root, the tree, and liberty is its fruit. Consequently, every man ought to look for his liberty, not to the beginning but rather to the end of history, and we may say that the real and effectual emancipation of every individual human being is the true and great aim, the ultimate goal of history.

Liberty and Self

(. . .) The materialist, realist and collectivist definition of liberty (. . .) is this: man only becomes man and achieves consciousness only to the extent that he realizes his humanity within society and then only through the collective endeavors of the society as a whole: he is released from the yoke of external nature only through that collective or social toil which alone has the capacity to turn the face of the earth into a haven favoring humanity's development: and without such material emancipation there can be no intellectual and moral emancipation for anyone. He cannot free himself from the yoke of his own nature, that is to say, he cannot subordinate his own body's instincts and movements to the instructions of his increasingly developed mind, except through education and training: but both of these are eminently and exclusively social things; because, but for society, man would have stayed forever a wild beast or a saint, which amounts to pretty much the same thing.

In the end, the isolated man cannot attain to consciousness of his liberty. Being free, in the case of man, means being acknowledged, deemed and treated as such by another man, by all of the men surrounding him. So freedom is not a phenomenon of isolation, but of mutual contemplation, not a factor for exclusion but rather a factor for liaison, the freedom of every individual being nothing more than the mirror image of his humanity or his human rights in the consciousness of all free men, his brothers, his equals.

I cannot claim and feel myself free except in the presence of and with regard to other men.

(. . .) I am truly free only when all human beings around me, men and women alike, are equally free. Far from being a limitation or negation of my freedom, the freedom of my neighbor is instead its precondition and confirmation. I only become truly free through the freedom of others, so that the greater the numbers of free men around me, and the more extensive and comprehensive their freedom, the more extensive and profound my freedom becomes. Conversely, it is the enslavement of men that opposes a barrier to my freedom, or, (and it amounts to the same thing), it is their brutishness that is a negation of my humanness because, to repeat myself, I cannot claim to be truly free myself except when my freedom, or — and this comes to the same thing — my human dignity and human rights, which consist of withholding obedience from any other man and determining my actions solely in conformity with my own beliefs, mirrored by the equally free consciousness of everyone, are reflected back to me by universal endorsement. Thus confirmed by everyone's freedom, my own freedom reaches out into infinity.

State and Government

(. . .) I have no hesitation in saying that the State is an evil, albeit a historically necessary evil, as necessary in the past as its utter extinction will sooner or later prove to be, as necessary as were men's primitive brutishness and theological meanderings. Historically, in every land it was born of the marriage of violence, rapine and pillage — in short, of war and conquest — with the gods successively invented by nations' theological fantasies. From its inception, it has been and remains to this day a divine sanction upon brute force and triumphant iniquity.

(. . .) Revolt against the State is a much easier undertaking, because there is in the very nature of the State something that is an incitement to revolt. The State is authority, force, the display of and fascination with force. It does not wheedle and does not seek converts: and every time that it dabbles in these, it does so with very bad grace: for persuasion is not in its nature which is, rather, to impose and compel. To what lengths it goes to conceal its nature as the lawful trespasser against men's wills, as the standing negation of their freedom. Even when it serves the good, it does it disservice and spoils it, precisely because it commands good, and any command provokes and inspires freedom to righteous revolt: and because the good, once it is commanded, becomes, from the vantage point of true morality, human (though not, of course, divine) morality, and in terms of human respect and liberty, the bad.

(...) Exploitation and government, the first affording the means whereby to govern, and representing the pre-requisite as well as the object of all government, which, in turn, guarantees and legalizes the power to exploit, are the two indivisible terms of all that goes by the name of politics. Since the beginning of history, they have indeed constituted the stuff of the life of States, theocratic, monarchical, aristocratic and even democratic. Previously and up until the great Revolution at the end of the 18th century, the intimacy between them had been disguised by the fictions of religion, loyalty and chivalry: but ever since the rough hand of the bourgeoisie tore away all the veils, which had in any case become fairly transparent, and ever since its blast of revolution scattered all of the empty conceits under cover of which Church and State, theocracy, monarchy and aristocracy had for so long managed, undisturbed, to perpetrate their historical vileness; ever since the bourgeoisie, wearying of being the anvil took its turn at being the hammer; ever since it ushered in the modern State — in short, that necessary connection has turned into a revealed truth, indeed, an incontrovertible truth as far as everyone is concerned.

Exploitation is the visible body and government the soul of bourgeois rule. And as we have just seen, the one and the other in such intimacy, are, in theoretical as well as practical terms, the necessary and faithful representation of metaphysical idealism, the inescapable consequence of that bourgeois doctrine that looks outside of social solidarity for the liberty and morality of the individual. That teaching results in exploitative government by a tiny number of the fortunate or elect, in exploitative slavery for the greater number and, for all and sundry, in negation of all morality and all liberty.

THE INTERNATIONAL REVOLUTIONARY SOCIETY OR BROTHERHOOD (1865)

The texts which follow are at once the least well-known and maybe the most important of Bakunin's anarchist writings. They do not feature in the six volumes of his Oeuvres, publication of which was undertaken by Bakunin's disciple James Guillaume between 1895 and 1913. They have not thus far been collated for the Archives Bakounine currently being published in the Netherlands and are not to be found in the monumental Life of Bakunin, hand-written in German, by Max Nettlau,[1] a work of which only a few rare autographed copies are to be found in the world's chief libraries. They are translated here from the language in which they were first written: French.

They represent a number of unconnected documents. As a result of which there is some duplication in their contents. But we have not seen fit to edit them insofar as their ideological passages are concerned at any rate, nor to attempt to revamp the order in which they are written. That would have been tantamount to impairment of the rich and powerful delivery of Bakunin's train of thought. One of these texts is entitled Revolutionary Catechism. It should not be confused with the Rules by which the Revolutionary *ought to abide* (more widely, and incorrectly, known under the title Revolutionary Catechism) wherein it is argued that "the end justifies the means." Bakunin's contribution to that amoral "catechism" dating from 1869 has, in any event, been challenged on the basis of the available evidence by the editor of the Archives Bakounine, Arthur Lehning.

The texts which we offer here were drawn up by Bakunin while in Italy in 1865. They represent the statutes and program of his International Revolutionary Brotherhood (or Society). This organization purported to be made up of a "worldwide family" and "national families." Its membership was divided into two categories: the "active brethren" and the "honorary brethren," in imitation of the practices of the Carbonari and the freemasons. However, it appears that the organization in question remained largely at the blue-print stage. As Arthur Lehning has pointed out, such programs and statutes mirror Bakunin's evolving thoughts, rather than "the operation of an organization." With which A. Romano agrees when he asserts that what was in fact at stake was "a secret pact between four or five friends: a spectral alliance."[2]

The handful of men who joined Bakunin in Italy in launching his "Brotherhood" were all, like Giuseppe Fanelli, former disciples of the republican Giuseppe Mazzini, from whom they had acquired their taste for and familiarity with secret societies. They had parted company with their mentor because they had concluded that his deism and his concept of a purely "political " revolution (which is to say, one bourgeois and bereft of social content) were obsolete.

The novelty in the "Brotherhood" program was not simply its socialist, internationalist content and its affirmation of the "right of secession," which was to be reiterated by Lenin, but also its libertarian provenance. As H.E. Kaminski has written, "issuing the watchwords of anarchy, it represents a counter to Marx's and Engels's Communist Manifesto, to which it is inferior in terms of its scientific reasoning, but of which it is the equal in terms of the fervor of its revolutionary enthusiasm." It is "the spiritual foundation of the whole anarchist movement."[3]

In the pages which follow there is a contradiction, apparently so at any rate. Sometimes Bakunin calls categorically for the "destruction of States": "The State," he avers, "must be destroyed root and branch," etc. but sometimes he sneaks the term "State" back into his line of argument. In which case he defines it as "the central unity of the country," as a federal agency. Nevertheless he continues to vent his spleen on "the nanny, transcendent, centralized State" and to denounce "the despotically centralistic pressures of the State." Which means that in Bakunin's view, there were States and States. Moreover, this same ambiguity is to be found in the writings of Proudhon, from whom Bakunin drank so deeply. Indictment of the State was the essential theme of Proudhonian thought. And yet the later Proudhon, the author of The Federal Principle (1863), a book written just two years before Bakunin's Program, also unashamedly uses the word "State" in the same federalistic, anti-centralistic sense with which Bakunin invests the term.

The Program of the Brotherhood

The International Revolutionary Society is to comprise two different organizations: the international family proper, and the national families: these latter must be everywhere organized in such a way as to remain always subject to the absolute leadership of the international family.

The International Family

Composed exclusively of international brethren, active and honorary alike, it is to be the keystone upon which our entire great revolutionary endeavor will depend. The success of the latter will thus hinge chiefly upon astute selection of the i[nternational] b[rethren].

In addition to the essential qualities which go to make up the serious revolutionary character of integrity, like bona fides, courage, prudence, discretion, constancy, fortitude, determination, boundless commitment, lack of vanity and selfish ambition, intelligence, practicality, the candidate must also have taken into his heart, will and mind all of the underlying principles of our *Revolutionary Catechism.*

He must be an atheist and join with us in demanding for this earth and for man that which religions have displaced into the heavens and made an attribute of their gods — truth, liberty, justice, happiness and goodness. He must acknowledge that, independent of all theology and divine metaphysics, morality has no other source than the group consciousness of men.

He must be, as we are, the enemy of the authority principle, every application and consequence of which he must despise, whether it be in the world of the mind and morality, or in the world of politics, economics and society.

He must love liberty and justice above all else and recognize, with us, that any political and social organization, founded upon the negation or merely upon some curtailment of this absolute principle of liberty, must, of necessity, lead to iniquity or disorder and that only rational and equitable social organization compatible with human dignity and human happiness is qualified to be that which will have liberty as its fundament, ethos, sole law and ultimate aim.

He must understand that there is no liberty in the absence of equality, and that attainment of the widest liberty amid the most perfect (de jure and de facto) political, economic and social equality, conjoined, is justice.

He must be a federalist, as we are, within and without his homeland. He must appreciate that the advent of liberty is incompatible with the existence of States. It follows that he must seek the destruction of all States and, at the same time, that of all religious, political and social institutions: such as established Churches, standing armies, centralized powers, bureaucracy, governments, unitary parliaments, universities and State banks, as well as aristocratic and bourgeois monopolies. So that out of the ruins of all this the free human society may arise at last, no longer organized, as is the case at present, from the top down and from center to periphery, by dint of a compelled unity and concentration, but rather starting from the free individual and the free association and autonomous commune, from the bottom up, and from the periphery to the center, by dint of free federation.

He must espouse, in theory as well as in practice and in the fullness of its implications, this principle: every individual, every association, every commune, every province, every region, every nation enjoys an absolute right of self-determination, to enter or not to enter into association, to enter into alliance with whomsoever they may wish, and to break off alliances without regard to supposed historic rights or the convenience of their neighbors: and he must be staunch in his belief that only when they are formed through the omnipotence of their inherent, natural attractions and needs, all enjoying the cachet of liberty, will these new federations of communes, provinces, regions and nations become truly strong, fruitful and indissoluble.

Consequently, he must simplify the so-called nationality principle, an ambiguous principle replete with hypocrisy and snares, the principle of the ambitious State of history, to arrive at the much greater, much simpler and only legitimate principle of liberty: every individual or collective body, being free or being entitled to be free, is entitled to be itself and nobody has the right to foist upon it his own dress, customs, language, views and laws: everyone should be absolutely free in his home. Which is what national rights, honestly understood, boil down to. Anything that goes beyond that point is not a confirmation of one's own national liberty, but rather a denial of the national liberty of one's neighbor. The candidate, then, ought to despise, as we do, all those narrow, ridiculous, freedom-killing and thus criminal notions of greatness, ambition and national glory, which are fit only for monarchy or oligarchy, and, today, suit the grande bourgeoisie, in that they assist it in deceiving peoples and in pitting them, one against another, the better to enslave them.

In his heart, patriotism, henceforth occupying a secondary place, must yield to love of justice and of liberty, and if need be, should his own homeland have the misfortune to depart from these, he will never hesitate to side against it: which he will do without undue discomfort, if he is truly convinced, as he ought to be, that there is no prosperity and political greatness for any country except through justice and liberty.

Finally he must be convinced that his country's prosperity and happiness, far from being in contradiction with those of every other country, instead require them for their own sake, that there is, between the destinies of all nations, a conclusively all-powerful solidarity, gradually turning the narrow and, in most cases, unjust sentiment of patriotism into a more comprehensive, more generous and more rational love of humanity, which will, in the end, establish a universal and world-wide federation of all nations.

He must be socialist in the fullest sense of the word as used in our revolutionary catechism and, with us, he must recognize it as legitimate and just, call for it with all his heart and stand ready to lend his every assistance to the triumph of an organization of society wherein every individual human being born, male or female, is afforded equal means of maintenance, education and training during his infancy and adolescence, and later, upon reaching the age of majority, is afforded those external facilities, that is, the same political, economic and social means to create his own well-being, by applying to work the various gifts and aptitudes with which nature will have endowed him and which equal instruction for all will have nurtured in him.

He must understand that, just the way that inheritance of misfortune which it cannot be denied, alas! is all too often nature's way, is everywhere rejected by the principle of justice, so, following the same logic of fairness, the inheritance of good fortune must also be rejected, since the dead, being no longer in existence, cannot write prescriptions for the living, and that, in short, equality of the economic, social and political circumstances from which every individual starts — the absolute prerequisite for the liberty of us all — is incompatible with hereditary ownership and with the rights of inheritance.

He must be persuaded that, labor being the sole producer of social assets, anyone enjoying these without working is an exploiter of another man's labors, a thief, and, work being an essential underpinning of human dignity, the only means by which man actually conquers and creates his freedom, all political and social rights must henceforth be extended to workers only.

He must acknowledge that the land, nature's free gift to one and all, cannot and ought not to be owned by anyone. But that its fruits, being the products of labor, ought to go solely to those who cultivate it with their own hands.

He must be convinced, as we are, that woman, different from man but not inferior to him, intelligent, hard-working and free as he is, should be declared his equal in all political and social rights: that in the free society, religious and civil marriage should be replaced by free marriage, and that the upkeep, education and training of all children should be a matter for everyone, a charge upon society, although the latter, while protecting them against either the stupidity, negligence or malice of their parents, need not remove them from these, children belonging neither to society nor to their parents but rather to their future liberty, and the authority of society should have no other aim, no other task with regard to them than to deliver to them and prepare them for a rational, manly education, founded exclusively upon justice, human respect and the cultivation of labor.

He must be revolutionary. He must understand that such a complete and radical transformation of society, necessarily entailing the ruination of all privileges, all monopolies and all established powers, will not, of course, be feasible by peaceful means: that, on those same grounds, it will have ranged against it all of the mighty, all of the rich and, on its side, in every country, only the people, plus that intelligent and truly noble segment of the youth which, though part of the privileged classes by birth, embraces the people's cause on the foot of its unselfish beliefs and fervent aspirations.

He must understand that that revolution, the sole and supreme objective of which will be the effective political, economic and social emancipation of the people, doubtless helped and organized by that youth, can, in the final analysis, be effected only by the people: that, all other religious, national or political matters having been utterly exhausted by history, there remains today but one question into which all others are subsumed and which is henceforth the only one with the capacity to set peoples in motion; the social question: that any so-called revolution, whether a revolution of national independence such as the recent Polish rising, or the one preached today by Mazzini, or exclusively political, constitutional, monarchist or even republican, such as the recent abortive revolt of the progressives in Spain — that any such revolution, being made outside of the people and thereby precluded from success unless it relies upon some privileged class representing no one's interests but its own, must, of necessity, be mounted against the people and will be a retrograde, noxious, counter-revolutionary movement.

Disdaining therefore and regarding as an inevitable mistake or brazen deception any secondary movement not having as its immediate and direct object political and social emancipation of the laboring classes, which is to say, the people, inimical to all compromise and reconciliation which from now on are impossible, and to any lying connivance with those who, by virtue of their interests, are the natural enemies of the people, he must see no salvation for his country and for the entire world other than in social revolution.

At the same time he has to appreciate that this revolution, cosmopolitan by its very essence, even as justice and liberty are too, cannot succeed unless, sweeping like a worldwide conflagration across all of the narrow boundaries of nations and felling States in its path, it encompasses the whole of Europe for a start and then the world. He must understand that the social revolution will, of necessity, turn into a Europe — and world-wide revolution.

That the world will necessarily split into two camps, the camp of the new life and that of the old privileges, and between these two opposing camps, formed, as in the days of the wars of religion, not now by a rallying of nations, but by a community of ideas and interests, there will necessarily ignite a war of extermination, without quarter or truce; that the social revolution, contrary in its very essence to the hypocritical policy of non-intervention which suits only the moribund and the impotent, will not, for the sake of its well-being and self-preservation, unable to survive unless it spreads, put up its sword before it has destroyed every State and every one of the old religious, political and economic institutions in Europe and across the whole civilized world.

That this will not be a war of conquest, but a war of emancipation, of forcible emancipation on occasion it is true, but always and for all that salutary in that its sole object and outcome will be the destruction of States and their age-old foundations, which, with the blessings of religion, have ever been the well-springs of all slavishness.

That the social revolution, once well ablaze in one place, will find fervent and formidable allies among the popular masses everywhere, even in the seemingly most hostile lands: these, just as soon as they grasp and gain palpable sense of its activity and its object, will not be able to do otherwise than throw in their lot with it everywhere: that, as a result, it will be necessary to pick for its initiation asuitable setting where it can withstand, unaided, the first onslaught of the reaction, after which, spreading beyond, it cannot fail but to succeed against all the wrath of its enemies, by federalizing and uniting into one formidable revolutionary alliance all of the countries which it will have drawn into its orbit.

That the elements of social revolution are even now sufficiently widely spread in all of the countries of Europe and that it is simply a question of collating and concentrating them in order to turn them into an effective power: that such should be the task of serious revolutionaries from every land brought together into an association both public and secret, with the dual objective of widening the revolutionary terrain and at the same time of laying preparations for an identical and simultaneous revolt in every one of the countries where revolt will be feasible initially, through a secret understanding between the most intelligent revolutionaries of those countries.

It is not sufficient that our candidate should understand all that. He must have a passion for revolution in his breast: he must be so enamored of liberty and of justice that he is seriously willing to make his contribution to their success, to the extent of making it a duty that he sacrifice to them his rest, his well-being, his vanity, his personal ambition and often his private interests.

He must be convinced that there is no better way to serve them than by participating in our endeavors, and he must know that, in taking his place among our number, he will be contracting with us the very same solemn commitment that we all make towards him too. He must have familiarized himself with our revolutionary catechism, all our rules and laws and pledge to abide by them at all times with scrupulous observance.

He must understand that an association with a revolutionary purpose must necessarily take the form of a secret society, and every secret society, for the sake of the cause it serves and for effectiveness of action, as well as in the interests of the security of every one of its members, has to be subject to strict discipline, which is in any case merely the distillation and pure product of the reciprocal commitment made by all of the membership to one another, and that, as a result, it is a point of honor and a duty that each of them should abide by it.

Moreover, whatever the differences in the capabilities of the international brethren, we will only ever suffer one master: our principle — and only one will — our laws, which we have all helped to frame, or which we have at least all consecrated equally by our free assent. While bowing respectfully before a man's past services and cognizant of the great usefulness which might be afforded to us by some by virtue of their wealth, others by their learning and still others by their lofty position and public, literary, political or social influence, then, far from seeking them out on account of these attributes, but rather deeming these to be grounds for diffidence, in that all men might bring into our ranks either the habit or the pretension to authority, or the legacy of their past, whereas we cannot countenance either the pretension, the authority or the legacy, always looking ahead and never backwards, and recognizing no merit or entitlement in any except the one who will most actively and determinedly serve our association.

The candidate will appreciate that none should enter into that [association] except to serve it and that, as a result, it is entitled to expect some positive usefulness of each of its members — absence of such usefulness, once duly registered and proven, resulting in exclusion.

In becoming one of our number, the new brother will have to make a solemn commitment to look upon his duty to this society as his primary duty, relegating to second position his duty to each member of the society, his brother. Those two duties must henceforth prevail, if not in his heart, then at least in his will, over all others.

Essential points of the national catechisms

The national catechisms of the different countries may thus vary upon all secondary points.

But there are essential and fundamental points which will have to be equally binding upon the national organizations in every country and which will, in consequence, have to furnish the common basis for all national catechisms. Those points are:

An isolated national revolution simply cannot succeed and so there is a need for an alliance and revolutionary federation between all peoples seeking liberty.

The impossibility of any such federation or alliance in the absence of a common program that satisfies the rights and legitimate needs of all nations equally and which, without regard to so-called historic rights, or for what is termed the necessity or welfare of States, or for national glories, nor for any other vain or ambitious pretense to predominance and strength, all things that a people ought to be capable of rejecting if it wishes to be truly free, will have equal liberty for all and justice alone as its sole principle and basis.

Such a program is incompatible, and liberty, equality, justice, cheap government, real welfare and emancipation for the laboring classes are incompatible with the existence of centralistic, military and bureaucratic States. It is absolutely essential that all of the States presently in existence in Europe (excepting Switzerland) be destroyed, as is root and branch demolition of all the political, military, administrative, judicial and financial institutions that today make up the life and power of States.

Abolition of all connection and all established or State-subsidized church, confiscation of all transferable and non-transferable assets of churches for the benefit of the provinces and communes, with this provision, that once all religion has become absolutely free and a matter exclusively for the personal conscience of the individual, the upkeep of each faith, whatever it may be, will thereafter be a matter for its faithful alone.

It is absolutely necessary that any country aiming to belong to this free federation of peoples should replace centralistic, bureaucratic and military organization at home with a federal organization rooted solely in the absolute liberty and autonomy of regions, provinces, communes, associations and individuals, with elective officials answerable to the people, and with arming of the nation, an organization that will no longer operate, as it does today, from the top down and from center to periphery, according to the unity principle, but rather from the bottom up, from periphery to center, in accordance with the principle of free federation, on the basis of free individuals who will form the associations and autonomous communes; of autonomous communes that will form autonomous provinces; of provinces that will make up regions, and of regions that, federating freely with one another, will form countries, which will in turn sooner or later make up the universal and world-wide federation.

There is a need for recognition of the absolute rights of secession enjoyed by every country, every region, every province, every commune, every association, as well as every individual, with this belief, that, once the right of secession has been recognized, de facto secessions will become impossible, because with national units having ceased to be the products of violence and historical falsehood, they will be formed freely on the basis of the inherent needs and affinities of their parts. Political liberty is not feasible without political equality. And the latter is impossible without economic and social equality.

There is a need for social revolution.

The extent and scope of that revolution will vary to a greater or lesser degree in every country, according to political and social circumstances and the measure of revolutionary development in each. However, in every country, certain principles will have to be proclaimed which alone have the capacity to interest the masses of the people and galvanize them, regardless of what their level of civilization may be. Those principles are the following:

The land belongs to everyone. But usufruct of it will belong only to those who till it with their own hands. Rents upon land are to be abolished.

All social wealth being produced only by labor, anyone enjoying it without working is a thief. Political rights should be reserved for honest folk only and will be available only to toilers.

Without spoliation of any sort, but through the unaided efforts and economic powers of the workers' associations, capital and the instruments of labor will pass into the possession of those who will apply them to the production of wealth through their own labors.

Every man should be the son of his endeavors and justice will not be done until such time as society is so organized that everyone will be entitled by birth to the same resources for upkeep, education and training and, at a later stage, the same external facilities for creating his own well-being through his own labors.

Insofar as this may be feasible in each country, marriage should be freed from the oversight of society and women afforded equality of rights with men.

No revolution could succeed in any country today unless it was simultaneously a political and a social revolution. Any exclusively political revolution, be it national and directed solely against foreign domination, or domestic and constitutional, or even should it have a republic as its objective, will, insofar as it consequently does not have immediate, effective, political and economic emancipation of the people as its primary objective, prove to be an illusory, phony, impossible, noxious, retrograde and counter-revolutionary revolution.

The revolution should not only be made for the people's sake: it should also be made by the people and can never succeed unless it implicates all of the rural as well as the urban masses.

Thus centralized by the idea and by the sameness of a program common to all countries: centralized by a secret organization that will not only mobilize all the parts of a country, but indeed many, if not all countries, according to a single action plan: centralized also by the synchronization of revolutionary upheavals in many rural and urban areas, the revolution will have to assume and thereafter retain a local character, in the sense that that it will not have to start from a huge concentration in one location of all of a country's revolutionary forces, nor ever take the Romanseque and bourgeois character of a quasi-revolutionary expedition, but igniting simultaneously all around a country, will take the form of a real popular revolution, in which women, the old and children will likewise take part and which will be invincible for that very reason.

That revolution may well be bloody and vengeful in its early days, when the people's justice will be enforced. But it will not long remain thus, and will never develop into systematic, cold-blooded terrorism. It will wage war on positions and things much more than on men, confident that things and the privileged, anti-social positions which they generate and which are much more powerful than individuals, constitute both the character and the strength of its enemies.

Thus, it will open with the universal destruction of all institutions and all establishments, churches, parliaments, courts, administrations, armies, banks, universities, etc. which constitute the very existence of the State. The State must be demolished root and branch and declared bankrupt, not merely in financial terms but in terms political, bureaucratic, military, judicial and of policing. But having gone bankrupt, having indeed gone out of existence, and having no means of meeting its debts, the State will no longer be in a position to compel anyone to pay his. That matter will of course be left to the individual conscience. At the same time, in communes and towns, everything that formerly belonged to the State will be confiscated for the benefit of the revolution: the assets of all reactionaries will also be seized and all legal papers consigned to the flames — whether they be trial papers, property deeds or debt records — and the whole paper mountain of civil, criminal, judicial or official records which may have escaped destruction will be declared null and void, and every individual left with his possessions untouched. Thus will the social revolution will be made, and, once revolution's foes have been stripped of all means of harming it, there will be no further need to proceed against them with bloody measures that are all the more offensive because they unfailingly invite a violent backlash, sooner or later.

While it will be carried out locally everywhere, the revolution will of necessity assume a federalist format. Immediately after established government has been overthrown, communes will have to reorganize themselves along revolutionary lines, and endow themselves with leaders, an administration and revolutionary courts founded upon universal suffrage and upon effective accountability of all officials before the people. In order to defend the revolution, their volunteers will at the same time form a communal militia. But no commune can defend itself in isolation. So it will be necessary for each of them to radiate revolution outwards, to raise all of its neighboring communes in revolt to the extent that they will rise up, and to federate with them for common defense. Between themselves they will of necessity enter into a federal pact founded simultaneously upon solidarity of all and autonomy of each. That pact will serve as a provincial charter. For the governance of common affairs, a government[4] and provincial assembly or parliament will of necessity be formed. The same revolutionary requirements induce the autonomous provinces to federate into regions, regions into national federations, nations into international federations. And order and unity, destroyed as the products of violence and despotism, will sprout again from the very bosom of liberty. There is a need for conspiracy and for a strong secret organization, revolving around an international focal point, to lay the groundwork for that revolution.

Notes to The International Revolutionary Society or Brotherhood

1. Max Nettlau (1864-1944), born in Vienna, but of German nationality, the indefatigable historian and historiographer of anarchism, a prolific and erudite author of numerous writings and articles and, notably, of this memorable life of Bakunin.
2. A. Lehning and A. Romano, in *La Premiere Internationale* (a symposium from 1964), CNRS, 1968, (pp. 284, 335 and 349).
3. H.-E. Kaminski, *Bakounine, la vie d'un révolutionnaire*1938, pp. 213-214.
4. In stapling this text by hand into the manuscript of his Bakunin, Max Nettlau saw fit to write in the word (sic) after the words "leaders" and "government."

An Internationalist Federalism

As was mentioned by James Guillaume, Bakunin had tried, unsuccessfully, to get the following text adopted by the Berne congress (September 1868) of the League of Peace and Freedom, a coalition of liberal, humanitarian bourgeois inclinations, of which he was himself a member: in it, there are a number of ideas earlier expounded in the program of the Revolutionary Federation above. This text, even more plainly than the former, is Proudhonian in inspiration, insofar as it makes the case for the federal principle as well as criticizing the nationality principle so dear to Napoleon III (whom Bakunin still supported at the time that he had rushed to the assistance of the Polish Uprising of 1863).

We are in the happy position of being able to announce that this principle [the federal principle] has been unanimously acclaimed by the Geneva congress. Switzerland herself, which in any event implements it today with such felicity, has indicated her unreserved support for it and embraced it and every one of its implications. Unfortunately, in the congress resolutions, that principle has been very badly phrased and is mentioned only in passing, first of all apropos of the League which we must establish, and further on, apropos of the newspaper that we are to issue under the title of the "*United States of Europe*," whereas, in our view, it ought to have had pride of place in our statement of principles.

This is a most irksome oversight which we must waste no time in remedying. In accordance with the unanimous feeling of the Geneva congress, we must proclaim:

1. That if liberty, justice and peace are to prevail in relations between nations in Europe, if civil war between the different peoples who make up the European family is to be rendered impossible, there is but one thing for it: to establish the United States of Europe.

2. That the States of Europe will never be able to be formed with the States as presently constituted, given the monstrous disparity that obtains between their respective strengths.

3. That the example of the now defunct German Confederation has demonstrated beyond controversy that a confederation of monarchies is a joke: that it is powerless to guarantee the populace either peace or freedom.

4. That no centralized, bureaucratic and therefore even military State, even should it call itself a republic, will be able seriously and sincerely to enter an international confederation. By virtue of its make-up, which will always represent a blatant or disguised negation of freedom at home, it would necessarily represent a standing declaration of war, a menace to the existence of its neighbor countries. Founded, in essence, upon an ultimate act of violence

— conquest — or as it is described in private life, robbery with violence, an act blessed by the Church of some religion, consecrated by the passage of time and thereby transformed into historic right, and relying upon that divine consecration of triumphant violence as if it were some exclusive, supreme title, every centralist State thereby stands as an utter negation of the rights of all other States, its recognition of them, in treaties that it concludes with them, only ever being prompted by political interest or by powerlessness.

5. That all members of the League ought in consequence to bend their every effort to reconstituting their respective homelands, so as to substitute for the old organization there, founded, from the top down, upon violence and the authority principle, a new organization with no other basis than the interests, needs and natural affinities of populations, and no principle beyond the free federation of individuals into communes, of communes into provinces, of provinces into nations and, finally, of the latter into, first, the United States of Europe and, later, of the whole wide world.

6. Consequently, absolute repudiation of everything going by the name of the historic right of States: all matters bearing upon natural, political, strategic or commercial borders will have to be regarded henceforth as belonging to ancient history and rejected vigorously by all adherents of the League.

7. Recognition of the absolute entitlement of every nation, large or small, of every people, weak or strong, of every province, every commune, to complete autonomy, provided that its domestic constitution is not a threat and a danger to the autonomy and liberty of neighboring countries.

8. The mere fact that a country makes up part of a State, even should it have freely decided to join it, in no way implies that it is under any obligation to remain attached to it forever. No perpetual obligation could be countenanced by human justice, which is the only one that can claim any authority among us, and we will never recognize any rights or duties other than those founded upon freedom. The right to free assembly and equal freedom to secede is the prime and most important of all political rights: without which confederation would be nothing more than centralization in disguise.

9. From all of the foregoing it follows that the League must openly shun any alliance of such and such a national faction of the European democracy with monarchist States, even should that alliance be designed to win back the independence or freedom of an oppressed country: such an alliance, which could not but lead to disappointments, would at one and the same time be a betrayal of the revolution.

10. Instead, the League, precisely because it is the League of Peace and because it is persuaded that peace can only be achieved and founded upon the closest and completest fellowship of peoples in a context of justice and freedom, must loudly proclaim its sympathies for any national uprising against any

oppression, be it foreign or native, provided that that uprising be mounted in the name of our principles and in the political and economic interests alike of the popular masses, though not with any intent to found a mighty State.

11. The League will wage war without quarter against anything going by the names of States' glory, greatness and power. In place of all these false and malignant idols to which millions of human victims are sacrificed, we will offer the glories of the human intellect as manifested in science and of a universal; prosperity founded upon labor, justice and liberty.

12. The League is to acknowledge nationality as a natural phenomenon, with an incontestable right to exist and freely develop, though not as a principle, every principle being required to display the characteristic of universality, and nationality being, instead, an exclusive and distinct phenomenon. The so-called nationality principle, as posited in our day by the governments of France, Russia and Prussia, and also by many German, Polish, Italian and Hungarian patriots, is merely a by-product which the reaction uses as a counter to the spirit of revolution: at bottom eminently aristocratic, even to the extent of scorning the dialects of illiterate populations, implicitly refuting the freedom of provinces and the effective autonomy of communes, and backed in every country, not by the masses of the people, whose real interests it systematically sacrifices to a supposed public good, which is never anything other than the benefit of the privileged classes, this principle articulates nothing except the alleged historic rights and the ambition of States. The right of nationality can therefore only ever be regarded by the League as a natural consequence of the supreme principle of liberty, ceasing to be a right the moment that it makes a stand against liberty, or even outside of liberty.

13. Unity is the goal towards which mankind strives irresistibly. But it turns lethal and destructive of the intelligence, dignity and prosperity of individuals and peoples, every time that it takes shape outside of a context of liberty, be it through violence, or under the authority of some theological, metaphysical, political or even economic notion. The patriotism that strives for unity outside of freedom is an evil patriotism, always noxious to the people's interests and the real interests of the country which it purports to exalt and serve, a friend, albeit often against its will, to the reaction — enemy of the revolution, which is to say of the emancipation of nations and of men. The League can recognize but one unity: the unity freely constituted through federation of autonomous parts into the whole, in such a way that the latter, no longer the graveyard where all local prosperities are forcibly interred, becomes instead the confirmation and well-spring of all these autonomies and all these prosperities. The League will thus vigorously attack any religious, political, economic and social organization that is not utterly imbued with this great principle of freedom: in the absence of which there is no intellect, no justice, no prosperity and no humanity.

CHURCH AND STATE

At this point we insert a philosophical-political text targeting the Church as the accomplice of the State, the purpose being to play up the diversity of Bakunin's thinking. The text dates from 1871 and is in fact a sequel to the text we reproduce in this book of the anthology as *The Paris Commune*. Like the title of that text, the title "Church and State" is of our own devising. The pamphlet from which they have both been lifted was in fact titled *The Paris Commune and the Idea of the State*. There is good reason for splitting that pamphlet into two parts as we have done: it is very often the case that Bakunin throws himself headlong at a topic and then, at some point in his essay, veers abruptly in order to tackle a quite distantly related or different matter, with precisely the same impetuosity. Which is precisely what happened when he came to write that pamphlet. Hence the liberty that we have taken with his text.

They say that reconciliation and universal fellowship of the interests of individuals and of society can never in fact be achieved, because those interests, being contradictory, are unlikely to counter-balance one another or even to reach accommodation. To such an objection, let me answer that whereas, up to the present, those interests have never been reconciled anywhere, this was because of the State, which has sacrificed the majority's interests for the sake of a privileged minority. Which is why this notorious incompatibility and this strife between personal interests and society's interests are nothing but trickery and a political lie, sprung from the theological lie that concocted the doctrine of original sin in order to bring man into dishonor and destroy whatever consciousness of his own self-worth he may have had.

That very same counterfeit notion of antagonistic interests was also incubated by the dreams of metaphysics which, as we know, is a close cousin of theology. Ignoring the sociability of human nature, metaphysics looked upon society as a mechanical and purely artificial aggregation of individuals, suddenly combining, under some formal or secret treaty, arrived at freely or under the influence of some superior force. Before combining into society, these individuals, endowed with a sort of immortal soul, enjoyed undiluted liberty.

But whereas the metaphysicians, especially the ones that believe in the immortality of the soul, assert that men are, outside of society, free beings, the inevitable conclusion from that is that men can only combine into society on condition that they forswear their freedom, their native independence and sacrifice their interests, personal interests to begin with, and then their local ones. The imperviousness of such renunciation and sacrifice of itself must be, ipso facto, all the greater according to the increase in society's numbers and the complexity of its organization. In which case, the State is the expression of all these individual sacrifices. Enjoying such an abstract, and at the same time violent, existence, it carries on, needless to say, making greater and greater trespasses against individual liberty, in the name of the lie that goes under the name of "the public good," although, self-evidently, it represents only the interest of the ruling class. In this manner, the State appears to us an inevitable negation and annulment of all liberty and every interest, whether personal or general.

It can be seen here that in metaphysical and theological systems everything is connected and self-explanatory. Which is why the logical defenders of these systems may and indeed should, with an easy conscience, carry on exploiting the masses of the people through Church and State. Lining their own pockets and indulging their every sordid whim, they can at the same time take consolation from the thought that their labors are for the glory of God, the victory of civilization and the eternal happiness of the proletariat.

But we who believe neither in God nor in the immortality of the soul, nor in free will proper, we contend that liberty ought to be understood in its completest and widest sense as the goal of humanity's historical progress. By some queer, albeit logical paradox, our idealist adversaries from theology and metaphysics make the idea of freedom the foundation and basis of their theories, only to arrive at the blunt conclusion that men's enslavement is indispensable. We, materialists in matters of theory, tend in practice to devise and render durable a rational and high-minded idealism. Our enemies, godly and transcendental idealists, lapse into a practical, bloody, squalid materialism, in the name of the same reasoning, according to which every development is a negation of the founding principle. It is our conviction that the entire wealth of man's intellectual, moral and material development, as well as his apparent independence, that all of it is the product of living in society.

Outside of society, man would not only not be free, but would not even have become truly man, which is to say a being possessed of self-awareness, sentient, thoughtful and with the gift of speech. Only the conjunction of intellect and collective endeavor could have compelled man to quit the savage and brutish condition which was his pristine nature, indeed his starting point for subsequent development. We are profoundly convinced of this truth — that men's entire lives, interests, tendencies, needs, illusions, even follies, as well as their violence, injustices and their every action, which may have the appearance of volition, merely represent the consequence of the inescapable forces at work in life in society. People cannot countenance the notion of independence from one another, without turning their backs on the reciprocal influence of the interweave of manifestations of external nature.

Within nature herself, that marvelous warp and weft of phenomena is certainly not achieved without tension. Quite the opposite. The harmony of natural forces emerges only as the authentic product of that continual tension that is the very essence of life and movement. In nature as in society, order in the absence of struggle amounts to death.

If order is natural and feasible in the universe, that is only because that universe does not function according to some preconceived system imposed by an over-arching will. The theological supposition of divine ordinance leads to a self-evident absurdity and to negation, not just of all order, but of nature itself. Natural laws are only real insofar as they are inherent in nature, which is to say, insofar as they are not ordained by any authority. Those laws are merely manifestations or fluid modalities of the development of things and of combinations of these greatly varied, ephemeral but real phenomena. Taken all together, they constitute what we call "nature." The human intellect and science took note of these phenomena, examining them experimentally, then codified them into a system and called them laws. But nature herself is above laws. She operates unconsciously, being herself a representation of the infinite variety of phenomena, inexorably manifesting themselves and repeating themselves. Which is why, thanks to such inexorability of action, universal order can exist and in effect, does exist.

Such order also appears in human society, which, apparently, evolves in a so-called anti-natural fashion, but which in fact is subject to the natural, inevitable progress of phenomena. Except that man's superiority over other animals and his capacity for thought introduce a special (and, let it be said, quite natural in this sense, that like every living thing, man represents the material product of the marriage and operation of phenomena) ingredient into its development. That special ingredient is reason, which is to say that capacity for generalization and abstraction, thanks to which man can project himself mentally, scrutinizing and observing himself, as if he were some remote and alien phenomenon. Setting himself equally above himself as above his surroundings, he comes to the extremity of perfect abstraction, the stage of utter nothingness. That outer limit of the highest abstraction of thought, that utter nothingness, is God.

Such is the meaning and the historical foundation of all theological doctrine. Failing to comprehend the nature and material causes of their own thoughts, not cognizant even of the conditions or natural laws particular to them, the first men to live in society could assuredly not have suspected that their absolute notions were merely products of their capacity for conceiving abstract ideas. Which is why they took the view that those ideas, derived from nature, were real phenomena before which nature itself would cease to count for anything. Whereupon they set about worshipping their fictional creations, their impossible notions of the absolute, and rendering every honor to them. But somehow a way had to be devised to make the abstract notion of nothingness or Godhead sensible. To that end, they inflated the concept of divinity and also endowed it with every good and bad quality and attribute which they had only ever encountered in nature and in society.

So much for the origin and historical development of all religions, starting with fetishism and ending with Christianity.

It is scarcely our intention to embark here upon a history of religious, theological and metaphysical absurdities, much less speak of the successive deployment of all of the divine incarnations and visions spawned by centuries of barbarism. It is common knowledge that superstition has always given rise to frightful misfortunes and compelled the spilling of rivers of blood and tears. Let us say only that all of these revolting vagaries of poor humankind were historical phenomena inevitable in the course of the normal growth and evolution of social organisms. Such vagaries spawned in society the fatal notion, enthroned in men's imaginations, that the universe was supposedly governed by a supernatural force and will. Century followed century and societies grew so accustomed to that idea that in the end they murdered within themselves any striving after a more far-reaching progress, and any capacity to achieve it.

The ambition, first, of a few individuals and then of a few social classes enshrined slavery and conquest as living precepts and more than anything else they planted the terrifying idea of divinity. After which, any society was impossible unless it boasted these two institutions as its foundations: Church and State. These two social scourges are defended by all doctrinarians.

These institutions had scarcely arrived in the world before two castes were suddenly organized: that of the priests and that of the aristocrats, who, losing no time, took care to inculcate deeply into the enslaved populace the indispensability, usefulness and healthiness of Church and State.

The object of all this was to swap brutish slavery for a lawful slavery, ordained and consecrated by the will of the supreme being.

But did the priests and aristocrats honestly believe in the institutions that they supported with all their might and with particular advantage for themselves? Were they simply liars and deceivers? No. My belief is that they were, at one and the same time, believers and impostors.

They too were believers because they shared, naturally and inevitably, in the vicissitudes of the masses, and it was only later, at the time of the demise of the ancient world, that they turned skeptics and shameless deceivers. There is another basis on which we may regard the founders of States as honest folk. Man always readily believes in whatever he wants and whatever does not run counter to his own interests. It matters not if he is intelligent and well-educated: out of self-regard and a desire to live alongside his neighbors and enjoy their respect, he will always have faith in whatever he finds agreeable and serviceable. I am convinced that, say, Thiers and the Versailles government strove at all costs to persuade themselves that by killing a few thousand men, women and children in Paris, they were saving France.

But while the priests, augurs, aristocrats and bourgeois, in ancient and in recent times, might well have been sincere believers, they were nonetheless sycophants. Indeed, it is unthinkable that they should have credited every one of the absurdities which go to make up faith and politics. I will not so much as mention the days when, as Cicero has it, "two augurs could not look at each other without laughing." Even in the days of ignorance and widespread superstition, it is hard to imagine the inventors of miracles, day in and day out, having believed in the authenticity of those miracles. The same may be said of politics, which can be encapsulated under the following axiom: "The people must be subjugated and fleeced in such a fashion that it does not complain too loudly about its fate, that it does not forget to submit and that it has not the time to turn its mind to resistance and rebellion."

How then, after that, could we imagine that folk who have turned politics into a profession and are conversant with its object, which is to say, injustice, violence, falsehood, treachery, murder — massive and individual — can have any honest belief in the art of politics and in the wisdom of the State as provider of social happiness? For all their cruelty, they cannot have grown silly to that degree. Church and State have ever been the great schools of vice. History attests to their crimes: in every place and at all times, the priest and the statesman have knowingly, systematically, implacably and blood-thirstily acted as the executioners of peoples.

But even so, how can we reconcile two seemingly so incompatible things: deceivers and deceived, liars and believers? That may appear logically a thing hard to do: in fact, however, which is to say in practical life, those qualities are very frequently found side by side.

The vast majority of people live in contradiction with themselves, amid continual misunderstandings: generally, they fail to recognize this, until some extraordinary occurrence shakes them out of their customary sloth and forces them to cast an eye over themselves and around themselves.

In politics and in religion alike, men are merely tools in the hands of exploiters. But the robbers and the robbed, the oppressors and the oppressed live side by side with each other, governed by a handful of individuals who are to be regarded as the real exploiters. These are the very same people, free of all political and religious prejudices, who are deliberate in their mistreatment and oppression. In the 17th and 18th centuries, up until the great Revolution erupted, as well as in our own day, they commanded in Europe and did pretty much as they pleased. We have to believe that their dominance will not endure for long.

While the main leaders are well aware of what they are doing in deceiving peoples and leading them to perdition, their henchmen, or the creatures of Church and State, zealously apply themselves to upholding the sanctity and integrity of those odious institutions. While the Church, according to what the priests and most statesmen have to say, is so necessary for the salvation of the soul, the State, in its turn, is equally necessary for the preservation of peace, order and justice, and doctrinarians of every persuasion declaim: "Without Church and without government, there is neither civilization nor progress."

It is not for us to expound upon the problem of eternal salvation, because we do not believe in the soul's immortality. It is our conviction that the Church is the thing most harmful for humanity, for truth and for progress. And could it be otherwise? Is it not to the Church that falls the charge of perverting younger generations, women especially? Is it not the Church which, by its dogma, its idiocy and its ignominy, tends to do logical reasoning and science to death? Is it not an affront to man's dignity, warping his notion of rights and of justice? Does it not mortify all that lives, does it not squander liberty, is it not the one that preaches eternal slavery of the masses, to the advantage of tyrants and exploiters? Is it not that implacable Church which tends to perpetuate the reign of darkness, ignorance, misery and crime?

Unless our century's progress is a misleading dream, we must have done with the Church.

Program and Object of the Secret Revolutionary Organization of the International Brethren (1868)

The following is the program, dating, without doubt, from autumn 1868, of the second of the secret brotherhoods which Bakunin had just launched at that time. It was the clandestine accompaniment to his International Alliance of Socialist Democracy, the latter being an organization which was public and which applied for admission into the International en bloc. In this text, attention will be drawn to Bakunin's condemnation of — not revolutionary constraint — but violence and terror when these are not useful, when they attack men rather than things and when they are, in effect, a distraction for those who dream of bloody revolution against men because of their own reluctance to contemplate a radical revolution against things. Bakunin had come to these conclusions in the light of study of the Terror of 1794 (more so than the Terror of 1793). On another count too, this program merits attention: in it Bakunin declares war on "authoritarian" revolutionaries. The guess is that even then the frictions between him and Marx were in the hatching.

The Association of the International Brethren seeks simultaneously universal, social, philosophical, economic and political revolution, so that of the present order of things, rooted in property, exploitation, domination and the authority principle — be it religious or metaphysical and bourgeois-doctrinarian, or indeed revolutionary in the Jacobin sense — not a stone upon a stone should be left standing in the whole of Europe to start with and then in the remainder of the world. To a cry of peace to the toilers and liberty to the oppressed, and of death to rulers, exploiters and overseers of all sorts, it is our desire that all States and all churches be destroyed along with all their religious, political, juridical, financial, police, university, economic and social institutions and laws, so that all these millions of impoverished, duped, enslaved, tormented and exploited human beings, once delivered of all their formal and informal directors and benefactors, collective and individual, will at last know complete freedom.

Persuaded that individual and social evil reside much less in individuals than in the manner in which things and social positions are organized, we will be humane as much out of a sense of justice as out of considerations of serviceability, and we will ruthlessly destroy positions and things so that we may spare men without the Revolution's being put in jeopardy. We refute free will and society's entitlement to impose punishment. Taken in its most humane and widest sense, justice itself is merely a — so to speak, negative and transitional — idea: it poses the social question but fails to think it through, merely indicating the only possible route to human emancipation, which is to say, to the humanization of society through liberty in a setting of equality: a positive solution can only be provided by society's being organized along increasingly rational lines. That much craved solution, the ideal of us all, is liberty, morality, intelligence and well-being for all, through fellowship of all, through brotherhood of man.

Every individual human being is the involuntary product of a natural and social context into which he is born, in which he has grown up and to whose influence he continues to be susceptible. The three major causes of all human immorality are: inequality, political, economic or social alike; the ignorance which is its natural product, and the necessary consequence of them both: slavery.

The organization of society being always and everywhere the sole cause of the crimes committed by men, it is evidently hypocritical or nonsensical for society to punish criminals, every punishment being based upon a presumption of culpability and criminals being at no time culpable. The theory of culpability and punishment is an outgrowth of theology, which is to say, the marriage of absurdity with religious hypocrisy. The only right which can afforded to society in its present transitional phase, is the natural right to murder the criminals of its own making, in the interests of its own self-defense, and not the right to sit in judgment of or to condemn them. That right will not even be a right in the strict sense of the word: it will, rather, be a natural phenomenon, baneful but inevitable, the emblem and product of the impotence and doltishness of the existing society: and the more that society manages to avoid recourse to it, the nearer will it be to its effectual emancipation. All revolutionaries, the oppressed, the suffering, the victims of the way in which society is presently organized and whose hearts are naturally filled with vengeance and hatred should bear it well in mind that kings, oppressors, and exploiters of all sorts are as blameworthy as the criminals produced by the masses of the populace: they are malefactors but not culpable, since they too, like ordinary criminals, are the involuntary products of society's current organization. There will be no need to marvel if, at the start, the risen people should kill many of them. That may well be an inevitable misfortune, as meaningless as storm damage.

But such a natural phenomenon will be neither moral nor useful. On that score, history is brimful of lessons: the horrifying guillotine of 1793, which could scarcely be accused of slothfulness nor of sluggishness, failed to eradicate the nobility of France as a class. The aristocracy, while not completely destroyed by it, was at least profoundly shaken, not by the guillotine, but by the confiscation and sale of its assets. And as a general rule it may be said that political blood baths have never killed off parties: above all, they have shown themselves to be powerless against the privileged classes, such is the extent to which power resides not so much in men as in the positions awarded to men of privilege by the organization of things, which is to say, the institution of the State and its implications as well as its natural basis, private ownership.

Thus, in the mounting of a radical revolution, one has to attack positions and things, destroy property and the State, in which case there will be no need to destroy men and to condemn oneself to the unfailing, inevitable backlash that never has failed — and never will — to trigger a slaughter of men in every society.

But if men are to be afforded the right to be human, without any danger's thereby being posed to the government, we must be ruthless with positions and things: everything will have to be demolished, primarily and above all property and its inevitable corollary, the State. Therein lies the secret of Revolution.

Small wonder that the Jacobins and Blanquists should have become socialists more out of necessity than out of conviction: for them, socialism is a means, not the end of the Revolution, in that they want dictatorship, which is to say, centralization of the State and the State will, as a matter of logical and inevitable necessity, lead them towards the reconstitution of property. So, as we say, it is only too natural that, having no wish to make a radical revolution against things, they dream of a bloody revolution against men. But that bloody revolution, based upon the erection of a mightily centralized revolutionary State, would inevitably result, as we shall prove at greater length anon, in the military dictatorship of a new master. So victory for the Jacobins or the Blanquists would spell the death of the Revolution.

We are the natural enemies of these revolutionaries — the would-be dictators, regulators and overseers of the revolution — who, even before the monarchist, aristocratic and bourgeois States of the present are dismantled, dream of the creation of new revolutionary States, every whit as centralistic as, and more despotic than the States in existence today, with their ingrained familiarity with order created by some authority from the top down and such a huge aversion to what strikes them as disorder and which is nothing more than the free and natural expression of the people's life: well ahead of a good and salutary disorder, they dream of its being curtailed and muzzled through the action of some authority that will be revolutionary in name only, but which will in effect be nothing but a fresh backlash in that it will amount to a further sentence upon the masses of the people, governed by decrees, to government by decree, to obedience and immobility and death, that is, to enslavement and exploitation at the hands of a new quasi-revolutionary aristocracy.

We understand the revolution to imply the unleashing of what are termed today evil passions, and the destruction of what is described in the same language as "public order."

Unafraid, we invoke anarchy, being convinced that out of such anarchy, which is to say, the comprehensive display of the people's life off the leash, must come liberty, equality, justice, the new order and the Revolution's very strength in the face of reaction. That new life, the people's revolution, will doubtless not be long in taking shape, but it will arrange its revolutionary organization from the bottom up and from the periphery to the center, in keeping with the principle of liberty, and not from the top down and from the center to the periphery, after the fashion of every authority, for it matters little to us whether that authority calls itself Church, Monarchy, constitutional State, bourgeois Republic or even revolutionary dictatorship. We despise them all and reject them all equally, as infallible sources of exploitation and despotism.

The revolution as we understand it will, from day one, set about the root and branch and complete destruction of the State and of all State institutions. The natural and necessary upshot of that destruction will be:

The bankruptcy of the State.

A cessation of recovery of private debts through State intervention, with every debtor being afforded the right to pay his own, should he so desire.

An end to payment of all taxes or levies upon any contributions, direct or indirect. Dissolution of the army, magistracy, bureaucracy, police and clergy.

Abolition of formal courts, suspension of everything described juridically as right, and of the exercise of those laws.

In consequence, the abolition and burning of all property deeds, records of inheritance, sale or gift, of all trial records, and, in short, of the whole mountain of judicial and civil papers. Everywhere and in everything the fact of revolution will supersede State-created and -guaranteed rights.

All productive capital and instruments of labor are to be confiscated for the benefit of toilers' associations, which will have to put them to use in collective production.

Seizure of all Church and State properties as well as precious metals from individuals for the benefit of the federated Alliance of all labor associations, which Alliance will constitute the Commune. In return for confiscated assets, the Commune will issue every person thus divested with their essential needs, and later they will be free to earn more by dint of their own effort, if they can and if they so desire.

As regards organization of the Commune, there will be a federation of standing barricades and a Revolutionary Communal Council will operate on the basis of one or two delegates from each barricade, one per street or per district, these deputies being invested with binding mandates and accountable and revocable at all times. Thus organized, the Communal Council will be able to choose separate executive committees from among its membership for each branch of the Commune's revolutionary administration.

The capital is to declare itself in rebellion and organize itself as a Commune which, having once destroyed the authoritarian nanny State, which it was entitled to do in that it was its slave as was every other locality, will abjure its right or rather any pretension to govern or overrule the provinces.

An appeal will be issued to all provinces, communes and associations, inviting them to follow the example set by the capital, to reorganize along revolutionary lines for a start, and to then delegate deputies to an agreed place of assembly, (all of those deputies invested with binding mandates and accountable and subject to recall), in order to found the federation of insurgent associations, communes and provinces in furtherance of the same principles and to organize a revolutionary force with the capability of defeating the reaction. Not official revolutionary commissioners in any sort of sashes, but rather revolutionary propagandists are to be despatched into all of the provinces and communes and particularly among the peasants, who cannot be revolutionized by principles, nor by the decrees of any dictatorship, but only by the act of revolution itself, that is to say, by the consequences that will inevitably ensue in every commune from complete cessation of the legal and official existence of the State.

The nation State is to be abolished, in this sense, that every foreign country, province, commune, association or indeed isolated individual which might have rebelled in furtherance of the same principles are to be received into the revolutionary federation without regard to the current borders of States, even should they belong to different political or national set-ups, and those provinces, communes, associations or individuals which will have sided with the Reaction are to be excluded from it. Thus it is through the very act of extrapolation and organization of the Revolution with an eye to the mutual defenses of insurgent areas that the universality of the Revolution, founded upon the abolition of borders and upon the ruins of States, will emerge triumphant.

Henceforth, there can be no successful political or national revolution that does not translate as social revolution, and no national revolution that does not turn into universal revolution, precisely because of its radically socialist character and destruction of the State.

Since it is the people which must make the revolution everywhere, and since the ultimate direction of it must at all times be vested in the people organized into a free federation of agricultural and industrial associations, the new revolutionary State — being organized from the bottom up through revolutionary delegation and embracing all countries that have revolted in the name of the same principles, without regard to the old borders or for differences of nationality — will have as its object the administration of public services and not the governance of peoples. It will represent the new fatherland, the alliance of the world revolution against all reactionaries combined.

That organization precludes any notion of dictatorship and supervisory leadership authority. But if that revolutionary alliance is to be established and if the revolution is to get the better of the reaction, then, amid the popular anarchy that is to represent the very life-blood and energy of the revolution, an agency must be found to articulate this singularity of thought and of revolutionary action. That agency should be the secret worldwide association of the International Brethren.

That association starts from the basis that revolutions are never made by individuals, nor even by secret societies. They are, so to speak, self-made, produced by the logic of things, by the trend of events and actions. They are a long time hatching in the deepest recesses of the popular masses' instinctive consciousness, and then they explode, often seeming to have been detonated by trivialities. All that a well-organized society can do is, first, to play midwife to the revolution by spreading amongst the masses ideas appropriate to the masses' instincts, and to organize, not the Revolution's army — for the people must at all times be the army — but a sort of revolutionary general staff made up of committed, energetic and intelligent individuals who are above all else true friends of the people and not presumptuous braggarts, with a capacity for acting as intermediaries between the revolutionary idea and the people's instincts.

The numbers of such individuals, then, need not be huge. A hundred tightly and seriously allied revolutionaries will suffice for the whole of Europe. Two or three hundred revolutionaries will be enough to organize the largest of countries.

NO GODS, NO MASTERS: VOLUME 2

MIKHAIL BAKUNIN

Controversy with Marx

In the preceding text, references to the political thinking of the "marxians" are still veiled and no one is mentioned by name. Relations between Bakunin and Marx within the First International only really turned sour after 1870 when Marx who had at first and very advisedly let the workers have their say, abandoned his role as advisor and hidden mastermind behind the International in an attempt brazenly to harness the organization for the benefit of his "authoritarian" and "anti-anarchist"[1] school of political thought. It was from that point that he came into open conflict with the libertarian socialists grouped around Bakunin. The strife between them led to a split in the International at the congress in The Hague in 1872, a split deliberately contrived by Marx, who saw to it that the Bakuninists were condemned without right of appeal and expelled.

1. The Excommunication of the Hague[2]

Letter to the Brussels newspaper La Liberté.
October 5, 1872, Zurich

Dear Editors,

Having published the sentence of excommunication which the marxian congress in The Hague has just passed on me, you will assuredly see the justice of carrying my reply. Here it is.

The triumph of Mr. Marx and his cronies has been complete. Assured of a majority which they had been long in building and orchestrated with much skill and care, if not with much regard for the principles of morality, truth and justice which are so readily encountered in their speeches and so rarely in their deeds, the marxians have cast aside their mask and, as behooves men enamored of power, as ever in the name of that sovereignty of the people which is henceforth to serve as stepping stone for all pretenders to governance of the masses, they have daringly proclaimed the enslavement of the people of the International.

Were the International less lively, had it been founded, as they imagine, only upon the organization of directing centers, and not upon the real solidarity of the effective interests and aspirations of the proletariat of every country in the civilized world, upon the spontaneous and free federalization of workers' sections and federations, independently of any government tutelage, the decrees emanating from this noxious congress in The Hague, the all too complaisant and loyal embodiment of marxian theories and marxian practices, would have been sufficient to do it to death. They would have rendered ridiculous as well as odious that magnificent association, in the founding of which, I am pleased to record, Mr. Marx had played a part as intelligent as it was vigorous.

A State, a government, a universal dictatorship! The dream of a Gregory VII, a Boniface VIII, a Charles V and a Napoleon, resurrected in novel forms, but still with the same pretensions, in the camp of the socialist democracy! Can there conceivably be anything more ludicrous, but also more repugnant?

To allege that a group of individuals, even should they be the most intelligent and most well-meaning of individuals, will have the capacity to perform as the brains, the soul, the directing, unifying will of the revolutionary movement and the economic organization of the world's proletariat, is such an affront to common sense and historical experience, that one wonders, in amazement, how a fellow as intelligent as Mr. Marx could have come up with it.

The popes at least could plead the absolute truth which they claimed to hold in their hands through the grace of the Holy Spirit and in which they were required to believe. Mr. Marx cannot enter that plea, and I will not do him the injury of supposing that he imagines that he has scientifically devised something approaching absolute truth. But, as soon as the absolute is ruled out, there can be no infallible dogma where the International is concerned, not by reason of political theory nor by virtue of formal economics, and our congresses ought never to lay claim to the role of ecumenical councils enunciating principles binding upon all members and believers.

There is but one law truly binding upon all affiliates, individuals, sections and federations of the International, of which that law constitutes the only true basis. It is, in its fullest sense, in all of its implications and applications, the international solidarity of workers of all trades and all lands in their economic struggle against the exploiters of labor. It is exclusively in the actual organization of that solidarity, through spontaneous action of the toiling masses and through absolutely free federation (all the mightier for its being free) of the toiling masses of every language and nation, and not in the unification of them through decrees and under the baton of any government, that the real and living unity of the International resides.

Who can doubt but that out of this broader and broader organization of the militant solidarity of the proletariat versus bourgeois exploitation the proletariat's political struggle against the bourgeoisie should emerge and indeed emerges? The marxians and we are at one on this score. But immediately there arises the matter which so profoundly separates us from the marxians.

Our reckoning is that the, necessarily revolutionary, politics of the proletariat should have as its sole and immediate object the destruction of States. We cannot understand how there can be talk of international solidarity when there is this desire to preserve States, unless the reference is to the universal State, which is to say, universal slavery. Like the great emperors and popes, the State, by its very nature, is a breach in that solidarity and thus a standing cause of war. Nor can we comprehend talk of freedom of the proletariat or true deliverance of the masses within the State and by the State. State signifies domination, and all domination implies subjection of the masses, and as a result, their exploitation to the advantage of some governing minority.

Not even as revolutionary transition will we countenance national Conventions, nor Constituent Assemblies, nor provisional governments, nor so-called revolutionary dictatorships: because we are persuaded that revolution is sincere, honest and real only among the masses and that, whenever it is concentrated in the hands of a few governing individuals, it inevitably and immediately turns into reaction. Such is our belief, but this is not the time to expand upon it. The marxians subscribe to quite contrary ideas. As befits good Germans, they worship the power of the State, and of necessity also the prophets of political and social discipline, the champions of order established from the top down, always in the name of universal suffrage and sovereignty of the masses, who are marked down for the privilege and honor of obeying leaders, elected masters. The marxians acknowledge no other emancipation than the one they expect from their so-called people's State (**Volksstaat**). They have so little enmity for patriotism that their International even flies, all too often, the colors of Pan-Germanism. Between Bismarck's politics and marxian politics there is doubtless a very palpable difference, but between the marxians and us there is a yawning gulf. They are governmentals and we are anarchists, come what may.

Such are the two main tendencies which have the International at present divided into two camps. On the one side, there is only, strictly speaking, Germany: on the other, there are, to varying degrees, Italy, Spain, the Swiss Jura, much of France, Belgium, Holland, and, in the very near future, the Slav peoples. These two tendencies clashed at the congress in The Hague and, thanks to Mr. Marx's great deftness, thanks to the quite contrived organization of its latest congress, the Germanic tendency has carried the day.

Does that mean that the awful issue has been resolved? It has not even been properly discussed: the majority, voting like a well-drilled regiment, has overwhelmed any discussion with its vote. So the contradiction remains, as acute and menacing as ever, and Mr. Marx himself, for all of the intoxications of success, doubtless does not delude himself that he can have rid himself of it so slickly. And even if he had entertained such a mad hope for a moment, the closing of ranks by the Jura, Spanish, Belgian and Dutch delegates (not to mention Italy which did not even deign to send its delegates to this congress, which was all too blatantly rigged), a protest so moderate in form but essentially all the more energetic and telling, must have quickly disabused him.

Obviously, this protest is merely a very weak foretaste of the formidable opposition which is going to erupt in every country authentically imbued with the principle and passion of social revolution. And this whole storm will have been whipped up by the marxians' very unfortunate obsession with making the political question a fundamental, a binding principle of the International.

Indeed, between the two tendencies indicated above, no conciliation is feasible today. Only the practice of social revolution, great new historical experiences, the logic of events can bring them around, sooner or later, to a common solution: and, strong in our belief in the validity of our principle, we hope that the Germans themselves, the workers of Germany, not their leaders, will then end by joining with us to tear down these people's prisons called States and to condemn politics, which is in fact nothing more than the art of dominating and fleecing the masses.

But, for today, what can we do? Resolution and reconciliation being impossible today on the political terrain, we must show mutual tolerance and afford each country the unchallengeable right to follow whatever political inclinations it may choose or which seem to it best suited to its particular circumstances. Excluding, in consequence, all political matters from the binding platform of the International, we must look exclusively to the terrain of economic solidarity for the unity of that great association. That solidarity unites us, whereas political questions necessarily divide us.

It is certain that neither the Italians, the Spanish, the Jurassians, the French, the Belgians, the Dutch nor the Slav peoples, those historic foes of Pan-Germanism, nor indeed the proletariat of England or America[3], will ever bow to the political tendencies foisted upon the proletariat of Germany by the ambition of its leaders. But supposing even that, in consequence of this disobedience, the incoming General Council[4] slaps an interdict upon all these countries and that some new ecumenical council of the marxians excommunicates them and declares them excluded from the body of the International, will the economic solidarity which necessarily, naturally and in fact is obtained between the proletariat of all these countries and Germany's have diminished any?

If the workers of Germany mount a strike, if they rebel against the economic tyranny of their bosses, or if they revolt against the political tyranny of a government which is the natural protector of capitalists and other exploiters of the people's labors, will the proletariat of all the countries excommunicated by the marxians stand idly by and gaze upon this struggle with indifference? No. It will give all of its meager funds and, what is more, will offer all of its blood to its brethren in Germany, without asking them in advance the character of the political system to which they believe they have to look for their deliverance.

Therein resides the true unity of the International: it resides in the shared aspirations and spontaneous movement of the popular masses of every land, and not in any government, nor in a uniform political theory imposed upon those masses by a general congress.

This is so self-evident that one would have to be blinded by the lust for power not to grasp it.

I can imagine, perhaps, crowned or uncrowned despots having possibly dreamt of ruling the world, but what am I to say of a friend of the proletariat, a revolutionary who purports actually to be desirous of the emancipation of the masses, who, by posing as the director and ultimate arbiter of all revolutionary movements which may erupt in various countries, ventures to dream of the proletariat of all those countries being made subject to a single thought, conceived in his own head?

I account Mr. Marx a very serious revolutionary, if not always a very honest one, and believe that he really does seek the revolt of the masses; and I wonder how he contrives not to see that establishment of a universal dictatorship, be it collective or individual, of a dictatorship that would serve, so to speak as the chief engineer of world revolution, regulating and steering the insurgency of the masses in every land the way one can steer a machine, that establishment of such a dictatorship would, by itself alone, be enough to kill the revolution, and stymie and miscarry all popular movements. Which is the man, which the group of individuals, however gifted their minds, who would dare flatter themselves that they could even encompass and comprehend the infinite multitude of diverse interests, tendencies and actions in every country, every province, every locality, every trade, the vast array of which, united, but not made uniform, by a great shared aspiration and by a few fundamental principles which have already penetrated the consciousness of the masses, will constitute the coming social revolution?

And what is one to think of an international congress which, in the so-called interest of that revolution, foists upon the proletariat of the entire civilized world a government endowed with dictatorial powers, with inquisitorial and pontifical right to suspend regional federations, and ban whole nations in the name of a so-called official principle that is nothing more than Mr. Marx's own brainchild, transformed by the vote of a rigged majority into an absolute truth? What to think of a congress which, in order, no doubt, to make its folly still more apparent, banishes this dictatorial government to America, after having packed it with probably very honest but obscure fellows, sufficiently ignorant and utterly unknown to itself? Our bourgeois enemies would be right, therefore, when they poke fun at our congresses and when they argue that the International Working Men's Association opposes old tyrannies only in order to establish a new one, and that, in order to replace existing absurdities worthily, it seeks to create another!

Notes to 1. The Excommunication of the Hague

1. See Miklos Molnar *Le Declin de la Premiere Internationale* Geneva 1963
2. Taken from *Oeuvres* Tome IV, pp. 342-351. The title has been added by us.
3. The resolutions passed at The Hague by a contrived majority were disowned by all of the International's component regional federations, to wit: 1. by the Jura Federation at its Saint-Imier congress (September 15-16, 1872); 2. by all of the French sections who were able, in spite of the Dufaure law, to meet and deliberate, by a congress of 23 delegates from the French sections (October 1872) among other occasions: 3. by the Italian federation (letter from its correspondence commission, December 1872) which, ever since its first congress in Rimini in August 1872, had broken off relations with the General Council: 4. by the Belgian federation, at its congress in Brussels (December 25-26,1872): 5. by the Spanish federation at its Cordoba congress (December 25-30, 1872) 6. by the American federation (resolution from the federal council at Spring Street, New York, January 19, 1873): 7. by the English federation at its London congress (January 26, 1873): 8. by the Dutch federation (the result of a poll reported by the Dutch federal council on February 14, 1873). The International had no sections in Germany, as they were forbidden by law: there the International could only count upon individual affiliates, directly affiliated with the General Council (note by James Guillaume).
4. The International's General Council, which had been based in London from 1864 to 1872, was removed, at the decision of the congress of The Hague, to New York, where Marx and Engels were counting upon finding compliant servants of their wishes.

2. Statism and Anarchy

The International Institute for Social History in Amsterdam has kindly allowed us to reprint the following extract from *Statism and Anarchy*, a work published in Russian in 1873 and never since translated into French: it constitutes Tome III of the *Archives Bakounine* published on behalf of the Institute in Amsterdam by E. J. Brill of Leyden (Netherlands). The translation into French is by Marcel Body.

On several occasions already we have expressed a very acute aversion to the theory of Lassalle and Marx which urges the workers, if not as a supreme ideal, then at least as their essential short-term objective, to establish a "people's State," which, as they themselves have explained, would be nothing but "the proletariat organized as ruling class." If the proletariat becomes the ruling class, over whom, may one ask, is it to rule? The fact remains that there will still be a class subject to that new ruling class, this new State, be it only, say, the rural rabble who, as we know, are not in good odor with the marxians,' and who, occupying the nethermost regions of civilization, will probably be guided by the proletariat of town and workshop: or indeed, if we consider the question in an ethnic light — say, in the Germans' case, the question of the Slavs — the latter will, on the same grounds, be in the same slavish subjection to the victorious German proletariat as that proletariat is with regard to its bourgeoisie.

Whoever says State necessarily says domination, and, consequently, slavery: a State without slavery, open or concealed, is inconceivable: that is why we are enemies of the State.

What is the meaning of "the proletariat organized as ruling class"? Does it mean that the proletariat in its entirety is to direct public affairs? There are around forty million Germans. Can those forty millions share in government and the entire people govern, in which case there will be no governed? In which case there will be no State: but, if there is one, there will be governed, there will be slaves.

In the marxian theory, this dilemma is dispatched very straight-forwardly. By popular government the marxians mean government of the people by means of a small number of representatives elected through universal suffrage. Election by the nation as a whole of so-called people's representatives and State leaders, which is the latest device of the marxians as well as of the democratic school of thought, is a lie that shrouds the despotism of the leading minority, a lie all the more dangerous because it is peddled as expressing the supposed will of the people.

Thus, no matter the angle from which we examine this matter, we are led to the same execrable result: government of the vast majority of the masses of the people by a privileged minority. But this minority, the marxians argue, will be made up of workers. Yes, to be sure, of former workers who, as soon as they become the people's governors and representatives, will stop being workers and will begin to look down upon the proletarian world from the heights of the State: they will then represent, not the people, but themselves and their ambitions to govern it. Anyone who queries that does not know human nature.

On the other hand, these elected representatives are going to be sincere socialists, and erudite ones to boot. The terms scientific socialist, scientific socialism, which are forever cropping up in the writings of the Lassalleans and marxians, themselves prove that the phony people's State is going to be nothing more than despotic government of the proletarian masses by a new, very tiny aristocracy of actual or alleged savants. The people, not being erudite, is to be spared the cares of government entirely and incorporated wholly into the herd of the governed. Some deliverance!

The marxians are alive to this paradox and, while conceding that government by savant, the most oppressive, most vexatious, most contemptible form of government possible, is going to be, for all its democratic forms, an outright dictatorship, take consolation from the thought that dictatorship is going to be temporary and short-lived. They contend that its sole concern and only object will be to enlighten the people and raise it, economically and politically alike, to a level where all government will promptly become redundant: and the State, once divested of its political character, which is to say, its authoritarianism, will automatically be transformed into a totally free organization of economic interests and communes.

There is a glaring paradox in all this. If their State is indeed a "people's State," on what grounds would it be abolished? And if, on the other hand, its abolition is necessary for real emancipation of the people, how could it be described as a "people's State"? In debate with them, we have drawn from them an acknowledgment that free organization of the toiling masses, freedom or anarchy, which is to say, organization from the bottom up, is the ultimate objective of social evolution and that any State, their "people's State" included, is a yoke, which means that, on the one hand, it fosters despotism and, on the other, slavery.

According to them, this statist yoke, this dictatorship is a necessary transitional phase on the way to complete emancipation of the people: anarchy or liberty being the goal, the State or dictatorship the means. So, in order to liberate the popular masses, we are to start by enslaving them.

For the time being, our polemic has stalled on this contradiction. The marxians argue that only dictatorship — theirs, of course — can establish the people's freedom: to which we reply that no dictatorship can have any aim other than lasting as long as it can and that it is only capable of fomenting slavery in the people which endures it and of schooling the latter in slavery: freedom can be conjured only by freedom, that is to say, by uprising by the entire people and by free organization of the toiling masses from the bottom up.

(. . .) While the socio-political theory of the anti-authoritarian socialists or anarchists leads them without fail to break utterly with all government, with all forms of bourgeois politics, and leaves them no option save social revolution, the contrary theory, the theory of the authoritarian communists and scientific authoritarianism lures and seduces its supporters, under the pretext of tactics, into endless compromises with governments and the various bourgeois political parties — which is to say, shoves them straight into the camp of the reaction.

(. . .) The crucial point in this program is (supposed) emancipation of the proletariat by the sole and exclusive means of the State. But for that to happen, the State has to agree to act as emancipator of the proletariat by loosening the yoke of bourgeois capital. How, then, is the State to be brought to this determination? There can be only two ways of bringing that to pass: the proletariat makes revolution in order to take possession of the State, the heroic course. Once it has taken over the State, it should, as we see it, destroy it immediately for it is the age-old prison of the proletarian masses: now, according to Mr. Marx's theory, the people not only should not destroy the State but should instead reinforce it, make it even mightier and place it, in this new form, at the disposal of its benefactors, tutors and educators, the leaders of the Communist Party — in short, at the disposal of Mr. Marx and his friends who will promptly set about liberating it after their fashion.

They are to take over the reins of government, because the ignorant people stands in need of proper tutelage: they will set up a single State Bank which is to concentrate into its hands the totality of commerce, industry, agriculture and even scientific output, while the mass of the people is to be divided into two armies: the industrial and the agricultural, under the direct command of State engineers who will make up a new, privileged erudite-political caste.

See what a role purpose the German communist school reserves for the people!

Notes to 2. Statism and Anarchy

1. We have chosen to use the term "marxians" here rather than "marxists" as the translator does, because Bakunin, when expressing himself in French, preferred the former term.

Bakunin and Marx on the Commune

Here are two splendid texts, one from Bakunin and the other from Marx, on the Paris Commune. They were both written in the wake of the defeat of the Commune (May 1871). Both expound a theme which they both deduced from the experience of the Commune, the first ever proletarian revolution: the theme of abolition of the State.

Bakunin's text contains nothing to startle. It is in fact quite consistent with the line he adopted in his earlier writings. In it one finds the distillation of libertarian socialism.

By contrast, there is more to surprise in the Address drafted by Marx on behalf of the General Council of the workers' International, to which marxians and Bakuninists alike belonged at the time. In fact, it is the product of the author's attempt to reconcile the two currents inside the International.

For that reason, it differs noticeably from Marx's writings of before and after 1871, and compares exceptionally well to Bakunin's writings. With hindsight, we can look upon it as one of the few bridges established between marxism and anarchism, as one of the very few attempts at a synthesis of "authoritarian" with libertarian thought.

In the Address, better known under the name *The Civil War in France,* Marx overhauled certain passages of the 1848 *Communist Manifesto.* Marx and Engels, the authors of that illustrious document, had set out therein their idea of proletarian revolution in stages. Stage one would be the capture of political power, thanks to which, "little by little," the means of production, the means of transportation and credit would be centralized in the hands of the State.

Only at the end of a protracted evolution, once class conflicts would have vanished and public authority been rid of its political character, would the whole of production be concentrated, not in State hands now, but in the hands of "associated individuals": in this libertarian style of association, the unfettered development of each would be the precondition for the free development of all.

Bakunin who, unlike the French socialists, had been conversant with the *Communist Manifesto,* in the German original since 1848, had not missed an opportunity to criticize this splitting of the revolution into two stages, the first of which would still be emphatically statist. He had criticized it in these terms: "Having become the sole proprietor (...) the State is also to be the sole capitalist, banker, sponsor, organizer and director of the whole of the nation's labors and distributor of its products. Such is the ideal, the underlying principle of modern communism."[1] And, elsewhere: "This revolution will consist of the expropriation, creeping or violent, of the current proprietors and capitalists, and of appropriation of all land and all capital by the State which, in order to be able to perform its great economic as well as political mission, will, of necessity, have to be very powerful and very tightly concentrated. The State is to administer and direct cultivation of the land through its appointed engineers commanding armies of rural workers organized and disciplined for such cultivation. At the same time, upon the ruins of all the existing banks, it will found a single bank that is a sleeping partner in all labor and the whole commerce of the nation."[2]

And again: "In Mr. Marx's people's State, we are told, there is to be no privileged class. Everyone is to be equal, not just before the law and politically, but in economic terms too. That, at least, is the promise, although I very much doubt that, given the manner in which it is tackled and the course intended, the promise can ever be honored. Thus, there is to be no privileged class any more, but an exceedingly complicated government, which will not be content to govern and administer the masses politically, as all of today's governments do, but which will also see to economic administration, amassing in its hands the production and fair distribution of wealth, cultivation of the soil, the establishment and expansion of factories, the organization and direction of trade and, finally, the investment of capital in production, by the sole banker, the State."[3]

Under the lash of Bakunin's criticisms, Marx and Engels felt a need to amend their overly statist thinking of 1848. Thus, in a foreword (dated June 24, 1872) to a new edition of the *Manifesto*, they conceded that "in many respects," they would now "rephrase" the passage in question from the 1848 text. And, remarkably, they cited in support of any such redrafting "the practical experiences, first of the February [1848] revolution, then, to a much greater extent, of the Paris Commune, when, for the first time, the proletariat held political power in its hands over a two month period." And concluded: "All of which means that, in places, this program is no longer up to the minute. The Commune in particular has supplied proof that the working class cannot rest content with taking possession of the existing machinery of the State in order to place it in the service of its own aims." The 1871 Address also announces that the Commune is "discovered at last, the political formula whereby the economic emancipation of labor can be brought about."

In his life of Karl Marx, Franz Mehring, an undisputed marxist, has himself stressed that the 1871 Address feting the Paris Commune was, on this score, somewhat of an amendment to the *Manifesto*, where elimination of the State had indeed been considered, but only as a long term process. Later, though, Mehring assures us, after the death of Marx, Engels, by then grappling with anarchist tendencies, had jettisoned the amendment in question and reverted to the old ideas in the *Manifesto*.[4]

The fact remains that the rather abrupt "about-turn" by the author of the 1871 Address must have aroused skepticism from Bakunin. Speaking of the Commune, he wrote: "So formidable was its impact everywhere that the marxians themselves, all of whose ideas had been overthrown by that insurrection, found themselves obliged to doff their hat to it. They went further: flying in the face of simple logic and their true feelings, they proclaimed that its program and its aim were theirs. It was a truly absurd travesty, but a necessary one. They had been forced into it, on pain of finding themselves cast aside and deserted by everybody, such was the extent of the passion aroused by that revolution in all and sundry."[5]

And Bakunin observed; "It appears that at the congress in The Hague [September 1872], Mr. Engels, taking fright at the despicable impression produced by the reading of a few pages from that *Manifesto*, had wasted no time in declaring that it was a superseded document, a theory which they [Marx and Engels] had since abandoned. If he said that, he was less than honest, for, on the very eve of that same congress, the marxians had striven to disseminate that document throughout every country."[6]

As for James Guillaume, Bakunin's disciple from the Jura, he reacted in similar terms to a reading of the 1871 Address: "This is an astonishing statement of principles, where Marx appears to have jettisoned his own program in order to come over to federalist ideas. Does that mean a real conversion by the author of *Das Kapital*, or at least a temporary seduction to which he succumbed under the pressure of events? Or was it a ploy on his behalf, designed to reap, through apparent support for the Commune's program, the benefits of the prestige attaching to its name?"[7]

In our own day, Arthur Lehning, to whom we are indebted for the erudite edition of *Archives Bakounine* currently being published, has stressed the contradiction between the ideas in the Address and all of Marx's other writings: "It is an irony of history that at the very moment when the struggle between the authoritarian and the anti-authoritarian tendencies was reaching its peak [inside the First International], Marx, reeling from the tremendous impact of the revolutionary uprising of the Parisian proletariat, articulated the ideas of that Revolution, the very opposite of the ideas for which he stood, and in such a way that they might almost be described as the program of the anti-authoritarian tendency against which he fought [inside the International] with tooth and nail (...) There is no doubt that the brilliant Address of the General Council (...) does not fit in at all with the elaboration of the system of 'scientific socialism'. *The Civil War* is, to the utmost degree, non-Marxist. (...) The Paris Commune had nothing in common with Marx's State socialism, but was rather more in tune with Proudhon's ideas and Bakunin's federalist theories. (. . .) The essential principle of the Commune, according to Marx, was that political centralization of the State had to be replaced by self-government of the producers, by a federation of autonomous communes to which had to be afforded. (...) the initiative hitherto devolved to the State.

The Civil War fully contradicts the other marxist writings where the withering away of the State is concerned. The Paris Commune did not centralize the means of production into State hands. The goal of the Paris Commune was not to let the State 'wither away' but rather to banish it immediately (...) The annihilation of the State was now not the inevitable conclusion to a dialectical historical process, of a higher stage of society, itself shaped by a higher form of production.

The Paris Commune obliterated the State, without fulfilling a single one of the conditions which Marx had previously stipulated as prefacing its abrogation (...) The Commune's defeat of the bourgeois State had not been designed to install another State in its place. (...) Its aim was not to found some new State machinery, but rather to replace the State by organizing society on economic and federalist foundations (...) In The *Civil War* [the Address], there is no mention of "withering away," but rather of immediate and utter extirpation of the State."[8]

Likewise, the marxologist Maximilien Rubel has conceded: "There is no denying that the idea which Marx framed of the conquest and suppression of the State by the proletariat found its definitive shape in his Address on the Paris Commune and that as such it differs from the idea offered to us in the *Communist Manifesto*."[9]

But there is nevertheless disagreement between the two scholars: Lehning, who, rightly or wrongly, regards Marx as an "authoritarian," alleges that the Address is a "foreign body" in marxist socialism, whereas Rubel, on the other hand, eager to discover a "libertarian" in Marx, contends that marxian thought found in the Address its "definitive form."

The fact remains, though, that in the striving today to work out some synthesis between anarchism and marxism, the Address of 1871 has to be regarded as a starting-point, a prima facie demonstration that it is feasible to reconcile fruitfully the two strands of thought, the authoritarian and the libertarian.

Notes to the Introduction to Bakunin and Marx on the Commune

1. Bakunin *Oeuvres* Tome IV, 1910, p. 62
2. Ibid. p. 381 - 382
3. Ibid. p. 476
4. Franz Mehring (1846–1919) *Karl Marx, Geschichte seines Lebens 1918*: and Lenin in *The State and Revolution* complained of "perversion" by Social Democratic "opportunism" of the "essential correction" which Marx had made to the *Manifesto*.
5. Bakunin, letter addressed to the Brussels newspaper *La Liberte*, dated October 5, 1872, in *Oeuvres*, Stock, Tome IV, p. 387
6. Ibid. p. 372
7. James Guillaume *Souvenirs de l'Internationale 1907*, Tome II, p. 192
8. Arthur Lehning "Marxism and Anarchism in the Russian Revolution," in the review *Die Internationale*, Berlin, 1923.
9. Karl Marx *Pages choisies pour une éthique socialiste* readings selected by Maximilien Rubel, 1948, introduction p. 4, note.

Bakunin: The Paris Commune[1]

(. . .) In the Paris Commune, revolutionary socialism has just essayed its first spectacular, practical venture.

I am a supporter of the Paris Commune which, though it has been massacred and smothered in blood by the henchmen of monarchist and clerical reaction, is all the livelier and more potent in the imaginations and hearts of Europe's proletariat: I am a supporter of it because it was a well articulated and daring rebuttal of the State.

It is an historical fact of immense implications that this rebuttal of the State should have manifested itself specifically in France, which has hitherto been par excellence the home of political centralization, and that Paris specifically, the center and historical creator of this great French civilization, should have been the one to take the initiative in this.

Paris, yielding up her crown and enthusiastically announcing that she was stepping down in order to bring liberty and life to France, Europe and the world at large;

Paris, reaffirming her historical powers of initiative by pointing out to all enslaved peoples (and which popular masses are not slaves?) the only path to emancipation and salvation;

Paris, dealing a death blow to the political traditions of bourgeois radicalism and affording revolutionary socialism a substantial basis;

Paris, earning once again the curses of every reactionary in France and in Europe;

Paris, burying herself in her ruins in order to signify a solemn repudiation of the triumphant reaction; redeeming, through her own misfortune, the honor and prospects of France; and proving to a comforted humanity that, while life, intelligence and moral firmness may have deserted the upper classes, they thrive in the fullness of their powers in the proletariat;

Paris, ushering in the new age, the age of definitive and comprehensive liberation of the masses of the people and their solidarity which henceforth will be quite substantial, criss-crossing and over-riding the borders of States;

Paris, doing patriotism to death and founding the religion of humanity upon her ruins;

Paris, proclaiming herself humanitarian and atheist, and substituting the great realities of social life and faith in science for fictitious gods: the principles of liberty, justice, equality and fraternity, those timeless foundations of all human morality, for religious, political and juridical morals;

Paris, heroic, rational and faithful, confirming her vigorous belief in the destinies of humanity, through her glorious demise and death, bequeathing it much more vigorous and lively to succeeding generations;

Paris, drowned in the blood of her most selfless children, is mankind crucified by the concerted international reaction in Europe, under the aegis of all the Christian churches and of the high priest of iniquity, the Pope: but the coming international, solidarity revolution of peoples will be Paris's resurrection.

Such is the true meaning, and such the beneficent, incalculable implications of the Paris Commune's two month life span and its never-to-be-forgotten collapse.

The Paris Commune was too short-lived, and in its inner development it was unduly hobbled by the deadly battle which it as obliged to wage against the Versailles reaction, for it to be able to — I will not say apply, but elaborate in theory — its socialist program. Also, and this has to be recognized, most of the members of the Commune were not, strictly, socialists and if they showed themselves to be such, this was because they were hopelessly carried away by the irresistible force of circumstances, by the nature of their environment, by the demands of their position, rather than by heartfelt conviction. In the Commune, the socialists, at the head of whom stood, of course, our friend Varlin, were but a very tiny minority; at most they numbered 14 or 15 members. Jacobins accounted for the remainder.

But, let us be clear about this, there are Jacobins and Jacobins. There are Jacobin lawyers and doctrinarians, like Mr. Gambetta, whose positivist, pompous, despotic and formalistic republicanism, having abjured the old revolutionary faith and retained nothing of Jacobinism save the cult of unity and authority, has delivered the people's France to the Prussians, and later to the home-grown reaction: and there are staunchly revolutionary Jacobins, heroes, the last honest representatives of the democratic faith of 1793, capable of sacrificing both their beloved unity and their cherished authority to the requirements of the Revolution, rather than accommodate their consciences to the insolence of the reaction.

These magnanimous Jacobins, at whose head stands Delescluze of course, a great soul and a great character, seek the success of the Revolution above all else: and as there is no revolution without the masses of the people, and since those masses today are eminently endowed with the socialist instinct and cannot mount any revolution other than an economic and social revolution, the authentic Jacobins, surrendering ever more to the logic of the revolutionary movement, must finish up becoming reluctant socialists.

Such indeed was the situation of those Jacobins who belonged to the Paris Commune. Delescluze and many another with him put their signatures to programs and proclamations, the general tenor and promises of which were positively socialistic. But since, for all their bona fides and good intentions, they were only socialists a lot more superficially enthused than converted in their heart of hearts, and as they had not had the time nor the ability indeed to overcome and banish from their minds a host of bourgeois prejudices which were at odds with their new-found socialism, it is understandable that, stymied by that inner turmoil, they were never able to move beyond generalizations nor take one of those decisive steps that might forever have severed their fellowship and all their connections with the bourgeois world.

This was a great misfortune for the Commune and for themselves: they were paralyzed by it and they paralyzed the Commune: but this cannot counted against them as a fault. Men are not transformed overnight, and cannot change either their nature or their ways at a whim. They proved their sincerity by going to their deaths for the Commune's sake. Who will dare require more of them?

They are all the more deserving of forgiveness in that the people of Paris itself, under whose influence they thought and acted, were a lot more instinctively socialist than socialists by belief or through considered reflection. Their every aspiration is comprehensively and exclusively socialist: but their ideas, or rather, the traditional expressions thereof cannot pretend to such loftiness. In the proletariat of France's larger towns and even in that of Paris, a lot of Jacobin prejudices, a lot of dictatorial and governmental idioms survive. The cult of authority, the necessary outcome of religious education, that historical source of all of the people's misfortunes, depravities and slavishness, has yet to be banished utterly from its heart. This is so true that even the people's most intelligent sons, the sincerest socialists, have yet to be delivered entirely from it. Root around in their consciences and you will find the Jacobin, and governmentalism, lurking in some dark recess, much shrunken, it is true, but not quite dead.

Also, the circumstances of the tiny number of convinced socialists who were part of the Commune were exceedingly difficult. Not feeling that they had sufficient support from the great bulk of the Parisian populace, for the International Association's organization, which was in any case very flawed, numbered only a few thousand individuals, they had to wage a daily battle against the Jacobin majority. And in what a setting at that! They had to find work and bread for some hundreds of thousands of workers, they had to organize and arm them and they had to monitor reactionary activity in a sprawling city like Paris, which was under siege, famished and prey to every filthy trick by the reactionaries who had successfully ensconced themselves in Versailles, with the permission and under the aegis of the Prussians. They had to counter with a revolutionary government and fight the government and army of Versailles, that is to say, in order to combat the monarchist and clerical backlash, they were obliged to set aside and sacrifice the basic premises of revolutionary socialism and organize themselves into a Jacobin counter.

Was it not only to be expected that, in such circumstances, the Jacobins, who were the stronger, in that they represented the majority of the Commune and who also possessed to an infinitely greater extent the political instinct, tradition and practice of governmental organization, should have enjoyed immeasurable advantages over the socialists? The astonishing thing is that they did not make a lot more capital out of it than they did, that they failed to invest the Paris uprising with an exclusively Jacobin character, and that they allowed themselves, instead, to be swept into a social revolution.

I know that many socialists, very conscientious about their theory, take our Paris friends to task for not having been socialist enough in their revolutionary practice, while all of the yaps of the bourgeois press on the other hand charge them with having abided only too faithfully by socialism's program. For the moment, let us leave the sordid complainants of that press to one side: let me point out to the inflexible theoreticians of emancipation of the proletariat that they are not being fair to our friends from Paris: for, between the finest theories and their implementation, there is a huge distance which cannot be bridged in just a few days. Anyone who had the good fortune to be acquainted with Varlin, say, to name only the one of whose death we can be sure, knows how impassioned, thought through and deep-seated were his and his friends' socialist convictions. These were men whose burning zeal, commitment and bona fides could never have been called into question by anyone who had dealings with them.

But precisely because they were men of good faith, they were full of self-doubt in the face of the immense undertaking to which they had devoted their thoughts and their lives: they were so disparaging of themselves! Also it was their conviction that in the social Revolution, which on this score as on every other is the diametrical opposite of political Revolution, the actions of individuals counted for virtually nothing and that the spontaneous action of the masses had to be everything. All that individuals could do was articulate, clarify and disseminate ideas mirroring the people's instinct, and, in addition, contribute through their unceasing efforts to revolutionary organization of the natural might of the masses, but no more than that: everything else ought to and can only be achieved by the people itself. Otherwise the upshot would be political dictatorship, that is, reconstitution of the State, privilege, inequality, all of the State's oppressions, and, by a roundabout but logical route, restoration of the political, social and economic enslavement of the masses of the people.

Varlin and all his friends, like all honest socialists, and, broadly speaking, like all toilers born and raised among the people, were very much subscribers to this perfectly legitimate prejudice against initiative continually emanating from the same individuals, against rule exercised by higher-ups, and, being above all else fair-minded, they trained this suspicion as much upon themselves as everyone else.

Contrary to the authoritarian communists' notion — a quite wrong-headed notion as I see it — that a social Revolution can be ordained and organized either by a dictatorship or by a constituent assembly issuing from a political revolution, our friends, the socialists of Paris, reckoned that only through ongoing spontaneous action of the masses, groups and associations of the people could it be mounted and prosecuted to its fullest extent.

Our friends from Paris were a thousand times right. For, in effect, what head, however inspired, or if one prefers to talk about a collective dictatorship, even one made up of several hundreds of individuals endowed with outstanding gifts, what brains are mighty enough and massive enough to encompass the infinite multiplicity and diversity of substantive interests, aspirations, wishes and needs, the sum of which represents the collective will of a people, and mighty and massive enough to devise a social organization capable of satisfying them all? That origination will never be anything other than a Procrustean bed upon which the more or less pronounced violence of the State will compel society to stretch out.

Which is what has always happened hitherto, and it is precisely this ancient system of organization through force to which the social Revolution must put paid by restoring their full liberty to the masses, groups, communes, associations and indeed individuals, by destroying, for once and for all, the historic cause of all violence, the might and very existence of the State which, when its downfall comes, must necessarily bring down with it all of the iniquities of juridical law along with all the lies of several cults, such law and such cults never having been anything other than the necessary consequence, in ideas as well as in substance, of all of the violence represented, guaranteed and fostered by the State.

It is self-evident that liberty is not about to be restored to humanity, and that the substantial interests of society, of the groups and of all the local organizations as well as all of the individuals who make up society, will not really be gratified until States are no more. Obviously, all the so-called general interests of society which the State is supposed to represent, and which in point of fact are nothing but the general and standing negation of the positive interests of the regions, communes, associations and the greater number of individuals subjected to the State, add up to an abstraction, a figment, a falsehood, and the State is like one huge butchery and like a vast cemetery where, in the shade and under the pretext of that abstraction, all of the real interests, all of the vital forces of the land come along generously and blithely to let themselves be hacked up and buried: and since no abstraction ever exists of itself or for itself, as it has neither legs to walk on, nor arms to create, nor stomach to digest the stream of victims fed to it, then plainly, just as the religious or celestial abstraction, God, in reality stands for the very positive, very substantial interests of a privileged caste, the clergy, its earthly counterpart, so that political abstraction, the State, stands for the no less positive and substantial interests of the class which is today the main, if not exclusive, exploiter class, and which, moreover, tends to assimilate all others — the bourgeoisie.

And just as the clergy is always divided and is today inclined to split even further into a very powerful, very wealthy minority and a very subordinate, passably impoverished majority, so the bourgeoisie and its several social and political organizations in industry, agriculture, banking and commerce, as well as in every administrative function of the State, financial, legal, academic, police and military, tends to divide further with every passing day into a truly dominant oligarchy and a countless mass of more or less vain and demeaned creatures, their lives a perpetual illusion, inevitably and increasingly driven down into the proletariat by an invisible force, the force of the current economic development, and reduced to serving as the blind instruments of that omnipotent oligarchy.

Abolition of Church and State must be the essential precondition for the real liberation of society: only after that can it and should it be organized differently, though not from the top down and in accordance with some ideal scheme devised by a few sages or savants, or indeed by means of decrees issuing from some dictatorial force or even national assembly elected by universal suffrage. Such an arrangement, as I have said before, would inevitably lead to creation of a new State, and, consequently, to formation of a governmental aristocracy, which is to say, a whole class of people having nothing in common with the mass of the people and, assuredly, that class would embark again upon the exploitation and subjection of it, on the pretext of the common good or in order to save the State.

The future organization of society must proceed from the bottom up only, through free association or federation of the workers, into their associations to begin with, then into communes, regions, nations and, finally, into a great international and universal federation. Only then will the true and enlivening order of freedom and general happiness come about — that order which, far from denying it, instead affirms and reconciles the interests of individuals and those of society.

Note to Bakunin: The Paris Commune

1. Taken from *The Paris Commune and the Idea of the State* (1871).

Karl Marx: The Paris Commune[1]

The cry of 'Social Republic!' to which the Parisian proletariat had launched the February revolution represented little more than a vague longing for a Republic that would not just abolish the monarchist form of class rule, but class rule per se. The Commune was the positive embodiment of that Republic.

Paris, the central seat of the former government power, and at the same time, the French working class's social stronghold, had taken up arms against the attempt by Thiers and his Rurals to restore and perpetuate the former governmental power bequeathed them by the Empire.

Paris was able to resist because, on account of the siege, it had got rid of the army and replaced it by a National Guard, the bulk of which was made up of workers. It was now a matter of turning this de facto state into a durable institution. The Commune's first decree, therefore, abolished the standing army and replaced it with a people in arms.

The Commune was made up of municipal councilors, elected by universal suffrage in the various arrondissements of the city. These were at all times answerable and subject to recall.[2] Most of its members were, naturally, workers or acknowledged representatives of the working class. The Commune was not to be a parliamentary body, but an active body, executive and legislature in one. Instead of carrying on as the instrument of the central government, the police were immediately stripped of their political powers and turned into an instrument of the Commune, accountable and revocable at any moment. The same was true of officials from all other branches of the administration. From Commune members down to the bottom of the scale, public service had to be repaid with a workman's wage. The traditional backhanders and commissions of high State dignitaries vanished along with those dignitaries themselves. The public services ceased to be the private preserves of the central government's henchmen. Not merely the city administration, but the whole of the initiative hitherto exercised by the State was transferred back into Commune hands.

With the standing army and the police, those material instruments of central government power, done away with, the Commune turned to the task of smashing the spiritual instrument of oppression, the priestly power: it decreed Church and State separated and all churches expropriated insofar as they constituted proprietorial bodies. Priests were despatched to the peaceful retreat of private life, there to live upon alms from the faithful, like their predecessors, the apostles. Every single educational establishment was thrown open to the people free of charge and simultaneously released from all Church or State interference. Thus, not only was education made accessible to all, but science itself was freed from shackles which class prejudices and governmental power had placed on it.

Court officials were stripped of that sham independence which had served only to disguise their squalid submission to every succeeding government, to which, one by one, they had pledged their loyalty, only to break it thereafter. Like every other public official, magistrates and judges were to be electable, accountable and revocable.

The Paris Commune of course was to have set the pattern for every great industrial center in France. Once Commune rule had been established in Paris and other secondary sites, the former central government would have had to yield in the provinces also to the self-government of the producers. In a short outline of national organization which the Commune was denied the time to develop, it is explicitly stated that the Commune was to be the political model even for the tiniest rural hamlet, and that in country areas the standing army was to be replaced by a people's militia with an extremely brief term of service. The rural communes in each department were to administer their shared affairs through a delegates' assembly in the departmental capital, and these departmental assemblies would in turn send deputies to the national delegation in Paris: delegates would be subject to recall at any moment and bound by the imperative mandate issued by their electors. Those few but significant duties retained by the central government would not be abolished, as has falsely and deliberately been claimed, but would be performed by communal officials, which is to say by officials strictly accountable.

There was to be no injury done the unity of the nation; instead it would be orchestrated by means of the communal Constitution; it would be made a reality through destruction of the State power which purported to be the embodiment of that nationhood, but which sought to remain independent of the nation itself, and superior to it, when it was really only a parasitical excrescence. While it was important that the purely repressive organs of the former governmental authority be lopped off, its legitimate functions were to be wrested from an authority that claimed a pre-eminence over society itself and awarded to accountable servants of society. Instead of deciding once every three or six years which member of the ruling class was to "represent" and trample the people underfoot inside Parliament, universal suffrage was to serve the people, organized into communes, the way individual suffrage serves any other employer on the look-out for workers and staff to run his business. And it is a commonplace that societies, like individuals, when it comes to genuine matters, generally manage to place everyone properly and, in the event of a mistake's being made, manage to make prompt amends.

Then again, nothing could have been more alien to the spirit of the Commune than the replacement of universal suffrage by some hierarchical investiture. Broadly speaking, it is the fate of entirely novel historical formations to be mistaken for the counter to older, even extinct forms, of social life, to which they may bear a certain resemblance. Thus, in this new Commune which shattered the power of the modern State, some have been intent upon seeing an evocation of the medieval communes, which to begin with, prefigured that State power and then became its foundation.[3]

The communal Constitution has mistakenly been interpreted as an attempt to break down into a federation of small States, (as Montesquieu and the Girondins dreamed about), that unity of great nations which, although originally engendered by violence, has now grown into a potent factor in social production.

The antagonism between the Commune and State power has wrongly been seen as an overblown form of the age-old struggle against over-centralization. Particular historical circumstances may, in other countries, have thwarted the classical development of the bourgeois form of government, as has happened in France, and, as in England, may have allowed the huge central organs of the State to ramify through corrupt *vestries*,[4] jobbing municipal councilors and ferocious welfare board administrators in the towns, and, in the counties, effectively hereditary justices of the peace.

The communal Constitution would have restored to the body of society all of the resources hitherto gobbled up by the parasitical State which feeds upon society and hobbles its freedom of movement. By virtue of that fact alone, it would have been the launching pad for France's regeneration.

(. . .) Implicit as a self-evident fact in the very existence of the Commune was municipal freedom: but henceforth it was no impediment to State power, which had been done away with. Only the mind of a Bismarck (...) could have come up with the idea of ascribing to the Paris Commune aspirations to that lampoon of the old French municipal organization from 1791 represented by Prussian municipal government, which degrades administration in the towns until these are mere secondary cogs in the Prussian State's police apparatus.

The Commune made a reality of that watchword of all bourgeois revolutions, cheap government, by abolishing these two great drains upon expenditure: the standing army and State officials. Its very existence supposed non-existence of the monarchy which, in Europe at any rate, is the usual burden and indispensable mask of class rule. It supplied the Republic with the basis of genuinely democratic institutions. But its ultimate objective was neither "cheap government" nor the "real Republic": these were merely its corollaries.

The multiplicity of constructions placed upon the Commune, and the multiplicity of interests making claims upon it demonstrate that it was a political form with every potential for expansion, whereas every form of government up to then had placed the emphasis on repression. And therein lies its true secret: it was essentially a working class government, the outcome of the producers' class struggle against the appropriating class, the political formula — at last discovered — which made economic emancipation of labor become feasible.

Notes to Karl Marx: The Paris Commune

1. Taken from *The Civil War in France* (1871)
2. For Kropotkin's critique of the Commune's system of representation, see below.
3. See below for Kropotkin's essay on the medieval Communes.
4. Parish councils.

Bakunin on Worker Self-management

I. On Cooperation[1]

(...) What is the International's aim? It is, is it not?, emancipation of the working class through solidary action of the workers of all countries. And what is the aim of bourgeois cooperation? The wresting of a small number of workers out of the common poverty, in order to turn them into bourgeois, to the detriment of the greater number.

(..) Let us suppose that a thousand men are exploited and oppressed by ten. What would one think if there were twenty, thirty or more in that thousand who said to themselves: "We are weary of being victims: but since, on the other hand, it is absurd to hope for everybody's salvation, as the prosperity of the small number absolutely requires sacrifice of the greater number, let us abandon our colleagues to their fate, and thinking of ourselves only, in order to become happy, let us in our turn become bourgeois, become exploiters?"

That would be treachery, would it not?

(...) Many of them are very well-meaning, not deceivers but deceived. Not knowing, not having ever seen or imagined any practice other than bourgeois practice, lots of them reckon that it would be legitimate warfare to resort to that same practice in order to combat the bourgeoisie. They are naive enough to believe that what murders labor may emancipate it, and that they, as well as the bourgeoisie itself, might deploy against the latter, the weapon by means of which the bourgeoisie grinds them down.

This is a great mistake. These ingenuous folk fail to appreciate the immense superiority afforded the bourgeoisie over the proletariat by monopoly of wealth, science and age-old practice, as well as the overt or covert but always active support of States and the whole organization of contemporary society. It would, thus, be a too unequal struggle for one to have any reasonable expectation of success in such conditions. Bourgeois weapons, being none other than unrestrained competition, the warfare of each against all, prosperity won at the cost of ruination to others, these weapons, these methods can serve only the bourgeoisie and would of necessity put paid to solidarity, the proletariat's only strength.

(...) We too seek cooperation: we are even convinced that cooperation in every branch of labor and science is going to be the prevailing form of social organization in the future. But at the same time, we know that it cannot prosper, develop fully and freely and encompass the whole of human industry, unless its foundation is equality, when all capital, all the instruments of labor, including the land, will have been handed back to labor as collective property.

So we look upon that requirement above all, and organization of the international power of the workers of every land as the main goal of our great association.

That accepted, far from being adversaries of cooperative undertakings at present, we regard them as in many respects necessities. At first, and this in our view for the moment is their chief advantage, they accustom the workers to organizing, conducting and running their affairs for themselves, without interference, whether from bourgeois capital or from bourgeois management.

It is to be wished that, when the time for social liquidation comes, every country and every locality should boast lots of cooperative associations which, if they are well-organized, and above all rooted in the principles of solidarity and collectivity and not in bourgeois exclusivism, will carry society from its current state through to a state of equality and justice without unduly great traumas.

But if they are to be able to perform that task, the International Association must stand over only those cooperative associations built upon its principles.

II. Worker Association and Collective Ownership[2]

The State, which has never had any task other than to regularize, sanction and — with the blessing of the Church — protect the rule of the privileged classes and exploitation of the people's labor for the benefit of the rich, must be abolished. Consequently, this requires that society be reorganized from the bottom up through the free formation and free federation of worker associations, industrial, agricultural, scientific and artistic alike, with the worker becoming at once artist and scientist, and artists and scientists also becoming manual workers, free associations and federations founded upon collective ownership of the land, capital, raw materials and the instruments of labor, which is to say, all large-scale property servicing production, leaving to private and hereditary possession only those items that are actually for personal use (. . .)

Notes to Bakunin on Worker Self-management

1. From the article "On Cooperation" in *L'Egalite* Geneva, September 21, 1869.
2. Taken from a letter of January 3, 1872 to Lodovico Nabruzzi. The title has been added by ourselves.

DIRECT ACTION AND LIBERTARIAN CONSTRUCTION FORESHADOWED

Dernier portrait de CÉSAR DE PAEPE

With Bakunin's disciples and successors James Guillaume, Cesar de Paepe, the Jurassians and Peter Kropotkin, we enter a phase of systematic exposition, of blueprints for an anarchist society.

Distilling and carrying on the work of its pioneers, anarchism now gets its second wind, so to speak. It strives to articulate in detail and with as much precision as possible the lineaments of the future organization of society, in the event of successful proletarian revolution: this is speculation in which Marx and his so-called "scientific socialist" school most often declined to indulge, haunted as they were by the obsession with putting distance between themselves and so-called "utopian" socialism.

Here, to be sure, the reader will find less literary panache and inspiration than in earlier writers. But those of us in the latter half of the 20th century who find ourselves with our backs to the wall of socialist achievement may delve into the social planning which appears below, not for the explosive eruption of ideas which we find in the speculations of the founding fathers, but for the, perhaps less stirring, solid and concrete matter. Having been largely put to good use by the French and Spanish anarcho-syndicalists of the first half of the 20th century, it may well, in this, the second half of that century, assist us in remaking the world.

For openers and by way of a foreword to what is to follow, here are some extracts from a report placed before the Basle congress of the First International on November 11, 1869, by the cabinetmaker Jean-Louis Pindy, delegate from the Paris Construction Workers' Trade Union. Pindy is the forerunner of several authors of social speculations featured in this volume. First, in fact, he outlines the prospects for dual federation — a federation of communes alongside a federation of trade unions with abolition of government and wage slavery as its corollary.

(. . .) We anticipate the workers organizing in two ways: first, a local grouping which allows the workers in the same area to liaise on a day to day basis: then, a linking up of various localities, fields, regions, etc.

The first mode: This grouping is in keeping with the political relations of the existing society which it replaces to advantage: thus far, it has been the approach adopted by the International Working Men's Association. Implicit in this state of affairs, where mutual societies are concerned, is federation of the local societies, helping one another out by means of money loans, organizing meetings to discuss social issues and, in concert, taking steps of mutual interest.

But as industry expands, another style of organization alongside the former becomes necessary. In every country, the workers sense that their interests are interlinked, and that they are being ground down one by one. For another thing, the future requires an organization that reaches beyond the precincts of the towns and, ignoring frontiers, establishes a sweeping reallocation of work around the globe: for this dual purpose, trades societies must be organized internationally: each trades body should maintain an exchange of correspondence and information within the country and with other countries (. . .) This sort of association becomes a factor for de-centralization, for no longer is it a matter of founding within each country a center common to all industries, but each one of them will be centered upon the locality where it is most developed: for example, in the case of France, while the colliers will be federated around Saint-Etienne, the silk workers will be federated around Lyon and the luxury industries around Paris. Once these two types of association have been established, labor organizes for present and future by doing away with wage slavery (. . .)

Association of the different corporations on the basis of town or country (. . .) leads to the commune of the future, just as the other mode of organization leads to the labor representation of the future. Government is replaced by the assembled councils of the trades bodies, and by a committee of their respective delegates, overseeing the labor relations which are to take the place of politics.

(. . .) We propose the following resolution:

"Congress is of the view that all workers should actively engage in the creation of strike funds in the various trades bodies.

As these societies take shape, it invites sections, federal groups and central councils to keep societies from the same corporation informed, so that they may proceed to formation of national associations of trades bodies.

Such federations are to have charge of gathering all information regarding their respective industry, overseeing the steps to be taken in concert, regulating strikes and working actively towards their success, until such time as wage slavery may be replaced by the federation of free producers."

The Debate between Cesar de Paepe (1842–1890) and Adhemar Schwitzguebel (1844–1895)

Cesar de Paepe by Miklos Molnar[1]

Without question, the most prominent of the Belgian delegates to the First International was Cesar de Paepe. Born in 1842 and dying in 1890, de Paepe was a witness to the grandeur and decline and then the resurgence of the Belgian labor movement. Son of a Belgian State official, de Paepe trained for a career in the law, but his father's sudden death compelled him to abandon his studies. He became a typographer under Desire Brismee and promptly the latter's colleague in the free thought movement. He joined the Societe des Solidaires (Fellowship Society) before joining with some new friends who included Voglet and Steens to launch the Le Peuple (People) society in 1861: this was a militant democratic association from which the Belgian section of the International Working Men's Association was to emerge four years later. From then on, up until his death, de Paepe, who had in the interim resumed his studies and qualified as a doctor, was in the forefront of the Belgian labor movement. We cannot rehearse every one of the phases of his busy life.[2] Let us note only that he was delegated to virtually every congress of the International where his addresses and speeches were among the most noteworthy.

Categorizing his ideology and political stance would be an even more daunting task than describing his life. Free-thinker, federalist, Proudhonist, collectivist, communist, anarchist, social democrat? What in fact was he? But what was the Belgian labor movement of his day, this "motley socialism, both mutualist and marxist, that goes under the name of collectivism" — to borrow Elie Halevy's felicitous but necessarily incomplete phrase?[3]

It strikes us that the two questions are really the same and that they cannot be answered on the sole basis of the classifications of "marxism," Proudhonist mutualism or anarchism in the Bakuninist sense. For de Paepe's thinking and that of his colleagues was, as well as being influenced by the great schools of thought emanating from Germany and France, tainted with the theories of Belgian thinkers like Potter and Colins,[4] and by workers' traditions going back to the days of the guilds. To be sure, de Paepe had periods when he was more or less Proudhonist and anarchist, but he also came under the sway of Marx's thought. But, reading his writings and speeches, we get the impression that, while inclining sometimes towards the one and sometimes towards the other tendency within the internationalist movement, de Paepe never wandered far from that Belgian collectivism which sought to reconcile the idea of collective ownership and the idea of freedom of the individual. In his questing after a system founded upon social justice and political liberty, de Paepe — or so we believe, at least — never made a definitive choice with regard to the proper means of bringing about this goal. The advocates of centralization often criticized his federalism, while anarchists took him to task for certain "statist" features of his system.

Likewise, de Paepe's attitude with regard to the choice between abstention or political activity was never categorical. Undecided at the time of the London Conference (September 1871), he turned "abstentionist" for a few years only to end up joining the Belgian socialist 'Youth' who prefaced the creation of the Belgian Workers' Party (POB) of 1885.

Let us note further that de Paepe's extremely conciliatory nature afforded him great suppleness when it came to taking a stand. A tolerant free spirit, he sought to pursue discussions through to a philosophical level which might facilitate an understanding which was not feasible in a climate of controversy.

Notes to Cesar de Paepe

1. From Miklos Molnar *Le Declin de la premiere Internationale* 1963.
2. See Louis Bertrand *Cesar de Paepe, sa vie, son oeuvre* Brussels, 1909. See also Bertrand's *Histoire de la democratie et du socialisme en Belgique depuis 1830* Brussels, 1906–1907, two vols. (note by Molnar).
3. In *Histoire du socialisme européen* Paris, 1948, p. 151, (note by Molnar).
4. The Baron Colin (1783–1859) in his chief works (*Le Pactes social* 1835, and *Socialisme rationnel* 1849) espoused an essentially collectivist socialism relying upon common ownership of the land. His chief disciple, Louis de Potter, published, among other things, a *Catéchisme social* in 1850.

On the Organization of Public Services in the Society of the Future[1] *by Cesar de Paepe*

Let us take as our starting point the present state of affairs, the public services as they currently are: then, let us strike from those services whichever of them a new social organization appears to make redundant; let us look at which public services the new requirements will necessitate, and those which, starting right now, are a palpably felt necessity: then let us ask to whom the performance of these various public services naturally and rationally falls. At which point, we are impelled to cast a glance over the overall economic trend, and ask ourselves if the thoroughgoing changes which that trend imposes or is going to impose upon certain industries, turn or are about to turn those industries into veritable public services: finally, we end by looking into how and in what manner public services in general ought to be performed in the future.

Management by Workers' Companies?

By whom ought the various public services to be organized and performed?

Here we find two great currents of thought, two downright antagonistic schools. As a general rule, one of these schools tends to abandon public services to the private enterprise of individuals or spontaneously formed companies, and thereby divests them, in a way, of their character as public services in order to turn them into private undertakings: so much for the laissez-faire school. The other, as a general rule, tends to place the public services under the direction of the State, the province (department or canton), or commune: this is the interventionist school. True, to begin with at any rate, the concession of the railways, mines, etc., to workers' companies would not display the same characteristic of runaway exploitation which has come to typify the financial concerns which presently hold the concession on these great public services. But let us not forget that the modern capitalist aristocracy too emerged from the third estate: let us not forget that, before they became what they are today, the great financial barons (or if not them, at least their fathers or grandfathers) were workers, but workers placed in a situation of privilege. Thanks to the unceasing improvements to mechanical agents, thanks to new industrial applications for the discoveries of science, thanks to reduction of running costs and the accumulation of capital which would follow from this expansion in mechanization and application of all sorts of scientific discoveries, it would not be long before these workers' companies, owners of enormously improved plant and enjoying a natural or artificial monopoly which society has left open to them, would dominate the whole economy, like their elder brothers, the finance companies.

Doubtless we will be told that concessions are granted only upon certain stipulations, and that the workers' companies, in accepting the concession, would be bound by contract. But the capitalists' companies to which the State has conceded collieries, railroad lines, etc., are bound by contract too: is that any impediment to their handing out fat dividends to their share-holders or plundering public assets as brazenly as you like? From the moment that the companies to which you grant any monopoly become owners of their work plant, where is the contract that is going to prevent them from improving that plant, reducing overheads, not replacing staff who die, and finally amassing capital — in short, from becoming a new privileged class? At best we should, in those circumstances, have the grim pleasure of substituting a worker aristocracy for a bourgeois aristocracy, even as our forebears substituted a bourgeois aristocracy for the old high-born aristocracy.

We will be told that the plant need not necessarily be the property of the company; that it can be supplied to the company by the greater social collective, and remain the inalienable property of the latter; whereupon the improvements resulting from the progress of civilization would bring benefit to the society as a whole: we grant that, but then these companies would no longer really be concessionary companies, but would be associate entrepreneurs simply bound to perform certain public services on behalf of society, as represented by the commune, province, canton or State, etc.

State Management?

Then again, among those who favor the transfer of all public services, or at any rate the most important of them, into the hands of public agencies and notably of the State, a fair number support that arrangement only on condition that the State be republican and democratically constituted, founded upon direct legislation or at least upon universal suffrage, and that it respect all political liberties: they would not favor it under a despotic or even merely monarchist regime. Not without reason, and for purely political reasons, they are afraid to bolster despotism's power even further, and as a result, they seek, momentarily, to leave completely to private industry a whole range of public services, such as education, insurance, the railroads, etc., which, from the economic point of view would better be entrusted to State care.

(. . .) Starting from the notion of the State as communicated to us by the history of every country, which is to say, from the despotic State, from the State which has everywhere to date been nothing more than the organized domination of a single family, huge caste or class over the multitude which is reduced to a state of legal and economic slavery, a great number of socialists have cried out: War on the State! They do not want to hear talk about the State in any form, no matter how interpreted. They declare very plainly that they seek the absolute destruction of the State, of all States: and the more logical among them, perceiving rightly that the commune is, in the final analysis, merely a mini-State, a State with a tinier territory, whose functions are performed on a smaller scale than ordinary States, declare that they want no more to do with the commune State than with the State proper. Upon their standard they have daubed the device: An-archy! Not "anarchy" in the sense of disorder, since on the contrary they believe in the possibility of arriving at true order through spontaneous organization of economic forces, but An-archy, in the sense in which Proudhon intended it, that is, absence of power, absence of authority, and in their minds, in the sense of abolition of the State, the terms authority and power being in their view absolute synonyms for the word State.

But alongside this traditional historical notion of the State, which, in fact, has thus far never been anything other than authority, power, and, further, despotism, (and the worst of despotisms at that, since it has always been exercised by an idle minority over the toiling majority), these socialists have taken account of a true fact and one that will become increasingly true, a fact that is one of the greatest economic phenomena of modern times: they have seen, in the chief branches of modern production, large industry increasingly replacing small-scale industry, centralization of capital, more and more massive application of collective effort and division of labor, the incessant introduction of mighty steam-driven machinery powering a host of tools and machines, tools hitherto isolated, now requiring that huge masses of workers be gathered into enormous factories, and that all of this cannot but add day by day to the domain of big industry. They have seen that in this great modern production, the isolated worker or artisan gives way to collective labor force, to workers' collectives; they have seen that these workers' collectives, faced with the allied capitalists whose interests are diametrically and openly opposed to their own, had of necessity to form themselves into resistance groups, into trades unions, and indeed implicate the workers of small industries in this movement: that association by trades must spread, and their conclusion is that such spontaneous organization of the working class had to furnish the basis for a new social grouping not unlike the spontaneous banding together into bourgeois communes in the Middle Ages: community of interests inevitably impelling trades bodies to spread in order to support one another, out of this grows a whole range of federations — at first local, then regional, then international. What is more, not content with these theoretical observations, they have embarked upon practice: like the English workers, they have founded trade unions, they have federated with one another, and they have, quite rightly, sought to found the International Association upon this federative economic basis. Thus they have embraced this grouping of workers' bodies which is rooted in the depths of modern economic life as a counter to the more or less artificial and obsolete grouping into purely political Communes and States, and predicted the imminent demise of these latter.

So far so good. But we wonder whether the workers' bodies, the associated trades bodies of the same locality, whether this Commune of proletarians, in short, on the day that it replaces today's official Commune or bourgeois Commune, will not act just like the latter vis-a-vis certain public services whose survival is essential to the life of society? We wonder whether, in the new Commune, there will be no need for security, a civil state, maintenance of roads and public squares, street lighting, drinking water in the houses, sewer maintenance, and a whole host of public services that we listed at the start of this work? Would there not be a need for workers' groups, the Commune's trades bodies, to select from among their number delegates to each of the public services, delegates charged with operating these various services, unless these groups prefer instead to act as a bloc in appointing a delegation to share management of these various services? In either instance, does that not saddle us with a local public service administration, a communal administration?

But all public services cannot be handled by a purely local administration, since many of them, and the most important of them at that, are by their very natures fated to operate over a territory larger than that of the Commune: is one Commune about to run the railways, maintain the highways, dam the rivers, channel the streams, see to delivery of mail and the despatching of telegrams to other localities, etc.? Obviously not! So Communes have to come to some arrangement, organize themselves into a Federation of Communes and choose a delegation to look after public services. Whether that delegation be appointed with a general remit to run all great regional public services, or with a special remit applicable to a particular service, matters not: in any event these delegates have to be in direct and ongoing contact with one another, so they still represent a regional or national public administration, the name having no bearing upon the thing. To start with, is it not more than likely that, for want of bases other than traditions and language, theses regions or nations would broadly correspond to the present nationalities, or, at least, to the chief great divisions of those nationalities, say, in the case of Great Britain, England, Scotland, Wales and Ireland? or, in the case of Switzerland, germanophone Switzerland and francophone Switzerland? or, in the Belgian case, Wallonie and Flanders (unless the latter, on account of especial affinities, linguistic, let us say, should rejoin Holland)?

And what is that regional or national Federation of communes going to be, in essence, other than a State? Yes, a State, for we should call things by their name. Except that this will be a federative State, a State formed from the bottom up. A state having at bottom, at its origins, an economic association, the grouping of trades bodies making up the Commune, and, in addition, having, no doubt, alongside its great public services administration directly emanating from the federated Communes, a Labor Chamber emanating directly from the general unions (in England they call them *amalgamated unions*) made up of local unions from the same trade federated at regional level.

"An An-Archic State"

The State is a machine; it is the instrument of the great public services. Like any other machine, this one too is essential for large-scale modern production and for substantial traffic in the products resulting from the same: like any other machine, the latter too has been murderous for the workers and has thus far always worked for the exclusive benefit of privileged classes. If there is to be an end of that, the workers must take over that machine. But in taking it over, let us check whether the State machine does not stand in need of important modifications so that it cannot injure anyone: let us check whether certain gears which bourgeois exploitation had overloaded do not need removing and others, which bourgeois carelessness had neglected, added: let us see indeed if it does not need to be established upon wholly new foundations. With those reservations, we can say: workers, the machine belongs to us, the State belongs to us.

Not that the word an-archy frightens us. On the contrary, the horror which an-archy strikes into the bourgeois class (a horror which seems to us to be a lot more in vogue among them than felt by the workers) means that it brings a smile to our lips and that we should be very sorry to drop the word. With the permission of our anarchist friends, therefore, we will not exactly reject the word, although strictly speaking it may not mean the same thing to us as it does to them. After all, the State, as we think of it and as we wish it to be, is not exactly an authority, a governmental system, something imposed upon the people by force or by guile, in short, an "*archy*," to use the Greek term. Is there anything very authoritarian about expressions like State postal service, State railway, State sponsored clearance of scrubland, etc.? We have no difficulty conceiving of a non-authoritarian State (we were going to say an an-archic State, but we desisted, because many of our readers would have regarded juxtaposition of those two terms as some sort of swearword). In fact, real authority certainly does not consist of the act of carrying out decisions taken, or implementing laws passed, or running public services in accordance with the law, but rather of the act of laying down and imposing law. Now, legislation may very well not be the handiwork of the State and may lie outside of its remit, either because laws are passed directly in the Communes or at some other level, or, because of the rounded education given to all and the single-mindedness resulting from that, society's laws one day become so self-evident to the spirit that they are no more in need of being passed than are the laws of astronomy, physics or chemistry.

And so, to the Commune fall the merely local and communal public services under the purview of the local administration appointed by the trades bodies of the area and operating under the supervision of all local inhabitants. To the State fall the more widespread regional or national public services, under the management of a regional administration appointed by the Federation of Communes and operating under the gaze of the regional Chamber of Labor. Is that all? No; there are and increasingly there will be public services which, by their very nature, are international or inter-regional (the actual names matter very little here). To cater for these there will have to be an international, and, we should say, voluntary federation that is universal, humanitarian or planetary, while conceding that, given the backwardness of the State among certain peoples, it will take quite some time before the reality can live up to these epithets. We need not indicate how this, the supreme constitution of humanity, would also need one or more agencies to run its universal public services: it would doubtless operate on the same basis as the ones we have mentioned with regard to the constitution of the State, and it too would doubtless have its international chamber of trades, made up of the mandataries of the international labor federations, some of which are even now starting to take shape at the instigation of the English trade unions.

Communism and "Anarchy"

But, we will, perhaps, be told (. . .) shouldn't (. . .) all branches of production be regarded as destined to be organized as public services? Can you not see that that would mean a descent into the most frightful communism!?

It is an astonishing thing, the power to frighten which lurks in certain words, when the idea which they articulate roams far and wide and is perfectly acceptable as long it is dressed up under some other name. This is the case with the word *an-archy*, which raises the hackles of our bourgeois, whereas the idea of indefinite whittling away of governmental functions and ultimately the abolition of government is the last word among the laissez-faire economists favored by these brave bourgeois! And it is the case with the idea of the State and State intervention in industrial affairs, where another type of person is concerned, who lumps together the official economists and the anti-State socialists, along with a central administration: the State, in short, is something which could very well have been managed without until the recent advent of large-scale modern production, but which has become and is increasingly becoming a social necessity in the face of large-scale output and large-scale traffic, as the usual organ of economic centralization, the usual manager of large industries which supply the raw materials for production and the great transport fleets to carry products to the consumer. So necessary is it that, without such economic centralization in the State's hands, economic forces would centralize anyhow in the hands of mighty companies which are out and out oligarchical States. The term communism has had the singular distinction of having been repudiated by socialists as a calumny, having been envisaged by economists as the last word in utopias, and in the bourgeoisie's eyes it appears as a theory consecrating ongoing theft and promiscuity, in short, the worst of blights.

As for ourselves, who are not frightened by the word "State," which some find so scary, any more than we are frightened by the word "an-archy" which others finds so horrifying, why should we take fright at the word "communism"? Even supposing that this word has no clearly defined meaning and does not convey a perfectly rational idea, it ought to be less of a fright to us than any other word: for communism, as envisioned in the past, has always been the form, sentimental or mystical maybe, but the vigorous and radical form to which the disinherited classes and their agitators, from Spartacus to Babeuf, have had recourse in order to articulate their age-old claims, and earn a hearing for their unceasing protests against misery and social iniquity. But the word communism also has a more precise meaning, in that it represents a genuinely scientific idea. Communism means common ownership, public ownership, social ownership.

Bourgeois State and Worker State

(. . .) We have seen that the State shoots us down, passes sentence upon us, imprisons us and shoots us once again, and we wish to divest the State of its judges, its jailers and its fusiliers. With our very own eyes we have seen that the State, even the present, bourgeois State, whenever it sought to produce on its own account instead of leaving production to companies of capitalists who have no aim other than to enrich themselves, produced a higher quality of product at cheaper cost than those companies: the State railways in Belgium and the postal service and the construction of seaports are all testimony to that. But what we have not seen, and what we or our offspring will see, is the workers' State, the State based on the banding together of free workers' Communes, assuming control once and for all of every large-scale social undertaking (. . .)

But what do we care for the anathemas pronounced against us from the official chairs of orthodox political economy?(. . .) What touches us a lot more closely is the instinctive repugnance felt towards any function entrusted to the State, any State intervention, by socialists who march side by side with us on every other score: between them and us, we believe, there is quite simply a great misunderstanding: perhaps the word State is the only point separating us from them: were that the case, we should willingly set the word aside, while declaring that we are retaining and even extending the thing, albeit under the more agreeable cover of some other designation: public administration, delegation from the federated Communes, etc.

But besides those who take us to task over the role we credit to the State, there are also those who will repudiate the role we attribute to the Commune. For Jacobins of every hue, the State is the great Everything, the god Pan, in which everyone has to live and move. For them, the State is not only a particular organ doubtless enjoying great importance and a lofty destiny, but is the whole body of society. These people cannot understand that one can enter life without a ticket of admission from the State, or that one can quit this world without a State passport: nor will they forgive us for having stripped the State of all its luster, all its splendor, its gleaming raiment, its splendid red and black robes, in order to dress it up in a miner's shirt or engine driver's jerkin: no more generals of the Republic, no more procurators of the Republic! But yet again, is this too the abomination of desolation?

Can you not see that making the Commune the lynch-pin of social organization is ridiculous? The Commune is merely a territorial sub-division of the department, just as the latter is a mere subdivision of the State: it is for the latter to appoint prefect and mayor, governor and burgermeister. Such is the will of the Republic, one and indivisible!

As for your autonomous Commune which, instead of being content to receive life from the State, claims instead that the State should emanate from it! As for your social Commune which seeks to turn the State into a mechanism of socialism, that is only an old incendiary whose exploits are known to us and whom we have butchered thrice already to cries of *Vive la Republique!* — in '93 with the guillotine, in June 1848 by fusillade, in May 1871 with grapeshot! Very well then, sirs, you great citizens of the Mountain! We concede that your thunderbolts may be a touch more terrible than those of your momentary allies, the high priests of the orthodox economic sect who make do with affording your exploits the approval of their science: in the name of freedom of labor, let the chassepot do its work, let the grapeshot do its work and let bullets puncture the flanks of the proletarian. . . . But, sirs, it is precisely because we are no longer willing to let ourselves be condemned, imprisoned, mown down or guillotined that we want no more of your judges, your henchmen and your executioners.

Instead of the Jacobin notion of the all-powerful State, we offer the idea of the liberated Commune, itself appointing all its administrators, with no exceptions: shifting for itself in respect of laws, justice and police. The liberal conception of the gendarme-State we counter with the notion of the State disarmed, but charged with educating the young and centralizing the great joint undertakings. The Commune becomes essentially the organ of political functions or what are described as such: law, justice, security, the guaranteeing of contracts, the protection of the incapable, civic society, but at the same time it is the organ of all local public services. The State in essence becomes the organ of scientific unity and of the great joint undertakings necessary to society.

Note to On the Organization of Public Services

1. Taken from Cesar de Paepe *De l'organisation des services publics dans la societe future* 1874, a report read to the Brussels congress of the (so-called "anti-authoritarian") International. The subtitles have been added by us.

The Question of Public Services Before the International Adhémar Schwitzguébel's reply to Cesar de Paepe.[1]

Adhémar Schwitzguébel (1844–1895), an ornamental engraver from the Swiss Jura and friend of James Guillaume, was one of the most active militants of the International's Jura Federation. In 1908 in Paris, James Guillaume published *Quelques écrits* by Schwitzguébel, from which the following text has been lifted. From a strictly anarchist viewpoint, it replies to Cesar de Paepe's report.

(...) In the light of what has been said already regarding the public services, it is manifest that two great schools of thought concerning reorganization of society are going to share the socialist world between them: the one inclines towards the workers' State, the other towards the Federation of communes.

Some are of the persuasion that, at the bottom of this great debate, it is simply a question of differing expressions of the same idea. But discussions regarding public services cannot leave any doubts on that score: we are dealing with two quite different things. That is what we shall strive to demonstrate. We shall examine the public services question from the viewpoint of the workers' State and from the viewpoint of the Federation of communes, and we shall conclude by setting it in the context of history and of the social Revolution.

The "Workers' State" Resembles the Present State

What is the idea underpinning modern States and by invoking which needs do supporters of the State justify its existence? The fact is that in all dealings between people, there are purely private dealings, but there are also essential relations of concern to one and all: hence the necessity for a public order, by means of which normal pursuit of public and general dealings between men can be guaranteed. Ponder well the Brussels memorandum, and you will find that the notion of the workers' State, by which it is informed, is, fundamentally, absolutely analogous with that of the current State.

Here come the objections: reorganized, directed and administered by the working classes, the State will have lost the oppressive, exploitative nature which it currently displays in the bourgeoisie's hands: instead of the political, judicial, police and military organization which it is at present, it is to be an economic agency, regulator of public services organized in accordance with social needs and the appliance of the sciences.

But let us take stock of the functioning of such a State. Lawful political action or the social Revolution have placed the running of the Commune and State in working class hands. What the laboring classes seek — emancipation of labor from all rule and all exploitation by capital — they can effect. The instrument of labor must become collective property, production must be organized, intercourse proceed, trade assist intercourse, and the present ignorance must be replaced by scientific and humane science and education: the existence of individuals and of society must be assured by hygienic conditions; public security must take the place of the current antagonism, the criminal interplay of hateful passions and brutal rivalries. The proletariat, having become dictator through the State, ordains collective ownership and organizes this for the benefit either of the Commune or of the State; it lays down the conditions upon use of the instruments of labor, in order to safeguard the interests of production, those of the producer groups, those of the Communes and of the State: then it prescribes the operation of exchange of produce, orchestrating and developing the means of intercourse: devises a program for training and education of the young, entrusting its implementation either to the Commune or to the State; it establishes a communal and general health service: and takes whatever steps may be necessary to guarantee public security in the Communes and in the State.

Thus, everything connected with social organization, the proletariat should first distinguish between what falls within the realm of private initiative and what falls within the realm of public initiative, what is private service and what is public service, what falls within the remit of the Commune and what behooves the State. Precisely as is standard practice today.

This task of distinguishing and disentangling the private from the public, of organizing everything public, everything falling under the remit of the Commune and the State, cannot be handled by the proletariat directly as a body. Its opinion, its general will is broken down and analyzed, and to that end, they have to be embodied by representatives who will take to the floor of parliament to put the case for their constituents. As is the practice today.

The "Workers' State' is No Solution

How will these workers' parliaments be constituted? By no other method than the famed universal suffrage. So there will still be a minority to whom the majority will lay down the law, or vice versa; for, given that the State is acknowledged as a necessary safeguard for public interests, the State's law will be binding upon everyone, and any who seek to evade it are to be treated as criminals. Here we find this workers' State, which was to have been organized to serve society's economic interests, rushing headlong into legislation, jurisdiction, policing, the army, formal schooling and the established church. The moment there is State law on the one hand, and on the other a diversity of interests to be satisfied, it is inevitable that there should be a majority or minority hostile to that law. If the State does not have the power to see to implementation of that law, it will not be observed and the action of the State will be scorned and nullified. So reason of State requires formation of a power with the capacity to eradicate any attempted rebellion against the State's constitution and laws. A whole judiciary to punish trespass against the basis, the order, the laws of the State: a police to oversee observance of the laws; an army to crush rebellion should any erupt, and to protect the State against trespass by other States — such are the necessary consequences of the underlying principle of the existence of the State.

If these public services, as they have hitherto been termed, are essential to the material existence of the State, formal schooling and the established Church are just as essential to its moral existence. The intellect has to accept such absolute domination by the State as the most natural thing in the world: so the whole of public education, by school and Church, is founded upon absolute respect for anything having to do with the State. And in the workers' State, which is credited with the essential characteristic of acting as economic regulator, the whole organization of property, production, exchange and intercourse will, in the hands of the majority or the minority which is to run things, be a weapon of domination every whit as powerful as the political, judicial, police and military functions performed by the bourgeois in power today. More so than the bourgeois, the workers, as masters of the State, will show no mercy to any trespass against their State, because they will believe that they have attained the ultimate ideal.

Thus, it does not seem to us that, the matter of social reorganization, the workers' State represents a solution consonant with the interests of humanity; the latter would not know emancipation, because the instrument of labor, the organization of labor, and certain public services would fall within the remit of the State or of the Commune; each individual would assuredly have greater guarantees of equitable allocation of the fruits of production, the blessings of improved training and education, the delights of social life than under the present state of affairs, but complete autonomy of the person and of the group would not be forthcoming, and if man is to know emancipation, he must be emancipated as worker and as individual.

(. . .) To broach the question of social reorganization in the terms of the formula offered for the consideration of the Brussels Congress, is, inevitably, to distract minds from the real terms of the question, and to make of the workers' State a foregone conclusion.

Two New Principles: Collectivism and Federalism

(. . .) Two principles, of immeasurable historical import, have emerged from the debates and internal squabbling which caused upset within our Association: the principle of collective ownership, as the economic basis of the new organization of society, and the principle of autonomy and federation, as the basis upon which human individuals and collectivities are banded together. To discover what the new organization of society might be, why not, instead of deliberating upon the necessary consequences of implementation of the two forenamed principles, muse upon what might be private service and what might become public service, and by whom and in what manner such public services might be performed? Resorting to rational argument, one might have been forced to say: we are confronted by a need to turn individual ownership into collective ownership: which is the most practical way of bringing about this change? It is the workers assuming direct control of the instruments of labor, which they employ to the advantage of the bourgeois and which they ought henceforth to turn to their own advantage. That revolutionary measure, practically superior to all decrees from dictatorial assemblies which might feel themselves qualified to direct the Revolution or the wholesale emancipation of the working classes: and spontaneous action of the masses of the populace, whence alone this may spring, is, right from the first acts of the Revolution, the practical assertion of the principle of autonomy and federation which becomes the basis of all social combination. Along with the bourgeoisie's economic privileges, all State institutions by means of which the bourgeoisie sustains its privileges will have foundered in that revolutionary storm.

Now let us examine the implications of such a Revolution for the reorganization of society. In any locality, the various trades bodies are masters of the situation: in such and such an industry, the implements employed are of minimal value: in another, they are of considerable value and a wider usefulness: if the group of producers employed in that industry are to be proprietors of the implements used, ownership of them may lead to a monopoly for one group of workers, to the detriment of other groups. The revolutionary necessities which have driven laboring groups into concerted action also commend to them federation agreements by means of which they mutually guarantee the gains of the Revolution: of necessity, these agreements will be communal, regional and international, and will enshrine sufficient assurances that no group may arrogate the benefits of the Revolution to itself alone. Thus, it seems to us that collective ownership ought to be at first communal, then regional, even international, according to the more or less general development and importance of such and such a branch of human activity, such and such a natural resource, such and such instruments of labor built up by preceding labor.

As to the constitution of groups of producers, the spontaneity of the revolutionary interests to which they owe their gestation is to be the starting point for their organization, and for the spread of their organization, with an eye to reorganizing society. Banded together freely for revolutionary action, the workers will stick to such free association when it comes to organization of production, exchange, commerce, training and education, health, and security: and just as, in revolutionary strife, the hostile attitude of one individual within such and such a group, of one group within such and such a commune, one commune within a region, one region in an international context, has failed to stall the onward progress of Revolution, so isolation, when it comes to expansion of the gains of the Revolution, will not be capable of halting the onward progress of the toiling masses operating without let or hindrance.

The State Replaced by the Federation of Communes

Let careful note be taken of the essential difference between the workers' State and the Federation of Communes. The State determines what constitutes public service and how that public service is to be organized: there we have human activity regimented. In the Federation of Communes, today the shoe mender works at home, in one room: tomorrow, thanks to the appliance of some discovery, shoe production can be multiplied a hundred-fold and simplified at the same time: shoe-menders will therefore band together, federate with one another and set up their workshops, their manufactories and thereby involve themselves in orchestrated activity. The same is true of every branch of human activity: that which is restricted organizes in a restricted way; that which is comprehensive, organizes in a comprehensive way, at the levels of group, commune and federation alike. This is experience, day to day practice placed in the service of human liberty and human activity.

In the context of such organization, what becomes of the public services of the present State, its legislation, its jurisdiction, its police, its army, its official schooling and official Church? The free contract replaces law: if there are disputes, these are judged by arbitration panels within the groups where the disputes originate: and as far as repressive measures are concerned, these now have no reason to exist in a society founded upon free organization — such and such a group's organization and action being incapable of harming me in any way, if there is parity of esteem for the organization and action of the group of which I am a member, in that such organization and action is hard to disentangle from the interests of emancipated humanity, once the Social Revolution has swept away all of the practical implications of bourgeois-ism. A security service may well still have a temporary usefulness but it cannot survive as an institution with the general, indispensable, irksome and oppressive remit which it enjoys under the present arrangement.

The Great Currents of the Social Revolution

There is no denying that, in terms of practicalities, the matter will be resolved according to the measure of socialist development in the laboring masses in each country, and in accordance also with the more or less decisive first steps of the Social Revolution. Today only the ignorant and people of bad faith dare argue that solution of the social question can be sought by means other than Revolution. We are pleased to record that our friends from Germany, in spite of the lawful character of their current socialist agitation, are in agreement with us upon this point. But the Revolution may come to pass in two ways: it may have as its immediate objective and also as the basis for its action, the working classes' conquest of political power within the State as it stands and conversion of that bourgeois State into a workers' State: then again, it may have as its immediate objective and as the basis of its action, destruction of every State and spontaneous, federative combination of all of the proletariat's revolutionary forces. While revolutionary action can vary from country to country, it is also liable to variation in the communes of the same country: here the Commune retains an authoritarian, governmental character, an aspect even of bourgeois-ism: elsewhere, there will be a clean sweep. If due account is taken of the current circumstances of the peoples of the different civilized States, and of the varying views still current on such matters, it will be understood that it is inevitable that the Revolution will be subject to extreme variation. Doubtless we shall see every socialist theory, communism, collectivism and mutualism, being implemented to a more or less restricted or comprehensive extent, according to whatever great currents the Revolution is to follow.

How could it be otherwise when today we see a great country like Germany clinging to the notion of the workers' State, and others, like Italy and Spain, clinging to the notion of a Federation of Communes? This diversity of revolutionary tendencies has given the bourgeoisie grounds for accusing socialism of impotence. With a modicum of foresight, however, it is easy to appreciate that, while there may be differences regarding the terms of a new organization of society, the working classes are more and more united on working to bring down the bourgeois edifice. And such difference cannot be a source of impotence: rather, it is a source of strength, in this sense — that workers' groups, implementing their own views and respecting the views of other groups, will, all of them, have all the more interest in the Revolution's succeeding.

In what respect will it halt the proletariat's revolutionary march, if the Germans make a reality of the workers' State, while the Italians, Spaniards and French make a reality of the Federation of Communes? And indeed if, in France, certain communes hold on to individual ownership while collective ownership prevails elsewhere?

The Federation of Communes Will Carry the Day

These reservations aside, it is nonetheless our firm belief that the organization best suited to serving the interests of humanity will eventually prevail everywhere, and that the first stirrings of revolution will prove crucial for subsequent development of the phases of the Revolution. We would even take this conviction so far as to declare that it is the Federation of Communes that will emerge from the Social Revolution with the greatest power.

This Federation of Communes has been taken to task for being an obstacle to achievement of a broad agreement, a complete union of the workers, and for not offering the same potential for action as a State, when it comes to revolutionary action.

But how are the workers' groups, freely federated within the International, to practice solidarity, accommodate one another and reach agreement? The fact is that the economic situation itself compels them to practice solidarity. What form will that take, once their action is no longer opposed by all of the hindrances the current order has to offer?

How comes it that the International grows in potential for action as long as it is a Federation, while it comes apart as soon as its General Council seeks to turn it into a State? It is because workers have a hatred of authority, and want to be free, and will only achieve that through practice of broad, comprehensive liberty.

Yes, our Association is proof of the promise of the principle of autonomy and free federation: and it is through implementation of that principle that humanity will be able to stride towards fresh conquests in order to guarantee moral and material well-being to all.

Note to The Question of Public Services

1. Report presented to the Jura congress held in Vevey, on August 1 and 2, 1875, by the Courtelary district Engravers' and Chequerworkers' Section. (All the subtitles have been added by us).

JAMES GUILLAUME (1844–1916)

JAMES GUILLAUME BY FRITZ BRUPBACHER[1]

James Guillaume was born on February 16, 1844, in London. His father, a Swiss from Neuchâtel, was a naturalized Englishman: his mother was French. His father's family lived in Fleurier in the Val-de-Travers. There, around 1815, his grandfather had founded a clock-making firm with a branch in London. He was a republican and had had to flee to the canton of Vaud in the wake of the disturbances in 1831. James Guillaume's father arrived in London at the age of twenty, a skilled clock-maker even by that date, to replace his uncle as branch manager. He was not an ordinary man and culture held rather more fascination for him than the watch business. Not content with mastering German and Spanish during his leisure hours, he also studied the natural sciences, in which he had an especial interest, as well as philosophy. In 1843, he married a young and highly cultivated woman who came from a family of musicians.

In 1848, after a Republic was proclaimed in Neuchâtel, James Guillaume's father, himself an enthusiastic republican, returned to Switzerland. He was soon appointed a judge, then prefect of the Val-de-Travers, and from then on concentrated exclusively upon public life. Elected State Councilor in 1853, he was returned again and again over a period of thirty five years.

James Guillaume was four years old then when he arrived in Switzerland. At the age of nine-and-a-half years, he entered grammar school, at the age of sixteen years, he matriculated into what is today called the academy, and stayed there until 1862. A somewhat undisciplined student, he was often in hot water with the school authorities who were royalist and religious. But whereas during the year he had blotted his copybook with his willful attitudes, he made up the lost ground in the examinations, always coming first. The important thing about his school career is not what he did in class — he did not listen to his teachers, having no confidence in them — but that he was determined to learn on his own and what was going on inside his head. He read every volume in his father's library, being enthused by the Ancient world, the French Revolution, philosophy and especially Spinoza and poetry ranging from Homer and Shakespeare through to Goethe and Byron, and was stirred by Rabelais, Moliere and Voltaire.

He was also much occupied by the natural sciences, astronomy, geology and entomology. He felt himself to be a poet and musician: he penned thousands of lyric verses, wrote plays and novels, and started work on an opera and an oratorio. Politics was another interest. In Neuchâtel the strife between republican and royalist was bitter. From that time on, Guillaume was fascinated by the history of the Revolution, and his heroes were drawn from among the Montagnards: Marat (himself a native of Neuchâtel), Robespierre and Saint-Just.

In September 1862, Guillaume traveled up to Zurich; he was to read philosophy, complete his education, and train as a teacher of Classics. He enrolled at the philological and pedagogical institute run by Köchly. Köchly and the aesthetician Vischer were the only teachers he ever had whom the young anti-authoritarian took seriously, and how! In Zurich, Guillaume familiarized himself with the German mind, its poets and philosophers. He also immersed himself in Greek literature. It was in Zurich that he began a translation of novelist Gottfried Keller's *The Folk from Sedlwyla*. Though Swiss, Keller was a superb writer of German. Guillaume was the first person ever to render Keller into French and his book appeared in 1864. As yet, socialism was virtually non-existent as far as he was concerned. When a slightly younger colleague confided that he had an enthusiastic admiration for Proudhon, Guillaume's reply was that Proudhon was a sophist.

In the spring of 1864, Guillaume was obliged to return to Neuchâtel. Much to his regret, he had to abandon his plans to make a study visit to Paris. As the year ended, he sat the examination for a teaching position in a trades schools and was posted to the Collège de Locle. (. . .) Bear in mind that he was not yet a socialist and that his life thus far had been spent amid studies and books. Now here he was transplanted into the world of laboring folk. He observed and his heart rebelled and his mind was incensed. He had a passion for truth, which ignited his passion for justice. He was struck by the futility of his classical education, and shrugged his shoulders as his mind wandered to his old plans for the future. Though a poet, he abjured song, as he now gave ear to the cries of living poetry. A historian, he wondered whether the Revolution was over, or indeed whether it had yet begun. To make his life worth the living, he meant to devote it to accessible education for the populace: for a start, he laid on evening classes for apprentices. He carried on reading all sorts of writers: Feuerbach, Darwin, Fourier, Louis Blanc, Proudhon. And, little by little, new ideas took shape inside his head. Erudite and philosophical, he had hitherto found equality conceivable only as Robespierre and Louis Blanc had conceived of it: since man had a soul, it followed that all souls were equal. But how was equality to be squared with Darwinism, with descent from animals, with the struggle for survival? And what became of morality if there was no free will? He was tortured by such questions for a long time: when, in the end, he bowed to negation of metaphysical free will, it left him calm and with solid ground underfoot.

His thinking lacked focus, however; and the socialist had not yet taken shape in the heart of the teacher and metaphysician. The French cooperative movement spilled over into Switzerland, and it was this that was to ignite the interest of the evening classes. In 1865, a section of the International was set up in La Chaux-de-Fonds: a people which had begun to help itself deserved a helping hand. It only remained for him to discover its living embodiment, commitment and patience, life and death sacrifice: such was the image which Guillaume admired and cherished in Constant Meuron, veteran of the Neuchâtel riots, a revolutionary and republican who had never known anything other than revolution and republic.

From then on, Guillaume was molded; he was eager to act and knew why to act. As to the how, he still dithered a little. He thought of becoming a village schoolmaster so as to get closer to the people; then of becoming a compositor, just as Constant de Meuron had turned his hand to the guilloche craft. He was talked out of both ideas after it was shown him that if he stepped down a class he would lose virtually all of the useful influence he might wield.

In the autumn of 1866, Constant Meuron and James Guillaume founded the Le Locle section of the International and Guillaume traveled to the Geneva Congress.

Thus far he had been committed to general education of the workers most often by means of history lectures (which later found their way into print) but also by means of dabbling in organizing cooperative credit and consumer cooperatives. He also played an active part in the political and parliamentary movement, but, like most of the Jura's Internationalists, he soon came to the conclusion that the working class had nothing to gain from that. The International's Congress in Lausanne and the Congress in Geneva of the League of Peace and Freedom, both held in 1867, modified Guillaume's thinking profoundly; in fact it was there that he came into contact with revolutionaries from all over Europe and there that he was converted to universal social revolution.

It was at this stage in his development that he made Bakunin's acquaintance in 1869 at the launching of the francophone Federation Romande. Their outlooks were quite compatible: the dream of a Stateless society where there would be no more government or constitution, where all men might be free and equal was something which had evolved from inside Guillaume and from external experience, before he ever met Bakunin. Yet, for each one of them, making the acquaintance of the other was a real event:

Guillaume wrote — "To Bakunin, I owe this, morally speaking: previously, I was a Stoicist, preoccupied with the moral development of my personality, straining to live my life in accordance with an ideal: under Bakunin's influence, I abjured that personal, individual quest and I concluded that it was better that the straining towards moral perfection should give way to something more humane, more social: renunciation of purely individual action, and a resolve to commit myself to collective action, looking to the collective consciousness of men acting in close concert in order to toil at a common undertaking of propaganda and revolution for the basis and guarantee of morality."

That he threw himself into this, we know. From 1866 to 1878, Guillaume lived only for the International. In 1868 he married Elise Golay. Let us respectfully salute the memory of the valiant young girl who placed her hand in that of the agitator and victim of persecution. From 1869 on, in fact, Guillaume was obliged to give up his teaching post in Le Locle, having clashed with the education authorities over his revolutionary activity. He became a compositor and stuck at that until 1872. To tell his story between 1866 and 1878 is to rehearse the story of the International: that is why his memoirs do just that. He was one of the most enthusiastic orators of that left, formed at the Congress of Basle, and which took shape as the authoritarians and anti-authoritarians parted company at the famous Congress in The Hague. When it comes to the development of Guillaume's ideas, then, setting on one side his personal capabilities both intellectual and moral, one cannot overstate the importance of the happiness he derived from living and operating among a working class whose spiritual activity was out of the ordinary. It is hard to distinguish what Guillaume gave his comrades from what he received from them. The Jura militants of that day truly were welded into one huge confession: they felt in common, thought in common and operated in common. They had no leaders and no led: only men of greater or lesser resolution and initiative, naturally gifted to a greater or lesser extent. But it would be a vain undertaking to try to establish where the work of one begins and where the work of another ends.

In this way, Guillaume became the intellectual emanation of a collective (. . .) There, in the Jura, the watch-makers and Guillaume together produced ideas which a later generation would rediscover and rename as revolutionary syndicalism.

From 1870 onwards, one can discern a clear opposition in western Switzerland between the two tendencies today described as social democratic and revolutionary syndicalist. The first falling-out came in 1870, at the Congress of the Fédération Romande in La Chauxde-Fonds: what was to occur on a larger scale in 1912 was seen there in microcosm. Guillaume was then editor of the organ of the "collectivists" (revolutionary syndicalists), *La Solidarité*, which survived until after the Commune and the crisis which then assailed the Jurassians. Later he was editor of the *Bulletin*, which replaced *La Solidarité*.

After the slaughter of the Commune, the conflict between authoritarian and anti-authoritarian inside the International grew more acute than ever. Marx attacked the anti-authoritarians and especially the Jurassians, at the London Conference. The upshot was that all anti-authoritarian elements were drawn together into even closer association, and hostilities worsened. We know that Bakunin and Guillaume were expelled from the International at the Congress in The Hague in 1872, when Marx and his colleagues reckoned that they had rid themselves of the anti-authoritarians' leading lights. This is not the place to go into the methods to which Marx resorted in order to encompass this end: the details of that can be found in Guillaume's *L'Internationale*.[2]

Even prior to The Hague, Guillaume had been to the fore, but, after that Congress, it becomes quite impossible to understand the subsequent development of the International without him.

The opposition facing Marx was a very motley crew; and if that opposition was to be focused and maintained, there was a need for an open mind capable of taking cognizance of lots of diverse personalities, if a concerted effort was to be feasible. Such was the role which Guillaume understood and performed so marvelously. The rarest of gifts in men, that on the one hand they should have clear, firm ideas of their own, and, on the other, that they should be able to accommodate themselves to the ideas of men differing from them and give them their due, was what set Guillaume apart. This is why he was so active in the intellectual strife within the International. Indeed, in everything he says and writes, one can sense an outstanding moral presence, equally free of fanaticism and of eclecticism.

(. . .) After 1870, the International was to perish under the pressure of economic and political developments, in spite of all its militants' efforts. The European workers' movement lost its self-consciousness and broke up into national movements. As in the rest of Europe, the spirit of revolt waned in the Jura too. The Bulletin edited by Guillaume as the organ of the Jura Federation and, for a few years at any rate, mouthpiece of the anti-authoritarian International, was forced to cease publication in 1878.

Notes to James Guillaume

1. Fritz Brupbacher (1874–1945), a medical doctor from Zurich, member of the Swiss Socialist Party from 1898 to 1914, at which point he was expelled. Thereafter he was a member of the Communist Party from 1920 up until he was expelled from that at the end of 1932. Essentially he always remained an anarchist and was forever making propaganda on behalf of sexual freedom. Published *Marx und Bakunin and 60 Jahre Ketzer* (an autobiography), books from which extracts have been translated into French as *Socialisme et liberté* (1955).
2. *L'internationale, documents et souvenirs (1864–1888)* four vols. 1905–1910.

IDEAS ON SOCIAL ORGANIZATION (1876) BY *JAMES GUILLAUME**

I. FOREWORD

Implementation of the ideas set out in the pages about to be read can only be achieved by means of a revolutionary movement.

It is not in one day that waters rise to the point where they can breach the dam holding them back: the waters rise slowly and by degrees: but once they have reached the desired level, the collapse is sudden, and the dam crumbles in the blinking of an eye.

There are, thus, two phenomena in succession, of which the second is the necessary consequence of the first: first, the slow conversion of ideas, needs and methods of action within the society; then, when the moment comes when this conversion is far enough advanced to be translated entirely into deeds, comes the abrupt and decisive crisis, the revolution, which is merely the culmination of a protracted evolution, the sudden manifestation of a change a long time in the hatching and become inevitable.

It will not occur to any serious-minded person to signal in advance the ways and means whereby the revolution, that indispensable overture to the overhauling of society, must be carried out. A revolution is a natural phenomenon, not the act of one or of several individual wills; it does not operate in accordance with any pre-determined scheme, but comes about through the uncontrollable impulse of necessities which no one may command.

So do not look to us for an outline revolutionary plan of campaign: we leave such childishness to those who still believe in the possibility and efficacy of a personal dictatorship in encompassing the work of human emancipation.

We shall confine ourselves to stating briefly the character which we should like to see the revolution have, if we are to avert its relapsing into the aberrations of the past. That character has to be above all else negative and destructive. It is not a matter of improving certain institutions from the past so as to adapt them to a new society, but rather of suppressing them. Thus, radical suppression of government, the army, the courts, the Church, the school, banking and everything connected with them. At the same time, there is a positive side to the revolution: it is the workers' assumption of ownership of the instruments of labor and of all capital.

We ought to explain how we envisage this assumption of ownership. First, let us speak of the land and the peasants.

---

*Chapter headings added by D. Guérin

In several countries, but particularly in France, the bourgeois and the clergy have long sought to gull and frighten peasants by telling them that the revolution aimed to take away their lands.

This is a foul lie by the enemies of the people. The Revolution seeks the very opposite: it aims to wrest the land from the bourgeois, the nobles and the clergy, in order to bestow it upon those among the peasants who have none.

If a tract belongs to a peasant, and that peasant works it himself, the revolution will not touch it. On the contrary, it will guarantee him free possession of it, and will release him from all charges weighing upon it. The land that paid a levy to the exchequer, and which was burdened by heavy mortgages, the revolution will emancipate just as it emancipates the worker: no more levies, no more mortgages; the land becomes free again, as does the man.

As for the lands of the bourgeois, the nobles and the clergy and the lands which the rural poor have tilled to this day for their masters, the revolution will wrest these back from those who stole them and restore them to their rightful owners, to those who cultivate them.

What will the revolution do in order to seize the land from the bourgeoisie, the exploiters and give it to the peasants?

To date, whenever the bourgeois made a political revolution, whenever they mounted one of these movements of which the sole upshot was that the people had a change of masters, they were wont to issue decrees and proclaim the wishes of the new government to the country: the decree was posted up in the communes, and the prefect, the courts, the mayor and the gendarmes saw to its implementation.

The authentically popular revolution will not be following that example: it will not draft decrees, will not require the services of the police and of the government administration. Not with decrees, with words written upon paper, does it seek to emancipate the people, but with deeds.

II. The Peasants

In this chapter we shall be examining the manner in which the peasants must organize themselves in order to extract maximum possible profit from their instrument of labor, the soil.

In the wake of the Revolution, here is the position in which the peasants will find themselves: some, who already had been small proprietors, retain the parcel of land which they carry on cultivating unaided, along with their family. Others, and these are the greater number, who were tenants of some big landlord, or mere waged laborers of some farmer, will have joined forces to seize a huge tract of land, and should cultivate it in common.

Which of these two arrangements is the better?

It is not a matter here of theorizing, but of taking the facts as our point of departure and establishing what is practicable immediately.

Approaching it from that angle, let us say for a start that the essential thing, the thing for which the Revolution has been made, has been achieved: the land has become the property of him who works it, the peasant no longer toils in order to profit an exploiter who lives off his sweat.

This great gain made, the rest is of secondary importance: the peasants may, should they so desire, divide the land into individual lots and assign one lot to each worker, or they may instead take the land under common ownership and band together to work it. However, although it may be secondary by comparison with the essential fact, the emancipation of the peasant, this matter of the best way to approach cultivation and ownership of the soil is also deserving of attentive scrutiny.

In a region which, prior to the Revolution, would have been peopled by peasant small-holders; where the nature of the soil is not such as to favor large holdings; where agriculture still clings to methods from the days of the patriarchs or where use of machinery is unknown or not widespread — in a region like that, it will be natural that the peasants should cling to the form of property to which they are accustomed. Each of them will carry on working his holding as he did in the past, with this sole difference, that his erstwhile servants (if he had any) will have become his colleagues and will share with him the fruits extracted from the land by their common effort.

Yet, the probability is that after a little while, these peasants who stayed small-holders will see the advantage to themselves of amending their traditional working arrangement. To start with they will combine in order to set up a communal agency charged with sale or exchange of their produce: then that initial combination will lead them to essay others not along the same lines. They will act in common to acquire various machines designed to facilitate their labors; they will assist one another in performance of certain tasks better performed when carried out quickly by a large number of hands, and they will doubtless end up imitating their brethren, the workers of industry and those from the large holdings, by deciding to pool their lands and form an agricultural association. But they will cling to the old routine for some years, and even though a whole generation may elapse in certain communes before the peasants resolve to adopt the collective ownership format, that delay will not pose any serious inconvenience; would that not be an end of the rural proletariat, and even within the communes clinging to the past, would there be anything other than a population of free workers living amid plenty and peace?

On the other hand, where big estates, and vast holdings account for a considerable number of workers, whose concerted and combined efforts are necessary for the soil to be worked, collective ownership prevails unaided. We will see the territory of an entire commune, sometimes even of several communes, composing only one agricultural venture, where the methods of large-scale farming will be followed. In these huge, farm-workers' communities, there will be no attempt, as the small peasant strives today upon his little parcel of land, to extract a host of different products from the same soil; we will not see, side by side, within the compass of a single hectare of land, a little stand of wheat, a little stand of potatoes, another of vines, another of forage, another of fruit trees, etc. By virtue of its external configuration, its exposure and its chemical composition, every soil has a special disposition for one variety of produce: thus, there will be no sowing of wheat on land suited to vines, no attempt to wrest potatoes from soil that would be better employed as pasture. Should it have land of just one sort, the agricultural community will engage only in the cultivation of one sort of produce, in the knowledge that cultivation on a large scale brings much more considerable results with less labor, and it will opt to secure the produce it needs through exchange, rather than produce only a small crop of inferior quality from soil not suited to the purpose.

The internal organization of an agricultural community is not necessarily going to be the same everywhere: there may be a rather wide variety according to the preferences of the combined workers; provided that they abide by the principles of equality and justice, they need consider only convenience and usefulness in this connection.

The management of the community may be conferred upon either a single individual, or upon a panel of several members elected by all of the membership: it will even be feasible for various administrative functions to be separated, each one entrusted to a special commission. The length of the working day will be fixed, not by some general law applicable nation-wide, but by decision of the community itself: the only thing is that, as the community is to be in contact with all of the agricultural workers of the region, it has to be accepted as likely that an agreement will be reached among all the workers upon the adoption of a standard practice on this score. The products of labor belong to the community and from it each member receives, either in kind (subsistence, clothing, etc.) or in exchange currency, remuneration for the labor performed by him. In some associations, such remuneration will be in proportion to hours worked; elsewhere, it will reflect both hours worked and the nature of duties performed; still other arrangements may be tried and put into practice.

This matter of distribution becomes quite a secondary issue, once the question of ownership has been settled and there are no capitalists left to batten upon the labor of the masses. We reckon, however, that the principle to which we should seek to approximate as closely as possible is this: **From each according to ability, to each according to needs.** Once — thanks to mechanical methods and the advances of industrial and agricultural science —

production has been so increased that it far outstrips the needs of society — and that result will be achieved within a few years of the Revolution — once we are at that point, shall we say, there will be an end of scrupulous measuring of the portion due each worker: each of them will be able to dip into the abundant social reserve, to meet all of his requirements, without fear of ever exhausting it, and the moral sentiment which will have grown up among free and equal workers will prevent abuse and waste. In the interim, it is for each community to determine for itself during the transitional period, the method which it considers most appropriate for distributing produce among its members.

III. The Industrial Workers

As with the peasants, there are several categories to be distinguished among the workers of industry. For a start, there are trades in which tools are virtually insignificant, where the division of labor is non-existent or just barely exists, and where, as a result, the individual worker can produce every bit as well as he would were he to work in concert. The professions of tailor, cobbler, etc., for example, fit that bill.[1]

Then there are the trades requiring cooperation of several workers, recourse to what is described as collective power, and which are generally followed in a workshop or chapel: the printworkers, cabinet-makers and masons are examples.

Finally, there is a third category of industry, where division of labor is taken much further, where production takes place on a mammoth scale and requires use of mighty machines and access to considerable capital. Examples are weaving, the metal-working plants, collieries, etc.

In the case of workers belonging to the first category, collective labor is not a necessity: and it will doubtless happen that in many cases, the tailor or cobbler may prefer to go on working alone out of his little shop. This is quite a natural thing, especially as in the smaller communes, there may be perhaps only a single worker belonging to each of these trades. Yet, and while not wishing to trespass in the least against the independence of the individual, our reckoning is that, where feasible, working in common is better: in the company of his equals, the worker has the incentive of emulation: he produces more, and plies his trade with more heart: in addition, working in common facilitates more useful monitoring of the whole by the individual, and of the individual by the whole.

As for the workers of the two other categories, obviously combination is forced upon them by the very nature of their toil: and as their instruments of labor are no longer simple tools for personal use only, but rather machines or tools, the use of which requires collaboration of several workers, ownership of that equipment cannot be other than collective.

Every workshop, every factory will therefore represent a workers' association which will remain at liberty to administer itself howsoever it may see fit, as long as the rights of the individual are safeguarded and the principles of equality and justice put into practice. In the preceding chapter, apropos of the agricultural workers' associations or communities, we offered, with regard to management, duration of working hours and distribution of produce, observations which are of course equally applicable to workers in industry, and which, as a result, we need not repeat. We have just said that, wheresoever we have an industry requiring somewhat complicated equipment and working in common, there had to be common ownership of the instruments of labor. But there is something that needs to be determined: is that common property to belong exclusively to the workshop where it operates, or should it instead be the property of the whole body of the workers of this or that industry?

Our view is that the latter of these solutions is the right one. When, for instance, come the Revolution, the printworkers of the city of Rome assume possession of all of that city's printworks, they ought immediately to meet in general assembly, there to declare that the range of printworks in Rome constitutes the common property of all Rome's printworkers. Then, as soon as possible, they ought to take another step, and show solidarity with the printworkers of the other towns in Italy: the outcome of this solidarity agreement will be the establishment of every printing works in Italy as collective property of the federation of Italian printworkers. Through this communalization, the printworkers right across Italy will be able to go and work in any of the towns in the country, and be assured of finding there the instruments of labor of which they will be entitled to avail.

But whereas, in our view, ownership of the instruments of labor ought to be vested in the corporation, we do not mean to say that, above the teams of workers making up the workshops, there is to be a sort of industrial government empowered to dispose of the instruments of labor as it deems fit. No: the workers of the various workshops do not at all abandon the instruments of labor captured by them to the care of a higher power called the corporation. What they do is this: under certain conditions, they mutually guarantee one another usufruct of the instrument of labor of which they have gained possession, and, by affording their colleagues from other workshops a joint share in that power, they receive in return a joint share in the ownership of the instruments of labor in the care of the colleagues with whom they have entered into the solidarity agreement.

IV. The Commune

The commune comprises the body of workers resident in the same locality. Taking as our model the commune, such as it exists in the vast majority of cases, and overlooking the exceptions, let us define the commune — as the local federation of producers' groups.

This local federation or commune is established with a view to furnishing certain services which are not the sole preserve of one corporation or another, but which affect them all, and which, for that very reason, are known as public services.

Communal public services can be summarized under the following headings:

a. Public Works[2]

All homes are the property of the commune.

Once the Revolution has been made, everyone carries on, temporarily, living in the same lodgings as before, with the exception of those families who were consigned to unhealthy or much too inadequate homes, and who are to be lodged immediately, through the good offices of the commune, in vacant apartments of homes previously the property of the rich.

The construction of new homes, containing healthy, spacious and comfortable lodgings, by way of replacement for the squalid hovels in the old popular districts, will be one of the prime tasks of the liberated society. The commune will turn its attention to this immediately, and in so doing it will not only be able to supply work to the masons', carpenters', locksmiths' and roofers' corporations, etc., but will also readily find useful occupation for that mass of folk who, living a life of idleness prior to the Revolution, have no trade; these can be employed as laborers on the huge building and excavation sites which will then open all over the liberated region, particularly in the towns.

These new lodgings are to be erected at everyone's expense — which means that, in return for labor performed by the various construction trades, the latter will receive from the commune the exchange bonds needed for them to be able largely to subsidize the upkeep of all their members. And since the housing will have been erected at the expense of all, it will have to be accessible to all which is to say that access to it will be free of charge, and that no one will be required to pay a levy or rent in return for the apartment he is to occupy.

Accommodations being free of charge, it seems that serious disagreements may arise from that, because no one will be willing to hold on to poor lodgings and everybody will be squabbling over the best ones. But we think that it would be wrong to think that serious problems would arise on that score, and here is the reason why. First, we ought to say that unwillingness to live in poor accommodations and yearning for better is assuredly a very legitimate desire: and it is precisely that desire, that we shall see arise very forcefully, which affords us an assurance that there will be vigorous steps taken everywhere to satisfy it, through the building of new homes. But until such time as they have been built, we will indeed have to be patient and make do with existing stock: as we have said, the commune will have taken care to met the most pressing needs by lodging the poorest families in the airy mansions of the rich: and, as for the remainder of the population, we believe that revolutionary enthusiasm will have engendered a feeling of unselfishness and self-denial which will ensure that everyone will be happy to bear, for a little while yet, the discomforts of unsuitable accommodations, and that it will not occur to anyone to take issue with a more fortunate neighbor who may, temporarily, have more agreeable accommodations.

After a short while, thanks to the vigor with which the builders, under the stimulus of widespread demand, will work, accommodations will become so plentiful, that every demand can be met: everybody will merely have to choose, in sure and certain knowledge that accommodation to his taste will be forthcoming.

What we say here is not at all as fanciful or wondrous as it might appear to those whose gaze has never looked beyond the horizon of bourgeois society: instead, it could not be simpler or more natural, so natural that it would be impossible for things to happen otherwise. In effect, with what ought the legions of masons and other construction workers to busy themselves, other than endlessly building comfortable accommodations truly worthy of occupation by the members of a civilized society? Will they need to build for years on end, before every family has its own? No. It will be a short-lived endeavor. And once they have finished, are they to fold their arms? No, of course not: they will carry on working: they will improve and refurbish existing stock, and gradually we will see the dismal districts, the narrow lanes, the unfit housing in our present towns disappearing: in their place will be erected mansions accommodating workers restored to their manhood.

b. Exchange

In the new society, there will be no more commerce, in the sense attached to that term today.

Every commune will establish an exchange agency, the workings of which we are about to explain as clearly as possible.

The workers' associations, as well as individual producers (in the sectors where individual production may continue) will deposit their products with the exchange agency. The value of these various products will have been fixed in advance by agreement between the regional trades federations and the various communes, on the basis of information which statistics will afford. The exchange agency will issue producers with exchange vouchers to the value of their products: these exchange vouchers will be acceptable currency throughout the whole territory of the Federation of communes.

Among the products thus deposited with the exchange agency, some are destined for use in the commune itself, and others for export to other communes, and thus for, barter against other products.

The former among these products will be shipped to the different communal bazaars, for the establishment of which temporary recourse will have been had to the most convenient of the shops and stores of the former merchants. Of these bazaars, some will be given over to foodstuffs, others to clothing, others to household goods, etc.

Products destined for export are to remain in the general stores, until such time as they are despatched to communes which are in need of them.

Here let us pre-empt one objection. We may perhaps be told: by means of exchange vouchers, the exchange agency in every commune issues the producers with a token of the value of their produce, and that before it has any assurance of those same products "moving." Should the products not "move," where would that leave the exchange agency? Might it not risk incurring losses, and is not the sort of operation entrusted to it high risk?

Our answer to that is that every exchange agency is confident in advance that the products it receives will "move," so that there cannot be any problem with its promptly issuing producers with their value in the form of exchange vouchers.

There will be certain categories of workers who will find it materially impossible to bring their products into the exchange agency: construction workers are one such example. But the exchange agency will nonetheless serve them as an intermediary: they will register there the various works they will have completed, the value of which will at all times have been agreed before-hand, and the agency will issue them with exchange vouchers to that value. The same will be true of the various workers employed in the commune's administrative services: their work takes the form, not of manufactured products, but of services rendered; these services will have been costed in advance and the exchange agency will issue them with the value of them.

The exchange agency's function is not just to receive products brought to it by the commune's workers: it liaises with other communes, and brings in products which the commune is forced to secure from outside, either to supplement their diet, or as raw materials, fuel, manufactured products, etc.

Such products drawn from outside are displayed in the communal stores, alongside local produce.

Consumers arrive at these various stores, brandishing their exchange vouchers, which may be split up into coupons of differing values: and there, on the basis of a standard tariff, they obtain all of the consumer items they may need.

So far, the account we have offered of the operations of the exchange agency does not differ in any essential from current commercial practice: in fact, those operations are nothing more than purchase and sale transactions: the agency buys produce from the producers and sells consumers consumer items. But we reckon that after a while, the exchange agencies' practices may be amended without any drawback, and that gradually a new arrangement will supplant the old: exchange proper will fade away and make room for distribution pure and simple.

Here is what we mean by that:

As long as a product is in short supply, and is found in the communal stores only in quantities smaller than the consumers could cope with, then one is obliged to introduce a measure of rationing into distribution of the item: and the easiest way to enforce rationing on consumers is to sell them the item, which is to say, to make it available only to those who will offer a certain price in return. But once, thanks to the prodigious expansion of production which will inevitably ensue as soon as work is organized along rational lines — once, shall we say, thanks to that expansion, this or that class of product far exceeds what the population could consume, then it will no longer be necessary to ration consumers; the sale transaction, which was a sort of brake upon immoderate consumption, can be dispensed with: the communal agencies will no longer sell products to consumers, but will distribute to them in accordance with the requirements claimed by the latter.

This substitution of distribution for exchange can be effected shortly in respect of all basic necessities: for the initial efforts of the producers' associations will be focused above all upon plentiful production of those items. Soon, other items, which today are still hard to come by and expensive, and are, as a result, regarded as luxury items, can, in their turn, go into large scale production, and thus enter the realm of distribution, which is to say, of widespread consumption. On the other hand, other items, few in number and of little importance (say, pearls, diamonds, certain metals) can never become commonplace, because nature itself limits availability; but as the high repute they enjoy today will no longer be attributed to them, they will scarcely be sought after, other than by scientific associations eager to deposit them in natural history museums or to use them in the manufacture of certain instruments.

c. Foodstuffs

The provision of foodstuffs is, in a way, only ancillary to the exchange facility. Indeed, what we have just been saying about the exchange agency is applicable to all products, including products specially destined for use as foodstuffs. However, we deem it useful to add, in a special paragraph, some more detailed explanation of arrangements to be made regarding distribution of the chief food products. Today the bakery, butchery, wine trade and colonial produce trade are at the mercy of private industry and speculators, who, through all sorts of frauds, seek to enrich themselves at the consumer's expense. The new society will have to remedy this state of affairs immediately, and that remedy will consist of elevating to the status of communal public service anything having to do with distribution of essential foodstuffs.

Let careful note be taken here: this does not mean that the commune commandeers certain branches of production. No: production proper remains in the hands of the producers' associations. But in the case, say, of bread, of what does production comprise? Of nothing except the growing of the wheat. The farmer sows and harvests the grain, and delivers it to the communal exchange: at which point the function of the producer is at an end. Grinding that grain into flour, turning the flour into bread no longer have anything to do with production; it is work comparable with the work performed by the various employees of the communal stores, work designed to make a food product, wheat, accessible to the consumers. The same goes for beef, etc.

So we can see: from the point of view of principle, there cannot be anything more logical than reincorporating the bakery, butchery, wine trade, etc., into the remit of the commune.

As a result, wheat, once it reaches the commune's shops, is to be ground into flour in a communal mill (it goes without saying that several communes may share the same mill): the flour is to be turned into bread in communal bakeries, and the bread will be issued to consumers by the commune. The same will be true in the case of meat: animals will be slaughtered in the communal abattoirs and butchered in the communal butcheries. Wines will be stored in the communal cellars and issued to consumers by specialist staff. Finally, other food crops will, according to whether they are for more or less immediate consumption, be stored in the commune stores or displayed in the markets, where consumers may come in search of them.

It is primarily with regard to this category of products, bread, meat, wine, etc., that every effort will be made to supplant the exchange arrangement with the distribution arrangement as quickly as possible. Once everyone can be assured of plentiful food supply, progress in the sciences, industrial arts and civilization in general will make giant strides.

d. Statistics

The communal statistical commission will have charge of collating all statistical information affecting the commune.

The various production associations or bodies will keep it constantly up to date with the size of their membership and with changes to their personnel, in such a way that instantaneous information may be available regarding the numbers employed in various branches of production.

Through the good offices of the exchange agency, the statistical commission will secure the most comprehensive data regarding production figures and consumption figures.

It will be through the statistics thus collected from all of the communes in a region, that it will be possible to strike a scientific balance between production and consumption: by working to such information, it will be possible to add to the numbers employed in branches where production was inadequate, and to re-deploy in those where productivity is excessive. It will also be thanks to them that we will be able to determine — granted not absolutely, but with sufficient practical accuracy — the relative worth of various products, which will serve as the basis for the exchange agencies' tariffs.

But that is not all: the statistical commission will still have to perform the tasks currently within the remit of the civil state; it will register births and deaths. We will not say marriages, because, in a free society, the willing union of man and woman will no longer be a formal act, but rather a purely private act in need of no public sanction.

Lots of other things fall within the statistical remit: diseases, meteorological observations, in short, everything which, happening on a regular basis, is susceptible to registration and calculation, and from the statistical analysis of which some information, and occasionally even some scientific law may be deduced.

e. Hygiene

Under the general heading of hygiene we have classed sundry public services the good operation of which is crucial to the maintenance of community health.

Pride of place has to go, of course, to the medical service, which will be made accessible by the commune free of charge to all of its members. Doctors will no longer be industrialists aiming to extract the fattest possible profit from their sick; they are to be employees of the commune, and paid by it, and their care is to be available to all who ask for it.

But the medical service is only the curative side of that sphere of activity and human knowledge concerned with health: it is not enough to cure illnesses, they should also be prevented. That is the function of hygiene properly so called.

We might go on to cite still other matters which should hold the attention and fall within the remit of the hygiene commission, but what little we have just said must by now be enough to give some idea of the nature of its functions and their importance.

f. Security

This service takes in measures necessary in order to guarantee the personal security of every inhabitant of the commune, as well as protect buildings, produce, etc., against any depredation and misadventure.

It is unlikely that there will still be instances of theft and banditry in a society where everyone will be able to live freely upon the fruits of his labor, and will find all of his requirements met in full. Material well-being as well as the intellectual and moral uplift that will result from the truly humane training afforded to all, will in any case make much rarer the sort of crimes that are the products of debauchery, anger, brutality or other vices.

Nevertheless, the taking of precautions in order to preserve the security of persons will not be a useless exercise. This service, which might — had the term not an excessively erroneous implication — be described as the commune's police, will not be entrusted, as it is today, to a specialist corps; every inhabitant will be liable to participate in it, and to take turns in the various security positions which the commune will have established.

Here no doubt, there will be speculation as to the treatment to be meted out in an egalitarian society to someone guilty of murder or other violent offenses. Obviously, a murderer cannot be allowed to go blithely on his way, on the pretext of respecting the rights of the individual and rebutting authority, nor can we wait for some friend of the victim to claim a life for a life. He will have to be denied his freedom and kept in a special establishment until such time as he can be returned safely to society. How ought he to be treated during his captivity? And in accordance with which principles will its duration be determined? These are delicate matters, upon which opinions are still divided. We shall have to trust to trial and error for a resolution of them: but even now we know that, thanks to the transformation which education will work upon character, crime will become very rare: criminals being now only aberrations, they are to be regarded as sick and demented; the issue of crime, which today occupies so many judges, lawyers and jailers, will diminish in social significance and become a simple entry under the philosophy of medicine.

g. The child is no one's property[3]

The first point to be considered is the question of the upkeep of children. Today, it is the parents who are charged with seeing to the nourishment and education of their children; this practice is the result of a bad practice which looks upon the child as parental property. The child is no one's property, but belongs to itself; and for the duration of the period when he is still incapable of looking to his own protection, and when, as a result, he may be exposed to exploitation, it is up to society to protect him and guarantee his unhindered development. It is up to society too to see to his upkeep: by subsidizing his consumption and the sundry costs incurred by his education, society is simply advancing him money which the child will reimburse through his labor once he becomes a producer.

Thus, it is society, and not parents, that should look to the upkeep of the child. That general principle accepted, we believe that we should refrain from prescribing in any precise and detailed way the form in which it should be implemented; we should be risking a lapse into utopianism; we must give freedom a chance and await whatever experience has to teach. Let us say only that with regard to the child, society is represented by the commune and each commune will have to decide upon the arrangement it deems best with regard to the upkeep of its children: in some places, preference will be given to the common life, elsewhere the children will be left to their mothers, up to a certain age at any rate, etc.

But this is only one facet of the question. The commune feeds, clothes and houses its children: who is to teach them, who will make men and producers of them? And according to which scheme will their education be administered?

To such questions our answer will be: children's education should be rounded, which is to say that it should develop simultaneously all bodily faculties and all intellectual ones, so as to turn the child into a rounded adult. This education should not be entrusted to a special teacher caste: everyone who has a science, an art or a trade to offer can and should be invited to impart it.

Two levels are to be distinguished in education: one when the child, between the ages of five and twelve years, has not yet attained the age to study the sciences, and when essentially it is a question of developing his physical attributes, and a second level when the child, aged between twelve and sixteen years, should be introduced to the several branches of human knowledge, while also learning the practice of one or several branches of production.

At the first level, as we have said, essentially it will be a mater of developing the child's physical faculties, strengthening the body and exercising the senses. Today, the task of exercising the vision, training the ear or developing manual dexterity is left to chance; by contrast, rational education will, by means of special exercises, set about making the eye and the ear as powerful as they have the potential to be; and, as for the hands, great care will be taken not to accustom children to being right-handed only: an effort will be made to make them as dextrous with the one hand as with the other.

At the same time as the senses are being exercised, and bodily vigor boosted by means of clever gymnastics, a start will be made on the cultivation of the mind, but in a quite spontaneous way: the child's head will be filled automatically by a number of scientific facts.

Personal observation, experience, conversations between children, or with the individuals charged with supervising their instruction will be the only lessons they will receive during this stage.

The school governed arbitrarily by a pedagogue, where the pupils sigh for freedom and outdoor games, is to be done way with. In their assemblies, the children will be completely free: they themselves will organize their games, their get-togethers and will establish a panel to oversee their work and arbitrators to resolve their squabbles etc. In this way they will grow used to public life, accountability, mutuality; the teacher whom they will have chosen of their own free will to deliver their education will no longer be a despised tyrant but rather a friend to whom they will listen with pleasure.

At the second level, the children, upon reaching the age of twelve or thirteen years, will, in a methodical way, study, one after another, the chief branches of human learning. Instruction will not be entrusted to the care of men who will make it their sole occupation: the teachers of this or that science will simultaneously be producers who will spend part of their time on manual labor: and every branch will number, not one, but a very great number of men in the commune who are possessed of a science and disposed to teach it. What is more, joint reading of good textbooks, and the discussions which will follow such reading will do much to reduce the importance currently attached to the personality of the teacher.

At the same time as the child is developing his body and absorbing the sciences, he will serve his apprenticeship as a producer. In first level education, the need to amend or modify play materials will have initiated the child into the handling of the major tools. At the second level, he will visit a variety of workshops, and soon, he will choose one or several specializations for himself. His instructors will be the producers themselves: in every workshop, there will be pupils and a part of every worker's time will be devoted to demonstrating working procedures to them. To this practical instruction a few theoretical lessons will be added.

In this way, upon reaching the age of sixteen or seventeen years, the young man will have sampled the whole range of human knowledge and will be equipped to proceed alone to further studies, should he so wish; in addition he will have learned a trade, whereupon he will enter the ranks of the useful producers, in such a way that, through his labor, he is able to repay to society the debt he owes it for his education.

It remains for us to say something about the child's relations with his family.

There are people who contend that a social organization formula that makes the child's upkeep incumbent upon society, is nothing short of "destruction of the family." That is a meaningless expression: as long as it requires the cooperation of two individuals of opposite sex to procreate a new-born child, there will be fathers and mothers, and the natural bond of kinship between the child and those to whom he owes his existence cannot be stricken from social relations.

The character alone of this bond must necessarily undergo change. In ancient times, the father was absolute master of the child, enjoying the right of life or death over it: in modern times, the paternal authority has been limited by certain restrictions, so what could be more natural if, in a free and egalitarian society, what remains of that authority should be completely eclipsed and give way to relations of unalloyed affection?

We are not claiming, of course, that the child should be treated like an adult, that all of its tantrums command respect and that whenever its childish wishes conflict with the rules established by science and common sense, the child should not be taught to yield. On the contrary, we are saying that the child is in need of direction; but in its early years that direction should not be vested exclusively in its parents, who are often incompetent and generally abuse the power vested in them. The object of the education received by the child being to equip it as quickly as possible for self-direction by comprehensive development of all its faculties, then obviously no narrowly authoritarian tendency is compatible with such a system of education. But because the relations of father and son will no longer be those of master and slave, but rather those of teacher and pupil, of older friend and younger one, is it conceivable that the mutual affection of parent and child should suffer by that? Is the opposite not the case when we will have an end of these enmities and frictions of which today's family has so many examples to offer, and which are almost always caused by the tyranny the father wields over his children?

So, let no one come along and say that the liberated, regenerated society is going to destroy the family. On the contrary, it will teach the father, mother, and child mutual love, mutual regard and respect for their mutual rights: and at the same time, above and beyond the family affections which encompass only a narrow circle and which sour if they remain exclusive, it will infuse hearts with a loftier, nobler love, love for the whole family of man.

A Federative Network

Departing now from the narrow ground of the commune or local federation of producers' groups, let us take a look at social organization as it is complemented, on the one hand, by establishment of regional corporative federations embracing all workers' groups belonging to the same branch of production: and, on the other, by establishment of a Federation of communes.

(. . .) We have already indicated briefly what a corporative federation is. Within the bosom of the present society, there are organizations bringing all of the workers in a trade within the compass of the same association: the federation of typographical workers is one example. But these organizations are only a very flawed foretaste of what the corporative federation should be in the society to come. The latter will be made up of all producer groups belonging to the same branch of labor; they band together, not, now, to protect their wages against the rapaciousness of the bosses, but primarily in order to assure one another of use of the instruments of labor in the possession of each of their groups and which, by mutual agreement, are to become collective property of the corporative federation as a whole; furthermore, by federating one with another, the groups are empowered to exercise a constant watching brief on production, and, as a result, to add to or subtract from the intensity thereof, in reflection of the needs manifested by society as a whole.

Establishment of the corporative federation will be effected extremely simply. In the wake of the Revolution, the producer groups belonging to the same industry will be alive to the need to send delegates to one another, from one town to another, for fact-finding purposes and in order to reach accommodations. Out of such partial conferencing will emerge the summoning of a general congress of the corporation's delegates to some central venue. That congress will lay the groundwork of the federative contract, which will then be put to all of the groups of the corporation for approval. A standing bureau, elected by the corporative congress and answerable to it, will be designed to act as intermediary between the groups making up the federation, as well as between the federation per se and other corporative federations.

Once all branches of production, including those affecting agricultural production, are organized along such lines, a vast federative web, taking in every producer and thus also every consumer, will cover the country, and statistics regarding production and consumption, centralized by the bureau of the various corporative federations, will make it possible to determine in a rational way the number of hours in the normal working day, the cost price of products and their exchange value, as well as how many of these products have to be made in order to meet consumer demands.

People accustomed to the empty bombast of certain alleged democrats may perhaps ask whether the workers' groups should not be called upon to take a direct hand, through a vote by all members of the corporative federation, in the settlement of these various details: And when we respond negatively, they will protest at what they will term the authority of the bureau, empowered to decide matters of such gravity for themselves and to take decisions of the highest importance. Our response will be that the task with which the standing bureau of each federation will have been charged has nothing to do with the wielding of any authority: in fact it is simply a matter of collecting and collating information supplied by the producer groups: and once this information has been gathered and made public, of deducing the necessary implications it holds for working hours, the cost price of products, etc. That is a simple arithmetical calculation, which cannot be done in two different ways or produce two different results: there is but one result possible from it; that result can be checked out by every person for himself, because everyone will have the data before him, and the standing bureau is simply charged with registering it and publishing it for all to see. Even today, the postal administration, say, performs a service rather analogous with the one to be entrusted to the corporative federations' bureau, and it would not occur to anyone to complain of abuse of authority just because the post office should decide, without reference to universal suffrage, how letters are to be classified and grouped into packets for delivery to their destination as speedily and economically as practicable.

Let us add that the producer groups making up a federation will take a hand in the bureau's doings in a manner a lot more effective and direct than mere voting: in fact, it is they who will supply the information, all the statistical data that the bureau merely collates, so that the bureau is only the passive go-between by means of which groups communicate with one another and publicly register the results of their own activities.

The vote is a suitable means of settling matters that cannot be resolved on a scientific basis, and which ought to be left to the whim of the balance of numbers, but in matters liable to precise scientific resolution, there is no need for a vote; truth is not balloted, it is simply registered and then overwhelms everybody by virtue of its obviousness.

But thus far we have shown only one of the facets of extra-communal organization: and alongside the corporative federations the Federation of communes should be established.

No Socialism in One Country

The Revolution cannot be confined to a single country; on pain of death, it is obliged to subsume into its movement, if not the whole world, then at least a considerable portion of the civilized countries. Indeed, today no country can be sufficient unto itself: international relations are a necessity of production and consumption, and they could not be severed. Should the neighboring States around a country in revolution manage to impose an impregnable blockade, the Revolution, being isolated, would be doomed to perish. Thus, as we are speculating on the hypothesis of the Revolution succeeding in a given country, we must suppose that most of the countries of Europe will have made their revolution at the same time.

It is not essential that the new social organization installed by the Revolution, in every land where the proletariat will have overthrown the rule of the bourgeoisie, should be the same in every particular. Given the differences of opinion which have thus far surfaced between the socialists of the Germanic countries (Germany, England) and those of the Latin and Slav countries (Italy, Spain, France, Russia), the likelihood is that the social organization adopted by the German revolutionaries, say, will differ on more than one count from the organization espoused by the Italian or French revolutionaries. But such differences have no bearing upon international relations; the basic principles being the same in both cases, relations of friendship and solidarity cannot but be established between the emancipated peoples of the various countries.

It goes without saying that the artificial frontiers created by existing governments will collapse before the Revolution. Communes will band together freely according to their economic interests, linguistic affinities and geographical situation. And in certain countries, like Italy or Spain, which are too huge to form only one agglomeration of communes, and which nature herself has split into several distinct regions, there will doubtless be, not one, but several Federations of communes set up. Which will not signify a breach in unity, a reversion to the old atomization into small, hostile, isolated political States; their interests will be all of a piece and they will enter into a pact of unity with one another, and this voluntary union, rooted in genuine usefulness, in a community of aims and needs, in ongoing exchange of good offices, will be tight and solid in a way quite different from the sham unity of political centralization established by violence and with no raison d'être other than exploitation of the country for the benefit of one privileged class.

The compact of unity will not be established only between the Federations of communes within the same country: the old political frontiers having become redundant, all of the Federations of communes, by and by, will enter into this fraternal alliance, and, once the principles of the Revolution have carried all before them in the whole of Europe, the great dream of the fraternity of peoples, achievable only by Social Revolution, will have become a reality.

Notes to Ideas on Social Organization

1. It should be noted, however, that even in these trades, the larger-scale industrial approach to production may be applied to make savings in time and labor. What we say about them is therefore applicable only to the transitional period. (Note by J.Guillaume)
2. The sub-headings which follow were added by James Guillaume
3. The sub-headings below have been added by ourselves.

PETER KROPOTKIN (1842–1921)

PETER KROPOTKIN *BY MAX NETTLAU*

His youth, education, days as an officer and as an explorer in Siberia, his life of science and toil in Petrograd, in short, his life from (December 9) 1842 up until the end of the 1860s is all there in his *Memoirs*.[1] From very early on, he was a tireless worker and researcher, and even in an oppressed and backward Russia he found things to occupy and utterly enthrall him. He got wind of the current of opposition which, under a thousand guises and countless nuances, was the constant companion of omnipotent absolutism, fighting it and monitoring it unremittingly, and never setting aside its weapons; he quickly came to know real science and to become a passionate lover thereof his whole life long, and he was also impressed by what might be termed the grandeur, richness and promise of Siberian Russia. Those were propitious times, for, between the ages of fifteen and twenty five, he witnessed the great liberal and radical awakening that came in the wake of Nicholas I's death; he saw natural science attain its apogee through the great works of Darwin and other contemporaries, and his travels in Siberia greatly widened his horizons.

(. . .) We know that at one point he turned his back on a life of science, just as he had earlier turned away from a military career and a life at court — and committed himself with that same intensity which marked his every action, to the cause of the people. He entered the Russian revolutionary movement and there, from the outset, belonged to the select group of authentic revolutionaries.

(. . .) In the spring of 1872, he traveled to Switzerland, where, in Zurich, he first immersed himself in mountainous socialist literature, the sort of stuff which never made it into Russia. On account of the fact that his brother who was already in Switzerland held to the very moderate views, (especially in practical matters) of Lavrov and other like-minded connections, he was forewarned against Bakunin, whom he did not go to see; then again, on reaching Neuchâtel and the home of James Guillaume, the latter had been forewarned about Kropotkin, so that there was no rapprochement with the anarchists towards whom he could feel himself being drawn, nevertheless.

When he asked Guillaume whether he ought to stay in Switzerland, the latter advised him to return to Russia. He did in fact go back, and threw himself more whole-heartedly than ever into revolutionary work. He paid the price for this: dressed as a workman, he would give talks to secret workers' groups and this resulted in his being arrested. Whereupon his less public activity was uncovered, his organizing work and correspondence, as well as the boldly revolutionary scheme he had drawn up for reorganizing Russian propaganda in all of its forms. He had another scheme too, to travel into Southern Russia where the circles were rather more radical, and to broach the idea of agrarian terror. He correctly saw that the moderate party was surreptitiously frustrating his efforts. In the end, he was wrested away from this frantic activity (for his propaganda activity always went hand in hand with science and his work) by his arrest and after fleeing (. . .) he arrived in Scotland in 1876 and made his way to London.

But what was he going to do in London, where the socialist movement had been well and truly extinct for some years by that time? After a short trip to Switzerland, he made another trip, there to remain this time. Finally, he realized his dream of 1872, to live in the Swiss Jura, where the intelligent, independent workers had done so much to sustain and spread anti-authoritarian ideas in the International. Certain events had brought him closer to James Guillaume, although their differing characters never allowed them to share any real intimacy and friendship. But James Guillaume was by then deferring somewhat to more restless though less consistent minds like Paul Brousse,[2] who was an anarchist in those days, and with whom Kropotkin got along more easily.

In the course of this work on behalf of the International, he worked for the Jura and for Spain, yet still found the time to draft their first anarchist program for German workers in Switzerland. Similarly, Paul Brousse drafted and wrote (for translation) for the first German anarchist newspaper of that time which was published out of Berne. And in Guillaume's absence, he even edited the *Bulletin jurassien* and passed the first article calling for "propaganda by deed" (in as many words, too), an article penned by Paul Brousse.

A congress happened to take him to Belgium, to Verviers (in September 1877), but, in order to avoid harassment, he traveled to Paris, there to embark upon his research into the French Revolution. He made a trip to Spain (summer 1878), to Barcelona and Madrid, and managed to smooth over a disagreement that divided Morago's terrorist group (Madrid) and Viñas's revolutionary syndicalist group (Barcelona): in point of fact, both these groups were anarchist.

Paris at that time was none too hospitable towards anarchist Internationalists and he soon moved to Geneva.

It was there that, at the beginning of 1879, his favorite offspring, *Le Révolté*, was launched (on February 22) (. . .) There it was that he published that long series of articles, which might have appeared disconnected, in that they mirrored developments of the time, but which lent themselves so well to being collected into pamphlets published and translated times beyond number, before publication in book form as *Paroles d'un Révolté*, because the entire series had been thought out and written in accordance with a pre-arranged scheme.

For a time to follow, Kropotkin's life was an eventful one. He was deported from Switzerland over an article which had been written by Cafiero. He spent another very bleak period in London, where he also attended the London International Revolutionary Congress (in 1881). He was reduced to living in Thonon, in Savoy, unable to re-enter Switzerland and increasingly threatened on the French side where the vigor of anarchist propaganda in Paris and Lyon had triggered an urge to strike at its very heart through its most committed propagandists. Kropotkin too was caught up in this dragnet and was arraigned in the despicable trial in Lyon — the anarchists' declaration, drafted by him, is worth re-reading — and Clairvaux prison and, I think, the very same cell as the aged Blanqui, became his last fixed abode in France. Freed after several years under an amnesty at the start of 1886, he was able to stay only a short time in Paris, and for the next thirty years he was to dwell in England, only to return to Russia in the spring of 1917, under Kerensky.

In England, where he spent six years in Harrow-on-the-Hill, a considerable distance from London, he moved house (to Bromley, Kent) to get a little closer and moved again before moving away once and for all (to Brighton), leading a studious life of tedious work, a life without apparent incident, but he managed to find a number of outlets for his activity, which are worth looking at.

In terms of propaganda, there was still *La Révolté* — in which the series of informative articles collected under the title *The Conquest of Bread* was published: later, there was *Les Temps nouveaux* Soon there would be the English monthly *Freedom*, from October 1886 on.

But there was another route by which he could develop his ideas. For years he had been writing about Russia, her revolution and her prisons, etc., in the Newcastle *Chronicle*, penning letters to the *Times* and highly fastidious articles in *Nineteenth Century*. Thus, the latter great review also carried articles setting out anarchist ideas. *The Scientific Basis of Anarchy* and *Anarchy to Come* saw publication there in 1887. Then, from 1888 to 1890, Kropotkin turned his attention to economic issues in articles which were to make up *Fields, Factories and Workshops* (Paris 1910). Thereafter he identified anarchy in nature — not the savage anarchy of the struggle for survival, but the altruistic anarchy and solidarity of mutual aid (articles from 1890 to 1896 and 1910), out of which came his book *Mutual Aid* (Paris, 1906). He concluded this topic with a few articles challenging Darwinism (1910 and 1912), before tackling his last great theme, ethics, in articles during 1904 and 1905, of the follow-up to which I know nothing[3], if indeed it has appeared. I do know however that this very daunting work was interrupted by his research into the French Revolution of 1793 and the Russian Revolution of 1905, as well as by his frequent illnesses, countless other ventures and, above all, by the restrictions of all sorts imposed upon him by a weakness that increased with his years.

Two trips to the United States and Canada gave a boost to his memoirs *About a Life* (1902), written for an American magazine, and to published lectures like Russian Literature (1905).

The Russian Revolution of 1905 gave final shape to his studies of the French Revolution, which had already been condensed in smaller publications and in the hefty tome *The Great French Revolution* published at last in 1909.

His historical works, scientific works and marxist polemics focused his interest upon the beginnings of socialism and the history of anarchist ideas. A tremendous entry in the *Encyclopedia Britannica* and the book *Modern Science and Anarchy* (Paris 1913) testify to that.

Notes to Peter Kropotkin

1. *Autour d'une vie* 1902
2. Paul Brousse (1844–1912), physician, anarchist at first and disciple of Bakunin, member of the Jura Federation. In 1877 in Chaux-de-Fonds, along with Kropotkin, he launched a secret society which he called "our international intimacy," made up of Internationalists of various origins, a continuation of the secret Brotherhood founded by Bakunin in 1865. Around about 1880 he switched from anarchism to reformist socialism and became an advocate of "possibilism," a euphemism for opportunism.
3. In fact *Ethics* was published, unfinished, after Kropotkin's death.

THE ANARCHIST IDEA[1]

1. Scrupulous examination of the current economic and political situation, leads us to the conviction that Europe is striding rapidly in the direction of a revolution: that this revolution will not be confined to just one country, but, erupting everywhere, will spread, as in 1848, to neighboring countries and will inflame more or less the whole of Europe: and that, while assuming different characters among different peoples, according to the historical stage they are passing through and according to local circumstances, it will nevertheless have this overall distinguishing feature: it will not be merely political, but will also and above all be an economic revolution.

2. The economic revolution may assume a variety of characters and differing degrees of intensity among different peoples. But the important thing is, regardless of what its character may be, that the socialists of every country, capitalizing upon the disorganization of powers in time of revolution, should bend their every effort to achieving, on a large scale, a change in the property system, through plain and simple expropriation of the present owners of large landed estates, the instruments of labor and all sorts of capital, and through all such capital being taken over by the cultivators, the workers' organizations and the agricultural and municipal communes.

The act of expropriation should be carried out by the workers of town and countryside themselves. It would be a profound error to wait for any government to do it: for history teaches us that governments, even when they have emerged from the revolution, have never done anything other than give legal sanction to accomplished revolutionary facts, and indeed, that the people had to wage a protracted battle with these governments in order to wrest from them assent for the revolutionary measures for which it had been calling loudly over periods of restlessness. Moreover, a measure of that importance would remain a dead letter unless it had been freely implemented in every commune, in every stretch of territory, by the interested parties themselves.

3. The expropriation of social capital and the taking of it into common ownership should be carried out wheresoever such action is feasible and as soon as the opportunity presents itself, without inquiring into whether the whole or most of Europe or of such and such a country is ready to embrace the ideas of collectivism. The drawbacks which would ensue from partial realization of collectivism will largely be made up for by its advantages. The deed having been done in a given locality, that itself will become the most potent method for propagating the idea and the mightiest engine for mobilization of the localities where the worker, little disposed to embrace these

collectivist notions, might yet hesitate to proceed with expropriation. Moreover, it would be tedious to go into a discussion of whether it may or may not be necessary to wait until the ideas of collectivism have been accepted by the majority before putting them into practice, for it is certain, that unless they set themselves up as a government which would shoot the people down, the doctrinarian socialists will not prevent expropriation from proceeding in those localities most advanced in terms of their socialist education, even should the great mass of the country remain in a condition of inertia.

4. Once expropriation has been carried through, and the capitalists' power to resist been smashed, then, after a period of groping, there will necessarily arise a new system of organizing production and exchange, on a restricted scale to begin with, but later more comprehensive, and that system will be a lot more attuned to popular aspirations and the requirements of coexistence and mutual relations than any theory, however splendid, devised either by the thinking and imagination of reformers or by the deliberations of some legislative body. However, we believe that we are not mistaken in predicting right now that, in francophone Switzerland at least, the foundations of the new organization will be the free federation of producers' groups and the free federation of Communes and groups of independent Communes.

5. Should the revolution set to work immediately upon expropriation, it will derive from it an inner strength that will enable it to withstand both the attempts to form a government that would seek to strangle it and any onslaughts which might emanate from without. But, even should the revolution have been beaten, or if expropriation has failed to spread to the extent we anticipated, a popular uprising launched on that basis would do humanity the immense service of accelerating the advent of the social revolution. While contributing (like all revolutions) a measure of immediate improvement to the lot of the proletariat, even if defeated, it would render impossible thereafter any other uprising that would not have expropriation of the few for the benefit of the many as its point of departure. A further explosion would thus of necessity lead to an end of capitalist exploitation, and, with the departure of that, to economic and political equality, work for all, solidarity and liberty.

6. If the revolution is to bear all of the fruits which the proletariat is entitled to expect of it after centuries of unceasing struggles and holocausts of victims sacrificed, then the period of revolution must last for several years, so that the propagation of new ideas should not be confined solely to the great intellectual centers, but should reach even into the most isolated hamlets in order to shake the inertia which is necessarily evident in the masses prior to their turning towards a fundamental reorganization of society, so that, at long last, the new ideas should have the time to be developed further, as the true advancement of humanity requires.

So, far from seeking to establish immediately and in place of the authorities overthrown, some new authority which, having been born in the initial stages of the revolution, when the new thinking is only just beginning to stir, would of necessity be essentially conservative: far from aiming to create an authority which, representing phase one of the revolution, could not help but hobble the free development of subsequent phases, and which would inevitably tend to immobilize and circumscribe, socialists have a duty to thwart the creation of any new government and instead to arouse those popular forces destructive of the old regime and at the same time generative of the new organization of society.

7. This being our conception of the coming revolution and the goal we intend to achieve, it follows that during the preparatory period through which we are passing today, we ought to concentrate all of our efforts upon widespread propaganda on behalf of the idea of expropriation and of collectivism. Instead of consigning these principles to some corner of our minds, and proceeding to talk to the people of nothing but the business of so-called politics (which would amount to an attempt to lay the mental groundwork for an eminently political revolution, palpably neglecting its economic aspect, the only one capable of investing it with sufficient strength) we ought instead, always and in every circumstance, to spell out those principles at length, demonstrating their practical implications and proving their necessity; we ought to make every effort to prepare the popular mind to embrace these ideas, which, odd though they may seem at first glance to those filled with politico-economic prejudices, readily become incontrovertible truth for those who discuss them in good faith, a truth which science is today beginning to grasp, a truth often acknowledged by the very people who publicly resist it.

Working along these lines, without letting ourselves be dazzled by the momentary and often contrived success of the political parties, we work at infusing the masses with our ideas: all undetectably, we are effecting a shift of opinion in the direction of our ideas; we bring together the men we need to propagate these ideas on a wide scale during the period of effervescence towards which we are striding: and we know from the experience of human history that it is precisely in periods of effervescence, when dissemination and transformation of ideas takes place at a rate unknown in periods of transition, that the principles of expropriation and collectivism can spread like wildfire and inspire the broad masses of the people to put these principles into practice.

8. If the revolutionary period is to last for a number of years and if it is to bear fruit, it is absolutely necessary that the coming revolution should not be restricted to the larger towns only: the uprising aimed at expropriation must take place primarily in the countryside. So there is a need to set about preparing

the ground in the countryside right now and not rely upon the revolutionary élan which might, in a period of effervescence, radiate from the towns into the villages.

As a temporary stratagem and as an experiment, the Jura sections ought to make it their duty to undertake, in villages adjacent to the towns, ongoing propaganda in favor of expropriation of the land by the rural communes. As there have been experiments along these lines already, we are in a position to state that they have borne more fruit than had been expected at the outset. Trial and error will show the best way to proceed, and how this propaganda might be extended. Difficult though things might be to begin with, a start should be made without further delay. Furthermore, we could not recommend too highly that a study be made of the peasants' uprisings in Italy and the revolutionary propaganda currently being conducted in the villages of Spain.

9. While urging that our efforts be concentrated upon widespread propagation, in all its forms, of the ideas of expropriation, we do not mean to say that we should miss opportunities to agitate on all matters pertinent to the life of the country and going on around us. On the contrary: we think that socialists ought to avail of every opportunity that arises to launch economic agitation, and it is our conviction that every agitation launched upon the terrain of the struggle of the exploited against the exploiters, however narrowly circumscribed its initial theater of action, the aims it pursues and the ideas it advances, can prove ground for socialist agitation, unless it falls into the clutches of ambitious schemers.

So it would be a good idea for sections not to scorn the various issues agitating the workers of the district for the sole reason that these matters have but very little to do with socialism. On the contrary, by taking a hand in all these issues, and by capitalizing upon the interest which these arouse, we might work to broaden the scope of the agitation, and, while sticking to the practicalities of the matter, seek to broaden theoretical notions and awaken the spirit of independence and revolt in those taking an interest in the resultant agitation. Such participation is all the more necessary in that it offers the only way of combating the wrong-headed opinions peddled on every such occasion by the bourgeoisie, and of preventing the workers' agitation from going down a road absolutely contrary to the workers' interests, as a result of activities carried out by ambitious persons.

10. As anarchists' efforts ought to be directed at undermining the State in all its parts, we cannot see the usefulness of our setting ourselves up as a political party which would strive to ensconce itself in the ramifications of government, in the hope of one day claiming its share of the inheritance of the present governmentalism. We believe that the best way of shaking this edifice

would be to escalate the economic struggle. But we believe too that it would also be a good idea to have an eye out at all times for the acts and feats of those who govern us, to study diligently those political issues which interest the laboring people, and to let slip no favorable opportunity to point up the incompetence, hypocrisy and class self-interest of existing governments, as well as the vicious and noxious character of governmental rule. Let us wage war on the State and its representatives, not so as to take a seat in its deliberations, as the political parties do, but in order to undermine the force they oppose to the worker's aspirations and in order to hasten their inevitable downfall.

11. Convinced that the mode of combination that will become a reality in the near future (in francophone Swiss territory at any rate) will be the Commune, independent of the State, abolishing the representative system from within its ranks and effecting expropriation of raw materials, instruments of labor and capital for the benefit of the community, we hold that there is a need for serious study of the collectivist Commune and discussion of the part which anarchists may play in the struggle currently incubating on the political and economic terrain, between the Communes and the State.

Notes to The Anarchist Idea

1. This was a report delivered by Peter Kropotkin, using the alias of Levashoff, to the Jura gathering on November 1, 1879. It was printed in the Geneva newspaper *Le Révolté*.

The 1880 Congress of the Jura Federation

The next year, 1880, saw a congress of the Jura Federation meet in Chaux-de-Fonds, in the Swiss Jura. Ever since the split in the workers' International at The Hague in 1872, the Jura Federation had acted as the spokesman for the "anti-authoritarian" libertarian socialism inherited from Mikhail Bakunin. Below the reader will find:

1) Lengthy excerpts from the minutes of the congress carried in the October 17, 1880 edition of the newspaper *Le Révolté*, and, in particular, Kropotkin's contribution.
2) Extracts from the memorandum (or "program") submitted to the congress by the Workers' Federation of the Courtelary District.[1]
3) Finally, the report submitted to the congress by the Italian Carlo Cafiero, on the subject of "Anarchy and Communism."

These texts allow us to distinguish two divergent schools of thought within the Jura Federation: one, represented by Kropotkin, Cafiero, etc., openly professed libertarian communism. The other, more cautious and less ambitious, whose spokesman was Adhémar Schwitzguébel, still clung to use of the term collectivism.[2]

What was the difference between these two tendencies?

In theory, collectivism merely wanted to see the means of production taken into common ownership and it left the workers' associations free to determine how the products of labor might be distributed, a faculty which in fact boiled down to remuneration for labor being a function of work performed. Libertarian communism, on the other hand, aimed to take into common ownership not just the means of production, but also consumer goods, and to distribute products thereafter in abundant supply on the market, free of charge, in accordance with the formula: "To each according to his needs." This was what James Guillaume had suggested back in 1874. (See above)

The objections to communism of the supporters of collectivism were primarily on grounds of opportunity. As Adhémar Schwitzguébel, who professed to be an anarchist-communist himself, said:

> Thus far, the communist idea has been misunderstood among the populace where there is still a belief that it is a system devoid of all liberty.

Objections from the supporters of libertarian communism inimical to the word collectivism also derived from the fact that in 1880 the latter term had lost the sense which had commonly been given to it in the First International.

Reformists no longer understood collectivism to mean taking of the instruments of labor into common ownership in a revolutionary and general way, but rather an evolutionary, parliamentary socialism.

Notes to the Introduction to The 1880 Congress of the Jura Federation

1. This was founded on September 1, 1868 through the amalgamation of the Sonvilier section and about twenty local sections from the Saint-Imier Valley. Adhémar Schwitzguébel had already reported to the Basle congress (1869) on the progress of this federation.
2. Max Nettlau *Bibliographie de l'anarchie* (no date) p. 58.

Minutes of the Jura Federation Congress (1880) (Extracts)[1]

(. . .) The congress was held in Chaux-de-Fonds on October 9 and 10, 1880.

Comrade Kropotkin reports, having attended a meeting of the Geneva section, that the latter held that the program was much too long to be made effective use of in popular propaganda.

Moving on then to discussion of the program, he says that for some time past socialism has been in fashion, and even where one might least expect to hear it, people have been heard to say: "We too are socialists!" We also have socialists of every hue, red and pink, blue and green, white and even black. All who acknowledge the necessity of some modification to the relations between capitalists and workers, however anodyne, have staked a claim to the description socialists.

We need not concern ourselves about those who claim to be socialists with the specific object of hobbling socialism's development. Let us leave those to the side for one moment. But if we were to examine all the other schools of socialism — reformist, statist, democratic, etc. — and if we were to compare them against anarchist socialism, we very readily perceive one idea constituting a clearly defined difference between these various schools and us. Namely, our conception of the work which the revolution is due to carry out.

Among all the evolutionary socialists and even among some revolutionary socialists, there is one common notion. They do not believe in an imminent great revolution, or indeed, if they do, they are persuaded that that revolution is not going to be a socialist revolution: "Come the next upheaval," they say, "the people is not going to be ready yet to carry out a serious revolution in the system of ownership: that is why the point is to first carry out a political revolution that will offer every opportunity for preparing minds for a social revolution." If they are to be believed, it would therefore only come when our great-grandchildren are graybeards. Examine the writings of socialists of every persuasion and you will find that at bottom they are dominated by this idea, regardless of the language they may use to disguise the fact.

We could not protest too loudly against this idea, whereby faint-hearts strive in advance to set a term to the implications of the coming revolution. It is our firm conviction that expropriation will be the goal and driving force behind the next European conflict, and we ought to bend our every effort to ensuring that that expropriation becomes an accomplished fact following the battle which we can all sense drawing near. It is expropriation, carried out by the people and followed by the tremendous shift in thinking which it will bring in its wake, which alone can invest the coming revolution with the requisite power to overcome the obstacles being erected in its path. It is expropriation that will have to serve as the point of departure for a new era of social development. And even should the efforts of our enemies, abetted in this by men who would even now tell the people "So far and no further!" succeed in defeating us, the very fact that we had made the attempt to take the whole of social capital and the products of labor into common ownership, albeit only within a restricted space, would be a salutary example presaging the ultimate success of the following revolution.

Expropriation, carried out by the people, once an uprising has thrown the power of the bourgeoisie into disarray: immediate seizure by producer groups of the whole of social capital: that is how we shall act come the next revolution, and it is primarily upon this point that we take issue with those schools of socialism which, at bottom, having no confidence in the people, seek to make the forthcoming revolution a mere change in the form of government, some of them, under the pretext of establishing the freedoms necessary for the socialist idea to prosper, and others of them, under the pretext of carrying out expropriation gradually, in piece-meal fashion, once they, the governments, judge that the right time has arrived.

If the Federation embraces the idea put forward by the Geneva section, that a summary of our program be published, might it not be a good idea for that summary to make more plain and explicit this essential difference between our party and the evolutionary schools?

Comrade Kropotkin further observes that use of the word collectivism in the program might be open to misinterpretation.

When that term was introduced into the International, it was invested with a meaning quite different from the one suggested by it today. With due consideration for the prejudices then existing in France against communism, which was understood to signify a monastic order walled up in a convent or barracks, the International opted for the word collectivism.

It also said that it wanted social capital to be taken into common ownership and groups to be completely free to introduce whatever system for distributing the products of labor they may regard as best suited to the circumstances. Today, an attempt is underway to imply that the word collectivism means something else: according to evolutionists, it means, not the taking of the instruments of labor into common ownership, but rather individual enjoyment of products. Others go further still and seek to restrict even the social capital which would have to be taken into common ownership: supposedly, this would extend only to land, mines, forests and means of communication. Furthermore, collectivists of this stripe would be ready to defend it at gun-point against those who would presume to lay hands upon it in order to turn it into collective property.

It is high time that there was an end of this misunderstanding, and there is only one way of achieving that: by jettisoning the word collectivism and declaring openly that we are communists, pointing up the difference existing between our conception of anarchist communism and the one peddled by the mystical and authoritarian schools of communism prior to 1848. That would be a better expression of our ideal, and our propaganda could not but be strengthened by it. It will benefit from the fillip afforded by the idea of communism, a boost that the idea of collectivism will never afford.

Comrade Elisée Reclus[2] supports comrade Kropotkin's remarks. In spite of all the explanations offered by the non-communist collectivists, he finds it impossible to comprehend how their organization of society would work. If the large plant, which is to say the land, and if all the secondary factories upon it are taken into common ownership, if work is performed by everyone, and the quantity and quality of products are due precisely to concerted endeavor, to whom might these legitimately belong, other than to the united body of workers? What rule is to serve as a guide for the distributive bookkeepers and help them determine the portion of the manna generated by the toil of mankind as a whole, preceding generations included, which is due to each person? Such distribution, effected at random or whimsically, cannot have any outcome other than the sowing of the seed of disagreements, strife and death in the collectivist society.

What is true and what is just is that products owed to the labor of all should be the property of all, and each person should be free to avail of his portion in order to consume it as he sees fit, with no regulation other than that emanating from the solidarity of interests and the mutual respect between associates. Moreover, it would be absurd to fear shortage, since the enormous loss of products caused by the current wastage of trade and private appropriation would have ceased at last. Fear is always a bad counselor. Let us have no fear about describing ourselves as communists, as in fact we are. Popular opinion has a logic to it: the collectivists have done well and universal common sense has grasped that appropriation of the land and of factories necessarily leads on to common ownership of products.

Comrade Reclus would also like to see congress express reservations regarding the paragraph in the Courtelary memorandum which relates to the Commune. No doubt local conditions are a very significant factor, and most of the groups will be established within the confines of existing communes: but it should be borne in mind that combination of revolutionary forces proceeds freely, outside of any communal organization. Up to now, communes have been only tiny States, and even the Paris Commune, insurrectionary below, was governmental at the top and retained the whole hierarchy of officials and employees. We are no more communalists than we are Statists: we are anarchists, remember, and we offer the best proof of that in our gathering today. We truly do hope to have a hand, however slight, in the revolutionary endeavor, and, whether we hail from Le Vallon, Geneva, Lausanne, France or Naples, we feel no attachment to any particular commune, nor to any State. The International does not recognize these borders.

Comrade Schwitzguébel declares himself an anarchist communist: if he accepts the program as just presented, which is to say, with collectivist ideas predominating, this is because he sees the populace as being rather more hostile than favorable to these ideas and because the drafting of a candidly communist program could only exacerbate that hostility; he remarks that there is a matter of appropriateness, so to speak, which needs to be investigated carefully. Thus far, the communist idea has been poorly understood among the populace where it is still believed to be a system devoid of all liberty. By his reckoning, there is a great preparatory work to be done to induce the populace to embrace communism.

Comrade Herzig, delegate from Geneva, finds that the program just outlined ascribes too many powers to the Commune and appears to want to replace the authority of the State, to which we stand opposed, by a new formula, that of the Commune — which would amount only to the decentralization of authority. Whereas it is true, as the program states, that the coming popular revolutions have their seat in the Commune and have the autonomy of the latter as their objective, we should not, for that reason, look to this new conception of Revolution for our way ahead, nor seek to get the upper hand in events: our duty is to see that new ideas utterly contrary to any principle of authority blossom in men's minds.

The program is open to the interpretation that political struggles should be conducted on a communal footing. We contest this view even when it might be proven that such struggles would help bring down the State, for, in order to launch them, we should necessarily have to walk the path of legality, which would be contrary to our principles and would imply their abandonment.

Comrade Cafiero, speaking of the revolutionary program, ventured to speak about communism (. . .) [3]

Comrade Pindy observes that not only can the idea of communism earn acceptance by the French worker, but communist sentiment is innate in him: if he styles himself at the moment a collectivist, this is on account of ridiculous stories that have been told ever since 1848 about the communism of that vintage. While the word communism is repugnant to him, he is nevertheless ready, in any circumstance, to practice the thing. Pindy himself has practiced it instinctively, but, in spite of that, to this day he holds that the word, but only the word, is repugnant to the French revolutionary workers. Then again, he declares that in order to expose the existing progressive pseudo-socialists, there is a case for explaining the true meaning of words, and for calling things by their proper name.

He has an idea that our program will achieve that aim.

Congress passes the following resolution which is to be appended to the program:

> Having listened to a reading of the memorandum published by the workers' federation of the Courtelary district, Congress recommends that publication to all socialists and all persons interested in social issues.
>
> Congress declares, however, that two points in the program could have been expressed more plainly.
>
> The ideas set out regarding the Commune are open to the interpretation that it is a matter of replacing the current form of State with a more restricted form, to wit, the Commune. We seek the elimination of every form of State, general or restricted, and the Commune is, as far we are concerned, only the synthetic expression of the organic form of free human associations.
>
> The idea of collectivism has given rise to mistaken interpretations which must be swept away. We want collectivism with all its logical consequences, not just from the point of view of collective appropriation of the means of production, but also from the point of view of enjoyment and collective consumption of products. Anarchist communism thus is going to be the necessary and inevitable

consequence of the social revolution and the expression of the new civilization that this revolution is to usher in.

We express our wish that scrutiny of this important matter may be resumed, taking as the basis of proof, application of these theories in a specific Commune, with due account taken of all of the constituent parts of that Commune, either as assets or difficulties in the implementation thereof.

Congress wishes to see, in the interests of workers' propaganda, publication of a pamphlet summarizing the memorandum presented by the socialist workers' Federation of the Courtelary district.

Notes to Minutes of the Jura Federation Congress

1. Carried in *Le Révolté* Geneva, 17 October 1880
2. Elisée Reclus (1830–1905) geographer and theoretician of anarchism, author in particular of *L'Evolution, la revolution et l'ideal anarchiste* 1898.
3. See below for the report on 'Anarchy and communism' by Carlo Cafiero.

Memorandum Submitted to the 1880 Jura Congress by the Courtelary District Workers' Federation

This program, a quite remarkable document, requires a short introductory note, in which we ought to underline a few points deserving of our attention.

For a start, it was drawn up by working men. It opens with the words "For us manual workers . . ." This was the decorative engraver Adhémar Schwitzguébel, writing on behalf of his comrades. These were workers who knew what they wanted. They bluntly spell out their views to the authoritarian socialists who flattered themselves that they would be taking power "in order to turn the present State into a communist State." And did not beat about the bush when they answered them thus: "We cannot share this outlook." And they expressly condemn the obstacle to progress represented, as they saw it, by the State, in a vivid phrase, inspired by the countryside in which they lived and labored: "Human society strides out, but the State is always a crock."

Yet these libertarians, supporters of the masses' spontaneity, had no worries about the activist minorities whom they regarded as indispensable in the steering of the social revolution: "Intervention (. . .) of the party possessed of a theoretical understanding of this revolution is a no less significant factor."

But, at the same time, the dangers of the successful revolution's being captured by leaders thrown up from within its own ranks did not escape them. They labored the necessity of acting in such a way that it "does not revert to operating to the advantage of the governing classes."

As good disciples of Bakunin and James Guillaume, but still ahead of their times, in that the anarchists of 1880 had not yet become syndicalists, they advocated a federation of trades bodies and sought a synthesis between commune and syndicate. They speculated: will the post-revolutionary commune be run by a general assembly of all its inhabitants or by local delegates from the various trades bodies? But, workers as they were, their penchant was rather towards the latter solution: it would be the local federation of trades bodies that would found the commune of the future.

Thus, problems which, in hard and fast form, confronted the Spanish libertarian communists, during the 1936 revolution, (See Volume III) had already been broached as long ago as 1880 by the manual workers of the Courtelary district.

Likewise, they anticipated one of the underlying principles of worker self-management: "In order to avert a relapse into the errant ways of centralized, bureaucratic administrations," it struck them that the commune locally, as well as the big public services nationally and internationally, ought not to be run by one single administration, but rather by different commissions, specializing in each sphere of activity. It is a structure which has prevailed in a number of self-managing communities in our own day.

The Program (Extracts)

"(. . .) For us manual workers, our task is dictated by the circumstances in which the laboring populations exist. Ours will be more of an indicative than a completed work. We shall set out that which we know; we shall voice our aspirations; we shall determine our demands; we shall conclude with the logic of popular common sense.

(. . .) In attacking the very foundations of bourgeois society, the social revolution will, by succeeding, consecrate fresh foundations for the development of human society. The work of peaceable progress, of successive piecemeal reforms will continue after the social revolution, as was the case with all of the great revolutions which have transformed the existential conditions of human societies.

That revolution is not just a theoretical construct: it is in the nature of things and is a development upon the existing situation that will bring it to pass. However, while the situation is the main element acting as the lever of revolution, the more or less intelligent and timely intervention of the party possessed of a theoretical understanding of that revolution is a no less significant factor. From that arises the need, not to wait for revolution to fall from out the skies, but to make preparations for it insofar as may be possible, to act in such a way that it does not revert to operating to the advantage of the governing classes.

(. . .) We find ourselves confronted by two very pronounced general trends. Some advocate the working classes' participation in current politics and their conquest of political power in the State. Others, on the other hand, call for abstention from political activity within the State.

It was differing theoretical notions of the political forms of the new society that founded the two schools, one of which stands for authoritarian socialism, and the other, anarchist socialism.

Unable to conceive of any form of politics other than the all-powerful, centralized State governed by an elective power, authoritarian socialism hopes to carry out the revolution in the system of ownership by taking over power in the State in order to turn the present State into a communist State.

We cannot share this outlook. The economic revolution sought by socialists is too profound a revolution for it to be able to be effected at the orders of some central power, whatever its strength and revolutionary vim. Decreed, it would remain a dead letter unless carried through by the people itself, right across the land. And even were the communist State to achieve a momentary existence, it would necessarily carry inside itself the seeds of destruction, because it would have resolved only one part of the social question, economic reform.

The whole question of attainment of human freedom — in its broadest sense — remains, because the State, by the very nature of its make-up and its manifestations, does not emancipate the human being but gobbles him up: the communist State, even more than the bourgeois State, would reduce the individual to a cipher and rule through force. As we see it, solution of the social question comprises, not just the most comprehensive possible achievement of material well-being for the benefit of, but also the achievement of the broadest measure of liberty for each and for all. It is on these grounds that we are not supporters of the communist State, and, as a result, we are the foes of a policy which is the logical avenue to such a State.

(. . .) Human society strides out, but the State is a always a crock.

Scrutiny of the contemporary situation furnishes startling proof of what we contend.

The statist socialist party, in order to operate politically on lawful terrain, had, unfortunately, but one option: to pocket its communist program and espouse a short-term practical program, on which basis it hoped to rally the masses: from the programs put forward by the democratic bourgeoisie, it borrows the salient points, affording them a socialist hue and thus have arisen the differing short-term policy programs of the lawful socialist party.

The bourgeois State would not countenance struggle even on this lawful terrain and the only country in Europe where this legal socialism was a power to be reckoned with, Germany, offers us the spectacle of a backlash right down the line: the retreat of the socialist party and its disorganization are the upshot of a whole protracted and powerful campaign.[1]

This statist political tactic thus does not strike us as the correct one. Let us take a look at the abstentionist approach. The anarchists, in broadening the social question and introducing into it, besides changes in ownership, the destruction of the State, were logically consistent in saying: since we seek destruction of the State, then, far from seeking to capture it in order to modify and transform it, we should instead be trying to create a vacuum around it, in order to undermine it with all the moral and material forces capable of making their contribution to this effort. Such are the origins of the contemporary abstentionist current. Unfortunately, common sense and theoretical logic rarely square with reality. While it is absolutely true, theoretically, that on the day the popular masses would refuse to appoint legislators, governments and State administrators, rejecting constitutions and laws and declining to pay taxes or perform military service, the State would have had its day in History, it is also no less true, on the other hand, that, in terms of practicality, most human beings are attached to something or other in the present society and in the State. It is through this practical bond, which is often trivial, that the whole system survives, sustained by the masses in spite of their discontent.

The State levies taxes and everybody aspires to pay less; it concerns itself with law enforcement and everybody wants proper justice at less cost; the State concerns itself with schools and parents seek good education for their children, at no cost to themselves; it concerns itself with the Church, and some want a liberal Church, some an orthodox or ultra-montane Church, while still others want the State to leave them free to follow no Church; the State concerns itself with policing, and everybody looks to it to guarantee his personal safety; it has a military organization, and many take it upon themselves to be soldiers, some as a career, some in a militia capacity; the State concerns itself with the roads, forests and water supply, and all these services have to satisfy the interests of the public; the State awards the right to appoint the government, the administrations, the law-makers, to vote institutions and laws and budgets and everybody takes pride in being a citizen-elector.

What with every individual caught up in one or several of these matters of practical detail, you have the entire mass hitched up to the system. Very few dare think and say that general services could as readily be provided directly by human society itself, freely organized.

(. . .) Three essential factors give us the authority to say that it is in the Commune that the social revolution will be at home. The old Jacobin revolutionary tradition has had its day, and, since the Paris Commune, a new revolutionary tradition has been building up around the idea of communal autonomy and federation. More and more, opinion is leaning towards this new political format, as the excesses of centralization are felt to be more of a burden by the populace everywhere; the development of the material situation as well as new currents of opinion lead on to the Commune and the federation of communes. Add to these general considerations the necessary consequences of our party's preparatory efforts, and we can assert that the people's insurrection will be hatched in the Commune.

Thus we ought to turn our attention to short-term revolutionary measures in the Commune.

The bourgeoisie's power over the popular masses springs from economic privileges, political domination and the enshrining of such privileges in the laws. So we must strike at the wellsprings of bourgeois power, as well as at its various manifestations.

The following measures strike us as essential to the welfare of the revolution, every bit as much as armed struggle against its enemies:

The insurgents must confiscate social capital, landed estates, mines, housing, religious and public buildings, instruments of labor, raw materials, precious metals, gems and precious stones and manufactured products:

All political, administrative and judicial authorities are to be deposed:

All legal intervention in the payment of collective or private debts and in the transmission of inheritance shall be abolished:

All taxes shall be abolished:

The army and police shall be stood down:

All documentation recording rents, ownership, mortgages, financial values and concessions shall be put to the torch.

These, it seems to us, must be the destructive measures. — What should the organizational measures of the revolution be?

Immediate and spontaneous establishment of trades bodies: provisional assumption by these of that portion of social capital proper to the functioning of their specialized area of production: local federation of a trades bodies and labor organization:

Establishment of neighborhood groups and federation of same in order to ensure short-term supply of subsistence:

Organization of the insurgent forces:

Establishment of commissions, on the basis of delegations from the groups, each with a specialization in running the affairs of the revolutionary Commune: a security commission against the revolution's enemies, a revolutionary strength commission, a commission to oversee social capital, a labor commission, a subsistence commission, a traffic service commission, a hygiene commission and an educational commission:

Establishment of external action commissions to work on the federation of all of the revolutionary forces of the insurgent Communes: to inspire, through revolutionary propaganda, insurrection in every Commune and region, and enforcement, on as wide a scale as possible, of measures appropriate to the destruction of the present order of things and to the well-being of the revolution:

Federation of Communes and organization of the masses, with an eye to the revolution's enduring until such time as all reactionary activity has been completely eradicated.

Collectivism strikes us (. . .) as the general form of a new society, but we shall strive with all our might to ensure that its organization and operation are free.

(. . .) Once trades bodies have been established, the next step is to organize local life. The organ of this local life is to be the federation of trades bodies and it is this local federation which is to constitute the future Commune. Will it be a general assembly of all inhabitants, or delegates from the trades bodies prior to referral to their particular assemblies, who will draw up the Commune's contract? It seems puerile to us to stipulate preference for one arrangement or the other: the two arrangements no doubt will apply, according to the traditions and particular importance of the Communes. We reckon it may be useful to say here that, broadly speaking, the more or less democratic practice of universal suffrage will increasingly pale in significance in a scientifically organized society, which is to say, one where hard facts and not meaningless artificial formulas will provide the basis for the whole life of society.

What are to be the powers of the Commune? Upkeep of all social wealth; monitoring usage of various capital elements — sub-soil, land, buildings, tools and raw materials — by the trades bodies; oversight of labor organization, insofar as general interests are concerned; organizing exchange and, eventually, distribution and consumption of products; maintenance of highways, buildings, thoroughfares and public gardens; organizing insurance against all accidents; health service: security service; local statistics: organizing the maintenance, training and education of children; sponsoring the arts, sciences, discoveries and applications.

We also want this local life in these different spheres of activity to be free, like the organization of a trade; free organization of individuals, groups and neighborhoods alike, to meet the various local services we have just enumerated.

In order to avert a relapse into the errant ways of centralized, bureaucratic administrations, we think that the Commune's general interests should not be handled by one single local administration, but rather by different commissions specializing in each sphere of activity and constituted directly by the interested-organizers of that local service. This procedure would divest the local administrations of their governmental character and would preserve the principle of autonomy in all of its integrity, while organizing local interests for the best.

(. . .) In the administration [of the] various overall [public] services, the principle of specialization shall apply as it does in communal administration, and we shall thereby avoid providing grounds for the criticism which has been made of anarchist socialism, that, in the organization of the general interests, it falls back upon a new form of State.

Notes to Memorandum Submitted to the 1880 Jura Congress

1. The allusion is to the period (after 1878) when Chancellor Bismarck was cracking down on the Social Democrats.

Anarchy and Communism
Carlo Cafiero's report to the Jura Federation

At the congress held in Paris by the Center region, one speaker, who stood out on account of his vitriol against the anarchists, stated: "Communism and anarchy are a shrieking mismatch."

Another speaker who also spoke out against the anarchists, albeit less vehemently, called out, while speaking of economic equality: "How can liberty be violated when equality exists?"

Well now! I hold both these speakers to have been mistaken.

It is perfectly possible to have economic equality without the slightest liberty. Certain religious communities are living proof of that, since the most complete equality obtains there, alongside despotism. Complete equality, in that the leader wears the same garb and eats at the same table as the others: only his right to command, sets him apart from them. And the supporters of the "people's State?" If they were not to run up against all sorts of obstacles, I am sure that they would eventually achieve perfect equality, but at the same time, also the most perfect despotism, for, let us not forget, the despotism of the present State would be magnified by the economic despotism of all of the capital which would have passed into State hands, and the whole thing would be multiplied by all of the centralization necessary to this new State. And it is for that reason that we anarchists, friends of freedom, propose to fight it to the bitter end.

Thus, contrary to what has been said, we are perfectly right to fear for liberty, even should equality exist: whereas there cannot be any fear for equality where true liberty, which is to say, anarchy, exists.

Finally, far from being a shrieking mismatch, anarchy and communism would shriek if they were not to be harnessed together, for these two terms, synonyms for liberty and equality are the two necessary and indivisible terms of the revolution.

Our revolutionary ideal is very simple, as may be seen: like that of our predecessors, it is made up of these two terms: liberty and equality. Except that there is one slight difference.

Learning from the travesties which all sorts of reactionaries have always made of liberty and equality, we have been careful to set alongside these two terms an expression of their exact value. These two precious currencies have been counterfeited so often that we must at last know and assay their precise value.

So, alongside these two terms, liberty and equality, let us place two equivalents whose plain meaning cannot give rise to equivocation, and let us state: "We want liberty, which is to say, anarchy, and equality, which is to say, communism."

Anarchy today is the attack, the war upon all authority, all power, every State. In the society to come, anarchy will be the veto, the prevention of the re-establishment of any authority, any power, any State; full and complete freedom for the individual who, freely and driven by his needs alone, his tastes and his sympathies, bands together with other individuals into a group or association; freedom of development for the association which federates with others within the commune or neighborhood; freedom of development for communes which federate within the region and so on; the regions within the nation; the nations within humankind.

Communism, the matter with which we are most especially concerned today, is the second point in our revolutionary ideal.

Communism, currently, is still attack; it is not the destruction of authority but is the taking into possession of all of the wealth existing world-wide, on behalf of the whole of humanity. In the society to come, communism will be the enjoyment by all men of all existing wealth, in accordance with the principle: **From each according to ability, to each according to needs**, which is to say, **From each and to each according to wish.**

It should be pointed out, and this is primarily an answer to our adversaries, the authoritarian or statist communists, that the appropriation and enjoyment of all existing wealth should, as we see it, be the doing of the people itself. The people, mankind, not being individually capable of seizing the wealth and holding it in their two hands, some have sought to conclude from that, it is true, that for that reason we have to raise up an entire class of leaders, representatives and depositories of the common wealth. But this is an opinion we do not share. No intermediaries, no representatives who always end up representing no one but themselves, no one to moderate equality, no more moderators of liberty, no new government, no new State, even should it style itself popular or democratic, revolutionary or provisional.

The common wealth being scattered right across the planet, while belonging by right to the whole of humanity, those who happen to be within reach of that wealth and in a position to make use of it will utilize it in common. The folk from a given country will use the land, the machines, the workshops, the houses, etc., of that country and they will all make common use of them. As part of humanity, they will exercise here, in fact and directly, their rights over a portion of mankind's wealth. But should an inhabitant of Peking visit this country, he would enjoy the same rights as the rest: in common with the others, he would enjoy all of the wealth of the country, just as he would have in Peking.

So the speaker who denounced anarchists as wanting to vest ownership in the corporations was well wide of the mark. A fine kettle of fish it would be to destroy the State only to replace it with a host of tiny States, to slay the single-headed monster only to make way for the thousand-headed monster!

No: as we have said and will never cease repeating: no go-betweens, no courtiers and no obliging servitors who always wind up as the real masters: we want all existing wealth to be taken over directly by the people itself, want it to be held in its powerful hands, and want the people to decide for itself the best way of putting it to use, either for production or consumption.

Yes, communism is feasible. Each person can very well be left to avail at will of what he needs, since there will be enough for everyone. There will no longer be any need to require more labor than the individual is willing to give, because there will still be a sufficiency of products for the next day.

And it is thanks to this abundance that labor will lose the ignoble character of slavishness, leaving it solely the charms of a moral and physical need, like the need to study and live alongside nature.

This is not at all to argue that communism is possible: we can affirm its necessity. Not only can one be a communist, but one has to be one, on pain of falling short of the goal of revolution.

Indeed, once the instruments of labor and raw materials have been taken into common ownership, if we were to cling to private appropriation of the products of labor, we should find ourselves obliged to retain money, the root of more or less sizable accumulation of wealth, according to the greater or lesser merits, or rather, greater or lesser shrewdness of the individual. In which case equality would have vanished, since anyone who contrived possession of more wealth would already, by virtue of that very fact, have raised himself above the level of the others. It would require just one more step to be taken for counter-revolutionaries to introduce rights of inheritance. And in fact, I have heard one socialist of repute, a self-styled revolutionary, who argued in favor of individual ownership of products, eventually declare that he could see nothing wrong with society's countenancing transmission of these products by way of inheritance: according to him, the matter was of no consequence. For those of us who are intimately acquainted with where the accumulation of wealth and its transmission through inheritance has taken society, there is no room for doubt on this score.

But individual claim upon products would not only restore the inequality between men: it would also restore inequality between the various types of work. We should see the immediate re-emergence of "clean" and "dirty" work, "uplifting" and "degrading" work and the former would be performed by the wealthier, leaving the latter as the lot of the poorest. In which case it would no longer be vocation and personal taste that would decide a man to pursue such and such an activity rather than another: it would be interest, the expectation of earning more in such and such a profession. This would lead to a renaissance of idleness and diligence, merit and demerit, good and evil, vice and virtue, and consequently, of "reward" on the one hand, and of "punishment" on the other, along with law, judge, underling and prison.

There are socialists who persist in arguing the notion of individual ownership of the products of labor, on the basis of a sense of fairness.

Curious delusion! With collective labor, which foists upon us the necessity of large-scale production and widespread mechanization, with modern industry's ever increasing tendency to avail of the labor of preceding generations, how could we determine which morsel is the product of one man's labor and which the product of another's? It is utterly impossible and our adversaries acknowledge this so readily themselves that they wind up saying; — "Well then! Let us take time worked as the basis for distribution." But at the same time they themselves confess that this would be unfair, since three hours of Peter's work can often be worth five hours of Paul's.

There was a time when we used to describe ourselves as "collectivists," in that that was the word distinguishing us from the individualists and authoritarian communists, but, basically, we were quite simply anti-authoritarian communists, and by calling ourselves "collectivists," we sought to use that name to express our idea that everything should be held in common, with no differentiation being made between the instruments and materials of labor and the products of collective labor.

But one fine day we witnessed the emergence of yet another stripe of socialists who, reviving the errant ways of the past, began to philosophize, and draw distinctions and make differentiations on this score, and finally ended up as apostles of the following thesis:

"There are" — they say — "use values and production values. Use values are those which we employ to meet our personal needs: they are the house where we live, the provisions we eat, the clothes, the books, etc., whereas production values are those of which we make use for production purposes: the workshop, the hangar, the byre, shops, machines and all sorts of instruments of labor, the land, raw materials, etc. The former values which serve to meet the individual's needs — they say —ought to be in individual hands, while the latter, the ones which serve us all for production, should be held collectively."

Such was the new economic theory devised, or rather, revived, to order.

But let me ask you, you who award the lovely title of production value to the coal which fuels the machine, the oil that lubricates it, the oil that illuminates its operations, why do you withhold that description from the bread and the meat upon which I feed, the oil with which I dress my salad, the gas that illuminates my work, and everything that serves to sustain and keep going that most perfect of all machines, the father of all machines: man?

Would you class among production values the meadow and the byre which shelters the oxen and horses and yet exclude the homes and gardens which serve the noblest of all animals: man?

Where is your logic in that?

Moreover, you who have made yourselves apostles of this theory, are perfectly well aware that this demarcation does not exist in reality, and that, if it is hard to trace today, it will vanish utterly on the day when we are all producers as well as consumers.

So, as we can see, it was not that theory that could have given fresh strength to advocates of individual ownership of the products of labor. This theory achieved only one thing: it gave away the game of these few socialists who sought to blunt the thrust of the revolutionary idea; it has opened our eyes and shown us the necessity of declaring ourselves quite bluntly communists.

But finally let us tackle the one and only serious objection that our adversaries have put forward against communism. They all agree that we are inevitably moving towards communism, but they note that we are just at the beginning of this and, products being in insufficient supply, rationing and sharing will have to be introduced, and the best way to share out the products of labor would be one based upon the amount of labor performed by each individual.

To which we reply that in the society to come, even when rationing might be required of us, we should remain communists; which is to say that rationing should be based, not upon deserts, but upon needs.

Take a family, that model of communism on a small scale, an authoritarian rather than a libertarian communism, it is true, though, in our example, that changes nothing.

Inside the family, the father brings in, say, a hundred sous a day, the eldest son three francs, a younger son forty sous, and the youngest of all just twenty sous per day. They all bring the money to the mother who holds the purse-strings and feeds them all. They all contribute varying sums, but at dinner, each one helps himself as he likes and according to appetite; there is no rationing. But bad times come, and straitened circumstances force the mother to cease leaving the distribution of dinner to individual preference and appetite. Rationing has to be introduced, and either at the instigation of the mother, or by everyone's tacit agreement, the portions are reduced. But lo! this rationing is not done in accordance with deserts, for it is the youngest son and the child especially who receive the larger part, and as for the choicest cut, that is reserved for the old lady who brings in nothing at all. Even in times of scarcity, this principle of rationing according to needs is observed in the family. Would it be otherwise in the great family of mankind in the future?

(. . .) One cannot be an anarchist without being a communist. Indeed, the slightest hint of limitation carries with it the seeds of authoritarianism. It could not show itself without promptly spawning law, judge and gendarme. We have to be communists, because the people, which does not understand the collectivists' sophisms, has a perfect grasp of communism, as friends Reclus and Kropotkin have already indicated. We must be communists, because we are anarchists, because anarchy and communism are the two essential terms of the revolution.

Declaration of the Anarchists Arraigned Before the Criminal Court in Lyon by Kropotkin January 19, 1883

What anarchy is and what anarchists are, we are about to say.

Anarchists, gentlemen, are citizens who, in an age when freedom of opinions is being preached on every side, have deemed it incumbent upon them to recommend unrestrained freedom.

Yes, gentlemen, around the world, we are a few thousand, a few million workers who demand absolute freedom, nothing but freedom, freedom entire!

We want freedom, which is to say, we claim for every human being the right and wherewithal to do whatsoever he may please, and not to do what does not please them: to have all of their needs met in full, with no limit other than natural impracticability and the equally valid needs of his neighbors.

We want freedom and we hold its existence to be incompatible with the existence of any power, whatever may be its origins and format, whether it be elected or imposed, monarchist or republican, whether it draws its inspiration from divine right or popular right, from the Blessed Blister or universal suffrage.

Because history is there to teach us that all governments resemble one another and are much of a muchness. The best ones are the worst. The greater the hypocrisy in some, the greater the cynicism in others! At bottom, always the same procedures, always the same intolerance. Not even the seemingly most liberal among them does not hold in reserve, beneath the dust of its legislated arsenals, some splendid little law on the International, for use against irksome opponents.

In other words, in the eyes of anarchists, the evil resides, not in this form of government as against some other. But in the very idea of government as such, in the authority principle.

In short, our ideal is to see the substitution for administrative and legal oversight and imposed discipline, in human relations, of the free contract, constantly liable to review and dissolution.

Anarchists thus intend to teach the people to do without government just as it is beginning to learn to do without God.

It will learn to do without property-owners too. Indeed, the worst of tyrants is not the one who throws you into a dungeon, but the one who keeps you hungry: not the one who takes you by the throat, but the one who seizes you by the belly.

No liberty without equality! No liberty in a society wherein capital is a monopoly in the hands of a minority that shrinks with every passing day and where nothing is shared equally, not even public education, even though this is paid for out of everyone's pocket.

We hold that capital, the common inheritance of humanity, in that it is the fruit of the collaboration of past generations and present generations, ought to be accessible to all, so that none may be excluded: and so that no one, on the other hand, may lay claim to a fragment at the expense of everyone else. In short, what we want is equality: de facto equality by way of a corollary to, or rather, essential precondition for liberty. **From each according to abilities, to each according to needs**: that is what we truly and earnestly yearn for: that is what shall be, since there is no prescription that may prevail over demands that are both legitimate and necessary. That is why we are marked down for every calumny.

Rascals that we are, we demand bread for all, work for all: and independence and justice for all, too!

PAROLES D'UN RÉVOLTÉ BY KROPOTKIN (1885)[1]

THE DECOMPOSITION OF STATES

When, following the collapse of medieval institutions, the incipient States put in an appearance in Europe and consolidated and expanded through conquest, guile and murder — they did not, as yet, meddle in other than a tiny range of human affairs.

Today, the State has come to meddle in every aspect of our lives. From cradle to grave, it smothers us in its embrace. Sometimes as central State, sometimes as provincial- or model-State, occasionally as commune-State, it dogs our every step, looming at every street corner, overwhelming us, gripping us, plaguing us.

It legislates our every action. It constructs mountains of laws and ordinances in which even the most cunning lawyer can no longer keep his bearings. Daily it creates further ramifications which it clumsily fits to the patched-up old mechanism, and manages to construct a machine so complicated, so hybridised, so obstructive, that it disgusts even those charged with operating it.

It creates an army of employees, of tight-fisted spiders who know nothing of the world save what they can see through the murky windows of their offices, or from their absurdly scrawled paperwork, a dismal band with but one religion, the religion of money, and but one preoccupation, clinging on to some party, be it black, purple or white, provided it guarantees maximum promotion for minimum exertion.

The results are only too familiar to us. Is there a single branch of State activity that does not disgust those unfortunate enough to have dealings with it? A single branch in which the State, after centuries of existence and patching-up, has not furnished proof of utter incompetence?

Note to Paroles D'un Révolté

1. Taken from Pierre Kropotkin *Paroles d'un Révolté* 1885.

FROM THE MEDIEVAL COMMUNE TO THE MODERN COMMUNE

The text which follows is one of Kropotkin's most important ones, one that has also exercised the greatest influence, notably over Spanish libertarian communism. But it has not always been properly understood. Too many Spanish anarchists saw Kropotkin as having sought to revive the communes of the Middle

Ages, and they were quick to identify this supposed reversion to the past with the tradition, still lively in the countryside in their own homeland, of the primitive, particularist and free peasant community.

In fact, such a construction placed upon Kropotkin's remarks is, in part at least, mistaken. Indeed, the author never tires of insisting, as indeed Marx does in *The Civil War in France*, upon the essential differences he detects between the commune of the past and that of the future. In our age of railways, telegraphs and scientific advances, the commune will, he argued, have a very different aspect from the one it had in the twelfth century. It will not be designed to replace the local lord, but rather, the State. It will not confine itself to being communalist, but will be communist. Far from having a tendency to "retreat within its walls," it will seek "to spread, to become universal." And Kropotkin is categorical in stating that, in our day, "a tiny commune could not survive a week": it will be confronted by an overwhelming need to contract alliances and to federate.

But it is here that the thinking of the anarchist theoretician is at its most elastic and accommodates the idealistic and parochial constructions which his future Spanish disciples thought themselves entitled, much later on, to place upon it.

In Kropotkin's estimation, every commune is not part of just one federation of communes, which cherishes liberty above all else, but of all manner of federative links which overlap, interweave and superimpose themselves one upon another, an attractive prospect, to be sure, and an intoxicating one for anyone who prizes liberty above all else, provided that it proves to be compatible with planning along modern lines.

In the same way, Kropotkin is attractive when he moves on from the communes proper, which is to say, the local communes, to the affinity groups which can no longer be tied to a given territory and whose members would be "scattered over a thousand cities and villages," and where, after the fashion of Charles Fourier, "a given individual will find his needs met only by banding together with other individuals sharing the same tastes."

Here there is a direct line of descent between Kropotkin and those Spanish libertarian communists who, at their congress in Zaragoza in May 1936, were to wallow in nostalgia for a golden age, for the "free commune" and support for the parochial focus upon the *patria chica*, and, on the very eve of an imminent social revolution, dwelt, with undue emphasis, upon the affinity groups of nudists and naturists, "refractory to industrialization."

It has been stated elsewhere that these naive and idealistic notions, invoking Kropotkin, would be vigorously resisted by one eminent Spanish anarcho-syndicalist economist, Diego Abad de Santillan.[1] In the view of the latter, "free communes" could not be viable, from the economic point of view. "Our ideal" — he explained — "is the commune combined, federated and integrated into the overall economy of the country and of other countries in revolution (...) A socialized, directed and planned economy is imperative and fits in with the evolution of the modern economic world.

Note to Introduction to From the Medieval Commune

1. Daniel Guérin *L'Anarchisme* 1965: Santillan *El Organismo económico de la Revolución* 1936: See also Volume III of this anthology.

When we say that the social revolution ought to proceed through liberation of the Communes, and that it will be the Communes, utterly independent and released from the oversight of the State, which will, alone, be able to provide the requisite context for revolution and the wherewithal for its accomplishment, we are taken to task for trying to resuscitate a form of society long since overtaken and which has had its day. "But the Commune" — we are told — "is a relic from another age! By trying to tear down the State and replace it with free Communes, you have turned your gaze upon the past and would transport us back to the high middle ages, re-igniting the ancient quarrels between them and destroying the national unity so dearly won over the course of history!"

Well now, let us examine this criticism.

First, let us note that any comparison with the past has only a relative value. If, indeed, the Commune we seek was really only a reversion to the medieval Commune, would we not have to concede that today's Commune could scarcely assume the same shape it took seven centuries ago? Now, is it not obvious that, being established in our day, in our age of railways, telegraphs, cosmopolitan science and the quest for pure truth, the Commune would be organized along lines so very different from those which characterized it in the twelfth century that we should be confronted with a quite novel phenomenon, situated in new conditions and necessarily entailing absolutely differing consequences?

Furthermore, our adversaries, the champions of the State, in its various guises, ought to keep it in mind that we might make the very same objection to them.

We too could say to them, and with considerably more reason, that it is they who have their gazed fixed upon the past, since the State is a formation every bit as old as the Commune. With this single difference: while the State in history stands for the negation of all liberty, for absolutism and arbitrariness, for the ruination of its subjects, for the scaffold and for torture, it is precisely in the liberation of the Communes and in the revolts of peoples and Communes against States that we discover the finest pages that History has to offer. To be sure, if we were to be transported into the past, it would not be back to a Louis XI or a Louis XV, or to a Catherine II, that we should look: it would, rather, be to the communes or republics of Amalfi and Florence, to those of Toulouse and Laon, Liege and Courtray, Augsburg and Nuremburg, Pskov and Novgorod.

So it is not a matter of bandying words and sophisms: what counts is that we should study, closely analyze and not imitate [those] who are content to tell us: "But the Commune, that is the Middle Ages! And damned as a result!" — "The State represents a past record of misdeeds" — we would reply — "So it is all the more damnable!"

Between the medieval Commune and any that might be established today, and probably will be established soon, there will be lots of essential differences: a whole abyss opened up by six or seven centuries of human development and hard experience. Let us take a look at the main ones.

What was the essential object of this "conspiracy" or "confederacy" into which the bourgeois of a given city entered in the twelfth century? The object was to break free of the seigneur. The inhabitants, merchants and artisans, came together and pledged not to allow "anyone at all to do wrong to one of them and treat him thereafter as a serf": it was against its former masters that the Commune rose up in arms. "Commune" — says one twelfth century writer quoted by Augustin Thierry — "is a new and despicable word, and this is what is meant by the term: persons liable to tallage now deliver only once a year to their seigneur the rent which they owe him. If they commit any crime, they can be quit of it through payment of a legally prescribed fine: and, as for the levies in money customarily inflicted upon serfs, they are wholly exempt from those."

So it was very much against the seigneur that the medieval Commune revolted. It is from the State that today's Commune will seek liberation. This is a crucial difference, since, remember, it was the State, represented by the king, which, later, noticing how the Communes sought to register their independence from their Lord, sent in his armies to "chastise," as the chronicle has it, "the presumption of these idlers who, by reason of the Commune, made a show of rebellion and defiance of the Crown."

Tomorrow's Commune will appreciate that it cannot any longer acknowledge any superior: that, above it, there cannot be anything, save the interests of the Federation, freely embraced by itself in concert with other Communes. It knows that there can be no half-way house: either the Commune is to be absolutely free to endow itself with whatever institutions it wishes and introduce all reforms and revolutions it may deem necessary, or else it will remain what it has been to date, a mere subsidiary of the State, chained in its every movement, forever on the brink of conflict with the State and certain of succumbing in any ensuing struggle. It knows that it must smash the State and replace it with the Federation, and it will act accordingly. More than that, it will have the wherewithal so to do. Today, it is no longer just small towns which are hoisting the flag of communal insurrection. It is Paris, Lyon,

Marseilles, Cartagena, and soon every great city will unfurl the same flag. And that, if ever there was one, is an essential difference.

In liberating itself from its Seigneur, was the medieval Commune also breaking free of the wealthy bourgeois who, through sale of merchandise and capital, had amassed personal fortunes inside the city? Not at all! Once it had torn down the towers of its seigneur, the town dweller soon watched the rise within the Commune itself of the citadels of rich merchants determined to bring him to heel, and the domestic history of the medieval Communes is the history of a bitter struggle between rich and poor, a struggle which, inevitably, ended with intervention by the king. With aristocracy expanding more and more within the very bosom of the Commune, the populace, now fallen, with regard to the wealthy seigneur from the upper city, into a servitude which had previously been his status with regard to the lord outside, realized that the Commune was no longer worth defending: it deserted the ramparts which he had erected in order to win his freedom and which, as a result of individualist rule, had become the boulevards of a new serfdom. With nothing to lose, it left the rich merchants to look to their own defenses, and the latter were defeated; unsexed by luxury and vice, enjoying no support from the people, they were soon compelled to yield to the injunctions of the king's heralds and handed over the keys to their cities. In other communes, it was the rich themselves who opened the gates of their towns to the imperial, royal or ducal armies, in order to forestall the popular vengeance hanging over their heads.

But will the primary concern of the nineteenth century Commune not be to put paid to such social inequalities? To seize all the social capital amassed within its borders and make it available to those who wish to deploy it for production and to add to the general well-being? Will its first thought not be to smash the power of capital and banish forever any chance that aristocracy, which brought about the downfall of the medieval Communes, might raise its head? Will it mistake bishop and monk for allies? Finally, is it going to imitate ancestors who looked to the Commune for nothing more than the creation of a State within the State? Who, abolishing the power of the seigneur or king, could think of nothing better to do than reconstitute the very same power, down to the finest detail, forgetting that that power, though confined within the town walls, nevertheless retained all of the vices of its paragon? Are the proletarians of our century about to imitate those Florentines who, while abolishing titles of nobility or forcing them to be worn as a badge of disgrace, simultaneously allowed a new aristocracy, an aristocracy of the fat purse, to be created? Finally, will they do as those artisans did who, upon arriving at the town hall, piously imitated their predecessors and re-established that whole hierarchy of powers which they had so recently overthrown? Will they change only the personnel, and leave the institutions untouched?

Certainly not. The nineteenth century Commune, learning from experience, will do better. It will be a commune in more than just name. It will be, not just communalist, but communist: revolutionary in its policy, it will be revolutionary in matters of production and exchange too. It will not do away with the State only to restore it, and lots of communes will know how to teach by example, abolishing government by proxy, and fighting shy of commending their sovereignty to the happenstance of the polling booth.

Once it had shaken off the yoke of its seigneur, did the medieval commune seek to hit him in the source of his power? Did it try to rally to the assistance of the agricultural population which surrounded it and, equipped with weaponry which rural serfs did not have, place these weapons in the service of the wretches upon whom it looked proudly down from atop its walls? Far from it! Guided by a purely selfish sentiment, the medieval Commune retreated within its walls. On how many occasions did it not jealously close its gates and raise its drawbridges against the slaves who flocked in search of refuge, and let them be butchered by the seigneur, as it looked on, within arquebus range? Proud of its liberties, it did not think to extend them to those groaning outside. It was at this price, at the price of preserving its neighbors' serfdom, that many a commune earned its independence. Then again, was it not also in the interests of the great bourgeois of the commune to see the serfs from the plains stay bound to the land, ignorant of industry and commerce, and still obliged to look to the town for their supplies of iron, metals and industrial products? And whenever the artisan thought to stretch his hand beyond the walls separating him from the serfs, what could he avail against the wishes of the bourgeois who had the upper hand, a monopoly upon the arts of war and hardened mercenaries in his hire?

Now what a difference: would the victorious Paris Commune have made do with endowing itself with more or less free municipal institutions? The Parisian proletariat smashing its chains would have signaled social revolution, first in Paris and then in the rural communes. The Paris Commune, even as it was fighting desperately for its survival, nevertheless told the peasant: Seize the land, all of it! It would not have confined itself to words, and, if need be, its valiant sons would have carried their weapons to far-flung villages to assist the peasant with his revolution: to drive out the land-thieves, and seize it in order to place it at the disposal of all who wish and have the expertise to harvest its bounty. The medieval Commune sought to retreat inside its walls: the nineteenth century one seeks to range far and wide, to become universal. It has replaced communal privilege with human solidarity.

The medieval commune could ensconce itself within its walls and, to some extent, cut itself off from its neighbors. Whenever it entered into dealings with other communes, those dealings were most often confined to a treaty in defense of city rights against the seigneur, or a solidarity agreement for the mutual protection of commune citizens on long journeys. And when authentic leagues were formed between towns, as in Lombardy, Spain and Belgium, these leagues being far from homogeneous, and too fragile because of the diversity of privileges, promptly fragmented into isolated groups or succumbed under the onslaught of neighboring States.

What a difference with the groups that would be formed today! A tiny Commune could not survive a week without being compelled by circumstance to establish consistent relations with industrial, commercial and artistic centers, etc., and these centers in turn, would be sensible of the need to throw their gates wide open to inhabitants of neighboring villages, adjacent communes and distant cities.

Were a given large town to proclaim the Commune tomorrow, abolish individual ownership within its borders and introduce fully-fledged communism, which is to say, collective enjoyment of social capital, the instruments of labor and the products of the labor performed, and, provided that the town was not surrounded by enemy armies, within days convoys of carts would be pouring into the market place and suppliers despatching cargoes of raw materials from far-off ports: the products of the city's industry, once the needs of the urban population had been met, would go off to the four corners of the globe in search of buyers: outsiders would flood in, and everyone, peasants, citizens of neighboring towns, foreigners would carry home tales of the marvelous life of the free city where everyone was working, where there were neither poor nor oppressed any more, where everybody enjoyed the fruits of their labor, without anyone claiming the lion's share. Isolation need not be feared: if communists in the United States have a grievance in their community, it does not relate to isolation, but rather to the intrusion of the surrounding bourgeois world into their communal affairs.

The fact that today commerce and trade, overruling the limitations of borders, have also torn down the walls of the ancient cities. They have already established the cohesiveness which was missing in the middle ages. All the inhabited areas of western Europe are so intimately bound up one with another that isolation has become an impossibility for any of them: there is no village perched so high upon a mountain crest that it does not have its industrial and commercial center, towards which it gravitates, and with which it can no longer sever its connections.

The development of the big industrial hubs has done more.

Even in our own day, the parochial mentality could arouse a lot of frictions between two adjacent communes, prevent their allying with one another and even ignite fratricidal strife. But whereas such frictions may indeed preclude direct federation of these two communes, that federation will proceed through the good offices of the larger centers. Today, two tiny adjoining municipalities often have nothing to bring them really close: what few dealings they have would be more likely to generate friction than establish ties of solidarity. But both already have a shared hub with which they are frequently in contact and without which they cannot survive, and whatever their parish rivalries, they will be compelled to unite through the good offices of the larger town whence they obtain their provisions or whither they bring their produce: each of them will be part of the same federation, in order to sustain their dealings with that higher instance and in order to cluster about it.

And yet this hub could not itself acquire an irksome ascendancy over the surrounding communes. Thanks to the infinite variety of the needs of industry and commerce, all population centers already have several centers to which they are bound, and as their needs develop, they will form attachments to other centers capable of meeting these new needs. So various are our needs and so rapidly do they sprout that soon one federation will no longer suffice to meet them all. So the Commune will sense a need to contract other alliances and enter into another federation. Member of one group for the purposes of securing its food requirements, the Commune will have to belong to a second one in order to obtain other items it needs, say, metals, and then a third and fourth group for its cloth and craft goods. Pick up an economic atlas of any country at all, and you will see that economic frontiers do not exist: the areas where various products are produced and exchanged mutually overlap, interlinking and criss-crossing. Similarly, the federations of communes, if they continue to expand freely, would soon interweave, criss-cross and overlap, thereby forming a compact "one and indivisible" network quite different from these statist combinations which are merely juxtaposed, just as the rods of the fasces are grouped around the lictor's axe.

Thus, let us repeat, those who come along and tell us that the Communes, once rid of State oversight, are going to clash and destroy one another in internecine warfare, overlook one thing: the intimate bonds already existing between various localities, thanks to the industrial and commercial hubs, thanks to the numbers of such hubs, thanks to unbroken dealings. They fail to appreciate what the middle ages were, with their closed cities and caravans lumbering slowly along difficult roads overlooked by robber-barons; they overlook the flows of men, goods, mail, telegrams, ideas and affections hurtling between our cities like the waters of rivers which never run dry; they have no clear picture of the difference between the two eras they seek to compare one with the other.

Also, do we not have the example of history to prove to us that the instinct to federate has already grown into one of mankind's most urgent needs? The State need only fall into disarray some day for some reason or another, and the machinery of oppression falter in its operations and free alliances will sprout all unprompted. Let us remember the spontaneous federations of the armed bourgeoisie during the Great Revolution. Remember the federations that sprang up spontaneously in Spain and salvaged that country's independence when the State was rattled to its very foundations by Napoleon's conquering armies. As soon as the State is no longer in a position to impose enforced union, union sprouts by itself, in accordance with natural needs. Overthrow the State and the federated society will sprout from its ruins, truly one, truly indivisible, but free and expanding in solidarity by virtue of that very freedom.

But there is something else. For the medieval bourgeois, the Commune was an isolated State plainly separated from the rest by its borders. For us, the "Commune" is no longer a territorial agglomeration, but is instead a generic term, synonymous with a combination of equals acknowledging neither borders nor walls. The social Commune will very quickly cease to be a clearly defined whole. Each group from the Commune will of necessity be drawn towards other similar groups from other Communes; they will band together and federate with them through ties at least as solid as those binding them to their fellow townsmen and will constitute a Commune of interests whose members will be scattered across a thousand towns and villages. Such an individual will only find his needs met when he bands together with other individuals of similar tastes and resident in a hundred other communes.

Even today free societies are starting to cover the whole vast expanse of human activity. No longer is it just to satisfy his scientific, literary or artistic interests that the man of leisure sets up societies. And it is not just to prosecute the class struggle that one combines.

One would be hard put to discover a single one of the many and varied manifestations of human activity not already represented by freely constituted societies and their numbers are forever expanding as they daily intrude into new spheres of activity, even those hitherto regarded as the State's special preserve. Literature, the arts, the sciences, education, commerce, industry, trade, entertainments, health, museums, long-distance undertakings, polar expeditions, even territorial defenses, help for the wounded, defense against aggression and the courts themselves — on every side we see private initiative at work in the shape of free societies. This is the characteristic tendency and feature of the latter half of the nineteenth century.

Left unhindered and to itself, and with vast new scope for development, this tendency will serve as the basis for the society of the future. It is through free combinations that the social Commune will be organized and these very same combinations will tear down walls and frontiers. There will be millions of communes, no longer territorial, but reaching out a hand across rivers, mountain ranges and oceans, to unite individuals scattered around the four corners of the globe and the people into one single family of equals.

Kropotkin's Revolutionary Government

Part I

That existing governments ought to be abolished, so that liberty, equality and fraternity may no longer be empty words but become living realities: that all forms of government tried to date have been only so many forms of oppression and ought to be replaced by some new form of association: upon that, everyone with a brain and of a temperament at all revolutionary is agreed. To tell the truth, one does not even have to be very innovative to arrive at this conclusion: the vices of existing governments and impossibility of reforming them are too striking not to leap to the eyes of every reasonable onlooker. And as for overthrowing governments, it is common knowledge that at certain times this is encompassed without undue difficulty. There are times when governments collapse virtually unassisted, like a house of cards, under the breath of a rebellious people. This we saw in 1848 and in 1870: and we shall see it anon.

Overthrowing a government is everything as far as a bourgeois revolutionary is concerned. For us, it marks only the beginning of the social revolution. Once the machinery of State has been derailed, the hierarchy of officials thrown into disarray and no longer knowing in what direction to go, soldiers having lost confidence in their officers, in short, the army of capital's defenders once routed, then there looms before us the mammoth undertaking of demolishing the institutions which serve to perpetuate economic and political slavery. What are revolutionaries to do, once they have the opportunity to act freely?

To that question, the anarchists alone answer: "No government, anarchy!" All the others say: "A revolutionary government!" They differ only upon the form to be given to this government elected by universal suffrage in the State or in the Commune: the rest come down in favor of revolutionary dictatorship.

A "revolutionary government!" Those two words have a very curious ring to them in the ears of those who understand what social revolution ought to signify and what government signifies. The two words are mutually contradictory, mutually destructive. We have indeed seen despotic governments — it is the essence of every government that it is for reaction and against revolution and that it should have a natural tendency towards despotism: but a revolutionary government has never yet been seen, and with good reason. Because revolution, synonymous with "disorder," the toppling and overthrow of age-old institutions within the space of a few days, with violent demolition of established forms of property, with the destruction of caste, with the rapid change of received thinking on morality, or rather, on the hypocrisy which stands in its place, with individual liberty and spontaneous action, is the precise opposite, the negation of government, the latter being synonymous with the "established order," conservatism, maintenance of existing institutions, and negation of individual initiative and individual action. And yet we continually hear talk of this white blackbird, as if a "revolutionary government" was the most straightforward thing in the world, as commonplace and as familiar to everyone as royalty, empire or papacy!

That bourgeois so-called revolutionaries should peddle this notion is understandable. We know what they understand by Revolution. It is quite simply a fresh coat of plaster upon the bourgeois republic: it is the assumption by so-called republicans, of the well-paid posts currently the preserve of Bonapartists or royalists. At most, it is the divorce of Church and State, replaced by the concubinage of them both, confiscation of clerical assets for the benefit of the State and primarily of the future administrators of those assets, and perhaps, additionally, a referendum or some such device. But that revolutionary socialists should act as apostles of this notion, we cannot comprehend except by one or the other of two suppositions: either those who embrace it are imbued with bourgeois prejudices, which they have derived, unwittingly, from literature and especially history written by bourgeois for bourgeois consumption, and, being still pervaded with the spirit of slavishness, the product of centuries of slavery, they cannot even imagine themselves free; or else they want no part of this Revolution whose name is forever upon their lips: they would be content with a mere plastering job upon existing institutions, provided that it carried them to power, even though they would have to wait to see what had to be done to pacify "the beast," which is to say, the people. Their only gripe with those in government today is that they covet their places. With these, we need not bandy words. So we shall address only those whose mistakes are honest ones.

Let us open with the first of the two forms of " revolutionary government" proposed — elected government.

Royal or other authority having been overthrown, and the army of capital's defenders routed, ferment and discussion of public affairs and the urge to move forward are everywhere. New ideas crop up, the need for serious change understood: we must act and ruthlessly embark upon the task of demolition, so as to clear the way for the new life. But what would they have us do? Summon the people to elections, to elect a government without delay, to entrust to it the task which each and every one of us ought to be carrying out on our own initiative!

This is what Paris did after March 18, 1871. "I shall never forget" — a friend told us — "those splendid moments of deliverance. I had climbed down from my garret in the Latin Quarter to join that huge open air club which filled the boulevards from one end of Paris to the other. Everyone was debating public affairs; every personal preoccupation had been forgotten; buying and selling no longer came into it; everyone was ready to hurl himself body and soul into the future. Even some bourgeois, carried away by the universal enthusiasm, were happy to see the new world ushered in. "If it takes a social revolution, so be it! Let's hold everything in common: we are ready!" The elements of Revolution were present: it only remained now to set them in motion. Returning that evening to my room, I said to myself: "How fine humanity is! It is unknown and has always been slandered!" Then came the elections, the members of the Commune were appointed, and little by little the power of commitment, the enthusiasm for action faded. Everybody returned to his customary routine, saying: "Now we have an honest government, let it get on with it." We know what ensued.

Instead of shifting for itself, instead of striding ahead, instead of throwing itself boldly in the direction of a new order of things, the people, trusting to its governors, handed the care of taking the initiative over to them. That is the first, the fatal consequence of elections. So what will they do, these governors invested with the confidence of everyone?

Never were elections more free than the March 1871 elections. Even the Commune's adversaries have acknowledged that. The great mass of electors was never more imbued with the urge to hoist into power the best men, men of the future, revolutionaries. And it did just that. All revolutionaries of note were returned by formidable majorities: Jacobins, Blanquists, Internationalists, all three revolutionary factions were represented on the Council of the Commune. The election could not have returned a finer government.

The upshot of it all we know. Ensconced in the City Hall, charged with following procedures laid down by preceding governments, these fervent revolutionaries, these reformers found themselves stricken by incompetence and sterility. For all their good will and courage, they were not even able to organize Paris's defenses. It is true that the blame for this is today being heaped upon the men, the individuals: but it was not the personnel that lay at the root of this failure, it was the system they followed.

Indeed, when it is free, universal suffrage can, at best, result in an assembly representative of the mean of the opinions current among the masses at that point: and, at the start of the revolution, that mean has, generally, only a vague, the vaguest of notions of the task facing it, and no grasp of the manner in which it must be tackled. Ah, if only the bulk of the nation, of the Commune could agree, before the upheaval, upon what needs doing as soon as the government has been brought down! If that dream of the desk-bound utopians could but be realized, we would never even have had bloody revolutions: the wishes of the bulk of the nation having been stated, the remainder would have bowed to them with good grace. But that is not how things work. The revolution erupts well before any broad agreement can be arrived at, and those who have a clear notion of what needs doing on the morrow of the uprising are, at that point, only a tiny minority. The vast majority of the people still has only a vague notion of the goal it would like to achieve, and no great knowledge of how to march towards that goal, no great confidence in the route to take. Only once the change gets underway will the practical solution be found and clarified: and it will be a product of the revolution itself, a product of the people in action — or else it will amount to nothing, as the brains of a few individuals absolutely cannot devise solutions which can only be thrown up by the life of the people.

This is the situation mirrored by the body elected through the ballot box, even should it not display all the vices inherent in representative government generally. Those few men who stand for the revolutionary idea of the age find themselves swamped by representatives of past schools of revolution or of the established order. These men, who would be so sorely needed among the people, most especially in such times of revolution, for the widespread dissemination of their ideas and mobilizing the masses and demolishing the institutions of the past, are riveted there inside a room, debating endlessly in hope of wresting a few concessions from the moderates and to talk their enemies around, whereas there is but one way of changing their thinking, which is by getting on with practical efforts. The government turns into the parliament, with all of the vices of bourgeois parliaments. Far from being a "revolutionary" government, it turns into the biggest obstacle to revolution and, unless it wishes to go on marking time, the people finds itself forced to dismiss it and to stand down men whom it was acclaiming as its chosen ones only the day before. But that is no longer an easy undertaking. The new government, which has wasted no time in organizing a whole new administrative network in order to extend its writ and enforce obedience, has no intention of going so quietly. Keen to maintain its power, it clings to it with all the vigor of an institution which has not yet had time to lapse into the decomposition of old age. It is determined to return blow for blow: and there is only one way to dislodge it — by taking up arms and making revolution all over again, in order to dismiss those in whom it had once placed all its hopes.

And then what we have is the revolution divided against itself! Having wasted precious time on procrastination, it watches as its strength is sapped by internecine splits between friends of the young government and those who have grasped the necessity of doing away with it! All because of failure to realize that a new life requires new formulas: that one does not carry out a revolution by clinging to the old formulas! All because of failure to appreciate that revolution and government are incompatible, the failure to discern that one of them, however presented, is still the negation of the other, and that there is no revolution unless there is anarchy.

Part II

The same holds for that other form of "revolutionary government" recommended to us, revolutionary dictatorship.

The dangers to which the Revolution is exposed if it allows itself to be bridled by an elected government are so apparent that a whole school of revolutionaries has turned its back upon that idea completely. They realize that a risen people cannot, through the ballot box, saddle itself with a government that represents only the past and is only a ball and chain around the people's ankles, especially when there is this great economic, political and moral regeneration to be carried out, which we call Social Revolution. Thus they wash their hands of the idea of a "lawful" government, for the duration of a revolt against legality at any rate, and they call instead for "revolutionary dictatorship." They say: "The party which overthrows the government will forcibly supplant it. It will assume power and act in a revolutionary way. It will take the requisite steps to ensure the rising's success: it will tear down the old institutions: it will see to territorial defense. For those unwilling to recognize its authority, there will be the guillotine; and those, be they people or bourgeois, who refuse to carry out the orders it will issue to set the revolution's course, will face the guillotine too!" So argue the budding Robespierres, those who have taken heed of nothing in the great epic of last century except its days of decline, the ones who have learned nothing save the speechifying of the procurators of the Republic.

As far as we anarchists are concerned, dictatorship of a single individual or party — which boils down to the same thing — stands forever condemned. We know that a social revolution is not steered by the mind of just one man or one group. That revolution and government are incompatible, we know: the one must do the other to death, and the name under which government may go — dictatorship, monarchy or parliament — is of little account. We know that the secret of our party's strength and truth resides in its quintessential maxim: "Nothing good or durable is achieved except by the free initiative of the people, and all power tends to do that to death!" That is why the best of us, were their ideas no longer required to undergo the people's acid test prior to implementation, and if they were to become masters of that redoubtable mechanism, government, which empowers them to act upon a whim, would, within the week, deserve to be cut down. We know where all dictatorship, even the most well-meaning one, leads — to the death of revolution. And finally we know that this notion of dictatorship is still only a blighted by-product of that governmental fetishism which, like religious fetishism, has always perpetuated slavery.

But it is not to the anarchists that we are addressing ourselves today. We are speaking to those among the governmentalist revolutionaries who, misled by the prejudices of their education, are honestly mistaken and ask nothing better than to talk. So it is to these that we shall address ourselves, in their own idiom.

And, first, one general observation. Those who peddle dictatorship generally fail to realize that, by sustaining that prejudice, they are merely preparing the ground for those who will later cut their throats. There is, though, one phrase by Robespierre which his admirers would do well to remember. He never reneged upon the principle of dictatorship, but... "Heaven forfend!" he snapped at Mandar when the latter broached the matter with him, "Brissot would be a dictator!" Yes, Brissot, that cunning Girondin, ferocious enemy of the people's egalitarian tendencies, rabid champion of property (which he had once upon a time characterized as theft), Brissot, who would blithely have locked up the Abbaye Hebert, Marat, and all moderate Jacobins.

But those words were spoken in 1792! By which time France had been three years already in revolution! In fact, the monarchy was no more: it only remained to deliver the *coup de grace*; in fact, the feudal system had been swept away. And yet, even at that point, when the revolution was surging freely ahead, there was this counter-revolutionary, Brissot, standing every chance of being acclaimed dictator! And earlier, in 1789? It was Mirabeau who might have been hoisted into power. The man who offered his eloquence to the king for hire, this was the man who might have been hoisted into power at that point, had the risen people not imposed its sovereignty at pike-point. and had they not forged ahead through the *faits accomplis* of the Jacquerie, exposing the insubstantiality of any constituted authority in Paris or in the departments.

But the governmental prejudice so blinkers those who talk about dictatorship that they prefer to pave the way for the dictatorship of some new Brissot or Napoleon, rather than turn away from the idea of awarding a new master to men breaking free of their chains!

The secret societies from the time of the Restoration and Louis-Philippe have made a mighty contribution to the survival of the prejudice of dictatorship. Backed by the workers, the bourgeois republicans of the time mounted a long succession of conspiracies aiming at the overthrow of monarchy and proclamation of the Republic. Not cognizant of the profound changes which were needed in France, even if a bourgeois republican regime was to be established, they deluded themselves that through a far-reaching conspiracy they could some day topple the monarchy, seize power and proclaim the Republic. Over a period of almost thirty years, these secret societies toiled unceasingly, with unbounded commitment and heroic perseverance and courage. If the Republic emerged quite naturally from the February 1848 insurrection, this was thanks to these societies, thanks to the propaganda by deed which they had mounted over those thirty years. But for their noble efforts, the Republic would even now be impossible.

Thus, their goal was to seize power themselves and set themselves up as a republican dictatorship. But, with good reason, they never managed that. As ever, thanks to the ineluctable force of circumstance, it was not a conspiracy that brought down the monarchy. The conspirators had prepared the ground for its downfall. They had disseminated the republican idea far and near: their martyrs had made it the popular ideal. But the final push, the one that brought down the bourgeoisie's king once and for all, was a lot broader and a long stronger than any secret society might mount: it emanated from the mass of the people.

The outcome, we know. The party which had paved the way for the downfall of monarchy found itself excluded from events in City Hall. Others, too cautious to tread the paths of conspiracy, but likewise better known and more moderate, bided their time until they could seize power and occupy the position which the plotters intended to capture to the sound of cannon. The journalists, lawyers and good orators who worked on their good reputations while the real republicans were forging themselves weapons or perishing in dungeons, captured power. Some, being famous already, were acclaimed by the rubbernecks: others pushed themselves forward and were acceptable because their names stood for nothing, other than a program of accommodation to everyone.

Let no one tell us that the party of action is lacking in practical acumen: and that others can outdo them. No, a thousand times, no! As much as the movements of the heavens, it is a law that the party of action is excluded while schemers and prattlers take power. The latter are more familiar to the broad masses which mount the final push. They poll more votes, for, with or without news-sheets, and whether by acclamation or through the ballot box, there is, essentially, always a sort of unspoken choice made at that point by acclamation. They are acclaimed by all and sundry, especially by the revolution's enemies who prefer to push nonentities to the fore, and acclamation thus acknowledges as leaders persons who, deep-down, are inimical to the movement or indifferent to it.

The man[1] who, more than anyone else, was the embodiment of this system of conspiracy, the man who paid with a life behind bars for his commitment to that system, just before he died uttered these words which amount to a complete program: **Neither God nor master!**

Part III

The illusion that government can be overthrown by a secret society, and that that society can install itself in its place, is a mistake made by every revolutionary organization thrown up by the republican bourgeoisie since 1820. But there is evidence aplenty to expose this error. What commitment, what selflessness, what perseverance have we not seen deployed by the republican secret societies of Young Italy, and indeed all the enormous endeavor, all of the sacrifices made by Italian youth — alongside which even those of Russian revolutionary youth pale — all of the corpses heaped in the dungeons of Austrian fortresses and victims of the executioner's blade and bullets, yet the beneficiaries of all that are the schemers from the bourgeoisie and the monarchy. Rarely in history does one come across a secret society which has, with such meager resources, produced results as tremendous as those achieved by Russian youth, or displayed a vigor and an activity as potent as the Executive Committee. It has rattled tsarism, that colossus which had seemed invulnerable: and it has rendered autocratic government, hereafter, an impossibility in Russia. And yet, how ingenuous they are who imagine that the Executive Committee is to become the master of power on the day that Alexander III's crown rolls in the mire. Others, the prudent ones who labored to make their names while revolutionaries were laboring in the mines or perishing in Siberia, others, schemers, prattlers, lawyers, hacks who from time to time shed a speedily wiped tear before the tomb of the heroes and who posed as the people's friends — they are the ones who will step forward to take up the place vacated by the government and cry Halt! to the "unknowns" who will have done the spade-work of the revolution.

This is inevitable and ineluctable, and it cannot be otherwise. For it is not the secret societies, nor indeed the revolutionary organizations which will deliver the coup de grace against governments. Their task, their historical mission is to educate minds to their revolution. And once minds have been cultivated, then, abetted by external circumstances, the final push comes, not from the pioneer group, but from the masses left outside of the structures of society. On August 31 (1870), Paris turned a deaf ear to Blanqui's appeals. Four days later, he proclaimed the downfall of the government: but by then it was no longer the Blanquists who were the cutting edge of the rising, it was the people, the millions, who deposed the *décembriseur*[2] and feted the farceurs whose names have echoed in their ears for two years. When revolution is ready to erupt, when the scent of upheaval is in the air, when success has already become assured, then a thousand newcomers, over whom secret organization has never exercised any direct influence, rally to the movement, like vultures flocking to the battle-field for their share of the remains of the fallen. These help in the mounting of the final push, and it is not from the ranks of honest, incorrigible conspirators, but rather from among the prattling nonsense-talkers that they will draw their leaders, so imbued are they with the notion that a leader is necessary. The conspirators who cling to the prejudice of dictatorship are thus, unwittingly, laboring to hoist their own enemies into power.

But, if what we have just said holds true for revolutions or rather political riots, it is even more true of the revolution we want, the Social Revolution. Allowing some government to establish itself, some strong power which commands obedience, is tantamount to stunting the progress of the revolution from the outset. The good which government might do is negligible and the harm immeasurable.

Indeed, what is it about and what do we take Revolution to mean? Not a straightforward change of government personnel. Rather, assumption by the people of ownership of the whole of society's wealth. Abolition of all of the powers which have never ceased from hindering the development of humanity. But can this immense economic revolution be carried through by means of decrees emanating from a government? Last century, we saw the Polish revolutionary dictator Kosciuszko[3] order the abolition of personal serfdom: serfdom persisted for eighty years after that decree.[4] We saw the Convention, the all-powerful Convention, the terrible Convention, as its admirers call it, order that all the common lands recovered from the seigneurs be shared out on an individual basis. Like so many others, that order remained a dead letter, because, for it to be put into effect, it would have taken the rural proletariat to mount a completely new revolution, and revolutions are not made by decree. For the people's assumption of ownership of social wealth to become an accomplished fact, the people must have room to work and shrug off the servitude to which it is only too accustomed, and be given its head and proceed without awaiting orders from anyone. Now, it is precisely that which dictatorship — however well-meaning — will prevent, and at the same time it will be powerless to advance the revolution by one iota.

But while government, even an ideal revolutionary government, does not generate any new strength and represents no asset in the work of demolition we have to carry out, then all the less should we depend upon it for the task of reorganization which is to follow that demolition. The economic change that the social Revolution will bring will be so immense and far-reaching and will have to work such a change in all relationships currently based upon property and exchange that it will not be feasible for one individual or several to devise the social forms which must take shape in the society of the future.

The devising of new social forms can only be the collective undertaking of the masses. It will require the flexibility of the collective intelligence of the country to meet the tremendous diversity of conditions and needs which will sprout on the day that individual ownership will be done way with. Any external authority cannot be anything other than an impediment, an obstacle to this organizational undertaking which has to be carried out, and, from the outset, a source of discord and hatred.

But it is high time that the oft rebutted illusion of revolutionary government, which has so often cost us so dear, was jettisoned. It is time to tell ourselves once and for all and take to heart the political adage that a government cannot be revolutionary. The Convention is invoked: but let us not forget that the few mildly revolutionary measures taken by the Convention placed the seal upon acts carried out by the people which was at that point marching ahead, ignoring all government. As Victor Hugo said in his vivid style, Danton pushed Robespierre, Marat monitored and pushed Danton, and Marat himself was pushed by Cimourdain,[5] that embodiment of the clubs of the "enragés" and rebels. Like every government before and after it, the Convention was merely a ball and chain about the people's ankles.

The lessons of history here are so conclusive: the impossibility of revolutionary government and the poisonousness of what goes under that name are so self-evident that it would be hard to account for the passion with which a certain self-styled socialist school clings to the idea of government. But there is a very straightforward explanation. Socialists though they profess to be, exponents of this school have a view that differs very greatly from our own of the revolution we are called upon to carry out. For them as for all bourgeois radicals, the social revolution is rather a distant prospect not to be contemplated today. Though they dare not say it, what they have in mind, in their heart of hearts, is something quite different. What they have in mind is the installation of a government similar to the one in Switzerland or in the United States, with a few attempts to take into State care what they ingeniously describe as "public services." This is something akin to Bismarck's ideal or the ideal of the tailor who has been elected to the presidency of the United States. It is a ready-made compromise between the socialist aspirations of the masses and the appetites of the bourgeois. They would like comprehensive expropriation, but have not the courage to attempt it and put it off until next century, and, even before battle is joined, they are locked in negotiations with the enemy.

For those of us who understand that the time to strike a mortal blow against the bourgeoisie is drawing near: that the time is not far off when the people can lay hands upon the whole wealth of society and reduce the exploiter class to powerlessness: for us, as I say, there can be no hesitation. We shall throw ourselves into the social revolution body and soul, and since any government in our path, regardless of the hat it may be wearing, represents an obstacle, we shall render the ambitious hors de combat and sweep them aside the moment they venture to reach for the reins of our fortunes.

Enough of governments. Make way for the people, for anarchy!

Notes to Revolutionary Government

1. Auguste Blanqui (1805–1881), the great revolutionary who advocated the dictatorship of a minority. See the foreword to Vol I of this anthology.
2. Louis-Napoleon Bonaparte (Napoleon III) had seized power by coup d'état on December 2, 1851.
3. Tadeusz Kosciuszko (1746–1817) appointed dictator of Poland in 1794.
4. Proclamation of May 7, 1794, promulgated on May 30 . Had this decree been put into effect, it would indeed have spelled the end for personal slavery and patrimonial courts (Kropotkin's note).
5. Cimourdain, hero of Victor Hugo's novel *Ninety Three* 1873: See Kropotkin *La Grande Révolution* 1909: and Daniel Guérin *La lutte de classes sous la première République* (1793-1797) new edition, 1969.

Kropotkin
Anarchy: Its Philosophy, Its Ideal (1896) [Extracts]

That a society restored to possession of all of the accumulated wealth within it, can largely provide everyone with a guarantee of plenty, in return for four or five hours of effective, manual toil at production each day, all who have reflected upon the matter are unanimously agreed with us. If, from birth, everyone was taught the provenance of the bread he eats, the home he inhabits, the book he reads and so on, and if everyone was used to complementing brain-work with manual labor, in some sphere of manual production, society might readily accomplish this task, without even reckoning upon the streamlining of production which the more or less near future may hold for us.

Indeed, one need only reflect a moment upon the unprecedented, unimaginable squandering of human resources which takes place today, to realize what productivity a civilized society is capable of, with such a tiny measure of work by everyone and such grand enterprises as it might undertake which are presently out of the question. Unfortunately, the metaphysics that goes by the name of political economy has never concerned itself with that which ought to be its very essence, the economics of forces.

As to the potential wealth of a communist society, equipped as we are equipped, there can no longer be any doubt. Where doubts arise, is when we come to investigate whether such a society could exist without man's being subject in his every action to State control: whether, in order to achieve well-being, European societies need not sacrifice that tiny morsel of personal freedom which they have gleaned over the century, at the cost of so many sacrifices.

One socialist faction argues that such an outcome cannot be achieved without sacrifice of freedom upon the altar of the State. Another faction, to which we belong, argues instead that only through abolition of the State, through achievement of wholesale freedom of the individual, through free agreement, utterly free association and federation, can we arrive at communism, common ownership of our inheritance and common production of all wealth.

This is the issue taking precedence over every other at the moment and which socialism has to resolve, unless it wants to see all its efforts compromised and all its further development stymied.

If every socialist casts his mind back, he will doubtless call to mind the host of prejudices which sprang up in him when first he ventured to think that abolition of the capitalist system and private ownership of land and capital had become an historical necessity.

The same thing is underway today in him who hears tell for the first time of abolition of the State, its laws, its whole system of management, governmentalism and centralization likewise becoming a historical necessity: and that the abolition of the one is materially impossible without abolition of the other. Our entire education, provided, remember, by Church and State, in the interests of them both, bristles at the very idea.

Is it any the less correct, though? And in the slaughter of prejudices which we have already carried out for our emancipation's sake, must the State prejudice survive?

The working man, if he remains waged, would remain a slave of the one to whom he would be obliged to sell his strength, whether the purchaser be an individual or the State.

In the popular mind, among the thousands of opinions that float across the human mind, there is also a feeling that, if the State were to step into the employer's shoes as purchaser and overseer of the labor force, that would still be a hateful tyranny. The man of the people does not think in abstract terms, but rather in concrete terms, and this is why he feels that the abstraction "State" would, as far as he can see, take the form of numerous officials drawn from among his colleagues in the factory or workshop, and he knows where he stands with regard to their virtues: excellent comrades today, tomorrow they would turn into unbearable task-masters. And he looks around for that arrangement of society which does away with current ills without conjuring new ones into existence.

This is why collectivism has never captured the enthusiasm of the masses who always turn back to communism, but to a communism increasingly purged of the theocracy and Jacobin authoritarianism of the '40s, to a free, anarchist communism.

Let me go further. In continually spelling out my thoughts on what we have seen in the European social movement over the past quarter of a century, I cannot resist the belief that modern socialism is ineluctably fated to take a step forward in the direction of libertarian communism.

Kropotkin in the Russian Revolution

Although the anarchists' part in the Russian revolution will be dealt with in the second book of this anthology, we have to depart here from the chronological approach. In fact, in order not to split up Kropotkin's various writings, we have opted to skip a number of years and turn now to the important writings of the "anarchist prince,"[1] from the time that he returned to the land of his birth after the October revolution of 1917.

Letter to Georg Brandes[2] (1919)

Dearest friend:

At last, a chance to write to you, and I shall waste no time in seizing it, although I cannot be sure, of course, that this letter will reach you.

Both of us thank you from the bottom of our hearts for the fraternal interest you took in your old friend, when rumor had it that I had been arrested. There was absolutely no truth in that rumor, any more than in the tittle-tattle about the condition of my health.

The person who is to deliver this letter will tell you of the isolated life we lead in our little provincial town: at my time of life, it is materially impossible to participate in public affairs during a revolution, and it is not in my nature to dabble. We spent last winter in Moscow. We worked alongside a team of collaborators on the blueprint for a federalist republic. But the team was forced to break up, and I resumed a study of Ethics which I had begun in England fifteen years ago.

All that I can do now is offer you a general idea of the situation in Russia, which, in my view, is not properly reported in the West. Perhaps an analogy will account explain.

At present we are at the stage experienced by France during the Jacobin revolution, from September 1792 to July 1794, with this addition, that this now is a social revolution feeling its way.

The Jacobins' dictatorial approach was wrong. It was unable to create a stable organization and inevitably led on to reaction. But in June 1793, the Jacobins nevertheless brought off the abolition of feudal rights, which had begun in 1789 and which neither the Constituent nor the Legislative assemblies had been willing to complete. And they loudly proclaimed the political equality of every citizen. Two huge fundamental changes which swept around Europe during the 19th century.

Something of the sort is happening in Russia. The Bolsheviks are striving to introduce, through dictatorship of one faction of the Social Democratic Party, social ownership of land, industry and commerce. This change which they are straining to carry out is the underlying principle of communism. Unfortunately, the method by which they aim to impose, in a strongly centralized State, a communism reminiscent of Babeuf's, and bring the people's constructive endeavor to a halt, makes success utterly impossible. Which lines us up for an angry and nasty backlash. Even now the latter is trying to get itself organized so as to restore the old order, capitalizing upon the widespread exhaustion caused, first, by the war, and then by the famine we in central Russia are suffering and by the utter chaos existing in exchange and production — things inevitable during such a comprehensive revolution, carried out by decree.

In the West, there is talk of re-establishing "order" in Russia by means of armed intervention by the allies. Well, dear friend, you know what a crime against the whole social progress of Europe, in my view, was the attitude of those who toiled to break down Russia's power of resistance, which prolonged the war by a year, brought us German invasion under cover of a treaty, and cost rivers of blood in order to prevent all-conquering Germany from trampling Europe beneath its imperial boot. My feelings on this score, you are familiar with.[3]

And yet I protest as strenuously as I can against armed allied intervention of any sort in Russian affairs. Such intervention would result in an upsurge of Russian jingoism. It would bring back to us a chauvinist monarchy — the signs of it are already discernible — and, mark this well, it would inspire in the Russian people as a whole a feeling of hostility towards western Europe, an attitude which would have the saddest implications. The Americans have already grasped this.

Perhaps the belief is that by backing Admiral Koltchak and General Denikin,[4] one is supporting a liberal, republican party. But even that is a mistake.

Whatever the personal intentions of these two military leaders may be, the vast majority of those who have rallied to them have different aims. Inevitably, what they would bring us would be a return to monarchy, reaction and a bloodbath.

Those of the allies who have a clear vision of events ought therefore to turn away from any armed intervention. Especially if they genuinely do wish to come to the assistance of Russia, they will find plenty of opportunity elsewhere.

Across the vast expanses of the central and northern provinces, we are short of bread. We have famine, with all that that implies. An entire generation is wasting away. And we are denied the right to buy bread in the West! — How come? Is it the intention to give us back a Romanoff?

Everywhere in Russia we lack manufactured goods. The peasant pays crazy prices for a pitchfork, an ax, a handful of nails, a needle, a meter of any cloth at all. The four iron-clad wheels off a sorry-looking Russian cart go for a thousand rubles (equivalent, once upon a time, to 2,500 francs). In the Ukraine, things are even worse: there are no goods to be had any price.

Instead of playing the role that Austria, Prussia and Russia played in 1793 in relation to France, the allies ought to have pulled out all the stops to help the Russian people out of this dire situation. And rivers of blood would be spilled to send the Russian people back to the past, but it would not succeed. There is a new future to be built through the constructive articulation of a new life, which is already taking shape, in spite of everything and in which the allies ought to help us. Do not delay, come to the aid of our children! Come and help us in the constructive work required! And to that end, send us, not your diplomats and generals, but your bread, tools for the production of it and organizers who were able to be of such assistance to the allies over these five awful years in preventing economic chaos and repelling the Germans' barbarous invasion.

I am reminded that I should close this letter, which is overlong already. Let me do so by offering you a fraternal embrace.

Notes to Letter to George Brandes

1. George Woodcock and I. Avakumovic, *The Anarchist Prince; The Biography of Prince Peter Kropotkin.*
2. Georg Brandes (1842–1927) renowned Danish literary critic.
3. During the 1914–1918 war, Kropotkin had sided with the western empires against the central powers, in a declaration known as the "Manifesto of the Sixteen." This reneging upon anarchism's basic principles was disowned by anarchist communists. (See Volume III of this anthology)
4. Alexis Koltchak (1874–1920) White Russian general defeated and shot by the Bolsheviks: General Anton Denikin (1872–1947) another White Russian general, eventually defeated by the Bolsheviks.

How Communism Should Not be Introduced

A letter to the workers of western Europe
Dmitrov, Moscow guberniya. April 28, 1919

I have been asked whether I do not have a message for the workers of the western world. Assuredly, there is a lot to say and learn about the current events in Russia. As the message might be unduly long, let me just set out a few main points.

First of all, the workers of the civilized world and their friends in other classes ought to lobby their governments to abandon completely the notion of armed intervention in Russia's affairs, whether this be mounted overtly or in an underhand, military way or in the form of subsidies to different nations.

At this moment, Russia is undergoing a revolution as profound and important as those made by England in 1639-1648 and France in 1789-1794. Each nation ought to refuse the shameful role to which England, Prussia, Austria and Russia were reduced during the French revolution.

Furthermore, it should be remembered that the Russian revolution which is aiming to build a society in which the entire output of the combined efforts of labor, technical expertise and scientific knowledge would go wholly to the community itself is not a mere accident of party political struggle. It has been incubated over almost a century of communist and socialist propaganda, ever since the days of Robert Owen, Saint-Simon and Fourier.[1] And although the attempt to usher in the new society by means of a one party dictatorship may seem condemned to failure, it has to be acknowledged that the revolution has already introduced into our everyday life fresh ideas regarding the rights of labor, its true status in society and the duties of every citizen, and that these will endure.

Not just workers but all progressive elements in the civilized nations ought to cut off the support that they have hitherto given adversaries of the revolution. Not that there is nothing objectionable in the methods of the Bolshevik government. Far from it! But any armed intervention by a foreign power necessarily leads to a bolstering of the dictatorial tendencies of those in government and stymies the efforts of those Russians ready to help Russia, regardless of their government, in the restoration of its life.

The evils inherent in party dictatorship have thus been magnified by the war-time circumstances amid which that party exists. The state of war has provided the pretext for reinforcing the dictatorial methods of the party as well as its tendency to centralise every detail of life within government hands, the upshot of which is to halt the enormous ramifications of the nation's normal activities. The native evils of State communism have been multiplied ten-fold, on the pretext that all of the miseries of our lives are ascribable to intervention by foreigners.

I ought to point out, too, that if the Allies' military intervention persists, it will assuredly spawn in Russia a feeling of resentment towards the western nations, a sentiment of which use will some day be made in future conflicts. Even now that resentment is growing.

In short, it is high time that the nations of western Europe entered into direct relations with the Russian nation. And in this regard, you, the working class and most advanced elements in every nation, ought to have your say.

One more word on the overall situation. The restoration of relations between the European nations, America and Russia in no way signifies the Russian nation's supremacy over the nationalities making up the empire of the tsars. Imperial Russia is dead and will not return from the grave. The future of its different provinces lies in the direction of a great federation. The natural territories of the various parts of this federation are quite distinct, as any of us conversant with Russia's history, ethnography and economic life are aware. All efforts to unite under a central command the constituent parts of the Russian Empire — Finland, the Baltic provinces, Lithuania, the Ukraine, Georgia, Armenia, Siberia, etc. — are assuredly doomed to fail. So it would be useful, were the western nations to declare that they recognise the right to independence of each and every part of the former Russian Empire.

My view is that this trend will continue. I see coming soon a time when each part of this federation will itself be a federation of rural communes and free cities. And I believe, further, that certain parts of western Europe will soon follow the example of this movement.

As far as our present economic and political position is concerned, the Russian revolution, being the continuation of the two great revolutions in England and France, is trying to venture beyond the point where France stopped, when she managed to establish what was called de facto equality, which is to say, economic equality.

Regrettably, in Russia this attempt has been mounted under the strongly centralized dictatorship of one party, the maximalist Social Democrats. An experiment along the same lines was conducted by Babeuf's extremely centralistic Jacobin conspiracy. I have to tell you candidly that, in my view, this attempt to erect a communist republic upon a base of strongly centralized State communism, under the iron law of a one party dictatorship is heading for fiasco. We in Russia are beginning to learn how communism should not be introduced, even by a populace weary of the old regime and offering no active resistance to the experiment being conducted by the new governors.

The idea of Soviets, that is, of workers' and peasants' councils, first advocated prior to the attempted revolution of 1905 and promptly realized by the February 1917 revolution, once tsarism had been overthrown, the idea of such councils controlling the country's political and economic life, is a grand idea. Especially as it necessarily leads to the idea that these councils ought to be made up of all who, through their own personal effort, play a real part in the production of the nation's wealth.

But as long as a country is governed by a one party dictatorship, the workers' and peasants' councils obviously lose all significance. They are reduced to the passive role formerly played by the estates general and parliaments when these were summoned by the king and pitted against an all-powerful royal council.

A labor council ceases to be a free and substantial council when there is no press freedom in the land, and we have been in those circumstances for the past two years, supposedly because a state of war obtains. What is more, workers' and peasants' councils lose all significance when elections are not preceded by free electioneering, and when elections are conducted under the pressure from a party dictatorship. Of course, the usual excuse is that dictatorial legislation is inevitable as a means of combatting the old regime. But such law obviously becomes a retrograde step once the revolution buckles down to the construction of a new society upon a new economic foundation. It turns into a sentence of death upon the new construction.

The ways of overthrowing an ailing government are well known to history, ancient and modern. But when new forms of living have to be created, especially new forms of production and exchange, with no examples to imitate, when everything has to be built on the hoof, when a government that undertakes to issue every inhabitant with lamp glass and matches shows that it is utterly incapable of managing with its officials, no matter how many of the latter there may be, that government becomes irksome. It builds up a bureaucracy so formidable that the French bureaucratic system, which requires the involvement of forty civil servants before a tree felled by storms upon a national highway can be sold off becomes child's play by comparison. This is what we are learning in Russia today. And this is what you western workers can and should avoid by all means if you have the success of social reconstruction at heart. Send your delegates over here to see how a social revolution operates in real life.

The tremendous constructive endeavor which a social revolution requires cannot be performed by a central government, even if it is guided by something more substantial than a few socialist and anarchist hand-books. It takes expertise, brains and the willing cooperation of a host of local specialized elements, who, alone, can successfully address the range of economic issues as they affect the locality. Rejecting such cooperation and falling back upon the genius of the party's dictators is tantamount to destroying the independent agent such as the *trade unions* (known in Russia as professional unions) and local cooperative organizations, by turning them into bureaucratic adjuncts of the party, as is currently the case. But that is the way not to make the revolution, the way to render its making impossible. And the reason why I feel it my duty to place you on your guard against borrowing such directives.

The imperialist conquerors of every nationality may want the populations of the one-time Russian empire to remain for as long as possible in miserable economic conditions and thus condemned to furnishing western and central Europe with raw materials, while the western industrialists will pocket all of the profits that Russians might have been able to reap from their labors. But the working classes of Europe and America, as well as the intelligentsia of these countries, assuredly understand that violence alone could trap Russia in such subjection. At the same time, the sympathies which our revolution evoked everywhere in Russia and in America show that you were happy to salute Russia as a new member of the international confraternity of nations. And you will assuredly soon notice that it is in the interests of all the workers of the world that Russia should be freed as soon as possible from the conditions presently arresting her development.

A few words more. The last war ushered in new living conditions for the civilized world. Socialism will surely make considerable progress and new forms of more independent living will certainly be generated, with their foundations in local freedom and constructive initiative: these will be created either peacefully or by revolutionary means if the intelligent segments of the civilized nations do not collaborate in inevitable reconstruction.

But the success of that reconstruction will largely be dependent upon the chances for close cooperation between different nations. In order to bring this about, the working classes of every nation must be closely united and the notion of a great international of all the world's workers must be revived, not in the shape of a unity under the baton of a single party, as was the case with the Second International, and is again the case with the Third International. Such unions of course have every reason to exist, but outside of them, and uniting them all, there ought to be a union of all the world's trade unions, federated so as to deliver worldwide production from its present subjection to capital.

Notes to How Communism Should Not be Introduced

1. For Robert Owen and Saint-Simon, see volume I of this anthology. Charles Fourier (1772–1837) was a French "utopian" socialist, founder of the phalansterian school and theoretician of universal harmony.

Vilkens' Last Visit to Kropotkin (December 1920)[1]

Kropotkin is seventy eight years old. In spite of his years, his thinking has retained all of its lucidity. His steps are as sprightly as ours. His memory inexhaustible. He speaks to us of the days of the Commune and rehearses tiny details, as if it had all happened just yesterday. He also relates tales of his youth, when he explored Siberia and the borders with China, with the same liveliness as a young schoolboy.

(. . .) Now the conversation turns to the Russian revolution. More than ever, Kropotkin is confirmed in his opinions: with their methods, the communists, instead of setting people on the road to communism, will finish up making its very name hateful to them.

Sincere they may well be: but their system prevents them in practice from introducing the slightest principle of communism. And, noting that no progress is being made in the work of the revolution, he foresees from this "that the people is not ready to endorse their decrees, that it will take time and changes of course." This is reasonable: the tale of political revolutions told all over again. The saddest thing is that they do not recognize and refuse to acknowledge their mistakes, and each passing day wrests a morsel of the conquests of the Revolution away from the masses, to be gobbled up by the centralist State.

In any event, he says, the experience of the Revolution is not wasted on the Russian people. It has awakened; it is on the move towards better prospects. Four years of revolution do more to raise a people's consciousness than a century spent vegetating.

- What is you view of the future of the Revolution, and, as you see it, what force might profitably replace the Bolsheviks?

- We should not place undue emphasis upon the masses' refusing indefinitely to back the Bolsheviks. By their methods, they themselves force them to lose interest. But they have access to a mighty military machine which, in terms of discipline, plays the role of the bourgeois armies. In any case, the Bolsheviks will come to grief through their own mistakes and, through their policy, they will have helped the Entente install the reaction, which the people fears, because everybody would have something for which to answer to the Whites.

- And if, through some misfortune, that were to happen, do you think that the power of the reaction would be bolstered?

- I think not. At best, it might endure for a few years, but the people, momentarily beaten, would bounce back with a vengeance, and the new Revolution would have experience and would march in step with revolutionary achievements in Europe.

- And what ought to be the attitude of the world proletariat with regard to the present Revolution?

- Without a doubt, it should carry on defending it, not just verbally any more, but by actions: for the bourgeoisie's hostility will diminish in the face of a steadfast attitude from the working class. And for the world proletariat, it will also be a good training for revolution. But defense of the revolution should not be confused with idolatry: the world proletariat should make ready to overtake the Russian model and rid itself in advance of every impediment to the masses' effective participation and not let itself be gulled by false formulas.

Notes to Vilkens' Last Visit to Kropotkin

1. Taken from the newspaper *Le Libertaire* of January 28, 1921.

Emma Goldman's Recollections of Kropotkin[1]

[We were in Moscow] when we had word from Dmitrov to say that our old comrade Peter Kropotkin had been stricken with pneumonia. The shock was all the greater because we had visited Peter in July and had found him in good health and in good humor. He seemed younger and in finer fettle than we had seen him last March. His flashing eyes and vivaciousness had shown us that he was in excellent condition. The Kropotkins' property was delightful in the summer sunshine, with all the flowers and Sophie's vegetable garden in full bloom. Peter had spoken to us with great pride about his wife and her green fingers. Taking Sasha[2] and me by the hand, he led us, with childish high spirits, to where Sophie had planted a special variety of salad plants. She had managed to grow heads as big as cabbages, with deliciously curly leaves. He had dug the soil himself, but it was Sophie who was the real expert, he reiterated. Her potato crop last winter had been so good that there were enough left over to swap for forage for their cow, and indeed to share with their neighbors in Dmitrov, who had few vegetables. Our dear Peter had frolicked in his garden while he talked to us about all these things as if they were world-shaking events. Our comrade's boyish spirit had been contagious and he enchanted us all with his charm and gaiety.

In the afternoon, in his studio, he became again the sage and thinker, clear-sighted and perspicacious in his evaluation of persons and events. We had talked about dictatorship and the methods imposed upon the revolution by necessity and those inherent in the nature of the party. I wanted Peter to help me better to understand the situation which was threatening to puncture my faith in revolution and the masses. Painstakingly, and with the sort of tenderness lavished upon a sick child, he had tried to set my mind at rest. He claimed that there was no reason to despair. He understood my inner turmoil, he said, but he was confident that, in time, I would learn to distinguish between the Revolution and the regime. They were worlds apart and the gulf between them necessarily had to deepen as time passed. The Russian Revolution was much greater than the French and carried a more powerful message for the whole world. It had made a deep impression upon the life of the masses everywhere and no one could predict the rich harvest which mankind was going to reap from it. The communists who had committed themselves implicitly to the notion of a centralized State were doomed to misdirect the course of the revolution. Having political supremacy as their goal, they had inevitably become socialism's Jesuits, justifying any means just as long as it encompassed their ends. Their methods paralyzed the energies of the masses and terrorized folk. But without the people, without direct involvement of workers in the reconstruction of the country, nothing creative or fundamental could be achieved.

Our own comrades, Kropotkin had continued, had in the past failed to give due consideration to the fundamental elements of a social revolution. In any such upheaval, the basic factor was the organization of the country's economic life. The Russian Revolution was proof that we ought to have made preparations for that. He had come to the conclusion that syndicalism was probably about to supply what Russia most sorely needed: an instrument by means of which the economic and industrial reconstruction of the country might proceed. He was referring to anarcho-syndicalism, hinting that such an arrangement, with help from cooperatives, would rescue future revolutions from the fatal mistakes and ghastly suffering which Russia was enduring.

All of which flooded back to mind when I received the sad news of Kropotkin's illness. Leaving for Petrograd without having first paid another call on Peter was unthinkable. Efficient nurses were few and far between in Russia. I could tend him and render that service at least to my beloved mentor and friend.

I discovered that Peter's daughter, Alexandra, was in Moscow and about to set out for Dmitrov. She informed me that a very competent nurse, a Russian woman who had trained in England, had been placed in charge. Their little villa was already overcrowded and she advised me not to disturb Peter for the time being. Off she went to Dmitrov, promising to telephone me about her father's condition and whether there would be any point in my visiting.

Scarcely had I arrived back [in Petrograd] than Madame Ravish telephoned me to say that I was needed urgently in Dmitrov. She had had a message from Moscow asking me to come without delay. Peter had taken a turn for the worse and the family had begged her to tell me to come right away.

My train was beset by a terrible blizzard and we arrived in Moscow ten hours later than scheduled. There was no train for Dmitrov before the following evening and the roads were blocked by snowdrifts too deep for cars to pass. The telephone lines were down and there was no way to reach Dmitrov.

The evening train traveled with exasperating sluggishness, stopping repeatedly to take on fuel. It was four o' clock in the morning by the time we arrived. Along with Alexandrer Schapiro[3], a close family friend of the Kropotkins, and Lavrov, a comrade from the Bakers' Union, I rushed towards the Kropotkins' villa. Alas! We were too late! Peter had breathed his last an hour earlier. He had died at four o' clock on the morning of February 8, 1921. His devastated widow told me that Peter had asked repeatedly whether I was on my way and when I would be arriving. Sophie was on the verge of collapse and, thanks to the need to tend her, I forgot the cruel conspiracy of circumstances which had denied me the chance to render the slightest service to the man who had given such a powerful fillip to my life and work.

Sophie informed us that Lenin, upon hearing of Peter's illness, had despatched the finest doctors from Moscow to Dmitrov, as well as provisions and sweets for the patient. He had also ordered that he be kept briefed regularly about Peter's condition and that these bulletins be carried by the newspapers. What a sad dénouement, that so much attention had been lavished, as he lay upon his death bed, upon the man who had twice been raided by the Cheka and been forced to go into reluctant retirement for that very reason! Peter Kropotkin had helped prepare the ground for the Revolution, but had been denied a part in its life and development: his voice had rung out throughout Russia in spite of tsarist persecution, but it had taken a communist dictatorship to silence it.

Peter never asked and never accepted any favors from any government, and would countenance no pomp and circumstance. So we decided that there should be no State interference in his funeral, and that it should not be degraded by the attendance of officials. Peter's last days on earth would be spent surrounded by his comrades only.

Schapiro and Pavlov set out for Moscow to track down Sasha and the other comrades from Petrograd. Along with the Moscow group, these were to take charge of the funeral arrangements. I stayed in Dmitrov to help Sophie prepare her dead beloved for removal to the capital for burial.

(. . .) Right up to the day when he had been forced to take to his bed, Peter had carried on working, in the most difficult circumstances, upon his book on Ethics which he had hoped would be his life's crowning achievement. His deepest regret in his declining hours was that he had not had just a little more time to complete what he had begun years earlier.

In the three last years of his life, Peter had been cut off from all close contact with the masses. At his death, such contact with them was restored in full. Peasants, soldiers, intellectuals, men and women from a radius of several kilometers, as well as the entire Dmitrov community, flooded into Kropotkin's villa to pay final tribute to the man who had lived among them and shared their struggles and distresses.

Sasha arrived in Dmitrov with numerous Moscow comrades to help remove Peter's body to Moscow. The little village had never paid anyone such grand tribute as it did to Peter Kropotkin. The children had been most familiar with him and loved him on account of his playful, boyish nature. The schools closed that day as a sign of mourning for the friend who was leaving them. Large numbers of them gathered at the station and waved their hands in a farewell to Peter as the train slowly pulled out.

From Sasha, I discovered en route that the commission handling Peter Kropotkin's funeral arrangements, which he had helped run and of which he was the chairman, had already been the object of a lot of obstruction from the soviet authorities. The commission had been authorized to publish two of Peter's pamphlets and bring out a special edition of the bulletin in commemoration of Peter Kropotkin. Later, the Moscow soviet, chaired by Kamenev, demanded that the manuscripts for that bulletin be handed over to the censors. Sasha, Schapiro and other comrades objected, saying that that would delay publication. To buy time, they had promised that the bulletin would carry only commentaries upon Kropotkin's life and work. Then, all of a sudden, the censor remembered that he had too much work at the moment and that the bulletin would have to wait its turn. Which meant that the bulletin could not appear in time for the funeral, and it was obvious that the Bolsheviks were relying upon their usual delay tactics to hold it up until it was too late to serve its purpose. Our comrades resolved upon direct action. Lenin had often hijacked that anarchist idea, so why should the anarchists not reclaim it from him? Time was pressing and the matter was important enough to risk arrest over. They broke the seals which the Cheka had placed upon our old comrade Atabekian's printworks and our comrades worked like Trojans to prepare and get the bulletin ready before the funeral.

The homage paid to the respect and affection inspired by Peter Kropotkin turned Moscow into one enormous demonstration. From the moment the body arrived in the capital and was delivered to the trade union headquarters, through the two days when the corpse was on display in the marble hall, there was such a procession of people as had not been witnessed since the events of October.

The Kropotkin commission had sent a request to Lenin asking him to ensure that anarchists imprisoned in Moscow were temporarily released so that they could participate in the final tributes to their late mentor and friend. Lenin had promised to do so and the Communist Party's executive committee had instructed the Ve-Cheka (Russian Cheka) to release imprisoned anarchists "on their own recognizance" so that they might attend the funeral. But the Ve-Cheka was not, it seems, inclined to obey, either Lenin or the highest authority of its own party. It asked if the commission could guarantee the prisoners' return to prison. The commission offered its collective assurances. Whereupon the Ve-cheka declared that "there were no anarchists imprisoned in Moscow." In point of fact, the Butyrky and the Cheka's own cells were crammed with comrades of ours rounded up during the raid on the Kharkov Conference, even though the latter, by virtue of an agreement between the soviet government and Nestor Makhno, had had official authorization. Furthermore, Sasha had secured admission to the Butyrky prison and had spoken with about twenty of our imprisoned comrades. In the company of the Russian anarchist Yartchuk, he had also visited the Moscow Cheka's holding cells and spoken with Aaron Baron[4], who was acting at that time as the spokesman for a huge number of other imprisoned anarchists. Yet the Cheka persisted with its claim that there were "no anarchists imprisoned in Moscow."

Once again, the commission was obliged to resort to direct action. On the morning of the funeral, it instructed Alexandra Kropotkin to telephone the Moscow Soviet to say that this breach of promise would be publicly denounced and that the wreaths placed by the soviets and communist organizations were going to be removed, unless Lenin's promise was honored.

The great colonnaded hall was filled to overflowing: among those in attendance were several representatives from the European and American press. Our old friend Henry Alsberg, lately returned to Russia, was there. Another journalist, Arthur Ransome, was there representing the *Manchester Guardian*. They would certainly publicize the soviets' breach of promise. Since the world had been regaled about the care and attention lavished upon Peter Kropotkin by the soviet government during his final illness, publication of such a scandal had to be averted at any cost. Kamenev therefore asked for a delay and gave a solemn undertaking that the imprisoned anarchists would be freed in twenty minutes.

The funeral was delayed for one hour. The huge masses of mourners shivered in the cruel cold of Moscow, waiting for the imprisoned disciples of the great deceased to arrive on the streets. In the end, arrive they did, but there were only seven of them in the entire Cheka prison. Of the comrades in the Butyrky prison, not one. At the last moment, the Cheka assured the commission that they had been released and were on their way. The paroled prisoners acted as pall-bearers. With pained pride, they bore the remains of their beloved comrade and mentor. The vast assembly greeted them with an impressive silence. Unarmed soldiers, sailors, students, children, trade union organizations representing every trade, groups of men and women representing the intelligentsia, peasants and many groups of anarchists with their red or black banners, a host united without compulsion, put into order without command, followed the lengthy route, over the period of two hours, as far as the Devishy cemetery on the outskirts of town.

At the Tolstoy museum, the strains of Chopin's funeral march greeted the cortege, as did a choir made up of disciples of the seer of Yasnaya Polyana. In token of gratitude, our comrades dipped their banners by way of a tribute from one great son of Russia to another.

As it passed in front of the Butyrky prison, the procession halted a second time and our banners were lowered by way of a final salute from Peter Kropotkin to the brave comrades waving him farewell from their barred windows. Spontaneous expression of deep-seated grief was a feature of the speeches made at our comrade's graveside by men representing a variety of political persuasions. The dominant tone was that the loss of Peter Kropotkin signified the loss of a tremendous moral beacon, the like of which no longer existed in our country.

For the first time since my arrival in Petrograd, my voice was heard in public. It sounded curiously harsh to me and incapable of expressing all that Peter meant to me.

The grief I felt at his death was bound up with my despair at the revolution's failure, which none of us had been able to forestall.

The sun set slowly on the horizon and the sky, bathed in a dark red, formed a fantastic baldachino over the freshly dug earth now covering Peter Kropotkin's final resting place.

The seven prisoners released on parole spent the evening with us and made their way back to prison only late in the night. Not expecting them, the warders had locked the gates and retired for the night. The men practically had to force their way in, so amazed were the warders to see these anarchists crazy enough to honor a promise made on their behalf by their comrades.

In the end, the anarchists from the Butyrky prison had not made it to the funeral. The Ve-cheka had alleged to the commission that they had refused to attend, although they had been offered the opportunity. We knew this to be a lie, but even so I decided to pay a personal visit to our prisoners to hear their version of events. This involved the odious necessity of seeking the Cheka's leave. I was taken into the private office of the head Chekist, a young lad with a gun at his belt and another on his desk. He stepped forward with hand extended and a fulsome greeting of "Dear comrade." He told me that his name was Brenner and that he had spent some time in America. He had been an anarchist and of course he knew Sasha very well, and myself too and knew all about our activities in the United States. He was proud to call us comrades. Of course, now he was with the communists, he explained, for it was his view that the current regime was a step in the direction of anarchism.

The important thing was the revolution, and, since the Bolsheviks were working on its behalf, he was cooperating with them. But had I stopped being a revolutionary, given that I had declined to shake the fraternally outstretched hand of one of its defenders?

My answer to him was that I had never shaken the hand of a detective, much less of a policeman who had been an anarchist. I had come to gain access to the prison and wanted to know if my request would be granted.

(. . .) He got up and left the room. I waited for half an hour, wondering if I was a prisoner. It was happening to everyone in Russia, so why not me? Suddenly there were footsteps approaching, and the door opened wide. An elderly man, apparently a Chekist, gave me permission to enter the Butyrky prison.

Among a group of imprisoned comrades, I met several whom I had known in the United States: Fanny and Aaron Baron, Voline,[5] and others who had worked in America, as well as Russians from the Nabat organization whom I had met in Kharkov. A representative of the Ve-Cheka had called upon them, they said, and offered to release some of them, one by one, but not as a collective group, as had been agreed with the commission. Our comrades had bridled at this failure to honor the commitment given and had insisted that they should attend the Kropotkin funeral as a group or not at all. The man told them that he would have to report their demand to his superiors and would return shortly, with their final decision. But he had not returned. The comrades said that it was a matter of no importance because they had held their own meeting in memory of Kropotkin in the prison corridors, at which they had honored him with impromptu speeches and revolutionary songs. With the aid of other politicals, they had turned the prison into a people's university, Voline told me. They offered courses in science and political economy, sociology and literature and taught common law prisoners how to read and write. In fact, they had a lot more freedom than we on the outside enjoyed, and we ought to envy them, they wise-cracked. But they feared that this haven of peace might not survive much longer.

Notes to Emma Goldman's Recollections of Kropotkin

1. Taken from Emma Goldman, *Living my Life* 1934. Emma Goldman (1869–1940) was of Russian Jewish extraction: she emigrated to the United States in 1886 and there became an anarchist. An advocate of women's rights, birth control and individual and sexual freedom, she published a newspaper *Mother Earth* and later brought out her admirable memoirs as *Living my Life*. In 1919, with the anti-anarchist witch-hunt at its height, she was deported from the United States to soviet Russia. She stayed there up until the Kronstadt revolt (1921). Then she returned

to Europe and America, carrying on indefatigably with her writing and lecturing. In 1936 she visited Spain.

2. "Sasha," the familiar name of Alexander Berkman (1870–1936), also of Russian Jewish extraction, who emigrated to the United States in 1888. Seeking to support the strikers in their battle against professional strike-breakers, in 1892 he shot the steel magnate Henry Clay Frick in Pittsburgh, wounding him slightly. On March 1, 1893, he was sentenced to a prison term of 21 years, of which he served 14, staunchly defended by Emma Goldman. He was arrested and deported along with her in 1919 to Soviet Russia. In December 1921, after the crushing of the Kronstadt revolt and the execution of Fanny Baron, he left Russia for Germany and then on to France. In poor health, he committed suicide in Nice. He wrote *Prison Memoirs of an Anarchist* (1912) and *The Bolshevik Myth* (1922).

3. Alexander M. Schapiro (1882–1947), son of a Russian anarchist. Secretary of the Anarchist International Bureau after the International Anarchist Congress held in Amsterdam in 1907 (see Volume III of this anthology). During the Revolution he was, alongside Voline, editor of the newspaper *Golos Truda* (see Volume III) and was a member of the Commissariat for Foreign Affairs. The Bolshevik crack-down on the anarchists forced him to leave for Berlin in 1922, there to be the driving force behind the exiled Russian anarchist group. Later he lived in Paris, where he contributed to *Le Combat syndicaliste* before moving on to the USA.

4. Aaron Baron, anarchist, took part in the Russian revolution of 1905, was then banished to Siberia and escaped to the United States, returning to Russia in 1917: joint editor with Voline of the Kharkov newspaper *Nabat*: arrested by the Cheka along with his companion Fanya in November 1920, he was kept in prisons and concentration camps until 1938, before being rearrested and disappearing. Fanny Baron was shot by the Bolsheviks in September 1921.

5. For a biography of Voline, see Volume III.

<u>Kate Sharpley Library</u>

Comrades and Friends —
No doubt some of you will be aware of the work of the **Kate Sharpley Library and Documentation Centre**, which has been in existence for the last eight years. In 1991 the Library was moved from a storage location in London to Northamptonshire, where we are now in the process of creating a database of the entire collection. At the same time, a working group has been formed to over see the organisation and running of the Library. The catalogue of the Library material will be published by AK Press (Edinburgh).

The Library is made up of private donations from comrades, deceased and living. It comprises several thousand pamphlets, books, newspapers, journals, posters, flyers, unpublished manuscripts, monographs, essays, etc. , in over 20 languages, covering the history of our movement over the last century. It contains detailed reports from the IWA (AIT/IAA), the Anarchist Federation of Britain (1945-50), the Syndicalist Workers Federation (1950-1979) and records from the anarchist publishing houses, *Cienfuegos Press*, ASP and others. Newspapers include near complete sets of *Black Flag, Freedom, Spain and the World, Direct Actions* (from 1945 onwards), along with countless others dating back 100 years. The Library also has a sizeable collection of libertarian socialist and council communist materials which we are keen to extend.

The Kate Sharpley Library is probably the largest collection of anarchist material in England. In order to extend and enhance the collection, we ask all anarchist groups and publications worldwide to add our name to their mailing list. We also appeal to all comrades and friends to *donate* suitable material to the Library. *All* donations are welcome and can be collected. The Kate Sharpley Library (KSL) was named in honour of Kate Sharpley, a First World War anarchist and anti-war activist — one of the countless "unknown" members of our movement so ignored by "official historians" of anarchism. The Library regularly publishes lost areas of anarchist history.

Please contact us if you would like to use our facilities. To receive details of our publications, send a stamped addressed envelope to:

KSL
BM Hurricane
London WC1N 3XX
England

THE KATE SHARPLEY LIBRARY

The Friends of Durruti Group 1937-1939

by Agustin Guillamón; translated by Paul Sharkey

ISBN 1-873176-54-6; 128pp, two color cover, 6x9; $9.95/£7.95. This is the story of a group of anarchists engaged in the most thoroughgoing social and economic revolution of all time. Essentially street fighters with a long pedigree of militant action, they used their own experiences to arrive at the finest contemporary analysis of the Spanish revolution. In doing so they laid down essential markers for all future revolutionaries. This study — drawing on interviews with participants and synthesizing archival information — is the definitive text on these unsung activists. "Revolutions without theory fail to make progress. We of the "Friends of Durruti" have outlined our thinking, which may be amended as appropriate in great social upheavals but which hinges upon two essential points which cannot be avoided. A program, and rifles." — *El Amigo del Pueblo* No. 5, July 20, 1937

SCUM Manifesto

by Valerie Solanas

ISBN 1-873176 44-9; 64 pp, two color cover, perfect bound 5-1/2 x 8-1/2; $5.00/£3.50.

This is the definitive edition of the SCUM Manifesto with an afterword detailing the life and death of Valerie Solanas. "Life in this society being, at best, an utter bore and no aspect of society being at all relevant to women, there remains to civic-minded, responsible, thrill-seeking females only to overthrow the government, eliminate the money system, institute complete automation and destroy the male sex. . . . On the shooting of Andy Warhol: I consider that a moral act. And I consider it immoral that I missed. I should have done target practice." —Valerie Solanas

The Friends of AK Press

In the last 12 months, AK Press published around 15 new titles. In the next 12 months we should be able to publish roughly the same, including a collection of essays and interviews by Murray Bookchin, the first book from Jello Biafra, three books from members of Crass, a stunning new cyber-punk novel, and the animal rights revenge novel to end all novels, as well as a new audio CD from Noam Chomsky.

However, not only are we financially constrained as to what (and how much) we can publish, we already have a huge backlog of excellent material we would like to publish sooner, rather than later. If we had the money, we could publish sixty titles in the coming twelve months.

Projects currently being worked on include: Morris Beckman's short history of British Fascism; previously unpublished early anarchist writings by Victor Serge; Raoul Vaneigem's *A Cavalier History of Surrealism*; two volumes of the collected writings of Guy Aldred; first-hand accounts from Kronstadt survivors; an English translation of Alexandre Skirda's classic work on anarchist history and organization, and his acclaimed biography of Makhno, *The Black Cossack*; *History's Lost Orgasms*, a history of insurrection from antiquity to the present day; the autobiography of perennial revolutionaries, the Thaelmans; new collage work from Freddie Baer; the first translation in English (running to eight volumes) of the complete works of **Bakunin**; a new edition of the Ex's glorious Spanish Revolution book/CD package; a collection of prison stories from ex-Angry Brigader **John Barker**; new editions of 'outsider' classics *You Can't Win* by **Jack Black** and **Ben Reitman**'s *Boxcar Bertha*; a comprehensive look at the armed struggle groups of the 1960s and 1970s, both in Europe and North America; and much, much more. We are working to set up a new pamphlet series, both to reprint long neglected classics and to present new material in an affordable, accessible format.

The Friends of AK Press is a way in which you can directly help us to realize many more such projects, much faster. Friends pay a minimum monthly amount, into our AK Press account. There are also yearly and life-time memberships available. Moneys received go directly into our publishing.

In return, Friends receive (for the duration of their membership), automatically, as and when they appear, one FREE copy of **every** new AK Press title. Secondly, they are also entitled to a 10 percent discount on **everything** featured in the AK Press Distribution catalog, on **any** and **every** order.

To receive a catalog and find out more about Friends of AK Press please write to:

AK Press
PO Box 40682
San Francisco, CA
94140-0682

AK Press
P.O. Box 12766
Edinburgh, Scotland
EH8 9YE